THOMAS FLETCH[ER]

Presented by the Citizens
of Philadᵃ to Capⁿ Isaac Hull.

Chesnut Street

Manufacturer of
SILVER PLATE & JEWELLERY,
and Importers of
Clocks, Watches, & Fancy Goods.

PH[ILADELPHI]A.

SILVERSMITHS TO THE NATION

Thomas Fletcher and Sidney Gardiner
1808–1842

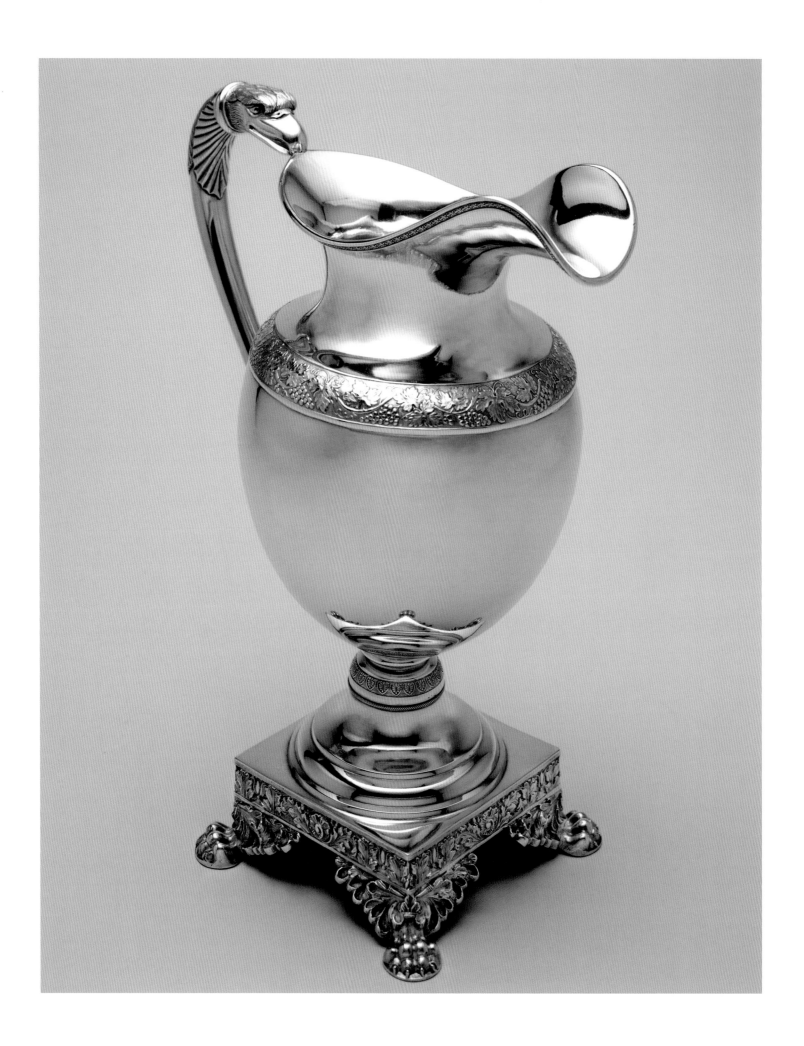

Silversmiths to the Nation

Thomas Fletcher and Sidney Gardiner
1808–1842

Donald L. Fennimore and Ann K. Wagner

With contributions from:

Cathy Matson
Deborah Dependahl Waters
Beth Carver Wees

ANTIQUE COLLECTORS' CLUB

ISBN: 978-1-85149-543-6

Principal financial support provided by:

Dr. Richard C. Weiss and Dr. Sandra R. Harmon-Weiss
The Henry Luce Foundation
National Endowment for the Arts
William Cullen Bryant Fellows of The Metropolitan Museum of Art

Additional financial support provided by:

The Americana Foundation
Mr. and Mrs. Richard Bressler
Mr. H. Richard Dietrich, Jr.
Friends of Winterthur, Inc.
Mr. Denison H. Hatch
Mr. Robert L. McNeil, Jr.
Roy J. Zuckerberg Family Foundation

Endpapers: See page 42
Frontispiece: See page 150
Title Page: See page 186
Contents Page: See page 172

British Library Cataloguing-in-Publication Data

A catalogue record for this book is available from the British Library

Origination by the Antique Collectors' Club Ltd., Woodbridge, Suffolk, England
Printed and bound in China

CONTENTS

FOREWORD

Elegant artistry, patriotic imagery, superb craftsmanship . . . these are but a few of the descriptors ascribed to the triumphal presentation silver created by the firm of Fletcher & Gardiner. Thomas Fletcher, an early nineteenth-century businessman and Sidney Gardiner, a silversmith, were driven by ambition and graced with the talent to capture the spirit of their time in silver and gold. Their Philadelphia firm revolutionized the significance of silver as a medium of public appreciation and commemoration, expressing the bravado and aspirations of a young, upstart country. In so doing, they introduced a new era in American silver.

The grand presentation pieces Fletcher and Gardiner created for heroes of the War of 1812 are without equal. The everyday silver they produced in abundance for dining and adornment spoke to the needs of an upwardly mobile class in the early 1800s. Outstanding examples of both can be seen throughout this exhibition catalogue, which is the first of its kind on this celebrated firm.

We are grateful to our colleagues at the Metropolitan Museum of Art, particularly Morrie Heckscher, for encouraging us to include as well thirty-six drawings from their permanent collection. The drawings correspond to many of the objects included here and are attributed to the Fletcher & Gardiner manufactory. Such direct correlations between blueprint and object are the delight of curators, scholars, and collectors.

This catalogue and its accompanying exhibition began more than thirty-six years ago when Donald Fennimore entered the Winterthur Program in Early American Culture and selected for his thesis topic the household silver of Fletcher and Gardiner. Like many of his counterparts in the program, Don went on to become a leading scholar of American decorative arts. He was curator of metalwork at Winterthur from 1971 until 2005, when he retired as curator emeritus. He taught the mysteries of metalwork to a host of younger scholars who succeeded in the Winterthur Program, myself included.

Impetus for this ambitious effort gained significant momentum when Ann Wagner entered the Winterthur Program in 2002. Fortuitously, Ann chose to explore Fletcher and Gardiner's presentation silver as her thesis topic, a perfect complement to Don's earlier work. Upon graduation, Ann joined the curatorial staff at Winterthur, whereupon she and Don proposed an exhibition and scholarly catalogue on these men and their remarkable silver. Winterthur was thrilled to endorse this effort.

It is therefore with deep satisfaction and pleasure that I welcome this addition to the long list of publications strengthening the distinguished tradition of research at Winterthur. This handsome volume, which satisfies not only the academic but also the aesthetic expectations of our museum audience, compellingly weaves the story of skill, artistry, and patriotism. It is a major contribution to American silver scholarship.

Leslie Greene Bowman
Director
Winterthur Museum & Country Estate

PREFACE

On February 14, 2003, Dr. Richard Weiss, a Winterthur Museum Trustee, and his wife, Dr. Sandra R. Harmon-Weiss, wrote a most interesting letter to Leslie Greene Bowman, the museum's director. They cited a passage from a letter sent more than one hundred years earlier (June 20, 1902) by John H. Buck, Curator of Metalwork at the Metropolitan Museum of Art in New York City, to Dr. Francis H. Brown, Boston resident, antiquarian, and member of the New England Historic and Genealogical Society. After asking for information on early Boston silversmiths, Buck concluded his letter by saying, "Why can not your Museum of Fine Arts get up an exhibition of old silver in the 'Fall' similar to the one of 'Book plates' that was so successful?"

Brown apparently took that suggestion to heart and spoke to Francis H. Bigelow, a student and writer on early American silver, who approached the MFA with a proposal to mount the first-ever exhibition of early American silver by a museum in the United States. The museum staff was receptive, and the result was an impressive "exhibition of three hundred and thirty-two pieces of American silver stamped with the marks of ninety American silversmiths of the seventeenth and eighteenth centuries." The prefatory note in the exhibition catalogue, entitled *American Silver*, records that "for the suggestion of the exhibition of early American Silver the Museum is indebted to Mr. Francis H. Bigelow, of Cambridge, who has also given much valuable aid in the arrangement of the pieces. The gratifying interest excited by the exhibition has resulted in the present memorial prepared by Mr. R. T. H. Halsey of New York. A technical description of the various pieces exhibited has been supplied by Mr. John H. Buck, Curator of Metal Work at the Metropolitan Museum of Art, also of that city."

Inspired by Buck's letter, Richard and Sandy Weiss wrote, "Could Winterthur consider a plan to 'get up' a similar exhibition on the 100th Anniversary of this enormously important primary exhibition?" They rightly noted the historic significance of the 1906 exhibition and catalogue as a catalyst that fed the nascent enthusiasm for early American silver. By posing their challenge, they recognized the role Winterthur has played for more than half a century in fostering the study of silver and other decorative arts of early America.

They also initiated a chain of events that culminated in a concerted effort on Winterthur's part to celebrate that heritage with the exhibition and catalogue *Silversmiths to the Nation: Thomas Fletcher and Sidney Gardiner, 1808–1842*. This volume presents the splendid work of Fletcher and Gardiner and, coincidentally, marks the upcoming anniversary of the firm's founding nearly two hundred years ago.

With a view to introducing the story of Fletcher and Gardiner and the climate in which they worked, we invited Cathy Matson, Professor of History at the University of Delaware and Director of the Program in Early American Economy and Society at the Library Company of Philadelphia, to contribute an essay about Philadelphia's economic climate at the time. We also invited Deborah Dependahl Waters, Senior Curator of Decorative Arts and Manuscripts at the Museum of the City of New York, to explore Philadelphia's precious metals community during Fletcher & Gardiner's era. The story of the firm, the partners, and their artistic legacy is addressed in the successive chapters. A final chapter, by Beth Carver Wees, Curator of American Decorative Arts at the Metropolitan Museum of Art, interprets a collection of drawings at the Met traditionally associated with the firm's work.

This catalogue represents the culmination of our long-standing admiration for Thomas Fletcher and Sidney Gardiner and the extraordinary silver and gold that emanated from their manufactory. The household, personal, and presentation objects they designed and produced epitomized the sentiment of their era. Their work stands today as the preeminent artistic record of the qualities that have come to be associated with the character of the United States of America. We derived great pleasure from working with this material and feel certain that readers will enjoy the insights it offers into the tumultuous formative period in this great country's history.

Donald L. Fennimore, Curator Emeritus
Ann K. Wagner, Assistant Curator of Decorative Arts
Winterthur Museum & Country Estate

ACKNOWLEDGMENTS

During the course of this project we have turned to many for assistance and advice. All have been generously forthcoming with both. We wish first to extend our sincere thanks to the individual and institutional owners of Fletcher & Gardiner silver and gold who have so carefully exercised their custodial responsibility for that wonderful legacy and graciously shared it with us.

We are especially grateful to Mrs. Frank J. (Marjorie) Bowden, Jr., Thomas Fletcher's great-great granddaughter, for not only lovingly shepherding records of Fletcher's personal and business life but also for generously sharing them with us. We also thank her children, F. Jay Bowden III, David Bowden, Rebecca Teal Lukens Bowden Guenther, and Nancy Fletcher Bowden Harris for their interest and enthusiasm.

To Morrison H. Heckscher we offer our thanks for encouraging us to give the Metropolitan Museum of Art design drawings a substantial presence in this catalogue and for providing important support for the exhibition. We are also grateful to Beth Carver Wees and Medill Higgins Harvey at the Met for many pleasant hours exchanging thoughts and insights about the Fletcher & Gardiner firm. Beth's extraordinary research and inquiry into the design drawings revealed more than any of us imagined and is summarized in her thoughtful essay and object entries.

The essays of Cathy Matson and Deborah Dependahl Waters contribute to this telling of Fletcher & Gardiner's story by exploring Philadelphia's economic and mercantile environment and the community of precious metals craftsmen they knew. We are particularly grateful to Beatrice B. Garvan and Gerald W. R. Ward for so willingly giving time, expertise, insightful commentary, and enthusiastic support of this project. Another resource was the work of Elizabeth Ingerman Wood, whose pioneering article on Thomas Fletcher was of immense help. Although she was not part of our ongoing dialogue, our research benefited from her publication.

For their support we extend our gratitude to generous colleagues and friends: David Atkinson, Elaine R. Bachmann, James G. Barber, Clara Bargellini, David Barquist, Carrie Rebora Barratt, Anne Bentley, The Rev. Catherine Brall, Michael K. Brown, James W. Cheevers, Maggie Christman, Kenneth Cohen, Stiles Colwell, David Conradsen, Ethyl Crawford, Gordon Crosskey, Gail F. Daly, John Davis, Ulysses G. Dietz, Davida Deutsch, Jeannine Disviscour, James Draper, Susan Drinan, Peter Drummey, Graham Duncan, Erin E. Eisenbarth, Julie Emerson, Nancy Goyne Evans, Valerie Faivre, Stuart P. Feld, Jean T. Fennimore, Robin Jaffee Frank, Ann Gillooly, Philippa Glanville, Alice Gordon, Ryan Grover, Laura Grutzeck, Fritz Hamer, Kirsten Hammerstrom, Alan and Simone Hartman, Christopher Hartop, Denison Hatch, Peter Hyland, Margaret K. Hofer, Jonathan Inslee, William Inslee, Robert Jackson, Catherine Jenkins, Eddie Jobe, Christina Keyser, Alexandra Alevizatos Kirtley, Michael Komanecky, Paul Allen Lambert, Margaret Lawson, Bruce Laverty, Michael Lewis, Bertram Lippincott III, Michael McAfee, Constance McPhee, Dean Meister, Joan Mertens, Ellen G. Miles, Rob Morgan, Roger Moss, Jeffrey Munger, Melinda T. Nasardinov, Cliff Nunn, Ruth Nutt, Tom Nutt, Fred Oakley, Sarah Papageorge, Kenneth Parker, Karen Parsons, Jane L. Port, Margaret and James Porter, Stuart Pyhrr, Jeffrey R. Ray, Edward Roehrs, Judy Rudoe, Bethany Sayles, Matthew Schultz, Bruce Schwarz, Jeanne Sloane, Jane Smith, Lewis Smith, Stephen Smithers, Michael Snodin, D. Albert Soeffing, Kevin Stayton, The Very Rev. John P. Streit, the late Charles V. Swain, Peter Tuite, William Voss, Kristen Wetzel, Lynne Wohleber, Lori Zabar, Ricardo and Janet Zapata, and Marilyn Zoidis.

Our colleagues at Winterthur Museum contributed much to this project. To Laszlo Bodo goes credit for many of the excellent photographs that form such an important part of this volume. Patricia Halfpenny offered significant encouragement and support during the course of the project, and Cheryl Payne gave unstintingly of her time and expertise. We thank Onie Rollins for her considerable help, enthusiasm, and support in shepherding this project to completion and also for her careful and sensitive editing of the manuscript. Thanks also to the late Janice Carlson, Cate Cooney, Wendy Cooper, Bert Denker, Linda Eaton, Grace Eleazer, Ron Fuchs, Leslie Grigsby, Emily Guthrie, Margaret Little, Jennifer Mass, Richard McKinstry, Susan Newton, Beth Parker-Miller, Laura Parrish, Tom Savage, Jim Schenck, Jeanne Solensky, Lois Stoehr, and Anne Verplanck for their assistance.

AUTHORS AND CONTRIBUTORS

Donald L. Fennimore, Curator Emeritus at Winterthur Museum & Country Estate, is an established and prolific author. He has published on all aspects of the metalwork medium, including the award-winning volumes *Metalwork in Early America: Copper and Its Alloys from the Winterthur Collection* (1996); *Campbell Collection of Soup Tureens at Winterthur* (2000); and *Iron at Winterthur* (2004). Mr. Fennimore recently retired after having spent thirty-four years at the museum.

Ann K. Wagner, Assistant Curator of Decorative Arts at Winterthur Museum & Country Estate, has lectured and conducted workshops on various aspects of metalwork. A former curatorial assistant in the Decorative Arts Department at Seattle Art Museum and graduate of the Winterthur Program in Early American Culture, she succeeds Donald Fennimore as metalwork specialist at Winterthur.

Cathy Matson, Professor of History at the University of Delaware, is also Director of the Program in Early American Economy and Society at the Library Company of Philadelphia. As a respected scholar, she has lectured, published, and edited numerous books and journals in the field, including *The Economy of Early America: Achievements and New Directions* (2005). Dr. Matson has also served as consultant for several PBS film presentations as well as theatre and documentary projects dealing with the era of the Early Republic.

Deborah Dependahl Waters is Senior Curator of Decorative Arts and Manuscripts at the Museum of the City of New York. She previously held positions with the New York State Council on the Arts, Christie's New York, and Winterthur Museum & Country Estate. Dr. Waters has written on a variety of topics related to the arts of the Mid-Atlantic region and, among others, served as author and general editor for the volume *Elegant Plate: Three Centuries of Precious Metals in New York* (2000).

Beth Carver Wees, Curator of American Decorative Arts at the Metropolitan Museum of Art in New York, is responsible for the collections of American silver, jewelry, and other metals. She lectures internationally; is an active member of the Silver Society, the American Ceramic Circle, and the American Friends of the Attingham Summer School; and has published numerous articles and catalogues, most notably *English, Irish & Scottish Silver at the Sterling and Francine Clark Art Institute* (1997).

Fig. 1.1 John Lewis Krimmel, *Pepper-Pot: A Scene in the Philadelphia Market*, 1811. Oil on canvas. Philadelphia Museum of Art, Gift of Mrs. Edward B. Leisenring, Jr. in honor of the 125th anniversary of the museum, 2001.

German by birth, John Lewis Krimmel became famous for his realistic depictions of life in rapidly expanding Philadelphia. This image captures the little-documented life of peddling on the streets and mingling of races and classes of Philadelphians.

Chapter 1
Philadelphia in the Early Republic
Cathy Matson

Visitors to Philadelphia during the first post-Revolutionary generation often portrayed a city of contrasts in which many residents anticipated unparalleled urban prosperity even as others grew uncertain about how to shape the city's social and cultural fabric. Indeed, the streets of Philadelphia offered a visual testament to uneven post-war recovery as late as 1810. And, as foreign observers noted, the burgeoning population of some fifty thousand residents shared the full range of contrasts that most European urban populations did. (Fig. 1.1) Throngs of new immigrants jostled for work opportunities and housing alongside the residents who were still struggling to recover from the war for independence. Outlying neighborhoods mushroomed with entrepreneurs, who set up shops that displayed a great range of imported goods, and craftsmen, who competed for opportunities at manufacturing and repairing household goods. In the densely packed city center, sailors mingled with peddlers hawking wares while the overflowing almshouse (Fig. 1.2) sat in stark contrast to the opulent townhouses of merchants such as Stephen Girard and Henry C. Pratt and manufacturers such as Manuel Eyre and William Massey. They, and some three-score other merchants and manufactures could by then rest assured that there was no better city than Philadelphia, the "pearl of the continent," in which to attract customers and hire skilled labor.[1]

Fig. 1.2 *Alms House.* From *The City of Philadelphia* (Philadelphia: William Birch & Son, 1800). Printed Book and Periodical Collection, Winterthur Library.

Although the almshouse never sheltered more than a small portion of the city's needy, it was widely applauded and bolstered the reputations of the same elite men who invested in shipbuilding.

Preparation for **WAR** to defend Commerce.

The Swedish Church Southwark with the building of the FRIGATE PHILADELPHIA.

Fig. 1.3 *Preparation for War to Defend Commerce.* From *The City of Philadelphia* (Philadelphia: William Birch & Son, 1800). Printed Book and Periodical Collection, Winterthur Library.

This massive 28-gun frigate was commissioned in 1800 and built at the Humphreys-Wharton shipyard just off the Delaware River. It answered the call by Congress for American preparedness for war.

This post-war generation remained dependent on commerce. (Fig. 1.3) The thicket of ship masts along the waterfront stood as mute testimony that some 25 percent of Philadelphia's population relied on foreign trade for both their livelihoods and the desirable commodities produced by strangers. Surpluses of flour, flaxseed, and timber products were being shipped to the familiar markets of the Caribbean, southern Europe, and the British Isles; by 1805 the value of goods leaving Philadelphia for these places rose to more than six times their pre-Revolutionary levels. Traders were also solidifying their connections to new ports such as Canton, Buenos Aires, Honduras City, Nootka Sound, Cape Horn, Hamburg, Bremen, and San Diego. The famous 1784 voyage to Canton of the *Empress of China*, which carried a cargo of ginseng and returned more than one year later with silks, porcelain wares, and

Eastern teas, brought its merchant investors some 30 percent profits. By the early 1800s, numerous ships were sailing from America for China each spring, and the goods returning to Philadelphia from more than fifty different world ports were processed by city craftsmen into "infant manufactures," packaged and delivered by its cartmen, sold by its retailers, and consumed by its eager and needy citizens.[2]

Philadelphia resident Stephen Girard's ascent provided an exceptional example of urban commercial fortunes. As a French sojourner who settled in the city by accident on the eve of the Revolution, Girard survived years of commercial uncertainty while trading with family and associates in New York, Saint-Domingue, Nantes, and Bordeaux during the 1790s. Only toward the end of that decade did he begin to profit from sales of Mid-Atlantic flour to starving French soldiers and

Saint-Domingue's revolutionaries in the Caribbean. Although his commercial risks were similar to those of many city merchants, Girard fared better in the long run due to fortunate choices in the face of adversity and a dogged refusal to retreat from commerce despite wars and revolutions. By the 1810s he had invested in a great complex of mines, canals, banks, ships, and philanthropic organizations, some of them his own creations.[3] (Fig. 1.4)

But even the best personal connections, knowledge of markets, and superior skill could not shield all entrepreneurs and international traders from the commercial disruptions of these years. Most merchants were far less successful than Girard and retreated from trade during the Napoleonic Wars in the 1790s, recurring bouts of yellow fever in the Mid-Atlantic region, and declining European demand for American foodstuffs at the end of the 1790s. Certainly, when the Jeffersonian embargoes during 1807–9 prohibited exports from American ports, the pace of commercial expansion that had emerged since 1801 slowed. Compounding these difficulties were the vagaries of credit and information in commerce. It still took six weeks on average for ships to cross the Atlantic Ocean, and privateers swarmed the Caribbean for a whole generation after the Revolution. During the episodic crises of the times, most merchants in Philadelphia lacked the capital to create new manufactures. Those who were not forced to retreat from commerce reinvested their profits in shipping and the fineries of a successful lifestyle or turned to real estate investment when fortunes were sufficient. The few who were successful circulated money and goods by lending to other merchants, speculating in foreign currencies, buying and selling bills of exchange, and promoting marine insurance. By the early 1800s, a handful of commercial leaders also began to move capital into small manufacturing enterprises.[4]

Although merchants were an influential leadership group in Philadelphia's early national years, they comprised only about 5 percent of the city's residents. A much greater number of Philadelphians enjoyed a moderately comfortable lifestyle, but even more survived just at the edge of household sustenance. Wholesalers, hustling between counting houses and docks, rubbed shoulders with new immigrants, while rural traders brought cartloads of agricultural goods to mills and docks for sale to residents and anonymous customers thousands of miles away. The dense commercial farming population around Philadelphia spurred the need for city artisans to make and repair farm wagons and tools, produce metal hand tools and leather goods, keep scores of retail shops,

Fig. 1.4 Benjamin Evans, *The Dwelling and Counting House of Stephen Girard as It Appeared at the Time of his Death, Dec. 26, 1831,* 1888. The Library Company of Philadelphia.

Stephen Girard lived and worked in this impressive complex of a red brick town house and two-story warehouse.

and vend wares throughout the city. The rich array of commodities produced by family members as well as seasonal hired workers and bound servants and slaves brought the majority of city residents only modest, and sometimes inadequate, incomes. Small "manufactories" processed and finished goods related to the region's agriculture or Caribbean plantation economies. For many years after the Revolution, most artisans experienced a slow pace of life in the city, and neighborly arrangements of buying and selling were flexible enough to accommodate small and unpredictable incomes.[5]

Between the wealthiest citizens and the majority of relatively poor working people there were rising entrepreneurs and traditional craftsmen steeped in highly skilled "arts." Optimistic writers around 1810 pointed to Philadelphia's four nail factories, thirteen breweries, six sugar houses, numerous grist and other mills, some dozen distilleries, a handful of dyeworks and tanneries, a few glass houses, numerous printers' shops, and eleven brush manufactories as signs of growth. In addition, a few small cotton and woolen mills, leather and pottery shops, harness and soap making establishments, carpet and saddle factories, and small machine parts establishments were set up on the fringe of the city during the worst months of the Jeffersonian embargoes, although working outside the home for wages was still less prominent among male workers than producing by the piece or the task.[6]

Tench Coxe, who wrote prolifically about manufacturing in the early 1790s, believed Americans had the means and the desire to overcome the post-war commercial problems and ultimately compete among the most advanced nations of the world. Cotton, he wrote, would not always be transported to England to serve its industrial revolution but soon would be part of a system of exchanges among the various regions of America that spurred textile production in the Mid-Atlantic. Merchants' investment capital, abundant water power, and numerous inventions would be important ingredients of America's rising manufacturing. As a complement to this kind of thinking, men such as Mathew Carey wrote that individual investors and immigrating skilled artisans would blend their capital into stock subscription companies, lotteries, transportation improvement companies, and small-scale "manufactories." Other writers agreed and added that rising "small men" would join in these new collective enterprises. Indeed, during the opening years of the nineteenth century, about 15 percent of artisans in the city followed such paths.[7] (Fig. 1.5)

But even collective efforts to raise capital sometimes fell short. By the second decade of the new century scores of appeals for aid reached municipal and state government legislators, who responded with helpful legislation and with outright grants to entrepreneurs.

WETHERILL & BROTHERS *WHITE LEAD MANUFACTORY & CHEMICAL WORKS.*
Corner of 12th & Cherry Streets Philadelphia

Fig. 1.5 W. L. Breton, *Wetherill & Brothers' White Lead Manufactory & Chemical Works. Corner of 12th and Cherry Streets Philadelphia.* From James Mease and Thomas Porter, *Picture of Philadelphia from 1811 to 1831* (Philadelphia: Robert DeSilver, 1831). The Library Company of Philadelphia.

Samuel Wetherill first developed his business skills as a house carpenter and builder but expanded during the Revolution into cotton manufactures, dyeing, and fulling. He was also one of the city's first importers of chemicals after the Revolution as well as a producer of white lead.

Fig. 1.6 "951–963 North Fifth Street." From Taylor sketch book, 1861. Joseph Downs Collection of Manuscripts and Printed Ephemera, Winterthur Library.

A large number of Philadelphia's resident poor and recent immigrants lived in housing along the alleyways behind major streets or in the rapidly expanding neighborhoods at the periphery of the city.

Philadelphians grew to appreciate how local banks could provide the loans that were so essential to starting new businesses in the city. Although the Bank of the United States lapsed in 1811, forty-one local banks operated in and around Philadelphia by 1815. But the effects of the War of 1812 and its aftermath nullified many of the positive effects of this government largesse and banking until the 1820s. The War of 1812 also sped up the separation between the city's elite investors and its less-successful artisans, whose access to bank credit diminished. Rapidly rising rents and the cost of living by war's end boded well for residents with capital to invest in new home construction along outlying streets, but in the shadow of Philadelphia's magisterial Federal-style institutions thousands of new immigrants lived in poverty. (Fig. 1.6) Textiles outworkers, who had felt the pinch of rising prices for raw cotton imported from the South, found it increasingly difficult to produce enough high-quality yarn to compete with factory spinners. Labor-saving machinery and unskilled female workers in proliferating small shops threatened the employment of skilled handloom weavers. On the waterfront, unemployment aroused racial tensions as hundreds of immigrants took on menial jobs. Scores of families became indigent and indentured their children or landed in the almshouse. Fully one-quarter of the city's population received some kind of poor relief, and the streets thronged with shabby oystermen's carts and rag pickers after the war.[8]

The end of war also exacerbated Philadelphia's relationship with other regions of the country and trading partners of other nations. After the first rush of consumer demand for goods from abroad, spurred by falling prices for European manufactured goods and a short period of rising demand in Europe for American food exports, the familiar gluts of imports in city warehouses, unpaid debts to storekeepers, and contracting credit plagued Philadelphians once again. Many road and canal projects now screeched to a halt, and the transportation linkages of Philadelphians to their

Fig. 1.7 Nicolino Calyo, *Manayunk,* ca. 1835. Watercolor and gouache on paper. Courtesy of Schwarz Gallery, Philadelphia.

This watercolor was produced by one of the most acclaimed landscape artists of the antebellum era. Although he traveled widely through Europe, Calyo spent most of his time in and around Baltimore, New York, and Philadelphia, recording economic transitions. The mills rising along the Schuylkill River just north of the city at Manayunk were at the core of Philadelphia's move toward factory production.

hinterlands remained relatively unchanged. But policy makers made few efforts to correct the gyrations of post-war credit and commercial troubles, and protective tariffs seemed woefully inadequate. Although the Second Bank of the United States was chartered in 1816, its directors made a series of decisions that hastened the next crisis. By mid-1818 Philadelphians entered another commercial slump. European crops began to recover from the devastations of the recent wars, and cotton manufacturers throughout Europe began to turn from southern American cotton (which Philadelphians helped carry across the ocean) to Indian sources. The Bank of the United States, drained already of specie to pay for part of the Louisiana Purchase debt and commercial debts abroad, had so overextended its loans to leading

merchants in the Northeast that vast networks of credit began to break down by the summer of 1818.[9]

As both banks and private lenders throughout the Mid-Atlantic scrambled to call in loans, grain harvests failed and yellow fever revisited the city once again in late 1818. By the next spring, Philadelphia was in the throes of a financial and commercial panic. Merchants sold ships and real estate to cover debts owed to foreign creditors, and new manufacturers closed scores of enterprises, throwing hired labor into unemployment. Of the nearly 10,000 residents reported to be employed in manufacturing during 1816, barely 2,000 of them worked in mid-1819. Rotting fruit lay heaped up in alleyways, fuel shortages left hundreds to live in freezing rentals, and large communities of homeless immigrants and African Americans built lean-tos when the almshouse closed its doors for want of funds.

The Panic of 1819 hastened a number of changes in Philadelphia. Shortened credit forced many importers and small entrepreneurs to cut back the quantity of imports but simultaneously to expand the variety of goods they carried in order sustain a customer base in the city—a practice that grew during the 1820s. In the textiles trades, handloom weavers and specialized dyers were increasingly replaced by new technologies, which less-skilled, lower-paid workers could operate. Factories themselves became easier to organize and capitalize than did craft shops, which required expensive hand tools and years of training. It would be many years, however, before textiles and other household imports made in Philadelphia would become comparatively cheaper than the equivalent British and European goods. In response to these market vagaries, many merchants shrank their importing businesses and devoted their time to retail sales or "jobbing" and commission sales for foreign merchants. Some shifted the risks of international trade into the new opportunities to trade with the North American interior, where there was a rising demand for necessities and fineries on the frontiers of New York, Pennsylvania, Kentucky, and Tennessee.[10]

As the city's population topped 120,000 in the early 1820s, the pace of change quickened noticeably. A serious decline of traditional craft relations in Philadelphia was accompanied by new canal and road projects that began to connect the city to its hinterlands more effectively; the rising number of stalls in markets on Second and Fourth streets signaled a revival of both rural productivity and middling incomes. The Erie Canal, opened in 1824, did not bring immediate anxiety to Philadelphia entrepreneurs because the nearly 500 ships entering and clearing the city annually seemed to symbolize the city's prosperity. But along with growth there were signs of weaknesses. The value of imports far exceeded the value of exports and re-exports many years during the 1820s and 1830s; moreover, Philadelphia's commercial lead had been taken over by New York City by the mid-1820s. The number of failures of young entrepreneurs grew much faster than the relative successes of importers.[11]

Philadelphia was still primarily a city of small manufactories and shops that were started with relatively modest amounts of capital. Small loans and family savings funded myriad investments in printing, machine parts, boatbuilding, leather tanning, food processing, or other businesses that employed just a few workers each. Of the thirty-nine textile establishments in 1820, only seventeen were large enough to be called factories, and most were sole proprietorships or small partnerships that outsourced

Fig. 1.8 *The Merchants' Exchange.* From *Views about Philadelphia* (Philadelphia: John T. Bowen, 1840), pl. 3. Joseph Downs Collection of Manuscripts and Printed Ephemera, Winterthur Library.

Within sight of Stephen Girard's bank (the former First Bank of the United States), this grand structure was begun in 1831 as a center for Philadelphia's business elite to meet. Merchants could watch ships approach the docks from the tower or conduct business downstairs. The building also housed a stock exchange, post office, marine insurance companies, coffeeshops, and newspaper vendors.

spinning to women and children in the city. The six mills in Philadelphia that were powered by water that year employed only about fifteen workers each, the majority of whom were children. The fortunes of mills along the Schuylkill and Delaware rivers rose and fell, and their doors closed frequently to the hundreds of immigrant workers dependent on them for jobs.[12] (Fig. 1.7)

The frigid winter of 1828–29 intensified a deep recession in the Mid-Atlantic region. Builders and small manufacturers halted work at many construction sites, forcing large numbers of immigrants into new neighborhoods beyond the Old City. Importing merchants complained bitterly about the amount of unsolicited goods being "dumped" on the city's docks by captains traveling from port to port without entry papers. Newspapers announced numerous failures in commerce and manufacturing during 1829 and 1830. And while paternalistic masters could still protect apprentices from the worst excesses of the slump, unskilled wage laborers fell through larger cracks than usual. The city continued to stratify along lines of incomes and degrees of personal success as well. Banks, brokerage firms, insurance companies, and fire companies proliferated, but so did small shops run by widows, soup kitchens, alcoves of watch and shoe repairmen, and unhoused orphans. The Board of Trade formed in 1833, the Merchants' Exchange was completed in 1834 (Fig. 1.8), and the imposing Walnut

Street jail provided physical testimony of the city's growth and its imposing institutions. In contrast, thousands faced higher rents and housing shortages, carrying "worthless bank notes" in their pockets and enduring the "noxious fumes" of paintmaking, tanning, or dyeing shops. Some of the greatest tensions, however, arose when the House of Refuge indentured hundreds of "idle, lazy, indolent, house-breaking scoundrels" to jobs formerly filled by the "honest, moral, and virtuous mechanics" who had taken years to develop their skills.[13]

Leading up to the devastating Panic of 1837, beauty and achievement mingled more noticeably than ever with the human and material costs of urban maturation in Philadelphia. (Fig. 1.9) Wherever one looked, ambitious efforts to build, develop, and expand overlapped with myriad personal setbacks and failures. Alongside imposing buildings there flourished an informal economy of peddlers, street vendors, day laborers, stablemen, and scavengers who had been forced down the economic ladder by subsistence crises, fuel shortages, and water pollution that sickened their children. Importers who brought the city's residents a widening array of goods were themselves often at the mercy of fluctuating international market prices. (Fig. 1.10) And although there were undoubtedly more small manufactories that attracted the admiration of foreigners and other Americans, family-owned shops and skilled custom work characterized a great deal of Philadelphia's employment through the 1830s. By that time, Philadelphia was certainly not the compact walking city it had been in the early years of the century, but the transformations that would create a metropolis noticeably more like the one we see today still lay largely in the future.

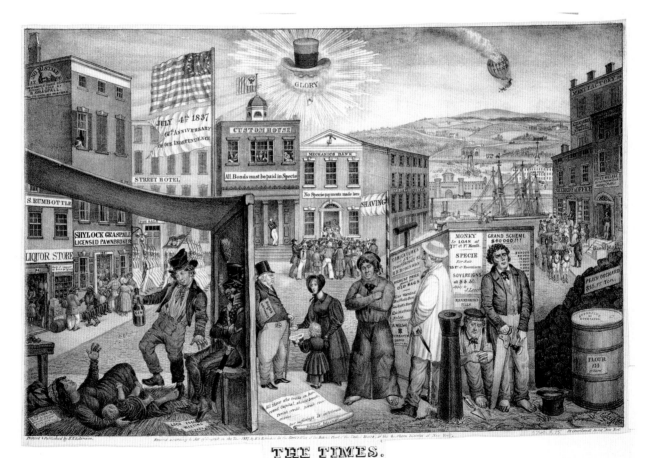

Fig. 1.9 Edward Clay, *Panic of 1837.* From *The Times*, 1837. The Library Company of Philadelphia.

In the center of this commentary on urban disaster wrought by the Panic of 1837, a woman and her child humble themselves to beg for relief from a broker, while in the background investors storm the doors of a bank where they had deposited their now-endangered savings.

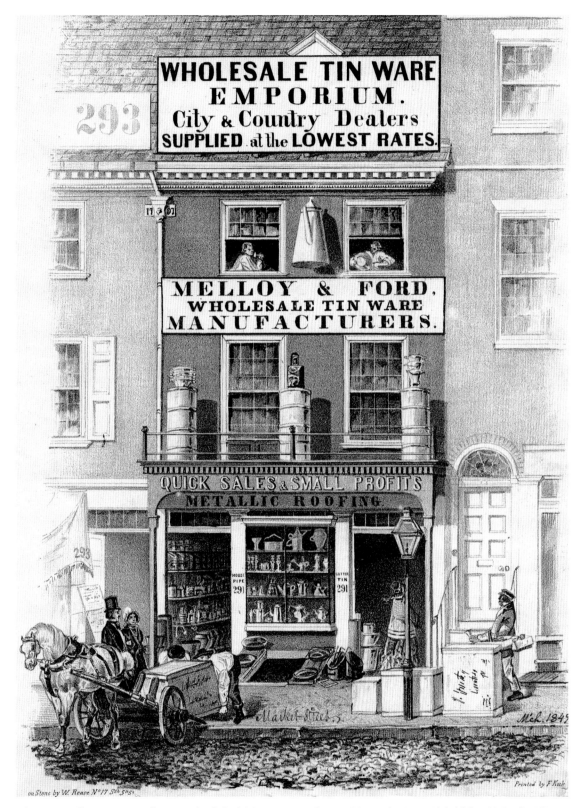

Fig. 1.10 William Rease, *Melloy & Ford, Wholesale Tin Ware Manufacturers, 291 Market Street, Philadelphia,* 1849. The Library Company of Philadelphia.

One of a number of small manufactories and retail stores lining the neighborhood streets after the Panic of 1837, this shop sold all manner of metalware. Notice that work and transport had changed little since late colonial times.

Fig. 2.1 Joseph Richardson, Jr., coffeepot (from coffee and tea set), ca. 1795. Winterthur Museum, Gift of Henry Francis du Pont, 1957.825.

Chapter 2
"Rich and Fashionable Goods": The Precious Metals Trades in Philadelphia, 1810–1840
Deborah Dependahl Waters

When silversmiths Thomas Fletcher and Sidney Gardiner moved their three-year-old partnership from Boston to Philadelphia in late 1811, they entered a city long supplied by talented local artisans who sold silver and gold objects of their own manufacture as well as English and Continental silver and silver-plated wares that they imported for resale. Dr. James Mease, author of *The Picture of Philadelphia* (1811), wrote that Philadelphians wrought the finer kinds of metals with neatness and taste and commented further: "but above all, the working of the precious metals has reached a degree of perfection highly creditable to the artists. Silver plate fully equal to sterling [the British standard, equivalent to 925/1000 parts silver], as to quality and execution is now made, and the plated wares are superior to those commonly imported in the way of trade."[1]

Within less than a decade, Fletcher and Gardiner came to dominate the regional and national markets for fine wrought silver. Such achievements were made possible in part by stylistic and technological transformations within the practice of silversmithing and allied trades and by shifts within the ranks of Philadelphia craftspeople engaged in such trades in the early decades of the nineteenth century. The precious metals trades in Philadelphia in 1810 constituted a mature artisan environment, one that had led the nation in the immediate post–Revolutionary War era in the adoption of the then newly fashionable classical style. The preface to a summary of 1810 Federal census returns noted that the increase of capital available to Americans, with the consequent extension of manufactures and commerce, had resulted in improved and increased production of precious metal objects nationwide. Accompanying figures reported that Pennsylvania produced more than one-third of the total value of the nation's output of gold, silver, set work (jewelry), and mixed metals.[2]

"The Urn Fashion"

In the first decades of government under the Federal Constitution, Philadelphia silversmiths and their patrons, like their American counterparts generally, embraced an international classical style. Born in Europe during the 1750s of a reverence for antiquity fueled by archaeological exploration and a rejection of the capricious extravagance of the rococo, classicism gradually became linked firmly to an eighteenth-century view of distinct, successive, national civilizations in which Greece and Rome rivaled each other as the summit of cultural achievement. As American citizens aspired to achieve democratic liberty, simplicity, and dignity guided by close study of classical political and philosophical texts, they also found inspiration in the "physical remains of antiquity, as reinterpreted by modern Europeans." Progress could be achieved by a proper emulation of the ancients not only in laws and customs but also in forms. Silver, with its malleability and its capacity for ready refashioning, was adaptable to such imitation. Despite the traditional association of silver objects with the aristocratic culture overthrown at the founding of the nation, genteel Philadelphians continued to acquire silver to mark civic or personal achievements or to use and display in dining rooms and parlors. The city's artisans and retail shops fulfilled consumer demand for objects incorporating the new style.[3]

Precious metals craftsmen glanced backward for inspiration only in the first phase of classical enthusiasm. From volumes such as *The Antiquities of Athens* by James Stuart and Nicholas Revett (London, 1762), the four illustrated folios by William Hamilton and Pierre d'Hancarville describing the collection of antique vases assembled by Hamilton (published from 1767 to 1776 and available at the Library Company of Philadelphia), and the decorative schemes and designs of British architect Robert Adam (as published in *The Works in Architecture*, beginning in 1773), silversmiths selected vessel forms, particularly the funerary urn, for beverage service components, sugar urns, and vases. (Fig. 2.1) They also chose decorative motifs—swags, rams' heads, paterae, husks, acanthus and laurel leafage—to use in bright-cut ornament (a type of engraving consisting of shallow, non-continuous gouges) or in moldings that emphasized the plain reflecting surfaces and straight structural lines of their objects. Catalogues for plate and plated wares issued by English manufacturers as well as imported sterling silver and silver-plated objects provided direct models for the new style. "The urn fashion" remained

Fig. 2.2 Joseph Lownes trade card, ca. 1790. American Antiquarian Society.

popular into the first decade of the nineteenth century.[4]

The presence of a silver urn in the hands of master silversmith William Ball as he led a group of thirty-five master, journeymen, and apprentice goldsmiths, silversmiths, and jewelers in Philadelphia's Grand Federal Procession commemorating the ratification of the Federal Constitution on July 4, 1788, only affirmed the triumph of the urn as both a vessel form and an emblem recognized by potential clients. Following Ball were silversmiths bearing a white silk banner that featured on one side the symbolic genius of America holding aloft a silver urn below a firmament filled with stars. The marchers referred to the perceived qualities of silver in their motto, which proclaimed: "The purity, brightness and solidity of this metal is emblematical of that liberty which we expect from the New Constitution."[5]

Technical innovations such as "flatting mills" to prepare sheet silver free from surface imperfections complemented the classical aesthetic demand for taut, smooth surfaces. Such mills, in use in Philadelphia as early as 1733, eliminated much of the labor-intensive hammer work required to forge sheet silver. Through much of the first quarter of the nineteenth century, craftsmen imported mills directly from England or purchased them from hardware merchants like Walton & Roberts or John Carrell & Son. Philadelphians preferred those of "Darwin's make," from England's largest producer of tools and equipment for silversmiths, but by 1812 craftsmen could buy locally made mills. Philadelphia-made presses to stamp out borders or handles were available by 1830.[6]

Artisans and Entrepreneurs

Silversmiths working in the classical style and utilizing manually powered equipment to assist in fabrication generally adopted either an artisan or an entrepreneurial approach to their craft. Aspects of each often appeared in the same firm successively. Staff size varied with the business model adopted by the master/owner and his relative economic success, with six or more workers marking the entrepreneurial manufactory. Surviving accounts and other records suggest that many artisans in the precious metals trades worked independently, with assistance from one or two apprentices and perhaps a wage-earning journeyman. Scattered manuscript census returns for 1810 taken by Philadelphia city ward record fifty-two master craftsmen in the precious metals trades. None had more than four males from the ages of 10 to 45 residing in their households. These men and boys probably worked in their masters' workshops.[7]

The master's workshop and home were often located on the same lot, with the retail "show shop" installed in the first-floor front room of his dwelling. The artisan master focused on the local market; produced fine goods to order for clients drawn from his circle of kinsmen, co-religionists, and business acquaintances; perhaps kept a small inventory of his own products as well as imported fancy goods and plated ware for ready sale; and performed a wide range of repair services. And as Philadelphia antiquary John Fanning Watson romantically reminisced, "Then almost every apprentice, when of age [usually 21 years], ran his equal chance for his share of business in his neighborhood, by setting up for himself, and, with an apprentice or two, getting into a cheap location, and by dint of application and good work, recommending himself to his neighborhood."[8]

Philadelphia-born Quaker artisan silversmith Joseph Lownes (1758–1820) served as mentor for a network of artisans and entrepreneurs active within the precious metals trades into the 1830s. By 1785 Lownes lived and worked in South Front Street, the address featured on his illustrated trade card of about 1790 (Fig. 2.2), which displayed forms and design vocabulary common to Philadelphia silversmiths while "the urn fashion" dominated production.[9]

By 1787 Lownes had at least two apprentices working with him, Joseph Head, a free black, and Samuel Williamson (1772–1843), who completed his apprenticeship in the spring of 1793. In addition to training Williamson and Head, Joseph Lownes also taught the silversmith's trade to his son Josiah Hewes Lownes and to his nephew Edward Lownes (1792–1834). With their assistance, the Lownes shop produced and sold tea and coffee equipage, tankards,

Fig. 2.3 Edward Lownes, pitcher presented to Dr. Philip Syng Physick, 1827. Winterthur Museum, 2000.26.

canns, flatware, and buckles and retailed imported plated wares as well. Clients included a fellow manager of the Pennsylvania Hospital, the widow of a former Philadelphia mayor, physician Benjamin Rush, marine insurance groups, and the fire insurance company that insured the Lownes dwelling and workshop. In 1798 Joseph Lownes acquired a house and lot at 124 South Front Street from the estate of goldsmith John David and resided there until his death.[10]

Edward Lownes left South Front Street in his first years as an independent artisan. By 1816 he had formed a short-lived partnership on South Second Street, then moved alone to South Third Street in 1817. In September 1819 he offered for sale a general assortment of silver plate, spoons, plated wares, jewelry, and fancy articles. His next newspaper advertisement, placed in May 1821, coincided with his move to the more fashionable Chesnut (now Chestnut) Street, a few doors below Fourth Street, on the north side, a stand previously occupied by silversmith, jeweler, and fancy-goods retailer James Black, who moved to Walnut Street. In 1824 Lownes joined his Chesnut Street competitors Thomas Fletcher, Sidney Gardiner, and Harvey Lewis as a founding member of the Franklin Institute.[11]

Edward Lownes adhered more closely to actual antique forms in his presentation silver than had earlier craftsmen working in "the urn fashion." They included an 1817 order for a pitcher from the Pennsylvania Agricultural Society to be given to Colonel John Hare Powel and an 1828 order from the Watering Committees of the City of Philadelphia for a pitcher to be presented to Fairmount Water Works engineer Frederick Graff (1774–1847). For a more personal presentation to Dr. Philip Syng Physick (1768–1837) in 1827, the donor and craftsman chose a classical ewer form mounted on a square pedestal base supported by paw feet (Fig. 2.3), suggesting familiarity with publications such as Thomas Hope's *Household Furniture and Interior Decoration* (1807) or Charles Heathcote Tatham's *Designs for Ornamental Plate, Many of Which have been Executed in Silver, from Original Drawings* (1806). Both the 1817 and the 1827 commissions are embellished with a cast border composed of grape leaves and grape clusters not unlike a similar border frequently employed on tea- and tablewares marked by Thomas Fletcher.[12]

Links between the Lownes family and that of silversmith Harvey Lewis (ca. 1783–1835) suggest plausibly that Lewis was apprenticed to Joseph Lownes. By 1804 Lewis had completed his training, appeared on the tax rolls, and had taken an apprentice of his own. The following year, he borrowed money from retired silversmith Joseph Richardson, Jr., to finance a partnership. That partnership had dissolved by March 5, 1811, when Lewis insured his newly built Second Street house with silversmith's wareroom on the north side of the lower story of the dwelling. A back building housed his workshop, at No. 2 South Second Street. Lewis alone repaid the sum due Richardson in November 1813. He subsequently sought premises in the city's most fashionable shopping precinct and in 1818 moved to 143 Chesnut Street, the location given in his advertisement published in Joshua Shaw's *United States*

Fig. 2.4 Harvey Lewis advertisement, 1822. From Joshua Shaw, *United States Directory for the use of travelers and merchants giving an account of the Principal Establishments of Business and Pleasure throughout the Union* (Philadelphia: James Maxwell, 1822), p. 3. Printed Book and Periodical Collection, Winterthur Library.

Fig. 2.5 Harvey Lewis, vase presented to Frederick Graff by the Watering Committees of the Philadelphia City Councils, 1822. The Historical Society of Pennsylvania, Gift of Miss Henrietta Graff, 1906, on deposit at The Atwater Kent Museum, HSP.T12.4.

Directory in 1822. (Fig. 2.4). The Lewis shop was not far from the shop of Thomas Fletcher and Sidney Gardiner at No. 130 Chesnut, on the southwest corner of Chesnut and Fourth streets.[13]

Lewis apparently maintained his business at the artisan level, despite his advertisement in Shaw's *Directory*. Repairs and fabrication of small silver items provided a portion of his income, as did flatware sales. He also attracted orders for fashionable silver tea- and tablewares and found a consistent patron in Elizabeth Willing Powel (1742–1830), widow of former mayor Samuel Powel, who also had patronized Joseph Lownes. In 1822 Lewis obtained a major civic commission from the Watering Committees of the Philadelphia City Councils for presentation to Fairmount Water Works engineer Frederick Graff. He provided a vase with swan handles in the current taste based on designs by French architect-designer Charles Percier (1764–1838) and his collaborator Pierre-François-Léonard Fontaine (1762–1853). Bas reliefs depicting the Water Works at Fairmount, and a river god, closely related to a sketch by

Graff and to the figure "Schuylkill Chained" executed by sculptor William Rush for the completed Works, personalized the vase.[14] (Fig. 2.5)

Although Lewis was still in business in August 1827, having advertised for his runaway apprentice, he resigned his seat on the board of the Franklin Institute "on account of indisposition" in January 1828. He did not continue silversmithing and was identified as a "Gentleman" in land records and directories from 1829 until his death near Newark, Delaware, in 1835. Edward Lownes probably bought out Lewis's business.[15]

Another working model, that of the entrepreneur eager to expand by exploiting wider markets, coexisted with that of the artisan silversmith. Entrepreneurially minded proprietors expanded production in part by establishing manufactories apart from their shops and living quarters and increasing their importation of fancy hardware, watches, and jewelry for wholesale and retail distribution. They sought to enlarge their markets outside the Philadelphia environs, often through advertising placed in newspapers, city directories, or traveler's guides, or by employing traveling salesmen. Samuel Hildeburn, of the wholesale and retail watchmaking and jewelry firm Hildeburn & Woolworths, called the latter the "travelling system," which his firm used to solicit orders and distribute merchandise among watchmakers, jewelers, and fancy-goods retailers throughout the South and West in the years 1816–18.[16]

One of the first to arrive in Philadelphia with an entrepreneurial dream was flamboyant goldsmith, jeweler, and hairworker Joseph Cooke, who came from England not later than 1786. By 1794 he had built one of the earliest commercial blocks designed for multiple use on the corner of South Third and Market streets. (Fig. 2.6) The interior of his 105-foot-front building was

finished "in the most elegant European style, with handsome mantels, marble chimney pieces, Venetian windows and doors, secret nailed floors, and elegantly palaced and ornamented round the roof." The fourth floor and garrets were suitable for lodging rooms; the second and third floors for public coffee rooms; and the ground floor for stores, "shelved, and countered in the newest stile." To work in the building, Cooke sought twenty to thirty journeymen in all branches of the precious metals trades as practiced in England— goldsmiths, silversmiths, jewelers, engravers, bucklemakers, plate-workers, spoonmakers, small-workers, lapidaries, chapemakers, five or six apprentices, a watchmaker used to jobbing, a foreman to manage the manufactory and instruct apprentices, and a partner able

Fig. 2.6 *South East Corner of Third, and Market Streets, Philadelphia.* From *The City of Philadelphia* (Philadelphia: William Birch & Son, 1800), pl. 10. Printed Book and Periodical Collection, Winterthur Library.

Fig. 2.7 Chaudron's & Rasch, coffee and tea set, 1809–12. Winterthur Museum, Gift of Mr. and Mrs. Henry Pleasants III in memory of Maria Wilkins Smith, 1975.80.1–.5.

to advance him £10,000 to finance his operations. But Cooke's vision proved too grandiose for Philadelphia. Unable to secure a partner, he offered his building for sale in 1795 and then proposed a lottery scheme in which the block and jewelry from his manufactory, at a total value of $400,000, were to be the prizes. Unable to sell 50,000 tickets at $8 each, Cooke's scheme failed. His building was demolished in 1838.[17]

More successful as an entrepreneur was former Lownes apprentice Samuel Williamson. An independent artisan craftsman by 1794, Williamson established his thriving manufactory on South Front Street, overlooking Dock Street, not far from the Lownes shop and home. There he parceled out silver for production to six men in January 1807, employed twelve craftsmen at different times in 1810, and engaged eleven in June 1811. He sold silver, plated ware, jewelry, and an occasional gold object to retail silversmiths in Boston, New York City, Philadelphia, Baltimore, and Georgetown, D.C. Major clients included Charles A. Burnett of Georgetown, N. Taylor & Co. of New York, and George W. Riggs of Baltimore.[18]

Then, without explanation, Williamson left the trade. The 1814 Dock Ward County Tax rolls show that silversmith William Seal was renting Williamson's former South Front Street property. On August 30, 1815, "the stock of a person declining business," including tea services, tumblers, flatware, and plated articles, was sold by auction from Williamson's old address. Williamson had moved to Uwchland Township, Chester County, Pennsylvania, where he had purchased two hundred acres of land in March 1814. He remained in rural Chester County until his death.[19]

The many French, Swiss, and West Indian Creole émigrés of the 1790s had a substantial impact on the precious metals trades in Philadelphia. A number of them—such as members of the interrelated Stollenwerck-Chaudron-Billon families that included watchmaker and jeweler (Jean) Simon Chaudron (1758–1846) and his successive partners watchmaker Charles Billon and silversmith Anthony Rasch—earned their livings by making and importing silver, jewelry, and watches based upon French designs. Chaudron, who was baptized in Vignory, Champagne, France, studied watchmaking in Switzerland and moved to Saint-Domingue (Haiti) in 1784. There he married Jeanne Geneviève Mélanie Stollenwerck, a daughter of coffee and indigo planter Pierre Hubert Stollenwerck, in 1791. After visiting Philadelphia in July 1790 and again in 1793, Chaudron joined his in-laws in that city, perhaps to escape the upheaval resulting from the Haitian slave rebellion. After the dissolution of a brief partnership with Swiss watchmaker and in-law Charles Frédéric Billon—which had operated as Charles Billon & Cie, Horlogers at 12 South Third Street—Chaudron retained the firm's premises. He offered for sale in 1802 a variety of marble and gilt timepieces, watches, jewelry, gold watch chains, seals, and keys, as well as claret, Saint-Domingue coffee, French silver objects, and one hundred stipple engravings of the apotheosis of Washington, "neatly framed," executed by John James Barralet (ca. 1747–1815). He also advertised Washington memorial rings for sale, with "an elegant portrait of the late illustrious General Washington" after a statue by French sculptor Jean-Antoine Houdon. By 1803 his billhead listed Chaudron as proprietor of a store selling clocks, watches, jewelry, and French china.[20]

Fig. 2.8 Simon Chaudron, soup tureen presented to Captain James Lawrence, 1813. The New-York Historical Society, Gift of Dr. Eugene H. Pool, 1942.544ab.

In 1809 silversmith Anthony Rasch (ca. 1778–1858) joined Chaudron to supervise a silver manufactory in Andrew Street, Hamilton Village, on the west bank of the Schuylkill River. Silver produced by the manufactory bore the mark "Chaudron's & Rasch" and often a quality designation "STER★AMERI★MAN"— for "Sterling, American Manufacture," both within banners, as struck on a coffee and tea service owned by the Dallas family of Philadelphia. (Fig. 2.7) The firm, like its artisan contemporaries Edward Lownes and Harvey Lewis, substituted more archaeologically correct models—like the tripod-base sugar bowl of the Dallas service in part modeled on the designs of ancient tripods rediscovered in sites such as the Temple of Isis in Pompeii—for the light derivative "urn fashion" forms of the 1790s and early 1800s. Silver objects became massive in scale. The gauge of the sheet metal increased in thickness. Bands of die-rolled and die-stamped ornament (here a guilloche centering a star motif) replaced labor-intensive engraved bright-cut borders,

and cast feet, finials, and handle sockets in bold floral or animal forms displaced urns and pineapples. Chaudron continued his sales operation at 12 South Third Street until January 1811, when S. Chaudron & Co. opened a new store at 9 South Third Street stocked with some two hundred pieces of sterling silver hollowware and a complete assortment of flatware from the manufactory. The Chaudron-Rasch partnership dissolved by mutual consent in August 1812.[21]

Simon Chaudron continued the Hamilton Village manufactory and his South Third Street retail store as S. Chaudron and Company. He secured orders from "The Citizens of Philadelphia" for a soup tureen (Fig. 2.8) for presentation to Captain Jacob Jones of the US *Wasp* following Jones's capture of the British brig *Frolic* on October 12, 1812, and for a soup tureen and pitcher for presentation to Captain James Lawrence (1781–1813) of the US Sloop of War *Hornet* following his capture of the British brig-sloop *Peacock* in late February 1813 off British Guiana. Chaudron employed classical nautical and war imagery in the ornament of the tureen, with cast bearded Neptune masks as handle supports and a toga-draped seated war goddess holding a warrior's shield and offering a laurel wreath to the victor as the cover finial. Despite these public commissions, Chaudron's creditors pressed him for repayment of debts. In a classified advertisement that appeared in *Relf's Philadelphia Gazette and Daily Advertiser* in November 1813, Chaudron publicly disclosed his predicament. Following his statement was the announcement of his assignees, who were to handle claims against Chaudron as well as receive payments due him. Three weeks prior to the assignment, Chaudron's collection of two hundred "actual" paintings of the "great masters," his print collection, and his four-hundred-volume French library were sold at auction.[22]

After the assignment, Chaudron did not resume business in his own name. Instead, his son Edward (1792–1836) advertised for four complete and well-recommended journeymen plate workers and spoonmakers and offered them constant employment and liberal wages from his father's address, 5 South Third Street, in March 1814. The 1816 Philadelphia directory listed Edward as a watchmaker and jeweler at 9 South Third Street.[23]

From 1815 through 1818, Simon Chaudron edited the French literary weekly *L'Abeille Americaine* and championed in the press the *Companie Agricola et Manufacturiere du Tombigbee*. In 1819 he and his family moved to Demopolis, Alabama, settling in the newly formed Vine and Olive Colony there. About 1825 he moved to Mobile, Alabama, where he advertised watch repairing at his lodgings on Dauphin Street. He remained in Mobile until his death in 1846.[24]

Chaudron's sometime partner Anthony Rasch had arrived in the port of Philadelphia from Hamburg in April 1804. In the petition for naturalization that he filed in 1811, he noted that he had resided outside Pennsylvania until 1809. He first appeared in the Philadelphia city directory in 1808, at 4 Watkins Alley. From 1809 until August 1812, Rasch managed the manufactory for Chaudron's & Rasch. When the partnership dissolved, Rasch opened a manufactory at 118 Market Street, between Third and Fourth streets. Rasch subsequently moved to the former premises of silversmith Joseph Anthony Jr.'s sons, Michael H. and Thomas, at 94 High Street, but continued his silver manufactory at various locations from 1813 to 1817. He produced elegant dining silver based on French models, including a pair of serpent-handle sauceboats. (Fig. 2.9) Settling at 165 Chesnut Street, one door below Fifth Street, in August 1817, Rasch traded as Anthony Rasch & Company, silver plate manufacturers and jewelers, in

partnership with George Willig, Jr. The firm became Rasch & Willig, Jun. in 1818. Despite optimistic advertisements, the partners made an assignment of their property in trust for the benefit of selected creditors effective September 1, 1819. The assignees immediately offered for sale below prime cost the entire stock in trade of the firm as well as the elegant store fixtures and the attached "complete Factory for manufacturing every description of silver plate." On August 5, 1819, the remaining three years of an excellent young chaser's term of service also were offered for sale.[25]

The assignees resorted to public auction to sell Rasch's personal tools and his household furnishings on September 11, 1819, along with the rolling mills, stamps or dies for making threaded spoons and forks, patterns, and scotch and pumice stone owned by the firm. Auction of the firm's stock and shop fixtures were to follow four days later, and the sale of stock continued on Friday, September 25, 1819. The assignees offered the goods remaining at 40 percent below prime cost together with the store fixtures again in January 1820, in hopes of closing the concern before the end of the month. Inclement weather postponed the closing, with the store fixtures—two elegant mahogany counters with drawers, three glass cases on each counter, and shelves embellished with looking glass and glass doors—still offered for sale in April 1820.[26]

While Rasch's assignees settled his Philadelphia affairs, he moved to New Orleans. There he advertised his newly established silver manufactory in January 1820. He noted "his late residence was Philadelphia, where the specimens of his workmanship and manner of business secured both approbation and confidence." To New Orleans he brought his own workmen. Rasch returned briefly to Philadelphia in 1820 to make arrangements to improve his New Orleans operation by bringing out "some more skillful workmen" but spent the remainder of his career in New Orleans.[27]

By 1820 the population of Philadelphia's city wards had reached 63,713. The number of workers employed in the precious metals trades kept pace despite an overall contraction in commerce and failures of specific partnerships (including that of Anthony Rasch and George Willig, Jr.) following the Panic of 1819. Surviving questionnaires completed for the 1820 Federal Census of Manufactures record that four Philadelphia firms had reached or exceeded the six-employee threshold that distinguished an artisan shop from a manufactory. Silversmith Joseph Pennel used the services of one man and five boys to produce silver coffee and tea sets, while jewelers Thibault & Brothers employed seven workmen and nine boys to produce jewelry with a market value of $40,000. Silverplaters Horn & Kneass noted that although they had employed as many as forty to fifty persons in previous years, with a weekly payroll of three to four hundred dollars, their 1820 labor force included only two men and seven boys, perhaps as a result of trade declines due to the effects of the Panic. The Fletcher & Gardiner manufactory reported the largest work force and most valuable output. This census documents the firm's dominance in the precious metals community in terms of number of employees and output in 1820. A rebound within the trades generally was recorded by compilers of the 1823–24 issue of the city directory, who located ten goldsmiths, silversmiths, and jewelers; thirty specialist silversmiths; forty-four jewelers; thirty-seven watchmakers; and forty silverplaters in the areas canvassed.[28]

Emerging Firms

Although links with the eighteenth-century and early nineteenth-century craft tradition dissolved quickly in the 1827 to 1835 period with the retirement of Harvey Lewis and the deaths of Sidney Gardiner, Joseph Richardson, Jr., and Edward Lownes, the reputation of excellence in workmanship and quality in metal standards that they and their associates had established found new champions in emerging firms operated by such partners as Curry and Preston, R. and W. Wilson, and Bailey and Kitchen. Employing mechanically assisted production techniques that Fletcher & Gardiner and other firms had used as well as extensive newspaper advertising, the newer enterprises sought to expand their product lines and their markets while accommodating client style preferences. The Wilsons and Curry and Preston stressed their craft backgrounds in their advertisements. John Curry and Stephen Preston had "been brought up to all the different branches of Silversmithing" and had carried on a manufactory for several years in Philadelphia prior to opening a retail store at 103 Chesnut Street, between Third and Fourth streets. Brothers Robert and William Wilson, sons and administrators of silversmith Robert Wilson (1766–1824), operated the Philadelphia Silver Spoon and Fork Manufactory at the northwest corner of Fifth and Cherry streets. They claimed to be "the only manufacturers in this city, who have been

Fig. 2.9 Anthony Rasch, pair of sauceboats, 1815–19. The Metropolitan Museum of Art, Sansbury-Mills Fund, 1959 (59.152.1–.2). Image © The Metropolitan Museum of Art.

Fig. 2.10 R. & W. Wilson, salts, 1825–46. Winterthur Museum, 1967.133.1, .2.

brought up to this business exclusively" and produced flatware and hollowware to four standards: "Crowns," "5 Francs," "Spanish dollars," and "Standard." (Fig. 2.10) Although both concerns stressed the low prices of their products, they also assured prospective clients that "work shall be made and finished in the handsomest manner." Curry and Preston noted too that they personally supervised their manufactory and employed none but first-rate workmen, while R. & W. Wilson utilized division of labor and "facilities and conveniences not equaled" in Philadelphia to enhance production capabilities. R. & W. Wilson and John Curry, successor to Curry & Preston, continued their rivalry into 1834 and faced new competition from Joseph T. Bailey and Andrew B. Kitchen, who had opened a store featuring watches, jewelry, silver plate, plated ware, and fancy goods at 136 Chesnut Street, two doors above the Second Bank of the United States, in the fall of 1832. Bailey & Kitchen only added to the concentration of precious metals shops, which had prompted a commentator in 1831 to note "the splendid repositories,

with which Chesnut Street particularly is embellished."[29]

On February 22, 1832, precious metals craftsmen joined fellow citizens in a civic procession celebrating the centennial of the birth of George Washington. Silversmiths, watchmakers, jewelers, silver chasers, and engravers organized a week prior to the event in a meeting held at the American Coffee House. A lottery determined the positions of the various trades in the line of march, with the precious metals workers leading the seventh division. A gold and silver watchcase manufacturer, not a silversmith, served as chief marshal of the division; his position reflected symbolic recognition of alterations in craft practices and product lines. A lithograph entitled *The Gold & Silver Artificers of Phila. in Civic Procession, 22 Feb. 1832* recorded their march past Thomas Fletcher's establishment and the edifice of the Second Bank of the United States on Chesnut Street. (Fig. 2.11) Artisans in parade uniforms followed a large open car, or float, drawn by six horses. On the car, men worked a coining press to mint medals honoring Washington.

The artisans distributed three thousand of the freshly minted medals to the assembled crowd and stamped a fine impression in gold for presentation to the Marquis de Lafayette and one in silver for inclusion in the cornerstone of the planned Washington Monument, when the procession came to Market Street, opposite the Old Court House.[30]

Figures prepared by economic historian Diane Lindstrom show the value added in manufacturing precious metals in Philadelphia in 1840 more than tripled the 1810 figures, escalating from $217,000 to $663,000. Precious metals comprised 5.9 percent of the city's total manufacturing value added in 1840, nearly three times the percentage achieved by New York craftsmen, whose product constituted only 2.1 percent of that city's total. Lindstrom suggests that New Yorkers

may have purchased precious metals along with other Philadelphia specialties such as drugs, medicines, paints, dyes, and cotton textiles with income earned from supplying commercial services to Philadelphians. This hypothesis is supported by contemporary commentators, including George G. Foster, who wrote in *The New York Tribune* on October 21, 1848: "In one feature, Chesnut-street fairly and decidedly outstrips Broadway: we mean the jewelry establishments. The displays of costly and magnificent silver plate, jewelry, and bijouterie in the windows of Chesnut-street are positively dazzling. We have never seen anything to approach them in any other city in the United States."[31] The newer firms emblematically held aloft the banners of the masters of 1788 and 1832 and the purity, brightness, and solidity of the metal they worked endured.

Fig. 2.11 M.E.D. Brown, *The Gold & Silver Artificers of Phila. in Civic Procession, 22 Feb. 1832.* The Historical Society of Pennsylvania.

Fig. 3.1 Lewis Veron Fletcher, portrait of Thomas Fletcher (his father), Philadelphia, ca. 1840. Oil on board. The Franklin Institute, 41-109, Gift of Mrs. Henry A. Thomson.

Chapter 3
Thomas Fletcher and Sidney Gardiner:
Their Lives and Work
Donald L. Fennimore and Ann K. Wagner

In stark contrast to their stature as co-owners of the premier silver manufactory in America during the first half of the nineteenth century, we know frustratingly little of Thomas Fletcher and Sidney Gardiner's early lives. Both trace their ancestries in America back through multiple generations to the seventeenth century.[1] Yet the information associated with their births and childhood that has survived provides little insight into the circumstances surrounding their first decade of life. Nor does it give any reason to imagine the two would ever cross paths, let alone merge their talents and achieve renown in their separate but related professions.

The Early Years
Thomas Charles Fletcher was born in Alstead, New Hampshire, on April 3, 1787, the seventh of fourteen children, to Timothy Fletcher, a farmer, and his wife Hannah (née Fosdick). Thomas led a somewhat peripatetic youth as evidenced by his parents' settling in Alstead (1778–91); Boston, where his mother was born (1791–93); and finally Lancaster (the place of his father's birth), Massachusetts (1793–1823).

Thomas spent the first four years of his life in Alstead, a farming community of fewer than one thousand inhabitants. That setting changed substantially when the family moved to Boston, more than fifteen times the size of Alstead, but then reverted to a town environment when they moved to Lancaster, about thirty-five miles northwest of Boston. That community, with about one thousand inhabitants who mainly supported themselves by farming, was home for the remainder of his youth. (Fig. 3.2)

Thomas's future business partner, Sidney Gardiner, was born on July 23, 1787, the third of six children, to John Gardiner, a physician, and his wife, Abigail (née Worth) in the village of Mattituck on the north shore of Long Island. Unlike Thomas, Sidney appears to have led a rather stationary youth, no doubt because of the community's need for his father's medical abilities as well as the Gardiner family's deep roots in the northeastern end of Long Island. Mattituck, a village containing twenty or twenty-five scattered dwellings as late as the 1840s, was a tiny community. Most of its inhabitants looked to Long Island Sound and the North Atlantic Ocean for their livelihood. That being the case, it might be presumed Sidney's youthful attentions were toward the sea, but that proved not so.[2]

Thomas and Sidney's worlds were disparate with regard to geography, economy, and familial influences. Even so, their lives were destined to intersect. That meeting took place in Boston probably about 1803, when they were in their mid-teens. It is likely that family influence and connections were responsible for the decision that Boston should be the place to launch their careers. Both had relatives there.

While the Gardiner family has long been associated with Gardiner's Island and its environs at the eastern end of Long Island, by the time of Sidney Gardiner's birth, their connections with Boston were long-standing. In 1635 Lyon Gardiner, the first of the family to come to America, had landed there and spent four years before moving to the island that bears his name. His time in Boston was productively spent for the town and inured the Gardiner name to those who remained. Subsequent generations of the family built on that association through marriage, notably with members of the Greene family.

Gardiner Greene (1753–1832), a descendant of one such union, rose to be a successful and wealthy Boston merchant with far-reaching and influential ties. It is possible he facilitated Sidney's decision to settle in Boston. He may have even proved a useful conduit in helping Sidney train to be a silversmith, since two uncles had been of that profession, Rufus Greene (1707–77) and Benjamin Greene (1712–76). A third member of the Greene family also practiced silversmithing in Boston. Samuel S. Greene (b. 1782) was a goldsmith on Ann Street at the moment Sidney Gardiner was apprenticing to the craft.[3]

Fig. 3.2 Henry Williams, portrait miniature of Thomas Fletcher, Boston, 1810. Watercolor on ivory. Yale University Art Gallery, Mabel Brady Garvan Collection.

Existing evidence strongly suggests that Thomas, unlike Sidney, had the benefit of a liberal education. He had excellent, legible penmanship and a command of the English language; he was well read and informed on a wide variety of subjects; and he was familiar with Latin and French. These accomplishments laid the foundation for several career options. He considered one in politics, as hinted in a written inquiry by his older brother, James Fosdick Fletcher, in New Orleans in March 1808.[4] However, Thomas decided to pursue a career as a merchant.

He did so under the tutelage of Boston merchant Joseph C. Dyer, who announced in the June 20, 1803, issue of the *Boston Gazette* that he had formed a partnership with Gibbs W. Eddy. The partners informed readers that they "have taken the Store, and the greater part of the Stock lately owned by Joseph Nancrede, No. 49, Marlboro' Street, where they offer for sale a large assortment of BOOKS and STATIONARY." In addition, they detailed an extensive assortment of watches, cutlery, fancy goods, London- and Parisian-warranted jewelry, and silver-plated wares. For the succeeding five years, during which the store moved to 48 Marlboro Street, Dyer and Eddy advertised regularly in the Boston newspapers.[5]

Their advertisements were typically lengthy and listed an extraordinary variety of imported goods including London-manufactured pearl and gold earrings, broaches, and lockets; Birmingham-manufactured gold watch chains and morocco-work boxes, whips, and spurs; and tortoiseshell combs. Among their offerings of plated wares were tea- and coffeepots, cake baskets, fish knives, and tea- and tablespoons from Sheffield and Birmingham. For those who could afford it, the partners carried comparable forms in English silver. Under the category of cutlery they had white and green ivory-handle, silver-mounted, fluted and plain table and desert knives and forks; corkscrews; silver-mounted pearl, buck, tortoiseshell, and buffalo-handle pen and pocket knives; and fine warranted and common razors. Their fancy goods included French gold and silver spangles, engraved and plain silver thimbles, opera and reading glasses, silver tooth and ear picks, morocco suspenders, and pocket books. Their military and sportsmen's equipage named silver-mounted sabers; cut-and-thrust swords with eagle heads, ivory grips, and American devices etched and gilded on the blades; London-manufactured dueling pistols; and red, blue, black, and white Ecclegrass plumes. The advertisements make clear that Dyer aggressively sought to attract the business of a broad segment of Boston's fashion-conscious clientele. In effect, he offered one-stop shopping, giving himself an edge over his competition. This was a lesson not lost on his perceptive apprentice, Thomas Fletcher. Some of the advertisements noted that "American manufactured . . . table, tea and salt Spoons; soup & gravy Ladles; tea Tongs, &c, &c, &c" could be had if wished, suggesting that Dyer emphasized imported rather than self-manufactured goods.[6]

On January 16, 1807, Dyer gave notice in *The Repertory* that he intended to leave for England with a view to giving up his business and pursuing other interests. He announced the sale of his inventory at greatly reduced prices. Several months later he acknowledged that he had to delay the sale "until the ensuing fall, when it will be entirely relinquished." That did take place, as announced in the January 14, 1808, issue of the *Boston Gazette* under the heading SALES AT AUCTION: "Joseph C. Dyer, Will commence the sale by Public Auction, at Warehouse, No. 49, *Marlboro'-street*, of his STOCK in TRADE, (which may remain unsold) on the 2d MONDAY (14th day) of March next, when the whole will be sold without reserve, to the highest bidder."[7]

In April 1808 watchmaker and aspiring merchant John McFarlane purchased a large portion of Dyer's fashionable goods and moved into his warehouse. He advertised a list of goods every bit as long as Dyer's, giving evidence to all readers that he intended to carry on as fully as his predecessor. McFarlane also noted that "GOLD NECKLACES . . . Silver Table and Tea SPOONS . . . LADLES . . . MUSTARD SPOONS . . . SALT SPOONS, &c. *of the first quality, manufactured particularly for the Store and warranted*" could be had. He closed with the statement "A Silver Smith wanted – apply as above."[8]

McFarlane first listed himself in the Boston city directories in 1796 and continued to do so on a regular basis, always as a watchmaker. With his acquisition of Dyer's business, he began his entrepreneurial career. Had he succeeded, he would have joined the ranks of many artisans who pursued upward mobility from the workbench into the ranks of businessmen. However, his ambitious beginning ended quickly in this venue, for almost five months to the day after he opened for business he placed the following advertisement in a local newspaper: "AT AUCTION On Monday, 3d of October, at WAREHOUSE, No. 48 Marlboro'-Street Will be sold without the least reserve JOHN McFARLANE'S whole STOCK IN TRADE . . . Terms of credit liberal, made known at sale." He appended his notice with a postscript stating that "those persons who may wish to purchase any . . . articles previous to the Auction, will be supplied at prices which cannot fail to give satisfaction."[9]

What brought about this shift is not known, but it might be presumed that finances were involved. Although this entrepreneurial excursion into the fancy hardware business was short-lived, its end signaled an opportunity. The timing was perfect for Thomas Fletcher and Sidney Gardiner to join forces, capitalize on the situation, and launch their business career.

The Boston Partnership

Fletcher outlined in detail the circumstances and arrangement of the partnership with Gardiner in a letter to his brother James Fosdick Fletcher, dated December 10, 1808:

> Mr. McFarland [sic] having determined on giving up business & selling his goods at auction, it became a necessary desideratum with me whether to become embargoed at Lancaster for an indefinite time or in defiance of embargo to commence business for myself. The former I could not contemplate without disgust and the latter seemed to require more tenacity & boldness than I possess. I thought of a partner. This mode of connection in business I have always [declined] but in this instance it appeared the least evil, or in fact the only resort. I found a <u>workman</u> in whose fidelity I could confide and who was a master of his profession. We made a bargain & took Mac's sale to supply ourselves with goods – our shop is opposite Broomfield's Lane. Our stock is about $6000. In the sale of McF's stock & the settlement of his account I found a task tedious & laborious and had, in addition to this, and in the same moment to select a stock, line & fit up a shop, arrange & mark my goods & prepare to open immediately. This you will perceive that not only the usual hours were busily employed but something borrowed from the season of accustomed rest. I have now however got settled & can conduct the business without much confusion or trouble ... Mrs. Legge ... told me that she had at length obtained a place for Sidney, but she was obliged to furnish him with everything but board.[10]

Fletcher's comments in this seminal letter document the origin of what was to become the most dynamic and influential silversmithing firm in the United States during the ensuing three decades. The letter also provides valuable insight into the energy he brought to overcoming a challenging situation for the purpose of advancing his career, a personality trait he would exercise many times.

At the same time that McFarlane closed his shop, a property a few doors away at 43 Marlboro Street was vacated by its lessee. Its size, location, and layout, with minor modification, suited it for the fancy hardware and silversmithing business, as evidenced by a bill rendered to the new partnership of Fletcher & Gardiner in November 1808:

Carpenter work done by Cushing & Jacob	
	86.40
do " " " Colburn	12.00
Building forge furnishing materials	12.50
31½ yards plastering at 40 cts	14.20
Mended do in front shop	2.50
Whiting front shop	1.00
Painting wall &c	1.50
Oct 31 for work done in back shop	7.00

The partners underwrote these improvements and made the property their first place of business, as announced in the November 7, 1808, issue of the *Boston Gazette* and the November 9, 1808, issue of the *Columbian Centinel*.[11] (Fig. 3.3)

Like the advertisements of their predecessors, Fletcher & Gardiner's went to considerable length to detail the inventory of imported goods in their wareroom, which offered fashion-conscious Bostonians the opportunity to acquire everything they might need without going elsewhere. This listing was preceded by notice that "their principal attention will be directed to the manufacturing of Gold and Silver Work of every description." This decision reflects the training and talent that Gardiner brought to the firm. The partners further proclaimed that "of the manufacturing branch they can speak with the fullest confidence, as the *whole attention* of one of the partners will be devoted to this part of the business, who hazards nothing in stating, that his work shall be, in every instance, equal to any imported." This emphasis speaks to their conviction that they saw themselves not merely importing foreign-manufactured goods but also manufacturing their own wares.

In their joint venture, Gardiner supplied the gold/silversmithing talent. Fletcher provided the marketing and managerial expertise, a role that evolved from his "having had the principal management of the business of ... Mr. Dyer and Mr. McFarlane ... for some time past." That, in turn, sprang from his apprenticeship

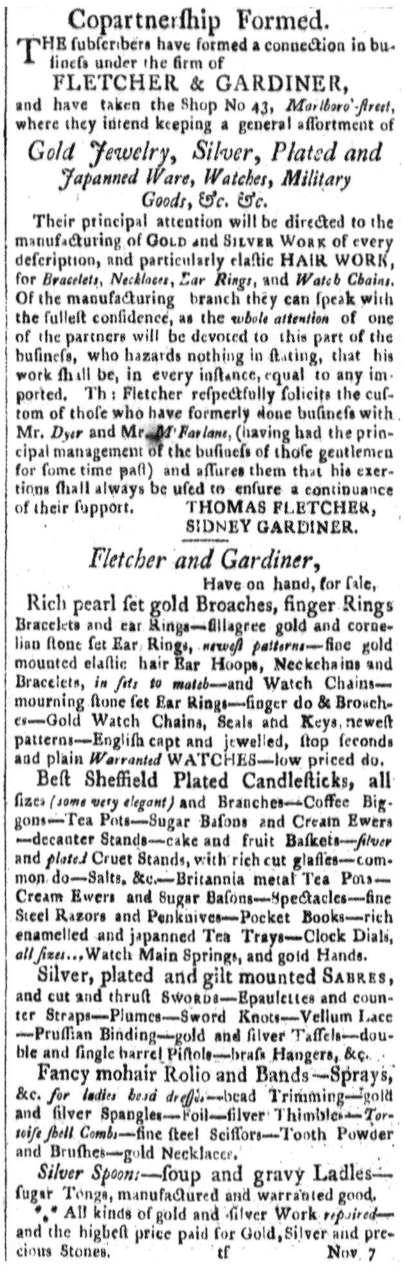

Copartnerſhip Formed.

THE ſubſcribers have formed a connection in buſineſs under the firm of

FLETCHER & GARDINER,

and have taken the Shop No 43, *Marlboro'-ſtreet*, where they intend keeping a general aſſortment of

Gold Jewelry, Silver, Plated and Japanned Ware, Watches, Military Goods, &c. &c.

Their principal attention will be directed to the manufacturing of GOLD and SILVER WORK of every deſcription, and particularly elaſtic HAIR WORK, for *Bracelets, Necklaces, Ear Rings*, and *Watch Chains*. Of the manufacturing branch they can ſpeak with the fulleſt confidence, as the *whole attention* of one of the partners will be devoted to this part of the buſineſs, who hazards nothing in ſtating, that his work ſhall be, in every inſtance, equal to any imported. Th: Fletcher reſpectfully ſolicits the cuſtom of thoſe who have formerly done buſineſs with Mr. *Dyer* and Mr. *M'Farlane*, (having had the principal management of the buſineſs of thoſe gentlemen for ſome time paſt) and aſſures them that his exertions ſhall always be uſed to enſure a continuance of their ſupport.

THOMAS FLETCHER,
SIDNEY GARDINER.

Fletcher and Gardiner,

Have on hand, for ſale,

Rich pearl ſet gold Broaches, finger Rings Bracelets and ear Rings—fillagree gold and cornelian ſtone ſet Ear Rings, *neweſt patterns*—fine gold mounted elaſtic hair Ear Hoops, Neckchains and Bracelets, *in ſets to match*—and Watch Chains—mourning ſtone ſet Ear Rings—finger do & Broaches—Gold Watch Chains, Seals and Keys, neweſt patterns—Engliſh capt and jewelled, ſtop ſeconds and plain *Warranted* WATCHES—low priced do.

Beſt Sheffield Plated Candleſticks, all ſizes *(some very elegant)* and Branches—Coffee Biggons—Tea Pots—Sugar Baſons and Cream Ewers—decanter Stands—cake and fruit Baſkets—*ſilver* and *plated* Cruet Stands, with rich cut glaſſes—common do—Salts, &c.—Britannia metal Tea Pots—Cream Ewers and Sugar Baſons—Spectacles—fine Steel Razors and Penknives—Pocket Books—rich enamelled and japanned Tea Trays—Clock Dials, *all ſizes*...Watch Main Springs, and gold Hands.

Silver, plated and gilt mounted SABRES, and cut and thruſt SWORDS—Epaulettes and counter Straps—Plumes—Sword Knots—Vellum Lace—Pruſſian Binding—gold and ſilver Taſſels—double and ſingle barrel Piſtols—braſs Hangers, &c.

Fancy mohair Rolio and Bands—Sprays, &c. *for ladies head dreſſes*—bead Trimming—gold and ſilver Spangles—Foil—ſilver Thimbles—*Tortoiſe ſhell Combs*—fine ſteel Sciſſors—Tooth Powder and Bruſhes—gold Necklaces.

Silver Spoons—ſoup and gravy Ladles—ſugar Tongs, manufactured and warranted good.

, All kinds of gold and ſilver Work *repaired*—and the higheſt price paid for Gold, Silver and precious Stones. tf Nov. 7

Fig. 3.3 Advertisement for the opening of the Fletcher & Gardiner firm in Boston. From *Boston Gazette*, November 8, 1808. Courtesy of Readex, a division of NewsBank, in cooperation with the American Antiquarian Society.

to Dyer, whom Fletcher fondly referred to as "my friend and former master."[12]

This business relationship, wherein a silversmith and merchant operated on equal footing, marks a significant shift away from the manner in which the precious metals business had been conducted during the two previous centuries. It speaks to the rise of the entrepreneur as the driving force in the American silver industry by the middle of the nineteenth century. Before that time, silversmiths entered business either under their own name as a small operation, as part of a larger shop with journeymen and apprentices, or in a contractual arrangement with another of the same profession.

Following the opening of Fletcher & Gardiner's manufactory and wareroom, the partners issued a number of advertisements in Boston's principal newspapers, asserting their place as the town's primary manufacturer of stylish jewelry and silverware with a comprehensive assortment of imported fancy hardware. At the end of December they advertised that they "continue to manufacture elastic hair festoon NECKLACES, with cornelian and pearl centers, and glasses for hair: Also Bracelets, Brooches, and Earrings to match; Gold Watche Chains, Seals, Keys, &c." A few weeks following, they noted that they "have just completed a set of Stamps for making 'Cestus Clasps' for the Waist; and can now accommodate [customers] at one or two day's notice." There followed the notice that they "will make any ornament, either from pattern or drawing, that may be wanted, and, having employed the best of workmen, they are confident of giving satisfaction in every instance." In June they advertised that they "have just received a supply of Pearls and Cornelians, and a variety of rare and beautiful gems, which they will manufacture into Ornaments of any kind." And one month later they let readers know that they "have for sale Ten thousand real pearls; 500 carnelians, 100 fine Topaz and a few diamonds—any of which they will manufacture into Ornaments."[13]

These notices, coupled with Gardiner's abilities as a jeweler/goldsmith and Fletcher's talents for marketing, drove the firm to quick success. Within two years they moved to better quarters at 59 Cornhill, as outlined in a letter Fletcher sent to Dyer: "We have removed from Marlboro' Street & fitted up the store formerly occupied by Mr. [William] Pelham at the corner of Cornhill Square & our shop is allowed to be the handsomest in the place. We find a material difference in sales, which have become double which we made formerly—We have thirteen workmen employed in our manufactory which we find succeeds beyond our expectations & we have every reason to hope that a few years of active industry will place us in a situation to command the respect of our fr[ien]ds the Eng[lis]h Manufacturers whose favors we have so long solicited."[14]

The partners announced the move in the October 6, 1810, issue of the *Columbian Centinel*, in which they reiterated their ability to fabricate any type of jewelry in addition to "Silver setts containing Coffee and Tea Pots . . . silver Pitchers, Tumblers [and] Porringers," thus marking their growing emphasis on the manufacture of silver goods equal to jewelry. There followed an advertisement on March 13, 1811, that they "have the pleasure of informing the public, that they have at present a complete and elegant assortment of Silver Tea Sets, consisting of Coffee and Tea Pots, Cream-Ewers, and Sugar-dishes, in sets to match, or single piece. They will also manufacture any article in the Silver-Plate [silver, not plated ware] line to any pattern, and of the first rate workmanship, at a reasonable price."

Within the space of three years, Fletcher and Gardiner had realized their most ambitious hopes. They had opened their shop and manufactory with acclaim and generated sufficient interest in their various lines of goods that Fletcher boasted: "We have now a 'beggardly account of empty boxes' having sold all our military goods, most of our Plated Goods, watches, &c. Our present stock does not exceed $6000 & I am happy to state that our debts do not am[oun]t to more than $4000 the whole of which I think we shall be able to pay off (except $1000 due old Dr G[ardiner]) as the notes become due."[15]

Surviving Financial Challenges

This success, however, was not achieved without a degree of tribulation. The partners' trials surrounding their plans for the business and the ensuing implementation revolved largely around money. Those challenges are amply noted in a letter Thomas wrote to his partner's father, Dr. John Gardiner, when the business opened.

> The proposal I made was that which I considered most conducive to the mutual interests of your sons [Sidney and Baldwin] and myself . . . & the knowledge I have obtained of the quality & prices of goods, during the five years I have been employed in this line, places it in my power to get such goods as are suited to the market, & at prices as low as charged as any that have been sent out to this country. This knowledge appears to me to be a more valuable acquisition than a capital, in as much as it gives me a decided superiority, in purchasing, as well as in selling over any man, however competent his funds, who has not been . . . doing business in this line. I have reflected on the [counter] proposal you have made, but [it] deranges the plan I had formed, & would place it out of my power to take a share in the business . . . I have made a proposition to Sidney . . . I am

> willing to consider the manufacturing branch of the business equal to my knowledge of trade, & to enter copartnership, on equal terms with him in profit & expense. Sidney to carry on the manufactory & I to transact the business of the selling shop. It is further proposed that Baldwin shall be with me a part of the time, (during which I shall use my exertions to make him acquainted with the mode of doing business) & the remainder of the time in the workshop. To this proposal your Son has agreed, & accordingly we have hired a shop & bought goods sufficient to make a decent assortment.[16]

Fletcher and Gardiner's ambitions outstripped their pocketbooks. If their hopes of a successful business were to be realized, they needed to augment their resources by seeking cash, credit, and goods from others. In this respect, both Joseph Dyer and John McFarlane were supportive.

Dyer was of material help, and McFarlane arranged for Fletcher and Gardiner to acquire a substantial portion of his stock on credit. This allowed the partners to open with enough goods to fill their shop and supply purchasers, even though they had little money of their own to invest. Such arrangements solved immediate problems, but in the end they incurred debts that had to be paid, as lamented by Thomas in a letter written a year later: "The whole of our notes to Mr. McFarlane are considerably overdue amounting to about $2500 a part of which has been due more than two months . . . What motive can he have for permitting us to trade on his capital? [It] cannot be for his own interest . . . we are every day basking in the favorable sunshine of one whose nearer approach could in a moment dissolve our little fabric to dust."[17]

Until the firm was able to generate sufficient cash flow to replenish stock and make a profit, it needed regular infusions of cash. Seeking that cash was a constant and necessary quest for Fletcher, who looked to his partner's father with a degree of misunderstanding and consequent frustration. Dr. Gardiner apparently had, or had access to, sufficient resources to underwrite a major portion, if not all, of the enterprise. Furthermore, from the content of Fletcher's letters to him, he indicated he was willing to be financially involved when the proposal was initiated. However, that support was slow to materialize. Evidence of the difficulties surrounding this is painfully apparent in a letter Thomas, not Sidney, wrote to Dr. Gardiner in 1809, a few months after the firm had opened: "Your letter to my partner of the 2d inst, has produced in me many unpleasant sensations. So very different does it appear from the language held out by you when in this place that I am at a loss how to construe your meaning, or to reconcile your present communication with the declaration made by you when you were here. If my recollection serves me, I understand you to say . . . that it was your intention to render the business in which your son and myself were engaged, every assistance in your power . . . I think I have the right to expect . . . that assistance . . . because it was expressly stipulated at the commencement of our connection."[18]

In the end the partners managed to obtain the needed cash and in so doing kept the business afloat. In fact, Fletcher proudly announced to his father at the one-year anniversary of the firm: "I have just finished my balance sheet and have ascertained to a certainty that I am worth (nothing perhaps you will say) you are mistaken—the nett profits of our business the year past has been upwards of eight hundred dollars. This sum is ours after paying $700 for repairing our shop and every other expense attendant on our business. You will no doubt be astonished when I tell you that, without a cent to begin with, I contracted debts the past year to the amount of $20,000—But thanks to an all ruling Providence, I have more than enough to pay every demand—My sales amount to more than $14,000 and my stock is worth at least $9,000."[19]

McFarlane, Fletcher & Gardiner

In spite of this early success, the quest for money continued, manifesting itself in evolving relationships. A significant event for the partners occurred November 19, 1810, when they dissolved their partnership and reincorporated it under the name McFarlane, Fletcher & Gardiner. The agreement stipulated that the "partnership [was] to continue 5 years." Fletcher was pleased with the arrangement, stating that Mr. McFarlane "brings into the concern a handsome Capital, and shares equally with us in profit and expense. Since this addition, our business is more extensive and more profitable than before & everything bids fair to encourage us except the constant interruptions of our commerce & intercourse with Europe . . . Our Manufactory is our greatest dependence, and that becomes daily more profitable."[20]

It seemed a perfect relationship that would take them forward for the next five years. But the partners hit an unforeseen snag, as noted by Fletcher: "Since this coalition has been in operation it has rec[eive]d the most cordial hatred & opposition from every member of the craft [in Boston]. Every method is resorted to - which

malice can invent to destroy the reputation & diminish the profit of the concern. But still we remain 'firm as the rock of ages' & defy the storm." In spite of the partners' resolve, the pressure on them from their competitors, presumably generated by envy and jealousy, built to the point where they decided to dissolve the partnership in August 1811. In retrospect, Fletcher lamented, "The business continued as usual by John McFarlane who assumes all responsibilities – Mr. Gardiner & myself are for the present 'on the wing.'"[21]

Fletcher and Gardiner were out of business, and not quite four years after they had established themselves with so much promise. Given the acrimonious circumstances and the hostile environment, it would have been tempting to write off the effort, go their separate ways, and seek alternate careers. However, the men discovered they enjoyed working with each other and were committed to a partnership in the precious metals trade. But they also concluded that they could not pursue their ambition in Boston. If they were to proceed, it would have to be elsewhere.

The Move to Philadelphia

Fletcher and Gardiner had both traveled to New York City and Philadelphia while considering their relocation. Fletcher offered an insight into their inclination when he wrote to his brother James, "We have it in contemplation to remove to Philadelphia."[22] In the end, the partners did determine to settle in Philadelphia. That decision was no doubt driven in part by the city's population—almost twice that of Boston at the time—and commercial activity, which was more than three times that of Boston. Another factor weighing against New York City was Philadelphia's long-standing reputation as an important center for the precious metals trade, which had been enhanced with the founding of the Federal Mint there in 1794.

Both Fletcher and Gardiner had made business trips to Philadelphia prior to this time, so they had some familiarity with the city on a personal level. During one of Gardiner's trips in early 1810, he wrote to Fletcher, "I am verry glade that I went to philad. [I] was in every place that looked like a jewellers shop but maid a mistack wounce got in to a tinmans shop but begged his pardon & promist never to do the like again. I enquired the price of all the silver mark [ed. I] found much difference in them. Charges [John Cauchois or Sampson Charpentier] & Shadrangs [Simon Chaudron, Philadelphia jewelers] is the loest you know I verry well quainted with Mr. Shadrang . . . I have made a bargain with him to let us have silver goods & pay a part in our work. He makes a beutiful monet I have ordered too sets to be maid light he makes all patterns for $2. the oz."[23]

On September 7, 1811, an advertisement appeared in the *Columbian Centinel*: "To be LET – The SHOP at No. 43 Marlboro' Street, now occupied for English Goods and Shoes. Possession given the first day of October next . . . Apply to Thomas Fletcher, 64 Cornhill." Shortly thereafter Thomas wrote to his father that "Gardiner & myself are going to Phila. We shall be ready to leave here in 3 or 4 weeks from this time." He wrote his next letter to his father on December 16, 1811: "I arrived in this place on the 10th of last month since which I have been so much occupied in filling up our store and purchasing goods that I have not been able to write . . . although the removal of our business here has been attended with a great expense we have every reason to believe we shall meet with success. We opened on the 2d of this month. Our store is No. 24 South Second Street."[24]

This move proved to be perhaps the single most significant decision Thomas Fletcher and Sidney Gardiner ever made as partners. It launched them into a realm of success that had existed only in their imaginations. More important, this juncture marks a watershed in the story of silver (and gold) in America. Fletcher and Gardiner revolutionized the significance of the precious metals in the United States as a medium of public appreciation and celebration of heroes. Silver and gold had a long and honorable tradition as a visible, tangible, and permanent record of significant events and people in this country. Even so, the monumental silver and gold artifacts that the Fletcher & Gardiner firm was to make in response to government and private commissions for the heroes of the War of 1812 had no precedent or counterpart in their grand scale, patriotic imagery, complicated fabrication, or multiple stylistic allusions. As such, the partnership gave shape to an era of American silver that spoke grandly to American's self-perception and the heightened sense of pride for those who represented the nation in the international as well as domestic arena.

This alone would have been enough to ensure the partners' place in history. However, their vision was as broad as it was high. In responding to numerous enthusiastic communal subscriptions for silver and gold monuments to American heroes, the partners realized that these same subscribers were also desirous of owning silver. Fletcher and Gardiner positioned themselves to fulfill that desire and met with a decades-long flood of orders, resulting in a large and impressive body of household and personal silver bearing their names.

Fletcher and Gardiner first publicly announced their arrival in Philadelphia in the December 19, 1811, issue of the *Aurora General Advertiser*.

NEW JEWELLRY STORE

Fletcher & Gardiner, Inform their friends that they have taken the Stand, No. 24, South Second Street, Lately occupied by Mr. [James] Vulcain, Where they intend carrying on extensively the Manufactory of Silver Plate And Jewellery, of every kind.

They have for sale a Handsome Assortment of Goods, In their line, which they offer very low, consisting of:-

Gold and Silver Watches, Plated Tea and Coffee Setts, Candlesticks and Branches, Sconces, Elegant Cut Glass and common Castors, Baskets, Salt Stands, Liquor Frames, Fish Knives, Rich strung Pearl Setts, comprising Necklace, Ear-Rings, bracelets, Broach and Wreath.

Pearl Set and Filagree Ear-Rings, Finger Rings, Bracelets and Broaches, Elastic Gold Necklaces, Bracelet Bands, &c.

Mourning Rings, Pins and Bracelets, Gold Chains, Seals and Keys, and a variety of low priced Jewellry and Plated Goods.

Silver spoons, Ladles, Tea Setts, and all other plate work made to order.

Cash paid for Diamonds, Pearls and other Gems.-Pearls elegantly set.

Though shorter than many of the advertisements they had placed in Boston newspapers, it differs little in content, noting that the partners were capable of supplying all kinds of jewelry and silver of their own make as well as plated wares, watches, and, by implication through the phrase "assortment of goods," other kinds of fancy hardware, which they imported. Concurrent with this newspaper announcement, the partners had a trade card printed to distribute to prospective customers.[25]

Newspaper advertisements, trade cards, and walk-in customers accounted for three principal means by which the partners fostered their new business in Philadelphia. A fourth avenue that necessitated collegial goodwill from one's competitors involved immersing themselves in the network of those who were involved in the precious metals trade in the city. Business connections that had been made with Philadelphia jewelers and silversmiths during trips from Boston must have been invaluable. Men such as Samuel Williamson, Simon Chaudron, Harvey Lewis, and Thomas Whartenby helped as the partners familiarized themselves with the geography of the city—which influenced where to locate for maximum visibility and accessibility—as well as the political and social landscape of Philadelphia. Both were critical to success in the precious metals and fancy hardware trades. Fletcher and Gardiner adeptly negotiated these hurdles associated with their resettlement to Philadelphia. Success soon followed, as confirmed in a letter Fletcher sent to his father on December 19, 1813, "I have no apology to offer for my long silence except the great pressure of business, which has been such for the last six months that I have not found leisure to write . . . We have plenty of work in hand."[26]

The War of 1812

Prior to and during Fletcher and Gardiner's preoccupation with building their names as a resource for those interested in silver and fancy hardware, events were taking place that would have a profound effect on their business. The War of 1812, in which the United States pitted itself against Great Britain, filled center stage. Events leading to that two-and-one-half-year conflict began shortly after the American Revolution but simmered toward a boiling point about 1803, with England's systematic impressment of American sailors on the high seas. That and other economic and political tensions between the two resulted in President James Madison asking Congress to declare war on Great Britain, which it did on June 18, 1812. There followed a series of engagements between American and British land and sea forces that ended in a stalemate. Even so, given the American navy's small size and lack of extensive training, several of its officer corps conducted themselves impressively under fire.

Among the more illustrious instances was the encounter between the American frigate *Constitution* and the British frigate *Guerrière* just off Cape Race, Newfoundland, on August 19, 1812. The captain of the British ship, James R. Dacres, fired broadside at long range, while the commander of the *Constitution*, Isaac Hull, held fire and maneuvered his position. In the evening Hull gave the order to fire. Within fifteen minutes he had shot away the *Guerrière's* mizzenmast and reduced its sails and rigging to a tangled wreckage. Two further volleys destroyed the *Guerrière's* mainmast and foremast, leaving the vessel totally helpless. Dacres then surrendered. After the crew was evacuated, the ship, damaged beyond recovery, was set afire.[27] Hull and his victorious crew returned to port amid great celebration.

The United States Navy enjoyed a number of such victories, but not without its share of defeats. When Americans did wrest a victory, much was made of it. One battle that gave particular cause for celebration occurred on Lake Erie, where an American squadron under the command of Oliver Hazard Perry approached a British fleet commanded by Robert H. Barclay on September 10, 1813. Perry, in the *Lawrence*, received the brunt of the British cannonade. Upon closing to pistol range with the British, his ship continued to endure fire,

killing or wounding all but 20 of his 103-man crew. Perry saw that the *Lawrence* was damaged beyond use and so had himself rowed one-half mile through a hail of shot to another of his ships, the *Niagara*, which was relatively unscathed. With it in the forefront of his remaining squadron, he resumed the onslaught. The British line was then so battered that they surrendered. Perry's victory gave the United States complete command of Lake Erie and thus control of the northwest flank of the country.[28]

The American public followed military engagements on land and sea with great interest. Their enthusiasm was one of a new nation testing its mettle. During the War of 1812, early naval successes were publicly celebrated. State legislatures strove to outdo one another by commissioning portraits, medals, silver services, and ornamental swords as well as voting cash awards for their native-born heroes. America's challenge to British naval power and national awareness of an international military presence were widely acclaimed by newspapers. Philadelphia, like other urban areas, hosted banquets and parades featuring painted fabric transparencies depicting specific victories, music, flags, and evening illuminations. Naval battle scenes painted and engraved by American artists were widely reproduced, even on handkerchiefs, tobacco boxes, and other personal items. Poets published rhapsodic praises, and musicians composed heroic tunes. And the tallest, weightiest, and most capacious silver objects ever produced in America to that date were created by the firm of Fletcher & Gardiner.

Presentation Urns

Gifts of silver in recognition of heroism or military service have a long history in Western culture, but citizens in this era of the young republic sponsored a form that was relatively unexplored in North American silversmithing—grand presentation urns. Customary trophies such as bowls or double-handle cups, typical of eighteenth-century prizes, no longer suited the vision of a war hero's "suitable plate" award. The taste for expansive expressions of gratitude in silver was matched by the significant funds raised for each gift. Groundswells of appreciation in urban areas promoted public-subscription campaigns to raise money. Heroes in the first wave of victories, Captains Isaac Hull and Jacob Jones, were both recognized by the citizens of Philadelphia with urns made by Fletcher & Gardiner.

Signatories to the subscription list that circulated in Philadelphia for Hull's victory agreed "to contribute the sum severally annexed to our names for the purpose of procuring a splendid piece of Plate to be presented to Captain Hull and another of less value to Lieut [Charles]

Morris in testimony of our warmest admiration and esteem". The list comprises 169 individuals and companies who pledged between $3 and $115. A committee of six Philadelphians—Commodore Richard Dale, U.S.N.; William Jones, merchant; George Harrison, Navy agent; Charles Biddle, Prothonotary of the City and County of Philadelphia; Thomas W. Francis, merchant; and John Sergeant, attorney at law—met on September 5, 1812, to confirm "that a piece of plate of the most elegant workmanship, ornamented with appropriate emblems, devices, and inscriptions be presented . . . to captain Isaac Hull."[29] That committee was also to determine the recipient of the commission. Philadelphia silversmiths Joseph Anthony, Jr., Simon Chaudron, John B. Dumoutet, Harvey Lewis, James Black, Thomas Whartenby, Joseph Lownes, John McMullin, and Samuel Richards were all reputable craftsmen, had worked in the city for a time, and possessed the skills to fabricate a tribute in silver.

Yet not one of the above-mentioned men received the commission, which amounted to the then-substantial sum of $3,000. This fact is somewhat surprising, particularly for Chaudron, Whartenby, and Lewis, all of whom were established craftsmen commissioned to make other silver for presentation to heroes of the War of 1812. It is worth noting that none of their names appear on the subscription list for the Hull silver, whereas Fletcher & Gardiner pledged $20. In so doing, they counted themselves among the "citizens of Philadelphia" who were underwriting this worthwhile project. At the same time, it is not unreasonable to presume that the partners saw an opportunity and, in a clever marketing strategy, offered their services to the committee members overseeing disposition of the project.

Their salesmanship paid off handsomely, as suggested by an advertisement the partners placed in the December 7, 1812, issue of the *Aurora General Advertiser*: "TO SILVERSMITHS WANTED IMMEDIATELY, two or three Journeymen Silversmiths, they must be good workmen and of steady habits." This need to bolster the shop staff with trained craftsmen surely sprang from the commencement of work on the Hull project as well as the need to fulfill existing orders.

Within a year, Fletcher could proudly proclaim to his father that "we have got our silver urn finished for Captain Hull – it cost $2200 – we have had thousands to view it, and it is allowed to be the most elegant piece of workmanship in this Country – we have plenty of work in hand – the Philadelphians don't like to see the Yankees get above them." He also wrote to his brother James that "our great work the Urn for Capt Hull is at last completed. It weighs 502 ounces pure silver and has cost nearly 2300 dollars. I need not tell you how proud it makes us. We do not fear a competition very soon – when will the public

Fig. 3.4 Fletcher & Gardiner, urn presented to Isaac Hull, 1813. Private collection (see cat. no. 10 for full description).

feeling be excited to this degree again? Others are in hand for Bainbridge, Jones, Morris, Biddle, & the Immortal Perry – we have them all to make."[30] (Fig. 3.4)

Fletcher and Gardiner's acquisition of the Hull commission marked another critical juncture in their careers. Had that not occurred, there is little doubt that the firm would have enjoyed a long and prosperous run. However, that award set into motion a series of decisions on the part of the public that propelled the firm to the zenith of its domain. The prestige engendered in the Hull commission was noted by patriotic citizens throughout the United States. It is little wonder, then, that when groups decided to honor their favored hero with a suitable piece of plate, they looked to Fletcher & Gardiner. When

Fig. 3.5 James H. Young and George Delleker (engraved by), Fletcher & Gardiner trade card, Philadelphia, ca. 1817. Joseph Downs Collection of Manuscripts and Printed Ephemera, Winterthur Library.

Fig. 3.6 James H. Young and George Delleker, re-engraved Fletcher & Gardiner trade card, Philadelphia, ca. 1830. Joseph Downs Collection of Manuscripts and Printed Ephemera, Winterthur Library.

Fig. 3.7 James H. Young and George Delleker, re-engraved Thomas Fletcher trade card, Philadelphia, ca. 1837. Joseph Downs Collection of Manuscripts and Printed Ephemera, Winterthur Library, Gift of the Friends of Winterthur.

citizens in Newport, Rhode Island, wanted to present their esteemed native son Commodore Oliver Hazard Perry with a silver testimonial for his victory on Lake Erie, they approached not a Boston, Providence, or New York silversmith but the Fletcher & Gardiner firm to create a piece of silver to be "executed in a manner very honorable to the taste of the subscribers."[31]

The grand urn commissions won by Fletcher & Gardiner were risky from a business point of view. Creating new forms of presentation silver demanded a big investment in design time since new casting molds and ornamental patterns had to be fabricated and talented journeymen had to be hired for special associated tasks. Traditional forms ill suited public need, which demanded fresh interpretations from American silversmiths. Thus, work time and labor were costly risks, and payment was often limited by the subscription amount before Fletcher & Gardiner knew how much the finished product might cost. The firm also risked disappointing the public. The pressures were ponderous.

Yet the firm embraced the challenge. The presentation silver they produced reveals their experiences along a learning curve in artistic design and business practices toward an impressive mastery of both. The partners absorbed design ideas from Philadelphia's artistic community and European sources, deliberately filtering and shaping to suit their own recognizable style. In response, the public renown gained through awards for War of 1812 heroes launched Fletcher & Gardiner as the premier silver manufactory in the United States. This reputation was invaluable and something the partners struggled to sustain throughout their careers.

In Philadelphia they continued to build, moving their shop to a more fashionable and advantageous address, 130 Chesnut Street. Fletcher's younger brother Charles wrote that "our shop is almost completed & will be by far, the handsomest in the City when completed. G[ardiner] says he intends it shall be the headquarters for the fashionable ton – & says that he intends to 'drive' business this fall."[32] At the same time, Fletcher and Gardiner had a trade card engraved with their new address and their *chef d'oeuvre*, the great urn for Isaac Hull. (Figs. 3.5–3.7)

On a larger scale they knew they had to cement and broaden business connections with counterparts and suppliers in England and on the European continent. Toward that end, Fletcher wrote to his brother James that "should peace take place during the ensuing autumn or winter, I shall no doubt leave here [Philadelphia] for Europe early in the Spring, where by the aid of certain funds to be there placed at my disposal I shall make such purchases as will give us a decided superiority in point of business to any in our line . . . My head is so full of vast projects & I shall never rest untill I have put them in execution."[33]

Fig. 3.8 Engraving of fused-plate cruet and caster frame of the type that influenced the design of Fletcher & Gardiner cat. no. 36. From Chris. Wilson & Co., *Book of Patterns* (London, ca. 1820). Printed Book and Periodical Collection, Winterthur Library.

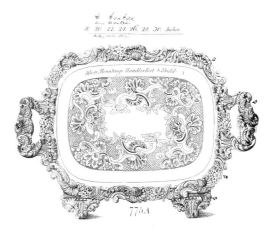

Fig. 3.9 Engraving of fused-plate tray of the type that influenced the design of Fletcher & Gardiner cat. no. 37. From Chris. Wilson & Co., *Book of Patterns* (London, ca. 1820). Printed Book and Periodical Collection, Winterthur Library.

Fletcher's First Trip Abroad

War between the United States and England did come to a close. Fletcher wrote his father on March 15, 1815, that "I have taken passage on board the Ship Superior . . . which leaves this port [Philadelphia] for Liverpool tomorrow . . . I expect to visit France before I return, and perhaps Germany and Switzerland, I cannot therefore inform you how long I shall be absent, but I suppose it will be about a year." He carried with him funds to purchase goods and establish a respectable correspondence: "Every facility has been afforded me and I have some of the best letters of credit that could be procured – I am going out solely on account of ourselves [Fletcher & Gardiner] . . . Sam[ue]l Williams Esq will be my friend and banker in London." As Fletcher most likely knew before he left for England and confirmed after he arrived, silver was no less expensive there. So he did not concern himself with the purchase of English silver but spent his time "going among the manufactories and in buying goods, in which I have been successful – I hope Gardiner & Charles will be as fortunate in selling them."[34]

The experience the partners had garnered in Boston and Philadelphia selling silver of their own make and retailing fancy hardware made by others served Fletcher well during his buying trip. That, and his innate sense of what would appeal to American sensibilities, enabled him to purchase wholesale a variety of goods, which he then sent to the store at 130 Chesnut Street. Silver-plated wares constituted a significant portion, with extensive purchases from Roberts, Cadman & Co; Kirkby, Waterhouse & Co; Watson, Pass & Co; and Watson, Bradbury & Co, all manufacturers in Sheffield, amounting to hundreds of pounds Sterling. The goods were detailed in advertisements in Philadelphia newspapers: "Plated Candlesticks, Rich plated and cut glass Castors, Chamber Candlesticks, Elegant Candlesticks and Branches with silver borders, Bread and Fruit Baskets, Tea and Coffee

Setts silver mounted, Decanter Stands, goblets, Flaggons, Waiters, Tea Urns, wine Coolers, Snuffers & Trays [and let it be known that these are] of entire new patterns, selected by one of the house."[35]

The mercantile connections Fletcher made on this trip with English manufacturers of plated wares remained vital for the duration of his firm's existence, as evidenced by ongoing advertisements in Philadelphia's newspapers. The firm had good reason to emphasize its offerings in silver-plated wares, for they were in great demand in the United States and had been since the 1750s, following the invention of fused plate by Thomas Boulsover in Birmingham, England.[36] These wares well suited a large segment of the American buying public; they looked like their English silver counterparts but cost significantly less. Consequently, the demand was considerable and promised impressive profit for anyone able to supply it.

A second and equally important advantage for importing fused plate was as a source of stylistic inspiration for the silver the firm was called upon to make. Although the partners had the artistic and technical ability to interpret a customer's verbal or written order in making silver, it was much more expedient for a local customer to select a plated object from their inventory and direct them to make one just like it in silver. For customers who were placing orders for silver from a distance, the partners selected in their stead. Relationships in the form and ornament of their work give evidence to the less expensive goods they were importing. (Figs. 3.8, 3.9)

While fused plate in the latest fashion formed a major part of Fletcher's purchases during his trip, he also sought a diverse category of goods that he knew would interest his customers. These were generally referred to as fancy hardware and consisted of both personal and household objects that were serviceable but by virtue of their style, material, or purpose reflected favorably on their owner's

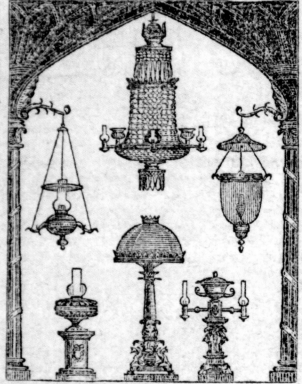

Fig. 3.10 Gardiner & Veron advertisement. From *Philadelphia Gazette and Daily Advertiser*, May 17, 1823. The Library Company of Philadelphia.

taste and status. Gold and silver pocket watches (from Robert Roskell in Liverpool); watch keys, seals, and penknives (from Thomas Nowill in Sheffield); men's shaving cases, ladies' work boxes, japanned tea trays, table china, and scissors (from James & Thomas Barlow in Sheffield); table knives and ornamental hair combs (from Samuel & George Dalton in Sheffield); fruit knives (from John Law in Sheffield); Britannia (from John Vickers in Sheffield); and glass for the table (from Biddle & Lloyd in Birmingham) all fell into this category.[37]

Many of these goods were intended for sale in the Fletcher & Gardiner shop. However, Fletcher realized this trip offered an unparalleled opportunity and therefore planned to create a network of separate but related businesses to be run by family members. He offered the kernel of his idea in a letter to his partner's younger brother, Baldwin: "In my several letters to my partner of May 11 [1815] & yesterday, I suggested to him a plan for a new establishment of w[hic]h you are proposed to be the principle. From the acquaintance I've already made w[it]h the manuf[acture]rs here, I'm convinced that it will be in my power to send out a much larger quantity of goods than can well be disposed of in our present establishment." While Fletcher couched the wording of this proposal to his employee in an objective and businesslike tone, he was much more enthusiastic in his letters to his partner: "Why should we lose the golden harvest which awaits us? Why should we not secure to ourselves to the greatest extent the benefits to be derived from my voyage across the Atlantic?"[38]

The Business Expands:
Gardiner, Veron & Company

Fletcher's vision, as outlined to Baldwin and another member of Fletcher's extended family, Lewis Veron, began with a second store in Philadelphia that would specialize in fancy hardware. Fletcher & Gardiner served as the parent firm and through its connections overseas supplied the new business with goods for a portion of the profit. After differences of opinion about the sharing of profits were resolved, the new firm, styled Gardiner, Veron & Company, opened its doors in 1816 at 98 Chesnut Street, Philadelphia.[39] (Fig. 3.10)

Their store offered an extensive inventory of goods that Fletcher felt would be of interest to style-conscious Philadelphians, including "almost every article in the *house furnishing* line." In most instances these were purchased wholesale or on credit, shipped to the United States, unpacked, inventoried, advertised, displayed, and sold to customers leaving no physical record of their connection with Thomas Fletcher and his extended familial network. This appears to have been intentional, as

Fig. 3.12 (below) Thomas Messenger & Sons, argand lamp, Birmingham, England, 1827–40. Retailed by Lewis Veron & Co., Philadelphia. Brass and glass. Dallas Museum of Art, The Faith P. and Charles L. Bybee Collection, Gift of Faith P. Bybee.

Fig. 3.11 (left) Embossed label on Thomas Messenger argand lamp, reading "LEWIS VERON & CO / PHILADELPHIA." Dallas Museum of Art, The Faith P. and Charles L. Bybee Collection, Gift of Faith P. Bybee. Photo courtesy of DAPC, Winterthur Library.

recorded in an order for lamps Fletcher placed with Birmingham lamp manufacturer Thomas Cox: "I wish the lamps now ordered to have <u>no name</u> on them. [Also] if you have a pattern book, I will thank you to send me one." Fletcher also ordered lamps from Thomas Messenger & Sons in Birmingham and Pellatt & Green in London. These were sold in his store and in Gardiner & Veron's. The latter did a thriving business in lighting, initiated by Fletcher, which continued after the partners separated in 1826, at which time Gardiner moved to New York City and Veron remained in Philadelphia. Many English lamps survive bearing embossed labels placed on the burner tubes by their manufacturers that read B. GARDINER NEW.YORK and LEWIS VERON & CO PHILADELPHIA.[40] (Figs. 3.11, 3.12)

English lamp, fancy hardware, and fused-plate manufacturers provided a veritable cornucopia of goods that Fletcher & Gardiner tapped for the American buying public. But it was not Fletcher's intention to exclude items made on the European continent. Therefore, following his visit in England, he traveled to Paris. He informed his parents in August 1815, that "I have found many goods that will answer our market and my business is such that it will be an object for me to remain here for some time – I shall not therefore return until spring." Toward that end Fletcher's "friend and banker in London," Samuel Williams, extended him credit between £1,000 and £2,000 for purchasing in France. A number of French goods are enumerated in newspaper advertisements, including epaulettes, plumes, vellum lace, gold and silver tassels, silk gloves, reticules, perfume, handkerchiefs, china figures representing the "4 elements" and "*la marchande de fleurs,*" and "about 5 doz[e]n gold watches of almost every size & quality [and] 12 doz silver watches." He further noted that he "pd Dubuc for clocks by F.W. [$] 780," [described as] "pendule, white marble & gilt," depicting "Chariot de Telemaque," "Terpsicore & Cupid," "Venus Coquille," "Sapho," and "figure of Washington with American devices."[41]

Artistic Inspiration

Another reason for Fletcher's trip, artistic inspiration, was referenced often in his letters and travel diary. He continually sought ideas he could turn to advantage in his Philadelphia manufactory. His journal recording expenses in Paris notes that he purchased a "catalogue of antiques" for $1.50, and a "sketch book" for $3.00, the latter to record useful things he saw for future reference. He also bought "antique engravings" for the substantial sum of $50.00. Yet that purchase pales in light of the $165.00 he spent with Parisian brass founders "Deniere & Matelin for Models," a firm celebrated for their exquisite gilt brass cases for mantel clocks.[42] It is likely Fletcher purchased figures and ornamental embellishments of the type that were affixed to these clock cases, believing they would serve him well in the design of silver after returning to Philadelphia.

Fletcher had also actively sought inspiration in England, noting in diary fashion that he "went to the British Gallery, Bouher's Panoramas – Mr. West's – Mrs. Linnwood's needlework &c." A particularly rewarding instance occurred during his visit to the celebrated English silversmithing firm of Rundell, Bridge & Rundell. He noted in his diary that "here I saw elegant silver chased work, the first I have met with . . . on going into the back room – I was shown cases filled with goods of the most costly kind . . . some wine coolers in the [antique] style & a candelabra formed of branches supported by figures of boys."[43]

The time Fletcher spent abroad purchasing goods and seeking artistic inspiration was invaluable to him in furthering his career, providing ideas for future creations, and advancing the competitiveness of the business. As noted by Sidney Gardiner in a letter to Fletcher ten months after his departure from Philadelphia: "Our goods cause so much [interest] this last week that I have not haded a moments time from morning till 11 at night to make any remarks on the goods – but I can tell you that [no] store ... in the United States looks so well as ours does at this time & the people flock around our windows & in the store as if they never had seen anything of the kind – your good [name] is better known at present than it would have been for a long time to come, if you had remained in Philad[elphi]a."[44]

New Manufacturing Processes

Fletcher also had a third item on his agenda during this trip—exploring manufacturing processes that had been incorporated into, and successfully supplanted, traditional craft techniques in the English silversmithing community, including the production of fused plate. Consequently, he devoted a significant amount of time to visiting English silver and fused-plate manufactories to study and record their workings. He wrote in his travel diary after visiting a shop in Sheffield that he saw a gravity-operated downfall press designed so that a "workman is enabled to raise it with one hand & strike up whatever he wishes with great facility." Several days later, he recorded that he went "to the rolling mill [where] the works are turned by steam – rolls cast iron – longest 3 ft & 12 or 14 in dia. . . . – here I saw the copper in bars about 6 in long & 1¼ in thick plated with silver about as thick as a wafer – when ready for use the silver is as thin as silk paper."[45] He carefully drew a small sketch of the rolling mill to accompany his description.

Fletcher also visited another manufacturer where he saw "downfall sliding weights and a vast quantity of steel dies used for striking up parts of articles of various kinds . . . the larger vessels are raised, soldered and swaged in the same manner as we do our silver work. The shells, and gadroons & other ornaments are stamped up from dies, and filled with soft solder . . . The whole process of manufacturing plated ware appears extremely simple and easily obtained by those [like us] who have been in the habit of making silver. The principal obstacles to such an establishment in our Country are first, the great capital required – secondly, the high price of labor."[46]

In spite of Fletcher's closing comment, he did do more than simply observe these techniques and processes. Following a visit to Matthew Boulton's works, he "called at Darwin's Manufactory of Steel Works, mills &c. [where he bought] a pair of 10 inch rollers with frame & wheels & pinions complete for 32½ - & two small mills besides a letter press which I intend to have altered for a cutting press. The whole cost £48.15." He planned to install "the rollers with frame" in his manufactory to roll silver into sheets, thereby speeding the process and lessening the cost to manufacture silverware for his customers. The "two small mills" he bought were different in purpose. They were destined for the production of ornamental borders. In order to serve as intended, they required rollers engraved with decorative designs around the perimeter. For that, Fletcher turned to a Sheffield die sinker and ornament maker, Mark Tyzack, who wrote to Fletcher that he had "received your parcel with Patterns enclosed for Two Borders and I will endeavor to have them done to your satisfaction, as well as the others before Order'd –

But respecting the time I cannot speak precisely for I have not yet got the rolls from Messrs. Darwin."[47] (Fig. 3.13)

Fletcher had been applying his time and talent to productive purpose while studying art and silver in England and France. He used his pencil not only to record his travels but also to create designs for decorative borders that, with the help of Tyzack and others of his ability, would figure so prominently in the construction and visual impact of silver emanating from the Fletcher & Gardiner manufactory. (Figs. 3.14, 3.15)

No. 1.—STAMPING THE TRIMMINGS.   No. 2.—SAFE WHERE DIES ARE KEPT.   No. 3.—ROLLING THE PLATES.

Fig. 3.13 *The American at Work, IV: Among the Silver-Platers.* From Randolph T. Percy, *Appleton's Journal* 5, no. 31 (December 1878), p. 483. Courtesy of Rutgers University.

An engraved roller (die) for making an ornamental border can be seen in the center (bottom) of this illustration.

Fig. 3.14 Preliminary drawing of rose-and-leaf border for die-rolled decoration on Fletcher & Gardiner silver. From Thomas Fletcher notebook, Thomas Fletcher Papers, Collection 39, The Athenaeum of Philadelphia.

Fig. 3.15 Preliminary drawing of shell-and-leaf and bound-laurel-leaf border for die-rolled decoration on Fletcher & Gardiner silver. From Thomas Fletcher notebook, Thomas Fletcher Papers, Collection 39, The Athenaeum of Philadelphia.

Return to Philadelphia: The Chesnut Street Shop

Having made many commercial connections, purchased great quantities of goods, and familiarized himself with production modes and the current styles developing in the most fashionable shops and manufactories in England and France, Fletcher returned to America in April 1816 and immediately began to capitalize on his overseas sojourn. By 1818 he was able to state that "after having spent more than a year in England & France & examined with critical attention the manufacturing establishments of those Countries, I have since my return devoted myself almost exclusively to the improvement of Manufactures at home, in which I have been tolerably successful. Our Plate and Jewellery establishment is in a flourishing state, notwithstanding the great influx of foreign articles of similar kinds."[48] The partners used the elevated reputation of their firm to pursue their ambitions on four fronts: expanding the operations of the manufactory, enlarging their network of familial retail stores, investing in manufacturing opportunities outside the precious metals, and fostering the level of American arts and manufactures in general.

The Fletcher & Gardiner shop at 130 Chesnut Street was well situated in the section of the city that served the financial community as well as those interested in fashionable goods. (Fig. 3.16) It was a Mecca of sorts, attracting large numbers of customers who sought goods for their household but also for resale in other businesses. As Charles Fletcher noted: "Our store is completely drained of all kinds of goods – a number of <u>dealers</u> are waiting until we receive a further supply of Birm[ingha]m plated ware – Thibault has already purchased of us $252 – & says he will buy at least $1000 more."[49]

The store and manufactory into which these retail and wholesale customers thronged was but two doors from the Second Bank of the United States. The Fletcher & Gardiner shop was a substantial brick building with two large show windows, one on either side of the entry door on the ground floor. There were two floors, each with three bays, and a dormered garret above. The building measured twenty-four feet across the front and forty-three feet deep. The first floor consisted of one large room, used as a jewelers shop and a hallway; the second floor was divided into two rooms and a passage; the third floor and garret were each divided into three rooms. In addition, the building had a piazza (stair hall) that provided access to the upper floors, which served as living spaces. Behind the piazza was a sitting room and kitchen. Located directly behind the store, separated by a three-foot wide alley, was the manufactory. Also made of brick, it stood three stories high, each floor containing one room only, with part of the first floor paved in brick. A third building, described

as a house and piazza, stood behind the manufactory, separated by another narrow alley. This building, also three stories high, included a garret. The first story had two rooms, one of which was a kitchen; the second floor was divided into three rooms, and the third story into two rooms separated from each other with a board partition.[50]

Of these three buildings, the salesroom and manufactory were a hive of activity during daylight hours. The firm employed a small army of journeymen and apprentices. Although their numbers rose and fell from time to time, they were typically substantial. The manufactory employed no fewer than sixteen apprentices during Fletcher's time in England and France. In addition, others worked in the salesroom. They expected these employees, many of whom probably lived in the building at the rear of the property behind the manufactory, to work a long day, judging from a comment Fletcher made in a letter to his wife, Melina: "Tell Baldwin [Gardiner] that his boys are not such early risers as he thinks they are – I past his store [in New York City] at a quarter before six [am] and it was not open," strongly suggesting that Fletcher wanted his employees to be fully engaged in work by that time of day.[51]

Fig. 3.16 M.E.D. Brown, *The Gold & Silver Artificers of Philadelphia in Civic Procession, 22 Feb. 1832* (detail). The Historical Society of Pennsylvania. The Fletcher & Gardiner manufactory and wareroom can be seen to the left.

The taking of apprentices in the goldsmithing and jewelers trades was a long-established practice when Fletcher and Gardiner opened their Boston business in 1808. The arrangement mandated that an apprentice give fully of his time and allegiance to his master for a specified period of time, as witnessed by the indenture in which Phineas Wittington bound his son, Samuel, to learn the art, trade, and mystery of a jeweler. It stipulated that Fletcher and Gardiner would assume responsibility for Samuel and teach him the essentials of the craft, in exchange for which the apprentice owed the partners three years of his undivided time and energy.[52] Signing such a document was a weighty responsibility for both parties. It was predicated on the belief that the master would have enough business to support himself and his apprentice for the duration of the latter's training.

Yet, such business arrangements were evolving in Philadelphia at this time, driven in part by the increasing involvement of the "entrepreneur," who, by investing capital, served as either agent for production or middleman between craftsman and consumer. Entrepreneurs invested for profit, not the perpetuation of a craft. To maximize prospects for success, they had to maintain flexibility, particularly with regard to business cycles and changing demand—the antithesis of apprenticeships. Fletcher and Gardiner were not insensitive to this fact and during the life of their firm appear to have adjusted their business accordingly. Although they supported sixteen apprentices in their manufactory in 1815, by 1820 that number had fallen to nine. At the same time they were paying nine employees.[53] By weaning themselves from the apprentice system and hiring paid workmen and women instead, all of whom answered to a shop foreman (Daniel H. Dodge from about 1819 to 1822 and George W. South thereafter until 1826), Fletcher and Gardiner protected their firm from unpredictable and potentially destructive fluctuations in demand for their goods.

Machine Production

Another evolutionary episode in which Fletcher and Gardiner participated involved the adoption of machine production to supplement or replace human effort. The incorporation of die-rolled borders into the partners' earliest silver and die-stamped jewelry suggests they either purchased borders or used machinery to a limited extent from the outset. However, they committed themselves heavily to the use of machines following Fletcher's explorations in English manufactories in 1815. Within a few years after that trip, they had incorporated hand mills for flatting silver, making ornamental borders, and cutting shapes as well as gravity-operated downfall presses for stamping jewelry, ornaments, and probably components such as lids for teapots, sugar bowls, and sauce tureens. Not

Fig. 3.17 *The American at Work, IV: Among the Silver-Platers.* From Randolph T. Percy, *Appleton's Journal* 5, no. 31 (December 1878), p. 484. Courtesy of Rutgers University.

This illustration shows a die-stamping machine. The worker is stamping bowl-shaped forms. The Fletcher & Gardiner manufactory used a similar process.

long thereafter, possibly encouraged by promotions like Thomas Hatt's exhibit in 1822 of a "STEAM ENGINE . . . driven with atmospheric air upon the precise principles of steam" at the Shakespeare Hotel opposite the State House in Philadelphia, Fletcher and Gardiner installed a steam engine in their manufactory. It replaced human and gravitational power in driving the firm's machinery, enhancing productive capacity and benefiting the firm's profit margin. Fletcher stated in a letter to Baldwin Gardiner in 1831 that "I have had about as much [business] as we could attend to with the power we have, your steam is on the high pressure principle, - ours on the low – my engineers are afraid of bursting their boilers if they move at a more rapid rate."[54] (Fig. 3.17)

In addition to lessening human effort, machinery fostered compartmentalization of labor. Given the demand that existed for spoons at this time, it made sense for Fletcher to invest in a machine to produce them quickly in quantity and train a workman to operate it exclusively. In so doing, he was assured of uniformity in his product and of keeping pace with orders. These employees, whom Fletcher identified as "spoonmakers," operated downfall presses. They were specialists whose focus was on a particular facet of the sequential efforts of production from inception to completion.[55]

Expansion Outside Philadelphia

Fletcher and Gardiner continually explored ways to expand their network in and outside the city, allowing them to supply an ever-increasing number of customers. In addition to the Gardiner & Veron partnership, brothers Charles and George Fletcher, who had been working in the Fletcher & Gardiner manufactory prior to 1813, joined forces in 1819 under their own names at 139 Chesnut Street. They maintained close connection with Fletcher & Gardiner but advertised regularly and independently, noting that they "have constantly for sale, a variety of Jewellery and Fancy Goods . . . mourning jewelry of every description and sets made of any pattern with hair handsomely plaited . . . miniature settings and lockets. . . and every article of Jewelry manufactured in the best manner, and without delay," stating also that "orders from distant jewelers [would be] made up at the lowest wholesale prices."[56] This marketing strategy ultimately sprang from the vision of an expanding network, with Thomas Fletcher and Sidney Gardiner at the center, that would connect them to greater numbers of customers in Philadelphia and others in more distant markets.

Charles and George dissolved their partnership in 1824 but continued to list themselves as jewelers in the Philadelphia directories at different addresses. George ultimately turned his attention to machine and calico engraving, but by the late 1820s Charles had assumed a significant new role in as a "travelling jeweller" for Fletcher & Gardiner in pursuit of business in markets outside Philadelphia. He visited New York and in 1829 wrote from Baltimore to his brother that "I think I could have sold a set of plate in Washington if I had taken one with me and plain shell end spoons several doz & some forks." The next day he noted, "Today I have visited most of the principal jewelers [in Baltimore] and invited them to call on me at Barnums [Hotel] – Mr. R[obert] Campbell called about 12 o'clock & bot for $10 – I opened all my goods & waited until 4 o'clock for more customers but <u>none came</u> . . . Mr. [Hugh] Gelston keeps but little silver plate but wishes to make an arrangement

with someone to supply him with new and handsome patterns . . . Saml Kirk is the principal plate worker here but his patterns are not handsome."[57]

The following month Charles was back in Washington and "sent two sugar dishes up to General [Andrew] Jackson's apartments this afternoon and have learnt that the ladies were well pleased with them & his private secretary sent me word that my house [Fletcher & Gardiner/Thomas Fletcher] should have a fair chance with the other applicants when it should be ascertained what articles may be wanted."[58] Through this aggressive marketing, Charles enabled the Philadelphia firm to offer its silver in every major metropolitan center along the northeastern seaboard. He served as an effective agent for the goods Fletcher & Gardiner imported and allowed the firm to keep abreast of news and trends that might affect its business.

Another of Thomas's brothers, Henry, was also instrumental in the firm's expansive efforts, but in a role complementary to that of Charles. He, too, began his career with the partners, apparently in the salesroom. However, that soon changed. While Fletcher was building inroads in the market for silver and fancy hardware along the eastern seaboard, he was exploring potential to the west. In response to a solicitation he made to William Pelham of Zanesville, Ohio, Pelham wrote to Sidney Gardiner that "in his letter to me Mr. F[letcher] mentions that you will probably have many articles which I might find it advantageous to deal in. I should think you would not have many such, as your assortments will be calculated for the refined taste of an opulent city, whereas my objects of trade must be necessarily limited to articles of necessity, suitable to the first stages of civilized life."[59] Never one to take no for an answer, Fletcher suggested to Henry that opportunity lay west.

Henry initially moved to Lexington, Kentucky, in 1817, where he established himself in the jewelry, silver, and fancy hardware business. But he struggled for ten years, ultimately turning to his brother, who advised that "a vast amount of goods goes out every year . . . through the regions west & south . . . If you would close your concern in Lexington this fall and remove to Louisville early in the Spring and open there a fresh stock of goods suited to the market it appears to me you could not fail of success . . . But I shall expect you to visit Philadelphia to select your stock . . . My silver plate manufactory goes on well and might be made useful to you by supplying you with spoons and tea setts."[60]

Henry did open a shop in Louisville in 1830. He advertised in the local newspaper, listing many of the same objects his brother offered in Philadelphia and welcomed orders for "sets of silverplate which would be executed in Philadelphia." His firm prospered and remained in business beyond his death in 1866. It did so because he took in his nephew, Charles Fletcher Bennett, as an employee in 1843. Charles became a full partner in 1854, and the name of the firm changed from Henry Fletcher to Fletcher & Bennett.[61]

Fletcher & Gardiner had yet another commercial connection, this one through Thomas's elder brother, James, who moved from Massachusetts to New Orleans shortly before Thomas aligned himself with Sidney Gardiner in Boston. Although separated by some 1,500 miles, the brothers remained close through their letters, in which they exchanged personal and family news. They also used these letters as a conduit for business. James wrote to Thomas in 1810, confirming that he had received a parcel of neck chains, filigree, earrings, gold buckles, and other jewelry from the latter that he would either sell or have sold for Fletcher & Gardiner. Shortly thereafter, Thomas wrote in return asking, "Will Carnelian beads, watch keys &c sell well [in New Orleans]? We have received a quantity of carnelian from the East Indies & should be glad to dispose of some of them, also some tortoise shell combs."[62] In addition, like Henry in Louisville, James took orders for jewelry that he had executed in Philadelphia. These and similar arrangements in which the men engaged throughout their lives proved profitable for both. Whereas Fletcher & Gardiner specialized in jewelry, silverware, and fancy hardware, James was a generalist, known as a commission merchant, who traded in anything that would turn a profit, including bales of cotton, barrels of oranges, sugar, tobacco, lead, flour, molasses, furs, and whiskey. Sometimes he involved his brother's firm in this business. Although such transactions did not constitute a large part of Fletcher & Gardiner's business, they added to the firm's profits, and the connections James made in New Orleans prior to his death in 1820 paved the way for substantial subsequent business in that region of the United States.

Political revolution set the stage for another of Fletcher & Gardiner's marketing ventures. Mexico's decade-long struggle for independence from Spanish rule culminated on August 24, 1821, when Augustín de Iturbide, a military revolutionary, and Juan de O'Donojú, representative for Spain, signed the Treaty of Córdoba. Eleven months later Iturbide was crowned Augustín I, Constitutional Emperor of Mexico. Among his first proclamations, Iturbide created an Imperial Order to recognize and reward Mexican subjects loyal to the monarchy—the National Order of Our Lady of Guadalupe. He further declared himself Grand Master of

Fig. 3.18 Augustín de Iturbide, Emperor of Mexico, wearing the National Order of Our Lady of Guadalupe made by Sidney Gardiner, 1822. Courtesy of Woodson Research Center, Fondren Library, Rice University.

the Order and had a badge designed to award to recipients.[63]

The emperor's representative, procuring badges for the Order, chose the Fletcher & Gardiner firm to fill the commission, as Gardiner outlined in a letter to his partner, who was in New York at the time: "Cortes [Cortez] sent for me this morning and read to me in presence of Capts Dallas and Allen, the account of the badge we made, and I can ashure you, it was very flattering to find that my first attempt should have proved so successful . . . the number to be made immediately is about 150."[64] He further wrote that Cortes strongly recommended Gardiner himself go to Mexico and fill the entire order. (Fig. 3.18)

Gardiner did just that. Within two months he wrote from Alvarado, Mexico, to Fletcher, "My passport introduces me as a person having been called in to the country by the government for the purpose of making the Order-imperial of Guadalupe." Given Fletcher and Gardiner's mercantile instincts, it is not surprising they both saw this as an opportunity to cultivate further business, as observed by Gardiner to his partner that "with energy on our part, I think we shall make money in the trade with the Mexicans." In anticipation of building that trade, Gardiner took a variety of goods with him. The partners determined that Mexican customers, in addition to jewelry, were most interested in knives, pocket books, topaz seals, sealing wax, but "it must all be red," quills, writing paper, swords, muskets, lamps, and lamp oil.[65] But they did not limit the scope of their trade goods, assuming instead the role of commission merchants handling anything that would make a profit.

The partners arranged with local agents to help them place their goods in the hands of potential consumers. Taylor, Sicard & Company served in this capacity in Veracruz, while the firm of Parrott & Willson did the same in Mexico City. These two centers appear to have been where Fletcher and Gardiner concentrated their marketing efforts, but they extended to other cities, including Tampico, Jalapa, Alvarado, and Puebla. This network served them well, but they had to deal with bureaucratic delays, political unrest, heavy import duties, graft, and theft. In addition, Gardiner and his brother-in-law Timothy Veron remarked that the weather was oppressive, and they complained constantly of sickness. Indeed, the latter eventually proved fatal for Gardiner. During his final trip to Mexico he succumbed to yellow fever. His obituary noted: "On the 11th of May [1827] Mr. SIDNEY GARDINER, of the House of Fletcher and Gardiner, of [Philadelphia], aged 40 . . . a skillful mechanic, and an enterprising merchant; ardent and zealous in the pursuit of business . . . among the first to engage in the Mexican trade, and had three times visited the Capital of Mexico [two in 1823 and one in 1827], but when on the eve of embarking for his native land, he fell victim to the fatal disease of Vera Cruz."[66] Although Gardiner's death did not immediately curtail his firm's involvement in the Mexican market, it did, in conjunction with financial difficulties, mark the eventual end about two years later.

The death was a severe personal loss to Fletcher, but he remained committed to the many projects he had envisioned during their partnership. In addition to marketing initiatives, these included involvement in manufacturing efforts unrelated to silver and jewelry.

Other Mercantile Initiatives

In 1818, flush with profits from their silver manufactory, Fletcher and Gardiner had invested in "a new and improved method of manufacturing Screws of wire, commonly called Wood Screws, at one operation, by Machinery lately invented in the United States and patented . . . [and] established a manufactory at the Falls of the Schuylkill . . . their intention . . . to supply the whole consumption of the country. In proceeding thus far, they have already expended thirty thousand dollars." Toward that end, in conjunction with partners John O. Stoddard of Philadelphia and Richard T. Leech of Pittsburgh, both merchants, they petitioned Congress to increase the import duty on wood screws, thereby enabling the firm to compete with Great Britain. Their petition followed two separate but related investments. The first was the purchase of a wire mill on the Schuylkill River from Ebenezer Hazard, gentleman investor, and Josiah White, ironmonger. The second was the purchase of rights to the patent for a machine to cut wood screws issued to Hazard and White by the United States Patent Office.[67]

The four partners were certain these investments, if protected by a federal duty, would allow them to nurture a nascent American industry and capitalize on the demand for a product that was sure to grow. Those expectations may well have been fulfilled and amply rewarded were it not for the fact that one of the partners, Stoddard, proved to be an investment adventurer who overextended himself, unbeknownst to Fletcher or Gardiner. Less than three months from the date of the petition to Congress, Stoddard declared bankruptcy with debts amounting to $340,797.12. A portion of his indebtedness was satisfied by the sale of real estate, but there remained an unpaid balance of almost $110,000, for which Fletcher and Gardiner, as his partners, became liable. Their liability proved a heavy burden, embarrassingly advertised in 1820 in Philadelphia's newspapers as "the valuable and extensive stock of Fletcher & Gardiner has been assigned . . . in trust for the benefit of all the creditors, without preference or distinction, [and] is now offered for sale."[68]

News of this event traveled quickly through commercial networks, causing numerous correspondents to express regret that Fletcher & Gardiner had been swindled. They further hoped that the debacle would not harm the reputation of the firm too greatly, as noted in a letter George Newbold, New York City merchant, wrote to silverplate manufacturer Watson & Bradbury in Sheffield, England, one of Fletcher & Gardiner's suppliers: "Fletcher & Gardiner expect to have all their old business arranged this summer [1821] so as to continue as formerly, but [I advise you] do not ship [any orders.] They might be the first house in the U.S. & in full credit from the manufactory of Silver Ware they carry on being the most extensive in the country & yet they cannot pay their bona fide creditors."[69] Fletcher and Gardiner found themselves in an untenable situation from which lesser men would have walked away. However, the partners honorably extracted themselves from the debt and forged ahead with the silver manufactory that had long been their mainstay.

Fletcher participated in two other separate but related investment schemes outside the realm of silver and fancy hardware. One involved a cotton factory in Norristown, Pennsylvania, which failed with the owner's bankruptcy. The other concerned Fletcher's old friend Joseph C. Dyer, who was living in England. Dyer asked Fletcher to help him obtain an American patent on two improvements he had made on roving machines. Fletcher was happy to accommodate his former master, but the seemingly straightforward task proved more vexing than either man envisioned. The patent office in Washington required not only detailed drawings but also a model. The latter, made in England, was unfortunately lost in shipment to America. Fletcher finally wrote Dyer in defeat that, after struggling with the matter for two years, "I have not been able to make any further progress in the business of the patent right."[70]

These and other manufacturing and marketing forays, though sometimes ending in failure and frustration, address the energy Fletcher and Gardiner brought to their business acumen as well as their willingness to risk money, effort, and even reputation on the chance to build commercial success. More broadly, these ventures testify not only to Fletcher and Gardiner's belief that the United States could match England as an industrial entity but also to the partners' desire to participate in that transformation. Fletcher and Gardiner took the initiative by encouraging the full spectrum of American arts and manufactures, not just those associated with their specialty, evidenced by a letter Philadelphia merchant/banker Samuel Jaudon wrote to Fletcher: "The convention of manufacturers & friends of manufactures at a meeting on the 5th [of January 1820] appointed you a delegate to represent this city [Philadelphia] in the Convention of Manufacturers which is to assemble in New York on the third Monday of Jan[uar]y."[71] This meeting foretold the incorporation of the New York Mechanic and Scientific Institution two years later.

Shortly thereafter, 1824, Philadelphia organized its own counterpart, The Franklin Institute of the State of Pennsylvania, for the Promotion of the Mechanic Arts—commonly known as the Franklin Institute. It has been observed that "of all the institutions established [in the United States] during the first half of the nineteenth century to advance technology, none was more successful than the Franklin Institute [which became] the most important technical organization in the country." Thomas Fletcher was one of the founders of the organization, and Sidney Gardiner was a member from its inception. On December 9, 1823, five men—Matthias W. Baldwin, machinist; Oren Colton, shuttlemaker; David H. Mason, engraver; and Samuel V. Merrick, fire engine builder—with Fletcher as the chair, met at the American Philosophical Society. These five formulated and passed two resolutions. The first was to form a "Society for the Promotion of the Mechanic Arts" and the second encompassed appointing a committee to draft a constitution and call a general meeting to which all those interested in belonging could attend. Fletcher, along with six others, constituted the committee responsible for drafting the constitution. An announcement of an invitation to attend a general meeting was placed in local newspapers.[72]

As scripted by its founders, the purpose of the Franklin Institute was to promote the useful arts by diffusing knowledge of mechanical science. This was accomplished by sponsoring lectures, building a collection, encouraging new inventions, and holding annual competitive exhibitions for which prizes were

awarded. Gardiner seems to have supported the Franklin Institute primarily through his membership and occasional service on the exhibition committee, but Fletcher served as treasurer, vice-president, and participant on the exhibition committee. Additionally, the partners contributed their wares to the annual exhibitions. In 1825 the Institute's American Manufactures Exhibition included silver pitchers and cake baskets made by Fletcher & Gardiner under the category "articles of jewellery, plate, &c." Adopting what would become standard tenor for official remarks about these wares, the report of that exhibition stated that "all of the above articles were considered to be of excellent workmanship, and very creditable to their makers, whose reputation is well established." The firm exhibited silver and jewelry again in 1831, 1836, and 1838. Of the second of these, the exhibition committee noted "There was an extensive assortment of [silver] from [Fletcher's] manufactory . . . which contributed much to enhance the splendor of the exhibition, but as Mr. Fletcher is an officer of the Institute, he is precluded from competition."[73] As such, the effort and expense he invested in submitting the products of his manufactory in these competitive exhibitions was philanthropic, intended not only to support the Franklin Institute but also to supply those seeking inspiration with emulative models. (Fig. 3.19)

Fletcher's dedication to, and support of, the Franklin Institute and its mission lasted his entire life. Evidence of that generosity was acknowledged by the Board of Directors in the minutes from a meeting of its officers shortly after his death in 1866: "Whereas Thomas Fletcher, one of the associates of the founder of the Franklin Institute, in bringing it into organized and useful existence . . . we shall ever cherish in our grateful remembrance, his services as Treasurer and Vice-President, and the hearty zeal which, during his active membership, he manifested for every measure that would promote the usefulness and prosperity of the Institute."[74]

Fig. 3.19 Christian Gobrecht, silver medal (obverse) awarded by the Franklin Institute for skill and ingenuity, Philadelphia, 1825–44. Winterthur Museum, 1984.27.

The Final Decade

Following Sidney Gardiner's death in Mexico in 1827, Fletcher remained at 130 Chesnut Street with the aid of a shop manager, overseeing everyday production of orders for jewelry and silver. He continued to seek and receive one-of-a-kind commissions for presentation silver and gold, including a number of gold-hilt swords given to military heroes by state and federal bodies. The most notable of the firm's swords, however, was not for an American. In June 1832, Fletcher received a letter from Calvin Durand, a merchant in New York City, informing him that "An order has been sent out by the merchants of Matanzas [Cuba] to have a superb sword made in this country to be presented by that body of citizens to the late G[ovenor] of Matanzas [Don Cecilio Ayllon], & are desirous of giving the order to such a person as will execute the same to their satisfaction, as well as to do honor to the manufacturer. They are willing to expend $1200 or thereabouts." There followed a flurry of correspondence between Fletcher, Durand, and John A. Grace of Newport, Rhode Island, who wrote Fletcher that:

> my friend Mr. Durand . . . has sent me a copy of your l[ette]r , , , respecting a sword . . . the ornaments must be Spanish & no Republican emblems of any kind can be admitted as the sword being presented to a distinguished Spanish off[icer] lately Governor of Matanzas. I have the Escutcheon of the City which with the initials C.A. worked into the <u>materials</u> of the blade; one in Spanish, the other in Latin or English . . . I presume the clasp of the belt sho[ul]d be a golden lion's head; & the belt itself, red or blue Morocco . . . The sword should be, I presume; strait & what in the British service is called a full dress 'Regulation Sword'- On the outer guard might be chased the Arms or Escutcheon of Matanzas – on the other one (to turn down) the C.A. might perhaps be placed . . . The Spanish motto is, 'Al Señor Don Cecilio por sus virtudes, el Comerico de Matanzas.' Great care must be had to write the above in a plain hand, & print it, so that y[ou]r. artists, who may not read Spanish – may make no mistake in any letter of it and spoil all. The Latin I contemplate is 'Et decus et pretium recti.' One motto on each side of the blade.[75]

Fletcher sent preliminary drawings for the sword to Grace, seeking comment and requesting their return. He felt it would take about four months to complete the commission. Later that month he wrote that the inscriptions Grace stipulated would be:

> etched on the blade together with military trophies & the Royal arms of Spain if I can obtain them in this city (probably the Consul General has them). The hilt I intend to make of fine gold (including the gripe), richly chased, the medallion enclosing the cypher, C.A. to be set with small rubies and topaz to correspond with the Spanish flag and the wreath to be chased in green gold. The collars around the neck of the gripe may be set with turquoise on the outward guards, the arms of Matanzas in bas relief, colored gold – military emblems on the scabbard mountings – diamond eyes to the lion head-&c. The blade will be the most difficult part of the business, and will probably cause the most delay . . . The colour of the Morocco should be Red and the ornamenting gold – corresponding with the national colours.[76]

With an understanding and agreement between the correspondents, Fletcher proceeded with the project, writing to Grace in April 1833: "If I had been less particular with the work, it might have been done a month sooner, but as it is to be seen and criticised in the great city of New York – and perhaps Cadiz and Madrid – I could not consent to give you anything less than the <u>best work</u> that I could have done in my establishment. Consequently some of the parts have undergone alterations to produce a good effect and where the work did not please me, I have had the gold melted and the parts made over again. The sword hilt is now complete and the scabbard will be done tomorrow or the next day. The Belt I shall have completed in the course of a week – but I should like to keep for a day or two to allow my friends an opportunity of seeing it before it goes hence never to return."[77]

Periodic high-visibility commissions such as these added greatly to the firm's fame, but they contributed much less to the profit margin than an ongoing and predictable demand for everyday goods. Fletcher struggled increasingly to maintain orders for jewelry and household silver that would keep his firm healthy, but matters beyond his control often affected this essential component of the business throughout the 1830s. One such incident involved an order from New Orleans for a large table service: "I have not been able to complete

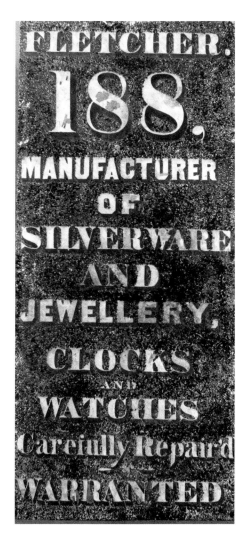

Fig. 3.20 (far left) Thomas Fletcher's trade sign, Philadelphia, 1837–50. Japanned and gilt tinned sheet iron. Private collection.

Fig. 3.21 (left) Thomas Fletcher's trade sign, Philadelphia, 1837–50. Japanned and gilt tinned sheet iron. Private collection.

Fig. 3.22 (above) Box with Thomas Fletcher's watch paper glued to the lid, 1837–50. Private collection.

[your esteemed order] owing to the disastrous state of things produced by the measures of Gen[era]l [Andrew] Jackson – his war against the U.S. Bank . . . This state of things made it necessary for me to discharge the greater part of my hands last winter for want of the material [silver] for them to work upon and funds to pay wages." Fletcher lamented in greater detail to his brother Levi: "The workshop back of 130 Chest. St. is almost deserted. Conrad [Bard, silversmith] & his two boys in one apartment and [George] Jacob [silversmith], Wm. Sharpe [jeweler] & a small boy in the other with an occasional visit from J[ohn] McPherson [die sinker] & E. Langton comprise the principal if not all the inmates of that once busy hive."[78]

To these difficulties another specter beset him involving the Bank of the United States. In July 1836 Fletcher wrote Francis Grillet that "I am full of business having sold out my house & store to the bank of the U.

States to be pulled down. We have to remove out all my goods and everything to do." He may or may not have sold his property voluntarily, as the bank was embroiled in the final phase of losing its charter and restructuring from a federal to a state institution. Regardless, Fletcher moved to 194 Chesnut Street, where his business was listed as Fletcher & Bennett, Fletcher having "taken into partnership [his] nephew [Calvin W.] Bennett [in 1835], who has been with me several years and had the principal charge of the retail business." This arrangement lasted only until January 3, 1837, after which Fletcher continued the business under his "own name . . . between 7th & 8th street." (Figs. 3.20, 3.21) Fletcher was fifty years old, and his glory days had passed. Nonetheless, he remained active in the jewelry and silversmithing business, doing so increasingly through communication with members of the trade who had been an important part of his business since the

Fig. 3.23 Gold one-half Johannes (obverse), Brazil, 1749. This coin was assayed, plugged, and counterstamped by Fletcher & Gardiner about 1816. Collection of Edward Roehrs.

beginning. This sometimes involved jobbing specialized services for commissions he had received and ordering wholesale finished goods from his counterparts.[79] (Fig. 3.22)

Another important, but little-heralded component of Fletcher's business that continued after the firm's heyday involved assaying specie for bankers, merchants, and others who needed to verify the purity of the alloys. In this regard, he wrote to Samuel Jaudon, "I have assayed the pieces of Gold furnished by you and find that they contain 116 grains each of pure gold, and 13 grains of alloy being in that respect consistent with the late law of congress regulating the coinage of gold." This highly specialized service, in which Fletcher determined to a precise degree the composition of precious metal alloys, covered not only American gold eagles and silver dollars but also coins issued by foreign countries. Consequently, agents in Valparaiso, Chile; Maracaibo, Venezuela; and Veracruz and Mexico City, Mexico, sent him specie for assay on a regular basis.[80] (Fig. 3.23)

In 1837, when Fletcher moved a few doors from 194 Chesnut to 188 Chesnut Street, it appears he did so fearing he might not be able to depend solely on the precious metals for his livelihood. That soon became a reality as he adapted space in the building for use as a hotel. Called the Morris House, it was a Temperance Hotel that provided rooms and baths to single persons and families on a transient as well as permanent basis. (Fig. 3.24) The downward spiral in which Fletcher's silversmithing and jewelry business was immersed at this time only worsened. By 1842 he had no choice but to close the door on that aspect of his life, as noted in a letter written to his son Lewis: "Our business affairs grow worse every day – thousands out of employment . . . Our assignee has had three sales at auction of our goods. They produced about one fourth of first cost. Nevertheless he seems determined to close up the business and when that is done I know not what to go at – My factory and tools are all gone – my store will soon be stripped and I am without the means of meeting my daily expenses."[81] (Fig. 3.1)

Those sales, advertised in the Philadelphia *North American and Daily Advertiser*, took place on May 31, June 7, and June 15, 1842. They mark the finale of Fletcher & Gardiner as the nation's premier manufactory of silver and jewelry to that time. But Fletcher still had to earn a living, which he attempted to do with his Temperance Hotel. By 1850 however, it too had failed. He wrote to

Fig. 3.24 Business card for the Temperance Hotel, 188 Chesnut Street, Philadelphia, when it was owned by Thomas Fletcher, 1837–50. Joseph Downs Collection of Manuscripts and Printed Ephemera, Winterthur Library.

Fig. 3.25 Photograph of Thomas Fletcher, ca. 1860. Private collection.

his brother Charles: "I am about to close business here by selling my furniture at auction – I have lost money by keeping the Morris House and am not able to fit it up for the coming winter. It is therefore safer to abandon it and let some other person take it. I have no means nor no business to engage in. I shall literally be 'turned out.' What business shall I pursue?" The answer for Fletcher ironically lay in his early inclination to enter politics. In 1852 he was elected to the office of Prothonotary of the District Court and wrote to his nephew Timothy that "I have become a fixture in the State House [and will remain so] for three years to come."[82]

Fletcher filled his days and earned what must have been a modest living in this way, while at the same time devoting a portion of his efforts to collecting old debts that, as recorded in his papers, sometimes extended back years. He also looked to family members he had helped in the past for support. He is last recorded in the Philadelphia city directories in 1855 as living without profession at 47 South 13th Street. He continued to live in the city for a time but divided his time between there and Delanco, New Jersey, on the Delaware River east of Philadelphia, where his son Thomas Sidney Fletcher lived. He so noted in a letter to his brother Henry, "I received yours of the 4th inst., but was in Delanco when it came, where I staid for a few days to help Thomas trim [grape] vines." (Fig. 3.25)

On November 14, 1866, at the age of seventy-nine, Thomas Charles Fletcher died at his son's house in New Jersey. And although his passing was without fanfare, it marked the end of a long and remarkable life—one that had recorded in silver a decidedly dramatic and tumultuous era in the early national history of America.[83]

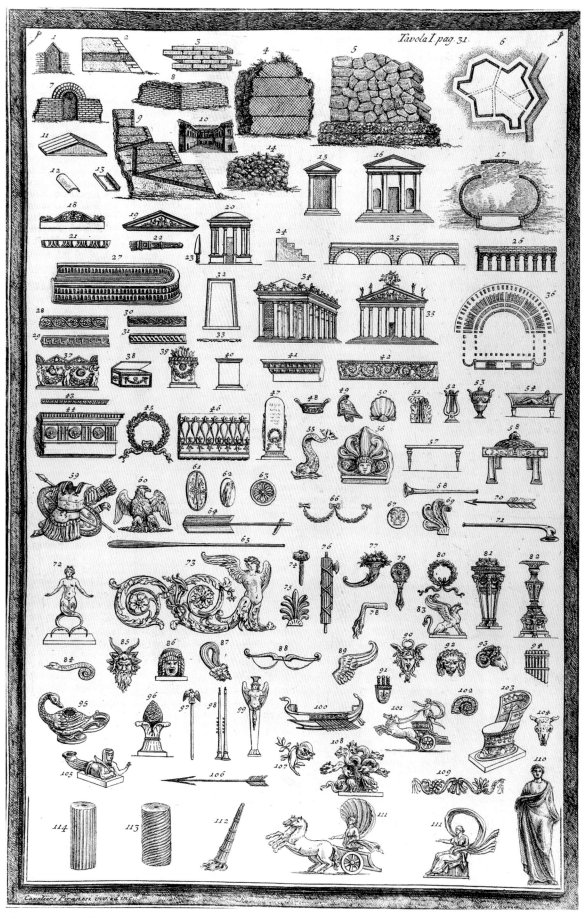

Fig. 4.1 *Tavolo I* (detail). From Giovanni-Battista Piranesi, *Diverse maniere d'adornare i cammini . . . e toscana* (Rome: Salomoni, 1769). Courtesy of University of Delaware Library.

Chapter 4
Fletcher & Gardiner: Seeking the Font of Antiquity
Donald L. Fennimore and Ann K. Wagner

When Thomas Fletcher embarked on the *Superior,* bound for England's port of Liverpool in 1815, the twenty-eight-year-old merchant cherished high professional and personal expectations for what he might accomplish on his first visit abroad. He planned to establish and strengthen connections with manufacturers to secure the most tasteful and suitable goods, thereby assuring his firm of what he considered to be "a decided superiority" over competitors at home. Examining fashionable silver and jewelry in Europe in order to sustain Fletcher & Gardiner's successful designs was also in the forefront of his mind. This voyage, and a second trip in 1825, conveyed Fletcher to the heady world of English and French cultures, industries, and arts—a privilege exercised by comparatively few American-born merchants of his era. His experiences abroad would have a lasting effect on the firm of Fletcher & Gardiner and the nation. As the ship sailed eastward, Fletcher noted his thoughts:

> at 5. P.M. took our departure from the light house with a light breeze from the S.W. – Thus after six years of anxious anticipation I am in a fair way to gratify my ardent wish to visit Europe & realize the projects which neither Embargo – non-intercourse – nor War, could ever drive from my imagination – but I begin to think as I have often before thought, that there is more pleasure in the anticipation than in the enjoyment – we know not the happiness we actually enjoy until deprived of it – these reflections arose insensibly in my mind as the sun sank slowly in the west and the land of my nativity gradually receded from my view.[1]

Fletcher's musings hint at his grand visions for the venture, yet they also convey his awareness that what lay ahead might not satisfy him as much as what he was leaving in his wake.

In addition to pragmatic reasons for crossing the Atlantic, Fletcher wanted to see Europe's fine arts and discover sources of artistic inspiration. His personal inclinations, coupled with the elevated status of ancient cultures in the minds and aesthetic sensibilities of those interested in the arts, many of whom were his clients,

extended Fletcher's mission well beyond meeting fancy-goods suppliers. When in London, his base was the Finsbury Square home of Samuel Williams, a merchant from Massachusetts and former U.S. Consul to Hamburg and London. Williams served as Fletcher's banker, providing credit advances in addition to the use of his home. Williams was also a collector and patron to artists.

Fig. 4.2 Thomas Fletcher, drawing, ca. 1815. Pencil on paper. Thomas Fletcher Papers, Collection 39, The Athenaeum of Philadelphia.

Fig. 4.3 Thomas Fletcher, drawing, ca. 1815. Pencil on paper. Thomas Fletcher Papers, Collection 39, The Athenaeum of Philadelphia.

At the time, he owned Gilbert Stuart's portrait of George Washington, which formerly belonged to the Marquis of Lansdowne.[2]

From March 1815 to April 1816 Thomas Fletcher was in constant motion. He visited manufacturers of silver-plated wares, jewelry, fancy goods, and porcelain tablewares, placing extensive orders in London, Birmingham, Sheffield, and Paris. Documents from this journey include letters to his family, bills for goods ordered, and a pocket-size calf-bound notebook for observations and informal records of transactions en route. The notebook preserves pencil drawings interspersed with notes about orders and calculations for profit yields. The drawings—including several ships under sail, profile portraits of a man and woman, a lobed vase and acanthus leaf, dolphins with entwined tails, an eagle perched upon a branch, silver border patterns, and Greek vases—indicate that Fletcher had an active interest in observing forms and nature, an abiding passion for the arts, and impressive amateur artistic abilities. (Figs. 4.2–4.4)

Fletcher's initial plans called for touring as far as Germany or Switzerland, but his actual itinerary did not extend beyond France, although it did include sightseeing as well as business. Admiration for the fine arts prompted at least one visit to a British paintings gallery, where he appreciated American-born artist Benjamin West's work. He also likely viewed works of antiquity acquired by Sir William Hamilton, then on view at the British Museum, and those installed for Napoleon Bonaparte in the Louvre. Fletcher also sought contemporary arts. While visiting the medieval cathedral in Lichfield, Staffordshire, he was particularly stirred by a funerary monument commemorating Anna Seward, a well-known poet, writer, and daughter of the canon. In a letter to his partner, he declared: "The finest specimen of modern sculpture I ever witnessed is the monument over the tomb of Miss Ann Seward – it is composed of white marble – an urn with a female figure weeping over it."[3] His opinion captures his enthusiasm for a modern artwork incorporating classical motifs. It also expresses his admiration for the sentiment conveyed by memorial arts, a taste shared by Americans of the era.

Antiquity in the Arts

In 1815 decorative arts inspired by antiquity remained the dominant artistic style in Britain, France, and parts of northern Europe. Architecture, sculpture, and vases were among the most influential and visible legacies of ancient cultures. Since the Renaissance, European architects had been designing palaces, public buildings, and private homes informed by antiquity. Architects and artists traveled to Italy and Greece, as did the wealthy on a Grand Tour, seeking authenticity and inspiration and amassing drawings or collections of artifacts. Contemporary artworks revived subject matter and forms that were two-millennia old.[4]

Fig. 4.4 Thomas Fletcher, drawing, ca. 1815. Pencil on paper. Thomas Fletcher Papers, Collection 39, The Athenaeum of Philadelphia.

Both Napoleon and England's Prince Regent (future George IV) energized the revival of classical styles with their own tastes and dynamic influences. By the time Fletcher journeyed to France, the grandeur associated with antiquity in Napoleon's imperial style had firmly imprinted itself on architecture, painting, sculpture, and the decorative arts. Napoleon's sophisticated employment of artistic patronage united his imperial iconography with French visual arts. His military campaigns fostered the recording of Egyptian monuments, hieroglyphics, and landscapes by archaeologist and artist Baron Dominique-Vivant Denon. Denon's five volumes devoted to Egyptian antiquities were among the most visible concentrations of images influencing the arts in that emerging taste.[5]

Likewise in Britain, artists created works reflecting the public's political, literary, and artistic interests in Greek, Roman, and Egyptian artifacts and historical figures. Poet John Keats's *Ode on a Grecian Urn* (1819) addressed an ancient vase: "O Attic shape! Fair attitude! with brede / Of marble men and maidens overwrought," capturing with verse what artisans created in many media. Goldsmiths supplying sophisticated table services, vases, and jewelry to Napoleon and the Prince Regent incorporated classical motifs into endless variations.[6] British sculptor and draftsman John Flaxman was one of numerous artists who cultivated his talents by residing in Italy and generating designs for manufacturers of decorative arts.

Fletcher surveyed gold, silver, and silver plate in London, Birmingham, and Paris as resources for his manufactory in Philadelphia with the same acquisitive energy that he selected the best manufactured goods for the store. He visited leading goldsmiths and jewelers, admired wares, purchased patterns perhaps in three-dimensional form and certainly in engraved drawings, and schooled himself in all current tastes. Knowing their workshop could produce silver and gold works at costs lower than they could be imported, Fletcher sought models of the highest standard to sustain their artistic preeminence.[7] His exposure to the royal goldsmiths' manufactories, observation of their collaborations with networks of specialist craftsmen, and appreciation for the scale of their production and patronage fueled his ambitions for expanding the Fletcher & Gardiner firm.

One of Fletcher's calls in London was the venerated shop owned by partners Philip Rundell and John Bridge. (Fig. 4.5) As royal goldsmiths, the Rundell, Bridge & Rundell firm enjoyed significant patronage from the Prince Regent as well as from titled and wealthy patrons in the United Kingdom and abroad. Fletcher experienced the shop during the era of that

Fig. 4.5 Rundell, Bridge & Rundell shop, Ludgate Hill, London, 1800–1825. Watercolor on paper. Courtesy of Sotheby's Photographic Library.

firm's greatest influence upon the British Empire's taste. Their inventory of luxury goods, jewelry, silver, and gold presentation works made a powerful and enduring impression upon him. The immediate remodeling of the Fletcher & Gardiner store in Philadelphia upon his return home is a more-than-coincidental testament to the impressions gathered in London. This influence extended further than the store's showroom, arguably even influencing Fletcher & Gardiner's mode of operations and vision for themselves to become the Rundell, Bridge & Rundell of North America.

Comparisons of some aspects of their business practices as well as the variety of goods they made suggest that Fletcher and Gardiner looked to the

Fig. 4.6 Digby Scott and Benjamin Smith (for Rundell, Bridge & Rundell), vase awarded to Thomas Lavie by the Patriotic Fund, 1805/1806. Courtesy of the Huntington Library, Art Collections, and Botanical Gardens, San Marino, California, 72.9.

London firm as a model, although Rundell, Bridge & Rundell commanded resources and patronage vastly exceeding those available in Philadelphia. Christopher Hartop has characterized the epoch of 1805 to 1825 as a significant period for Rundell, Bridge & Rundell, when their massive output of presentation vases, table services, tureens, candelabra, and swords produced intense collaboration among artists and designers—such as Flaxman and painter Thomas Stothard—and silver artisans.[8] The firm engaged established workshops in London to manufacture their silver and silver-gilt, with Paul Storr and the partnership of Digby Scott and Benjamin Smith in particular creating the most spectacular table services, vases, and lighting. By forming business arrangements with independent master craftsmen, Rundell and Bridge assured their firm the most talented artisans while being freed from the daily cares of managing a workshop.

Antiquity in Presentation Silver

Beginning in 1804 Rundell, Bridge & Rundell provided the Patriotic Fund (established by Lloyd's of London) with more than seventy silver presentation vases to reward outstanding valor during Britain's Napoleonic Wars.[9] Most vases are a lidded volute krater form with a lion finial and images of Britannia and a Greek warrior (Herakles) on opposite sides. The grandest, given for the Battle of Trafalgar, incorporated large bases enriched with sculptural figures. A more typical vase is one awarded to Captain Thomas Lavie for the capture of French frigate *La Guerrière*. Lavie's vase bears the marks of Scott and Smith, who supplied vases to the firm until 1809. (Fig. 4.6)

Just three years later American citizens endorsed their own practice of awarding monumental silver, vases, table services, and swords to military heroes of the War of 1812. Rather than being funded solely by insurance cooperatives or wealthy individuals, however, many awards in America were supported by subscription, whereby individual citizens united their funds, expressed their patriotism, and collectively recorded their self-awareness of a young nation forging a new history. The firm of Fletcher & Gardiner was at the forefront of this burgeoning cultural practice as designers and suppliers of such awards.

In an ironic turn, the firm's first major commission was for Captain Isaac Hull in recognition of his destruction of *La Guerrière*, which Captain Lavie's crew had captured from France in 1806. The urn that Fletcher & Gardiner created for Captain Hull launched the firm's association with splendid awards in silver for American heroes. (Fig. 4.7) At this time the firm also adopted the practice of prominently engraving their name on the outside of the base of presentation awards, after the manner of leading British and French goldsmiths.

In 1812, when Fletcher & Gardiner garnered the commission from the citizens of Philadelphia to produce the award for Hull, neither partner had personally seen the grandest works of silver from England or France. It follows that the monumental vase they created reveals a mixed lineage of design sources blended with their own invention. Perhaps motivated by patriotism and anti-British sentiment as much as style, the partners favored motifs in vogue in French Empire metalwork and in engravings of Greco-Roman antiquities.

The Fletcher & Gardiner silver of this era reveals a taste for austere Greek vase and vessel shapes; restrained ornamental borders such as the anthemion, guilloche, scallop shell, and floral or leaf patterns; and cast animal elements serving as spouts, handles, and paw feet. Similar details are found in French designs, particularly those of Napoleon's preferred team of Charles Percier and Pierre-

François-Léonard Fontaine. Their linear drawings, modeled upon archaeological artifacts, were disseminated in the 1812 publication *Recueil des décorations intérieures,* which inspired artisans in diverse media. Copies of their engravings were known in North America. Architect Benjamin H. Latrobe, an influential vice president of The Society of Artists of the United States and a proponent of Percier and Fontaine's interiors, endorsed French classicism and revivals of ancient Greek (Etruscan) design. The weight of France's leadership in the decorative arts was acknowledged in American artistic communities. Philadelphia, in particular, had a vibrant and cultivated French expatriate community. The arrival of Napoleon's brother, Joseph Bonaparte, and members of his family in 1815 carried a fresh wave of French style and culture into the city's circles.[10]

The overall form of the Hull vase, with a wide upper bowl and narrow pedestal on a platform base, resembles monumental sculptural tureens produced as part of lavish table services for Europe's aristocratic patrons. The ornamental motifs on the vase—the eagle finial, ram's head handles, paw feet, dolphins, bosses of Neptune's head, chased leaf passages on the bowl, frieze-like register, and anthemion on the plinth corners—link it to contemporary French interpretations of Greek classical design. (Figs. 4.8, 4.9) Specifically, the vase shares features with the Percier and Fontaine tureen-on-stand designed as part of a service for Empress Joséphine and fashioned by goldsmith Martin-Guillaume Biennais in 1806.[11] An engraving of this celebrated tureen, rather than the actual object, was most likely Fletcher & Gardiner's resource for designing the Hull vase. (Fig. 4.10)

It was not atypical for Fletcher and Gardiner or other American silversmiths to look to Europe's most ambitious designers for models. Yet, as their silver attests, the firm would regularly seek and alter prototypes to suit their own style. The Hull vase most obviously illustrates that practice, with the adaptation of the ornamental frieze depicting two kneeling, classically-draped women flanking the crowned "J" on Percier and Fontaine's tureen. Fletcher & Gardiner instead personalized Hull's vase with a chased panel depicting the triumph of his frigate, *Constitution,* over the British vessel and with female personifications of Fame and History flanking the scene. The powerful eagle on the lid, clutching a thunderbolt, enhances the vase's potent imagery of national power. In its scale, the Hull vase is a brilliant execution of bravura in American silver. If placed side by side, it would tower some ten inches above Empress Joséphine's impressive tureen-on-stand.

Like its contemporaries, the firm of Fletcher & Gardiner sought new motifs and forms from a variety of

Fig. 4.7 Fletcher & Gardiner, urn presented to Isaac Hull, 1813. Private collection (see cat. no. 10 for full description).

Fig. 4.8 Detail, Isaac Hull urn.

Fig. 4.9 Detail, Isaac Hull urn.

Fig. 4.10 *Pot-à-Oille.* From Charles Percier and Pierre François–Léonard Fontaine, *Recueil des décorations intérieures* (Paris: Chez les Auteurs, 1812), pl. 46. Printed Book and Periodical Collection, Winterthur Library.

Fig. 4.11 *A Vase from Piranesi.* From Henry Moses, *A Collection of Antique Vases, Altars, Paterae, Tripods, Candelabra, Sarcophagi, &c.* (London: H. G. Bohn, 1814). Printed Book and Periodical Collection, Winterthur Library.

printed designs sources, often combining ideas from more than one. The sources themselves transgressed boundaries of time and nationality with artists repeating motifs from earlier engravings. For example, another possible source of inspiration for ornament on the Hull vase—the rams' head handles and overlapping leaves chased into the bowl—is English artist Henry Moses's engraving after a vase first created by Italian draftsman and architect Giovanni-Battista Piranesi. (Fig. 4.11)

Rams' heads, however, were a prevalent motif on Roman stone altars, and such images were plentiful in engravings of the period and on silver table services, ormolu clocks, and furniture. Fletcher & Gardiner's design for the Hull vase blurs the distinctions among French, English, and antique Greco-Roman graphic sources. During his travels following the creation of the Hull vase, Fletcher selected engravings he judged suitable to be adapted for American-manufactured silver. The firm deliberately reinterpreted contemporary European and antique sources to suit their own style, sense of proportion, and American clientele.[12]

European and American craftsmen seeking authenticity drew upon models from antiquity in faithfully rendered engravings after classical Greek, Roman, and Egyptian objects. British collector Sir William Hamilton published his vast collection of antique vases, first in 1767–76 and again in 1791–95. Francesco Piranesi (Fig. 4.1), published *Le Monumens antiques du Musée Napoleon* in 1804–6 illustrating antique sculptures accumulated by Napoleon in the Louvre. Both sources made forms and subject matter available to artisans to adapt for their local markets. Also influential were the prolific and popular drawings of Giovanni-Battista Piranesi, scores of engraved designs for vases by British and European artists, and collections of decorative motifs intended for artisans in many disciplines, such as Rudolph Ackermann's *Repository of Arts*. Although scant information has survived about specific catalogues and engravings, there can be little doubt that both Fletcher and Gardiner had extensive libraries for men of their station. While abroad in 1815 and 1816, Fletcher acquired numerous models from a leading Paris brass founder and also purchased engravings and a "catalogue of Antiques" there; presumably he did the same in London.[13] When such purchases arrived at the Philadelphia establishment, they provided a fresh font of imagery for the manufactory. In addition to printed sources, Fletcher and Gardiner paid close attention to European tablewares and jewelry. One great advantage they possessed over other native-born American silversmiths was Fletcher's firsthand experience seeing completed silver and silver-gilt wares in the stores of French and British silversmiths.

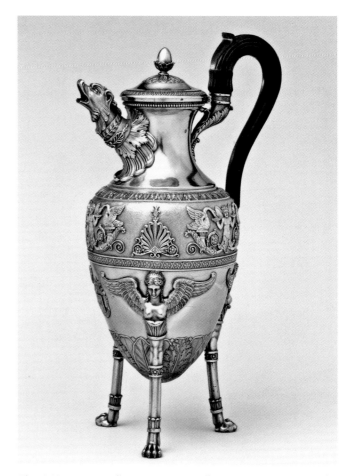

Fig. 4.12 Martin-Guillaume Biennais, coffeepot, Paris, 1797–1809. The Metropolitan Museum of Art, Rogers Fund, 1934 (34.12.1). Image © The Metropolitan Museum of Art.

Antiquity in Household Silver

The rigorous expressions of classical taste in silver and silver-gilt works by leading French goldsmiths, particularly Jean-Baptiste-Claude Odiot and Martin-Guillaume Biennais, influenced the form and ornament of Fletcher & Gardiner's silver. Both goldsmiths drew upon contemporary sources, including Percier and Fontaine, or collaborated with specialists to design their sculpture-rich tablewares and presentation works. Patrons of Parisian goldsmiths in the early 1800s responded to Napoleon's taste and ordered tea and coffee services with vase-shape bodies and ornament derived from antiquity. Prevailing designs for table services had opulent raised borders, cast or chased sculptural elements, and surface textures varying from highly polished to matte. A silver-gilt coffeepot created by Biennais conveys a strong classical aesthetic with an animal-figure spout, cast finial and leaf-shape handle mount, low-relief frieze encircling the body, and winged female busts over three paw feet. (Fig. 4.12) Likewise, a silver service created by Marc Jacquart with Greek vessel forms ornamented by mythological figures; animals on finials, spouts, and handle mounts; and with regimented

Fig. 4.13 Marc Jacquart, tea and coffee service, 1809–19. The Metropolitan Museum of Art, Purchase, Joseph Pulitzer Bequest, 1938 (38.12.1–.6) Image © The Metropolitan Museum of Art.

Fig. 4.14 Fletcher & Gardiner, tureen, 1817. The Saint Louis Art Museum, Funds given by the Decorative Arts Society and the Eliza McMillan Trust (see cat. no. 24 for full description).

lush borders represents the elegance and opulence of Parisian silver for aristocratic clientele. (Fig. 4.13)

Although American patrons might not request such costly tea and coffee services, a reflection of Fletcher's exposure to French style is seen in the firm's transition to a more sophisticated integration of antique forms and motifs in the firms' presentation and household silver.[14] An early opportunity to interpret Parisian tableware forms and ornament emerged with the commission from Baltimore's citizens for a 52-piece service for John Rodgers, which was completed following Fletcher's return from Europe. (Fig. 4.14) The two tureens from the Rodgers service, like all of the serving pieces, have presentation inscriptions under the bases, freeing the bodies for expanses of reflective surface and contrasting lush ornament. An applied border of grotesques and winged figures on the tureen lids echoes sources used for similar ornament on the pedestal of Jacquart's hot water urn and the frieze on Biennais's coffeepot.

The Rodgers service and a presentation vase made for Andrew Jackson, in contrast to the Hull vase, resemble European silver objects more so than printed sources. When these gifts were presented, each received press coverage. The Jackson vase was admired for its "uncommon taste and elegance" and the Rodgers service because it was "splendidly ornamented with borderings and embossed figures after the manner of the Egyptian and Grecian sculpturing." Fletcher was abroad when the firm began the vase that would be given to Jackson. The bowl's shorter body with a concave upper register ornamented with laurel boughs is a departure from the firm's previous War of 1812 vase shapes. The Jackson incorporated new sculptural elements such as the spiraling double-headed snake handles, the original eagle figures once bolted onto the plinth, and winged Egyptian-style feet supporting the magisterial plinth base. Eagles perched on thunderbolts, looking very much like those on Napoleon's imperial coat of arms, are mounted on the corners of the base. Grand French silver and silver-gilt tureens, such as one produced by Henry Auguste for Prince Vladimir Golitzin and Countess Natalie Chernyshev, incorporate similar elements. Fletcher's hand in the design for the Jackson vase is undocumented, although a letter he wrote to his brother in Philadelphia in 1815 captures his continuing involvement with presentation silver in the workshop: "If you can send me a sketch of the urn you are making and some other matters & things that I can turn to advantage – such as the portraits of our naval officers &c. it will be well."[15]

It is likely that direct interaction with European or British-trained artisans working in America, such as Jean Simon Chaudron, also exerted influence upon Fletcher & Gardiner's early silver designs. The partners cultivated relationships with talented foreign-born journeymen and other artists, many of whom flocked to the Mid-Atlantic states seeking patronage in the early 1800s. Evidence of one such connection, Italian-born sculptor Enrico Causici (Caucici), is preserved in a newspaper item from November 1816, just a few months after Fletcher's return from Europe. Causici advertised himself as a student of Antonio Canova, the famed Italian sculptor patronized by Napoleon. Causici traveled to Philadelphia to seek public commissions for sculptures and portraits of the nation's leading figures. He advertised that "specimens of his ability . . . may be seen at Fletcher and Gardiner's, corner of Fourth and Chesnut

streets."[16] Caucisi did not remain long in the United States but returned again in 1822 to produce sculptures for the Capitol, the figure of George Washington on the Baltimore Monument, and other work in New York. His connection with Fletcher & Gardiner encourages a hypothesis that he may have provided models for sculptural elements appearing on the firm's silver.

Adapting Antiquity for America

Occasionally, surviving documents clarify direct influence from French or English firms to Fletcher & Gardiner silver. One instance resulted from Fletcher's admiration for a silver vase produced for Rundell, Bridge & Rundell by Paul Storr. Known as the "Warwick," Storr's work was patterned after a massive marble vase constructed from archaeological fragments found at emperor Hadrian's villa at Tivoli. The vase was acquired by Sir William Hamilton, who transported it to England between 1776 and 1778. Hamilton persuaded his nephew George Greville, Earl of Warwick, to keep it,

Fig. 4.15 *The Warwick Vase.* From Giovanni-Battista Piranesi, *Vasi, candelabra, cippi, sarcophagi, tripodi, Lucerne, ed ornamenti antichi disegnati ed incisi dal Cav. Gio. Batt. Piranesi,* vol. I (Rome, 1778). The Metropolitan Museum of Art, Rogers Fund, transferred from the Library [41.71.1.12(2)]. Image © The Metropolitan Museum of Art.

Fig. 4.16 Paul Storr (for Rundell, Bridge & Rundell), vase, 1813–14. Courtesy of Koopman Rare Art.

thus giving the vase its name. Giovanni-Battista Piranesi's etchings of several views of this vase were published in 1778, and the form was successfully adapted into vases and wine coolers. (Fig. 4.15) Storr created pairs of "Warwick" wine coolers in silver and silver-gilt for at least a decade, several of which were ordered by Britain's Prince Regent.[17] (Fig. 4.16) Numerous published engravings of the reconstructed marble vase circulated, as did inspired renditions in fused plate, ceramics, and other materials, reinforcing its fame.

Fletcher's letterbook records a visit to the Rundell, Bridge & Rundell store in 1815: "Here I saw elegant silver chased work, the first I have met with . . . a fine vase copied from one in the possession of the Earl of Warwick . . . which was dug from the ruins of Herculaneum. [It] is beautifully made – it is oval, about ⅔d the size of that made for Hull, the handles are grape stalks and a vine runs all around covered with leaves & clusters of grapes – below are heads of Bacchus &c. finely chased – some wine coolers in the same style."[18]

Fig. 4.17a and b Fletcher & Gardiner, vases to honor DeWitt Clinton, 1824 and 1825. The Metropolitan Museum of Art (Left) Purchase, Louis V. Bell and Rogers Funds; Anonymous and Robert G. Goelet Gifts; and Gifts of Fenton L. B. Brown and the grandchildren of Mrs. Ransom Spaford Hooker, in her memory, by exchange, 1982 (1982.4ab) Image © The Metropolitan Museum of Art; (Right) Gift of the Erving and Joyce Wolf Foundation, 1988 (1988.199) Image © The Metropolitan Museum of Art (see cat. no. 43 for full description).

Fletcher's memory of this famous vase persisted. Ten years after he saw the form in London, Fletcher & Gardiner won the prestigious commission for two silver vases to honor New York Governor DeWitt Clinton and the completion of the Erie Canal. (Fig. 4.17) To create these ambitious works, Fletcher borrowed design foundations from Storr's vases. While retaining the overall form and twining grape-vine handles of the famous Warwick vase, Fletcher & Gardiner's versions eschewed the Bacchic heads and incorporated America-specific iconography. They adapted new design sources, such as prints depicting the canal projects and two classical frieze passages, to express Governor Clinton's, and New York's, participation in the progress of the world's arts and sciences.

More subtle and essential underlying forces shaping Fletcher & Gardiner's silver were the principles of proportion and design inherited from classical architecture. Illustrations of the five architectural orders had been promulgated with reprints of Andrea Palladio's *Four Books on Architecture* as well as treatises on their superiority and shared across national borders by generations of architects. (Fig. 4.18) In Philadelphia, prominent architects working in the Greek style included Latrobe, John Haviland, and William Strickland. Essays addressing classical architecture and numerous builders' handbooks were produced on both sides of the Atlantic.[19] One published in Philadelphia by Haviland, *The Builder's Assistant, Containing the Five Orders of Architecture,* illustrated more than 150 engravings by Hugh Bridport, an acquaintance of Fletcher and Gardiner. Like many others, Haviland's book championed the decorative elements and proportions of Greek and Roman architecture, advocating the clearness and simplicity of Greek composition.

In Philadelphia's artistic community, in which Fletcher

and Gardiner actively participated, enthusiasm for architecture, furniture, and interiors based upon Greek models was augmented by the influence of foreign-born artisans such as Latrobe. In 1811 Latrobe's oration to the Society of Artists in the United States extolled connections between Greek fine arts and the pursuit of liberty: "But if a conviction can be wrought, and diffused throughout the nation, that the fine arts may indeed be pressed into the service of arbitrary power, and – like mercenary troops, do their duty well while well paid – yet that their home is in the bosom of a republic; then, indeed, the days of Greece may be revived in the woods of America, and Philadelphia become the Athens of the Western world."[20]

Whether consciously pursued or inculcated through observation, much of Fletcher & Gardiner's silver reveals an awareness of the principles and motifs of classical architecture. In Palladio's view, using starting measurements (modules) based upon a column diameter assured harmony of all parts and created beauty. Fletcher & Gardiner employed ratios of proportion in the overall shape of silver objects, such as heights and diameters for different segments of a vase or pitcher and related measurements for a pedestal foot or plinth base. The firm also repeatedly created silver using basic geometry of circles, squares, and ovals for bodies and bases, interconnected in a ratio that suited the parts to the whole. Their decorative borders, such as the *ovolo*, or "egg and dart," of the Ionic order on vases and wine coolers were placed with consideration to scale and overall size of an object. The workshop's attention to classical design principles remained in place even as their silver adapted to changing fashions.

As this catalogue attests, the story of the firm's War of 1812 vases and ensuing commissions for presentation silver, gold hilted swords, and splendid table services benefited from Fletcher's personal interaction with the works of Europe's major goldsmiths. He and Sidney Gardiner possessed and cultivated the talent to create American silver that for the first time would rival the grand works of their contemporaries across the Atlantic.

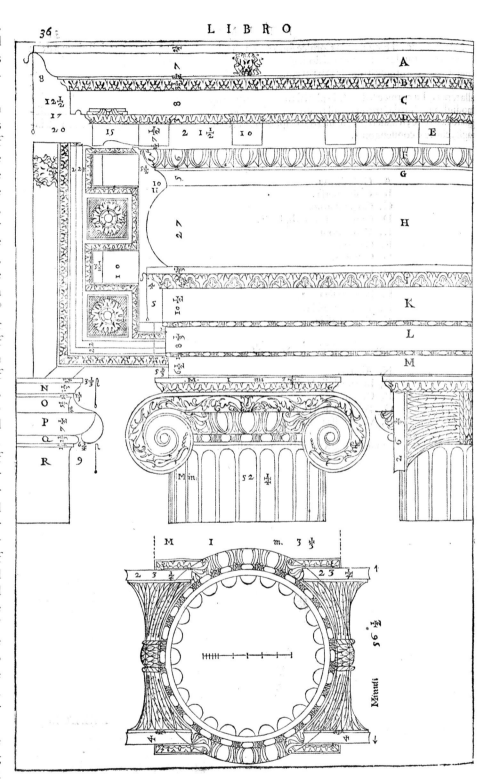

Fig. 4.18 *Dell' Ordine Ionico.* From Andrea Palladio, *Il Primo Libro dell'Architettura* (Venice: Appresso Dominico de'Franceschi, 1570), p. 36. Printed Book and Periodical Collection, Winterthur Library.

Fig. 5.1 Fletcher & Gardiner, pitcher, Philadelphia, 1815–20. Winterthur Museum, 1969.16 (see cat. no. 11 for full description).

Fig. 5.2 William Garret Forbes, oval sugar bowl, New York City, 1800–1810. Winterthur Museum, Gift of Marshall P. Blankarn, 1977.224. Isaac Hutton, octagon teapot, Albany, New York, 1805–17. Winterthur Museum, Gift of Carl Kossack, 1990.42.1. William Garret Forbes, oblong tea caddy, New York City, 1810–20. Winterthur Museum, 1967.231.

Chapter 5
Fletcher & Gardiner: Arbiters of Taste
Donald L. Fennimore and Ann K. Wagner

In 1807, the year before Thomas Fletcher and Sidney Gardiner opened their silver manufactory in Boston, British savant Thomas Hope, perhaps the most celebrated arbiter of taste in the early nineteenth-century English-speaking world, published *Household Furniture and Interior Decoration*. Hope identified what he felt were the essential qualities of good design and how those qualities should be incorporated into objects of all types so that every article, "however simple be its texture, and however mean its destination, is capable of uniting to the more essential requisites of utility and comfort . . . a certain number of secondary attributes of elegance and beauty, [that] may enable its shape and accessories to afford additional gratification, both to the eye and to the imagination."[1]

A proper expression of style in objects through a thorough understanding of historic precedents and sensitivity to proportion and design relationships was of central interest to Fletcher and Gardiner as they framed the utility and look of their silver. In this regard the partners were eminently well qualified; Gardiner was an adept and talented craftsman, and his partner was a connoisseur of impeccable taste. Their commingling of talents produced what are today considered to be icons of their era. Indeed, their firm's creations in silver and gold so well resonated with pubic sentiment at the time that their work was acclaimed and imitated throughout the United States.

However, there is scant reason to presume that Fletcher and Gardiner would rise to this influential status from the circumstances surrounding their entry into the silver business. Advertisements placed in Boston newspapers by silversmiths, jewelers, and fancy hardware importers often extolled the merits of objects that were made elsewhere, suggesting that the city's practitioners in the precious metals were regarded as neither innovative

Fig. 5.3 Fletcher & Gardiner, teapot with "rich borders *in relievo*," Boston or Philadelphia, 1808–15. Engraved with the crest and initial of the Appleton family of Boston. Private collection.

nor influential. Sheffield, England, New York City, and Philadelphia were among the more oft-cited names that Bostonians appear to have looked to for their cues in current fashion, as indicated by an advertisement placed in the April 27, 1808, issue of the *Columbian Centinel* by watchmaker John McFarlane: "Just received from Liverpool via New York . . . an elegant assortment of best Sheffield PLATED WARE." Another advertisement from jewelers Samuel Davis and Johnson Brown in the August 11, 1810, issue of the same newspaper cites that they had just received "elegant Philadelphia manufactured silver ware . . . with superb chaste work and figured borders," specifying features they felt Bostonians would favor. (Fig. 5.2) In the October 23, 1805, issue Joseph C. Dyer offered hollowware with "plain and rich engraved borders [in] oval, octagon and new oblong shapes, outlining options available for his customers.

When the Fletcher & Gardiner firm first advertised, they stated that manufacturing gold and silver would occupy their primary attention and that their work would be the equal of any imported. The partners remarked that they made fashionable silver with "rich borders *in relievo*" . . . and "rich Schell borders" . . . and they "will manufacture any article in the Silver-Plate line to any pattern and of the first rate workmanship."[2] (Fig. 5.3)

This last statement, issued in 1811, was a common claim expressed by many silversmiths, but it was one that could be interpreted as bravura on the part of the

partners. It invited challenging stylistic and technical commissions that could easily have exceeded their three years of experience in business under their own name. However, as evidenced by their response to just such a commission—the urn presented to Captain Isaac Hull by the citizens of Philadelphia two years later—they more than measured up to the promise that statement implied. In that commission, they created a silver object the likes of which had never been made previously in America. In so doing they caught the attention of the American public. The name "Fletcher & Gardiner" appeared in print throughout the United States as the creator of the heaviest, tallest, most ornate, elegant, and patriotic work in silver produced in the country to that date.

In its wake, the Fletcher & Gardiner firm became the darling of the fashionable world and was besieged with commissions for presentation, household, church, and personal silver and gold from Philadelphians as well as those in cities from New York, Boston, and Washington, D.C. to Columbia, South Carolina, and New Orleans. It might reasonably be presumed that many of these patrons were enamored of the fact that Fletcher & Gardiner had made well-publicized silver for Hull and wanted to own table- or teawares made by the firm. At the same time, these patrons were subscribing, consciously or not, to the partners' interpretation of current popular style.

That style, ultimately drawn from ancient Greek and Roman art and architecture, took hold in the United States during the nation's first blush of national self-awareness. The era evolved from the time in which the country's founders, rejecting monarchical rule, built a daring and experimental framework of republican democracy. Seeking historic precedent and moral justification, they "peered across the gulf of centuries to Greece and Rome, which they saw as the noblest achievements of free men aspiring to govern themselves." The resultant language of the American political system, crafted in emulation of the "prescriptive wisdom of antiquity," was peppered with terms such as senate, capitol, constitution, republic, democracy, and others with equally powerful conceptual associations.[3]

The language of the artifacts associated with this phenomenon conveyed those concepts in a tangible context that commingled impulses of nationalism and antiquarianism, affirming the United States as the new Rome. Current events of note—War of 1812 battles—were depicted on presentation silver. Motifs perceived as peculiarly American, such as the bald eagle, were incorporated into household silver along with those derived from the Greek Republic and Imperial Rome: acanthus leaves, tridents, dolphins, laurel wreaths, palmettes, lions, rams, gods, goddesses, and mythological creatures. This melding of motifs affirmed their users' awareness that the nation was making history as significant as that of revered ancient cultures.

As to be expected, the interpretation of American-inspired and ancient design concepts and their synthesis into objects by designers, silversmiths, chasers, engravers, and related craftsmen varied from individual to individual. Numerous factors impinged on the creation and character of any given work, among the more significant of which might be a maker's understanding of historic precedent and its suitability for adaptation, his sense of design and proportion, and technical proficiency. Those energetic and talented enough to closely study and master the vogue created artifacts that exhibited perceptual sensitivity and expressive genius. Their silver, whether grand celebratory monuments or everyday utensils, evinced clarity and vibrancy. Those at a greater intellectual or conceptual distance from the vocabulary in which they worked produced objects that were serviceable but wanting in the capacity to inspire admiration and imitation.

The contrast between an adequate expression and one that captures the essence and spirit of style is succinctly

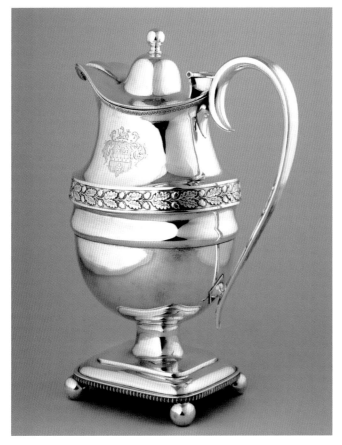

Fig. 5.4 Robert Shepherd and William Boyd, pitcher, Albany, New York, 1810–25. Private collection.

illustrated in pitchers created by Shepherd & Boyd and Fletcher & Gardiner. (Figs. 5.4, 5.1) These vessels, both executed in the current fashion, are equally serviceable. However, they diverge in their ability to impress viewers with the vigor of their interpretation. The Shepherd & Boyd example encompasses a pleasing but unremarkable character. The other, by contrast, might be described as "a most superb [piece] of plate . . . of the most substantial workmanship, and reflecting on the artists, Messrs. Fletcher and Gardiner, of Philadelphia, the highest degree of credit . . . It is splendidly 'ornamented with borderings and embossed figures after the manner of the Egyptian and Grecian sculpturings,' and it is universally admired."[4]

This testimonial, extolling a service the Fletcher & Gardiner firm made for War of 1812 naval hero Commodore John Rodgers, applies equally to the pitcher seen here and, indeed, to the partners' work in general. Admiring commentary of this type was repeatedly published during the firm's existence. Many acknowledged, usually with enthusiasm, that "Nobody in this 'world' of ours hereabouts can compete with them in their kind of work." The renown, with commensurate commercial success, that the firm achieved could not help but be noticed by others who sought a share of the market. Their success bred imitation, which remained an ongoing challenge throughout the life of the firm, as noted in his brother Charles's letter to Fletcher, who was traveling in England at the time: "I hope you will send us some new patterns of plate. It [is] time for us to get up something new and different from what is now made, as most of the silversmiths make our patterns." For the partners to maintain their competitive edge, they had to constantly create new and different interpretations so that their work would maintain its distinctive appearance.[5]

To accomplish this, Fletcher and Gardiner relied heavily on their traditional arsenal of hammer work, casting, chasing, and engraving, which was also employed by other silversmiths of their era. However, the Fletcher & Gardiner firm explored more innovative approaches not yet known to have been used by their competitors, exemplified by a five-piece service they created in 1823 that was "ornamented in a very splendid style and inlaid with platina." In another instance they fashioned a piece of presentation silver so that "the polish of the work is such, that all its ornaments are *multiplied by reflection* [against which they contrasted elements] in *frosted silver*." Yet another stylistic initiative involved devising sword hilts, scabbard mounts, and at least one frame for a portrait miniature of gold in contrasting colors of yellow, white, green, and red. The artisans in their manufactory

Fig. 5.5 Fletcher & Gardiner, detail of vase presented to Cadwalader Evans by the Schuylkill Navigation Company, picturing one of its bolt-on panels removed. The Historical Society of Pennsylvania (see cat. no. 58 for full description).

made silver-gilt and mastered the European practice of casting ornamental components for presentation vases and household wares using the lost wax process. Also, Fletcher & Gardiner adopted the new technique practiced by Parisian goldsmith Jean-Baptiste-Claude Odiot of bolting cast and chased sculptural elements to their work.[6] In this way the partners achieved the exceptional high degree of fit and finish characteristic of French silver of the era. (Fig. 5.5)

While the partners were adept at manipulating the style and overall character of their silver to keep it fresh, some of the techniques they used heightened the challenge. This was particularly true for the mechanized die-rolled and die-stamped aspects of their production. Die rolling and die stamping were a significant boon that allowed silversmiths to infuse a strong element of style into objects for a large and geographically expansive market. Both processes involved semi-mechanized (powered by individual effort) or fully mechanized (powered by water or steam) production, wherein multipart iron dies were used to make multiple replicas of a particular ornamental feature quickly and much less expensively than if done by hand. (Fig. 5.6)

Once made, these components could be soldered to the surfaces or incorporated into the bodies of teapots, pitchers, and other forms. They enabled silversmiths to produce complex, visually stunning, and stylish ornamental features with greater ease and speed and in larger quantity than their counterparts who relied on traditional hand techniques of hammering, chasing, engraving, and casting.

Die-rolling and die-stamping machinery offered another advantage as well—an owner could produce

more ornament than needed and sell the excess to others in the precious metals trade. Fletcher and Gardiner were aware of this possibility and appear to have served as a resource for die-rolled and die-stamped ornament. Fletcher underscored the availability and portability of this component of the manufactory's output when he wrote to his partner's younger brother Baldwin that "I forgot to bring with me the piece of rolled border for the sugar dish—it is the middle size."[7] The relationships that developed as a result between the Fletcher & Gardiner firm and other silversmiths benefited both. The partners had a wholesale market for their purposeful production overruns, and their silversmith customers had affordable access to fashionable decorative elements without having to invest in expensive machinery. Commercial relationships ensued wherein decorative components, designed and made under Fletcher and Gardiner's direction, became an integral part of the work of others.

Such relationships are traceable through close examination. Fletcher & Gardiner's "middle size" rose-and-leaf border that encircles the footed pedestal of one the firm's teapots (see Fig. 5.3) appears as the primary ornamental border in the body of a teapot marked by Boston silversmiths Jesse Churchill and Daniel Treadwell. (Fig. 5.7) In another instance, Baltimore silversmith Andrew E. Warner used a section of the same border on the base of a cream pot bearing his mark. (Fig. 5.8) The appearance of this border in three separate geographic locations traces commercial connections among the men. Furthermore, its presence on the Churchill & Treadwell teapot and the Warner cream pot suggests a hierarchical relationship in which the supplier partly determined the look of the recipient's work.

Exploiting this cooperative network, the Fletcher & Gardiner firm sold and/or traded die-rolled ornament to numerous craftsmen in Philadelphia and elsewhere. Those in Philadelphia include Conrad Bard, alone and in partnership with Robert Lamont; William Seal; George K. Childs; Edward Lownes; John McMullin; Harvey Lewis; and John T. Bailey and Andrew Kitchen. Outside the city, James Guthrie of Wilmington, Delaware; William Mannerback in Reading, Pennsylvania; John Musser in Lancaster, Pennsylvania; William Thomson, Christopher Giffing, Baldwin Gardiner, Thomas Richards, and Gerardus Boyce, all in New York City; Rufus Farnam and Richard Ward of Boston; James Reed of Murphreesboro, Tennessee; and Martha Miller and John Ewan in Charleston, South Carolina availed themselves of borders made in Fletcher & Gardiner's manufactory. In so doing, the silversmiths enlisted themselves in local, regional, and national networks with Fletcher & Gardiner serving as a source for die-rolled borders and, collaterally, the font for their style. The objects marked by these silversmiths, but with Fletcher & Gardiner borders, represent shared artistic responsibility. Although these silversmiths can be presumed to have taken full credit for the work stamped with their names, it was not wholly theirs. Authorship of the borders belongs to the Fletcher & Gardiner manufactory.[8]

The popularity of the partners' die-rolled borders sparked imitation by those who sought the same market and could afford to underwrite the requisite investment. A footed bowl marked by Philadelphia silversmith Thomas Whartenby with die-rolled rose-and-leaf border under the lip, closely imitates Fletcher & Gardiner's border. (Fig. 5.9) This and other imitative efforts by Edward Lownes and John Curry in Philadelphia; Samuel Kirk in Baltimore; Robert Keyworth in Washington, D.C.; and Ebenezer Moulton in Newburyport and Boston underscore the partners' influence on the mechanized component of silver design at the time.

On August 29, 1828, Baldwin Gardiner, who had been operating under his own name as a "merchant" in New York City, informed Fletcher that

> I have been applied to, to make a <u>Splendid Vase</u> & a <u>pair of Pitchers</u>, intended to be presented by the Citizens of New York, to Mr. Maxwell (the District Attorney) as a token of their respect and approbation of his course of prosecuting the late conspiracy cases, so called – The price to be paid for the <u>Vase & Pitchers</u>, from $800 to $1000 – These are the particulars. If you are disposed to make them, and in such a way as will answer my just expectations of profit, I shall be glad to have you undertake it – and I shall be satisfied <u>with a very small profit</u>; the more so to enable you to bestow the greater pains in <u>their elegant execution</u>, – for I shall look as much to the <u>honor of [the] thing</u> as to the profit – Of course, I shall expect to have my name stamped upon the bottom. In order, however, to let you see that I am frank and open on this point, I told Mr. Cary [John S. Crary] that I would apply to you, by name, to make them; and have told him that within a week, I would show him <u>your drawings</u> for such as is proposed to make. Mr. Cary told me that he had 'the say' in the business and that I should make them. None of the silversmiths here know that I have the

Fig. 5.6 Fletcher & Gardiner, section of a die-rolled rose-and-leaf border on a cake or fruit basket, Philadelphia, 1814. Ruth J. Nutt Collection of American Silver (see cat. no. 14 for full description).

Fig. 5.7 Jesse Churchill and Daniel Treadwell (marked by), teapot, Boston, ca. 1810. Die-rolled rose-and-leaf border attributed to Fletcher & Gardiner. Photograph by Taylor and Dull, N.Y. Courtesy of Historic New England.

Fig. 5.8 Andrew Ellicott Warner (marked by), cream pot, Baltimore, Maryland, ca. 1814. Die-rolled rose-and-leaf border attributed to Fletcher & Gardiner. The Maryland Historical Society, Gift of Mr. Fenton Boggs.

Fig. 5.9 Thomas Whartenby (marked by), footed bowl, Philadelphia, 1812–20. Die-rolled rose-and-leaf border imitative of Fletcher & Gardiner. Private collection.

order, as several of them would drop the hammer for me if they knew I sent to Philad. – and as soon as I am ready for such a courte on their part, I shall be very glad to have them. Please let me know your answer and if you intend to undertake them. Let me know how soon I may expect your drawings . . . N.B. I am now having made besides the 'opposition' vase for Mr. [Henry] Eckford – the two prize cups @50 $ ea for the successful Poems on the reopening the Bower Thea. And sets of plate for several persons & would heartily rejoice if I could throw it all in your hands.[9]

Fletcher's response to this request was a monumental "silver vase . . . said to be a most splendid article, not surpassed in design and finish in this country" that bears only the mark "B. GARDINER NEW YORK" on its underside. Given Gardiner's close, long-standing business and personal relationship with Fletcher, it might be imagined that this order was singular. It was not. Fletcher received numerous such requests. On June 8, 1831, Baltimore "watchmakers and jewellers" Robert and Andrew Campbell wrote him that "we wish you to make us as fast as possible two sets of plate consisting of Coffee, two Tea, one Cream Pot, sugar dish & slop bowl to each set. Make them of the large size and newest pattern, also as low as you can in price." In another instance Fletcher wrote in response to a letter of inquiry for a tea set from the Boston vendor of "lamps and silver ware," Alfred Welles, that "Yours of the 14th inst. is received . . . I will make a sett for you immediately provided you will allow me to draw upon you in advance [and] can finish you one set in about three weeks. The 5 pieces of the pattern you describe can be made for 175."[10]

Like the vase bearing only Baldwin Gardiner's mark, the silver Fletcher's manufactory made for Campbell, Welles, and others probably bore only the mark of the retailer. As such, those objects represent hidden artistic responsibility. It might be reasonably presumed that the merchant-craftsmen who ordered silver from Fletcher took full credit for the workmanship and artistry of the objects stamped with their names, but their role was only as vendor. While the "setts of plate" Fletcher made for Campbell and Welles are not presently known, a teapot bearing only the mark of Boston silversmith Newell Harding does survive. (Fig. 5.10) Although Harding could have made this teapot to match a Fletcher & Gardiner example (Fig. 5.11), it is likely that the firm fabricated it for Harding to mark and sell. The similarities of the teapots highlight the cited correspondence, helping to place the partners in a local, regional, and national network of silversmiths, jewelers, and watchmakers supplying not only silver components but also entire objects as well.[11]

For more than three decades, Thomas Fletcher and Sidney Gardiner's manufactory generated a rich and diverse body of silver and gold artifacts that they sold throughout the United States and beyond via networks of colleagues in the trades. Much of their work bears their stamped or engraved marks, but some was marked with the names of others. The latter presents a challenge in assigning due credit. At the same time, it validates the partners' influential presence in a complex and dynamic system that evolved to supply early nineteenth-century Americans with precious metals. To accomplish this with the level of success they achieved, Fletcher and Gardiner

had to orchestrate relationships with not only merchants, fancy hardware tradesmen, and other silversmiths but also with a full spectrum of specialist artisans, some of whom were employees and others independent jobbers.[12]

Regardless of which and how many individuals contributed to the creation of the silver and gold emanating from the Fletcher & Gardiner manufactory, the final product had a profound affect on all who saw it. As noted by John Linton of New Orleans: "I have rec[eive]d your . . . plate which has been opened & exhibited to the public & it affords me pleasure to say that it is much admired for the style and execution and is [commented] by every one as credit to your taste and a proof of great perfection."[13]

From this and other equally flattering comments directed toward Fletcher and Gardiner throughout their careers, it is apparent that the partners possessed the genius to identify and capture the essence of their era. At its most basic level, their silver attractively filled a need in the parlors and dining rooms of American householders. At a more abstruse but equally important level, the designs that took shape in their hands, and those of others they orchestrated, clearly resonated for all who struggled with the American identity and how best to express it in silver and gold. To Fletcher and Gardiner, therefore, fell the role of arbiter. The objects they created, both serviceable and artistic, document the ability of the partners to capture the spirit of their time in the precious metals. In response, a broad segment of Americans endorsed their genius through patronage. The Fletcher & Gardiner legacy serves as a compelling record of a formative era in American history as well as a high-water mark in the story of American silver and gold.

Fig. 5.10 Newell Harding (marked by), teapot, Boston, 1820–30. Probably made by Fletcher & Gardiner. Engraved with coat of arms and crest of the Channing family of Newport, Rhode Island. Private collection.

Fig. 5.11 Fletcher & Gardiner, teapot, Philadelphia, 1817. Engraved inside footrim: *From the family of George Gibbs to Walter Channing 1817.* Private collection.

Chapter 6
Design Drawings for Fletcher & Gardiner's Hollowware and Swords
Beth Carver Wees

In addition to the wealth of written documents that chronicle the partnership of Thomas Fletcher and Sidney Gardiner, an exceptional body of surviving drawings affords a rare glimpse into the creative process. These drawings comprise two distinct groups: one of thirty-two sheets depicting hollowware designs and another of four drawings for swords. Some are mere sketches while others are carefully detailed renderings. The circumstances surrounding their survival are unknown, but that these drawings relate to the firm's manufactures is certain.[1]

Several of the drawings were prepared for presentation to clients. Others were made as working drawings to assist the craftsmen. The presentation drawings are often fully finished, with volumetric shading and finely drawn ornamental details, although incomplete designs could also have been submitted for approval before being returned to the workshop for completion and annotation (see drawings 7, 8, 23). More generalized "pattern drawings" were adaptable for reuse within the firm's standard line of wares (see drawings 21, 22). In each instance the vessels were drawn full size, allowing the silversmith to measure his work in progress against the paper pattern; graphite grid lines on many of these drawings, as well as pinholes from a compass or calipers, indicate that they were used in that manner. Surface dirt, imbedded grime, stains, and tears further suggest their use as working drawings. On one occasion a drawing was copied onto a second sheet, perhaps to be retained as a workshop record (see drawings 24, 25).[2]

Most of these drawings were made in pen and ink—sometimes with wash—or in graphite. The use of rulers, compasses, and other mechanical drawing devices is evident, but ornamental details were often drawn freehand. Occasionally erasures are visible (see drawing 7). Two of the drawings are watermarked AMIES / & CO, for Thomas Amies's Dove Mill in Lower Merion Township, Pennsylvania (see drawings 1, 2). Of the remaining papers, several are of English manufacture, and nine of those bear J. Whatman watermarks. Graphite grid lines at the outer borders and uneven edges indicate that some of the sheets have been trimmed, possibly removing evidence of a watermark (see drawing 21). The dating of watermarks on English papers became mandatory after 1794. Now convenient for establishing a *terminus post quem*, these dates were originally required for calculating excise duties. Among the present group, dated watermarks range from 1811 to 1835. Two of the drawings, each on paste paper, are impressed with the blind stamp of an English paper supplier, illustrating a practice common among stationers at that time (see drawings 11, 13).[3]

Contemporary ink or graphite inscriptions provide additional context for the drawings, for example by identifying the form as a "Coffee Urn," "Wine Cooler," or "Plan of Lip A" (see drawings 7, 11, 13). In one instance the components of a tea and coffee service are listed—their respective weights itemized in troy ounces and pennyweight, the customary units for weighing precious metals—as well as the price per ounce (see drawing 3). Notations alongside a pitcher offer ornamental variations and their attendant costs, with small "x" marks indicating optional omissions. By interpreting these inscriptions we learn more about the process of manufacture. For instance, thicker silver was used when chasing was requested, thereby increasing both the weight and the cost of the finished object (see drawing 21). Rarely do the inscriptions and sketches on the versos relate to the drawings on the rectos, although they can occasionally provide helpful leads (see drawings 1, 2). Later inscriptions can also be instructive, but they are sometimes misleading. For example pencil notations on related drawings of two flagons, a chalice, and a paten are labeled "For a Boston, Mass. Church 1818," but at least one is drawn on paper watermarked 1835 (see drawings 23, 24, 25).

That these drawings were prepared for hollowware and swords marked by Fletcher & Gardiner or, after Sidney Gardiner's death, by Thomas Fletcher's firm is confirmed by comparison with surviving objects. Several of the drawings are virtually identical to extant pieces, and others are similar enough in form or decoration to be identifiable as their designs. But who actually drew them? None of the drawings for hollowware is signed, nor does corresponding documentary evidence survive, making attribution to a particular draftsman circumstantial at best. Of the sword drawings, one is inscribed at the lower right "Fletcher & Ben[nett] 1837" and another "Tho[s] Fletcher. / Phila[a] 1837," possibly suggesting a type of branding rather than a signature (see drawings 33, 34). The group of hollowware drawings belonging to the Metropolitan Museum has long been assigned to Thomas Fletcher, an as-yet-undocumented attribution. Fletcher's interest and involvement in the design of silver manufactured by the firm is apparent in his letters, where he comments on matters such as ornament for the cover of a vase or appropriate emblems on a sword. The pocket notebook that he carried on his travels through England and France is peppered with sketches of ships, antique vases, eagles, ornamental borders, and profile figures of fashionably dressed men and women, indicating his keen observational skills and artistic ability. Occasionally he comments on drawings being prepared for an order, but the question of authorship is never clearly addressed. On February 11, 1837, for instance, he wrote to a client, Mr. Thomas Smith: "I received your favor of the 28 ult. a few days since and have had sketches made of two patt[s] of silver pitchers, 4 patt[s] of silver tea setts and 2 patt[s] of silver forks . . . The sketches which I send are of our newest and most richly wrought patt[n]s."[4] His use of the phrase "have had sketches made" implies that the drawings were being produced by someone else, most likely a draftsman trained to turn design ideas into full-scale images.

Absent a signature or other documentation, determining the identities of such draftsmen is extremely difficult. They, like many others involved in the precious metals trade, belong to what Philippa Glanville has termed the "submerged membership" of the craft, individuals whose names are now lost to us.[5] The thirty-year time span of the present drawings as well as variations in technique and style—from the classical taste of the early nineteenth century to the more flowery rococo revival of the 1830s and 1840s—suggest that they could even represent the work of several different hands.

Occasionally the name of an outside artist is mentioned in the firm's correspondence. Writing in July 1815 to his brother Thomas, then traveling in England, Charles Fletcher provided news on a major commission: "Mr Bridport has just completed the drawing for Col. Armisted's [Armistead's] Urn – in the form of an Shell supported by 4 Eagles standing upon a round foot: the Body without any chasing." Thomas Fletcher's return reply requesting "a sketch of the urn you are making" hints at his oversight of this design. The "Mr Bridport" to whom Charles Fletcher referred was George Bridport, a London-born decorative painter who immigrated to the United States in 1808. Soon after his arrival in this country he was hired by architect Benjamin Henry Latrobe to serve as a draftsman on the

Baltimore Cathedral project (1808) and for ornamental painting at the United States Capitol (1808–9) and the handsome Philadelphia residence of William Waln (1808). In 1816 George and his brother Hugh established a drawing academy in Philadelphia. Having been contracted by Fletcher & Gardiner as the draftsman for the Armistead commission, the talented Mr. Bridport or artists affiliated with his academy could certainly have been hired for other such drafting projects. No documentary evidence, however, has materialized to confirm such an arrangement. A small watercolor image of one of the DeWitt Clinton vases was later painted by Hugh Bridport, with whom Thomas Fletcher was associated in the early years of the Franklin Institute. When the Institute opened a drawing school in the fall of 1824, architect John Haviland was appointed professor of drawing with Hugh Bridport as his assistant. Thomas Fletcher, one of the founders of the Institute and a longtime officer of the Board, would certainly have been well acquainted with these men.[6]

In engaging Mr. Bridport for the Armistead project, Fletcher & Gardiner would have been following a long-standing practice among eighteenth- and nineteenth-century English and Continental silver manufacturers, who routinely employed artists, architects, or sculptors to make design drawings for their silver. In London, for instance, the leading Regency firm of Rundell, Bridge & Rundell relied upon an extensive network of silversmiths and allied craftsmen to supply the many talents necessary to carry on its trade, all the while "maintaining a rigid control over the designs."[7] We have seen that the various artists, craftsmen, and manufacturers working in Philadelphia at this time formed a close-knit community, one within which Fletcher & Gardiner quickly became established. On the evidence of their surviving work, we know that they were affiliated with such Philadelphia artists as William Hooker, who signed the engraving on both the Isaac Hull and Oliver Perry urns (see F&G cat. nos. 10, 15); William G. Mason, whose signature appears on the United Bowmen's bowl (see F&G cat. no. 69); and Young & Delleker, who engraved the firm's handsome trade card with its depiction of the Hull urn. Among their fellow silversmiths, the name of Simon Chaudron figures intriguingly in this group of drawings.

Drawing no. 1, which depicts two ornamental motifs and a lengthy presentation inscription, is annotated on the reverse "Chaudron's Vase / 1810." A second drawing in the group, no. 2, depicts the actual vase rendered full size on two sheets of paper joined horizontally. According to the inscription, this monumental object was presented by a coterie of Pennsylvania and Maryland insurance companies to Captain Peter Dobel for his role in rescuing the ship *Asia* from "imminent peril" at the mouth of the Pearl River. The completed vase was exhibited to high acclaim in August 1810 at the Merchants' Coffee House in Philadelphia. Chaudron manufactured numerous presentation pieces and was commissioned to supply a soup tureen to Captain Jacob Jones of the *Wasp* as well as a soup tureen and pitcher to Captain James Lawrence of the US Sloop of War *Hornet*. But why would two drawings depicting a vase attributed to Chaudron have descended with the Fletcher & Gardiner drawings? In 1810 Sidney Gardiner had traveled from Boston to Philadelphia, where he visited a number of silversmiths and jewelers, among them Simon Chaudron. He wrote with enthusiasm to his partner Thomas Fletcher about a possible business arrangement: "I have made A bargain with him [Chaudron] to let us have silver goods & pay A part in our work . . . I have ordered too sets to be maid light . . . I gave him the patterns, you can mention to our Customers that we shall have them soon." Although the full extent of their relationship has not been determined, the likely exchange of goods and services is supported by evidence of shared designs, such as a sauceboat of 1812–20 marked by Fletcher & Gardiner (see F&G cat. no. 21) that is very similar to a pair by Chaudron.[8]

The rarity of surviving design drawings for early American silver bestows a special distinction on this collection. A group of twenty-one pen-and-ink drawings from the workshop of Annapolis silversmith William Faris provides the closest parallel to this group until the later nineteenth century. Also unsigned, the Faris drawings feature tea-, coffee-, and tablewares as well as a soup ladle, wine siphon, and spectacle frame. Like the Fletcher & Gardiner renderings, they are drawn full-size and display compass holes and pencil markings that suggest active workshop use. Few silver objects marked by Faris survive, making comparisons with the drawings more difficult, yet their very existence speaks volumes about the creative process behind the manufacture of silver. In both cases the drawings offer evidence of design choices guided by prevailing tastes in form, style, and contemporary use. Pinpointing direct influences is seldom an easy exercise. Just as the individuals whose designs culminated in these drawings cannot always be named, their sources can rarely be cited with complete confidence. Published volumes illustrating surviving antiquities; catalogues emanating from fused silver-plate manufactories in Sheffield, Birmingham, and elsewhere; silver and silver-plate objects imported into the United States; and the many skilled craftsmen who immigrated to this country seeking work in the precious metals trades all provided considerable inspiration for designers in early nineteenth-century Philadelphia.[9]

Thomas Fletcher's own artistic visions, enriched by his travels in England and France, as well as the firm's dedicated efforts to stay abreast of the latest fashions and technologies are made manifest in these drawings. Viewed as a group, and particularly within the context of the extraordinary objects and correspondence that survive, the design drawings for silver marked by Fletcher & Gardiner become an unexpected and invaluable resource for the study of American silver.

---

1. DRAWING FOR ORNAMENTS AND INSCRIPTION ON AN URN, ca. 1810

Inscriptions:

Recto lower left, in graphite: 13 (encircled)

Recto center bottom, in black and brown ink: to PETER DOBEL Esq. / In Testimony of the sense entertained of the manly & important services rendered by / him in contributing to the Rescue of the ship *asia* Captain Williamson from imminent / Peril at the mouth of the Tigris in the month of September 1807 this urn is Respectfully presented by / John Hollins President of the Maryland Insurance Company of Baltimore / Samuel Sterrett President of the Union Insurance Company of Baltimore / Alexander McKim President of the Baltimore Insurance Company / John Inskeep President of the Insurance Company of North America / James S Cox President of the Insurance Company of the State of Pennsylvania / Samuel W Fisher President of the Philadelphia Insurance Company / George Latimer President of the Union Insurance Company of Philadelphia / Thomas Fitzsimons President of the Delaware Insurance Company of Philadelphia / David Lewis President of the Phoenix Insurance Company of Philadelphia / Israel Pleasants President of the United States Insurance Company / John Leamy President of the Marine Insurance Company of Philadelphia / and a number of Individual Underwriters.

Verso lower left edge, in black ink: M M Lukens. Phila

Verso lower left, in brown ink: Chaudron's Vase / 1810
Pen and brown and black ink and white chalk on cream wove paper 13⅝ x 18⅝ in. (34.6 x 47.3 cm)
Watermark: AMIES / & CO (and a dove with an olive branch in its beak)
The Metropolitan Museum of Art Collection, The Elisha Whittelsey Collection, The Elisha Whittelsey Fund, 1953 (53.652.6) Image © The Metropolitan Museum of Art

This drawing depicts ornamental motifs and an inscription related to the urn pictured in Drawing 2. The sheet is in delicate condition and has been repaired in several locations using old writing paper. The panel enclosing the inscription is pricked on both left and right sides, presumably for guidance in keeping the lines of text straight.[10] Neither the scene of putti nor the eagle with spread wings appears on the finished drawing, although the putti scene could have been intended for the opposite side of the urn. The inscription was likely prepared for the vacant reserve on the front.

The inscription to Peter Dobel evokes the world of international shipping in the early nineteenth century. Described in contemporary newspapers as being "of Canton, formerly of Philadelphia," Dobel was captain of a number of ships traveling the eastern seaboard from Halifax in Canada to Kingston in Jamaica and to and from Canton. The specific incident referenced here occurred in September 1807, when the 497-ton ship *Asia*, under the command of Captain Williamson, ran into danger at Boca Tigris, the mouth of the Pearl River. According to the inscription, the urn was presented to Dobel by a long list of people representing eleven insurance companies as well as individual underwriters. Following the Revolutionary War, Americans began to establish their own insurance companies, modeled on British fire and marine insurers. The rescue of the *Asia* occurred at a time of transition, when the Embargo Act of 1807–9 and the War of 1812 disrupted shipping and dwindled premiums for marine insurers. It is no wonder that these Pennsylvania- and Maryland-based companies were grateful to Dobel for his part in saving their ship from "imminent peril."[11]

"Chaudron's Vase / 1810," inscribed in black ink on the verso, suggests that the urn was designed or manufactured by Philadelphia silversmith Simon Chaudron, with whom the Fletcher & Gardiner firm had certain business dealings.[12] The identity of "M M Lukens. Phila," also written on the verso, has not yet been determined.

2. DRAWING FOR A COVERED URN, ca. 1810

Inscription:
Recto lower left, in graphite: 12 (encircled)
Black chalk on white wove paper lined with tissue 33⅜ x 20½ in. (84.8 x 52.1 cm)
Watermark: AMIES / & CO (and a dove with an olive branch in its beak)
The Metropolitan Museum of Art, The Elisha Whittelsey Collection, The Elisha Whittelsey Fund, 1953 (53.652.7)
Image © The Metropolitan Museum of Art

This large drawing is executed on two sheets of paper joined horizontally and lined with Japanese tissue. The watermark AMIES / & CO, accompanied by a dove with an olive branch in its beak, appears twice on each sheet, indicating that the paper was produced at Thomas Amies's Dove Mill in Lower Merion Township, Pennsylvania. The left-facing dove, placed about 6½ inches from the lettered watermark, was Amies's standard device.[13]

The completed urn was exhibited in August 1810 at the Merchants' Coffee House in Philadelphia and was described in the contemporary press as "a superb and highly finished Vase." These newspaper accounts confirm the inscription detailed in Drawing 1: the vase was "intended as a present to Peter Doble [Dobel], esq. of Canton, in China, from the underwriters, as a token of their thanks, and approbation of the services rendered by him to the ship Asia, Williamson, of Philadelphia, when ashore in 1807, at the eastward of the Bocca Tigris." Furthermore, the notice in *Relf's Philadelphia Gazette* announced the name of the maker: "The Vase is from the manufactory of Chaudron & Co. of this city; and in point of elegance, chasteness and simplicity of execution, may vie with the best productions of the workshops of Europe." The covered urn is ornamented with such classical motifs as wave scroll, acanthus leaves, and swags of laurel. The cover finial is fashioned as a winged figure of Victory; the handles are reminiscent of ships' figureheads draped from the waist down in acanthus leaves; and the feet are eagles with wings spread. The panel of putti astride a dolphin continues the marine theme. Each element of the design alludes to the seafaring nature of Dobel's achievement or to the classical victor himself, about to be crowned with a laurel wreath. The peculiar configuration of the handles recalls French and Italian silver vessels of the early nineteenth century.[14]

3. DRAWING FOR A TEAPOT, 1812–20

Inscriptions:

Recto lower left, in graphite: 24

Recto lower left, in graphite: Whatman 1811

Recto lower left, embossed: JOHN PARSONS / (Royal Coat of Arms)

Recto right of handle, in graphite: 67, 1 2

Recto lower right, in graphite: Coffee Pot–oz 77 / Tea Pot–47.13 / Water pot–52.02 / Sugar Bowl–40.04 / Slop bowl–35.08 / Cream jug–19.06 / oz 271.13

Graphite on white wove paper 10⅜ x 16⅜ in. (26.4 x 41.6 cm)

Watermark: J WHATMAN/1811

The Metropolitan Museum of Art, The Elisha Whittelsey Collection, The Elisha Whittelsey Fund, 1953 (53.652.29) Image © The Metropolitan Museum of Art

Although drawn in faint graphite, this design for a teapot is carefully finished, with precise detailing and volumetric shading. The sheet itself has suffered significant wear, including tears, water damage, and evidence of a footprint. The watermark, J WHATMAN / 1811, runs vertically along the right side of the paper,

seen in reverse on the recto. An oval-shaped blind stamp in the lower left represents the stationer, whose use of the royal coat of arms was a patriotic gesture rather than an indication of a royal warrant.[15]

Decorative elements on this drawing read like a dictionary of ornament, including acanthus leaves, rosettes, an anthemion, and egg-and-dart borders. The swan's-neck spout terminates in a bird's head, as does the base of the handle.[16] According to the accompanying text, a silver teapot of this design would weigh 47 troy ounces 13 pennyweight, while a coffeepot made *en suite* would require 77 troy ounces. The annotated list of six different forms, amounting to more than 270 ounces of silver, served an important function for the silversmith by detailing the quantity of silver to be used, just as the full-scale drawings provided a ready gauge for measuring the work in progress. Weights were also important to the patron, who was billed at a per-ounce rate. In 1836, for example, Thomas Fletcher charged Mrs. Richard Ashhurst $2.31 per ounce for a six-part "tea and coffee sett" weighing 227 oz. 4 dwts., totaling $524.83 (see F&G cat. no. 42).

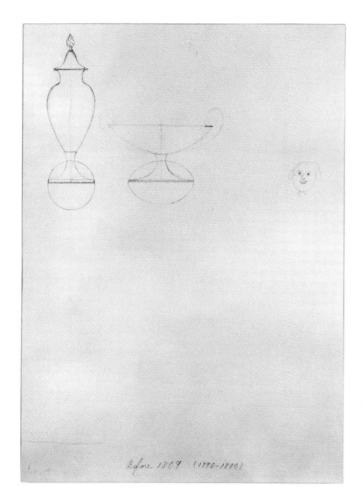

4. DRAWING FOR A COVERED CASTER AND A SALT, ca. 1815

Inscriptions:

Recto lower left, in graphite: 5

Recto bottom, in graphite: Before 1809 (1790–1800)

Graphite on cream wove paper $17^{13}/_{16}$ x 13 in. (45.2 x 33 cm)

The Metropolitan Museum of Art, The Elisha Whittelsey Collection, The Elisha Whittelsey Fund, 1953 (53.652.32) Image © The Metropolitan Museum of Art

This modest drawing for a classically inspired caster with flame finial and a two-handled salt dish reveals the tentative hand of someone working out ideas, perhaps for a more practiced draftsman to execute. The additional doodle on the right of a puckish face with toothy smile adds a playful quality to the drawing. Note the plans for a circular foot on the caster and an oval foot on the salt. The graphite inscription at the bottom, suggesting a date prior to 1809, is a later addition.

5. DRAWING FOR A COVERED URN, 1815–16

Inscriptions:

Recto on vase base, in ink: 8.JANUARY 1815.

Recto lower left, in graphite: 1 (encircled)

Verso center bottom, in graphite: Vase for Gen¹ Jackson

Pen and ink on cream wove paper 19¼ x 13⅜ in. (48.9 x 34 cm)

The Metropolitan Museum of Art, The Elisha Whittelsey Collection, The Elisha Whittelsey Fund, 1953 (53.652.4) Image © The Metropolitan Museum of Art

The work of an accomplished and confident draftsman, this drawing is a preparatory design for the monumental silver vase presented in 1816 by "the Ladies of South-Carolina" to their native son, Major General Andrew Jackson (see F&G cat. no. 22). In overall form and ornament it relates closely to the finished vessel. The coiled snake handles follow early nineteenth-century French and English models. Their precisely rendered scales recall designs by French decorative painter Jean-

Jacques Boileau for the London goldsmiths Rundell, Bridge & Rundell. The sturdy paw feet with sharply curved nails are reminiscent of Boileau's drawings as well as furniture designed by collector and connoisseur Thomas Hope. While the elegant band of laurel leaves draws our focus upward, it is in the densely rendered frieze below that the meaning of this presentation vase unfolds. There the artist portrays in brilliant shorthand fashion the victorious defense of New Orleans by General Jackson's forces. At left the American soldiers, identified by the fluttering stars and stripes, form a tightly regimented column, their muskets and cannon

discharging furious billows of smoke.[17] A rearing horse and rider gesture backward toward the retreating British troops, one of whom lies dead at the center of the frieze. The battle date of 8 January 1815 is inscribed above.

This drawing would have been part of the design process for a special commission rather than a standardized pattern drawing. The sheet has suffered numerous losses and cracks and appears to have been rolled. The artist is unknown, but the drawing was probably executed during Thomas Fletcher's travels abroad in 1815–16. Might this also be the hand of Mr. Bridport, as were the drawings for Colonel Armistead's punch bowl?[18]

6. DRAWING FOR A COVERED TUREEN, 1820–30

Inscriptions:
Recto lower left, in graphite: 3 (encircled)
Verso center, in graphite: 2 of this (above outer oval), 4 of this (above inner oval)
Graphite and an amorphous carbon-based material on wove paper 17⅞ x 13½ in. (44.8 x 34.3 cm)
The Metropolitan Museum of Art, The Elisha Whittelsey Collection, The Elisha Whittelsey Fund, 1953 (53.652.23) Image © The Metropolitan Museum of Art

Executed in graphite and chalk, this drawing for a covered tureen on claw feet appears to be by a different hand than most others in this group. The rendering is hard-edged yet sketchy, with cross-hatching and shading. The upper half of the sheet represents the tureen in plan. Compass holes on the plan as well as vertical and horizontal midlines were used for centering the design. The sheet has been cut down on both vertical sides, constricting the image.

The effect of restrained ornament against a smooth expanse recalls French and English tureens and entrée dishes of the early nineteenth century. The cover's leafy handle, fashioned as two C-scrolls, is a type routinely found on English silver and silver plate of the period. One of the sketches that Thomas Fletcher made while traveling in England and France in 1815–16 is of a similar handle, casually drawn on a page of shipping instructions. The narrow leaf-tip bands on the tureen relate to the die-rolled borders used, for example, on two tureens presented to Robert M. Lewis, outgoing president of the Chesapeake & Delaware Canal Company in 1836.[19]

8. DRAWING FOR AN URN, 1825–35

Inscription:
Recto lower left, in graphite: 30
Graphite on tan wove paper 17³⁄₁₆ x 12⅞ in. (43.7 x 32.7 cm)
The Metropolitan Museum of Art, The Elisha Whittelsey Collection, The Elisha Whittelsey Fund, 1953 (53.652.14) Image © The Metropolitan Museum of Art

Although more carefully delineated than the wine cooler on a pedestal foot (Drawing 7), this drawing of a calyx krater-shape urn or vase with overlapping leaves and ribbon-tied laurel borders appears to be by the same hand. The use of horizontal and vertical grid lines is similar, as is the representation of only the left-hand side of the vessel. Even the small bacchic head, which serves here as the base of the applied handle, is a profile version of the same model.

7. DRAWING FOR A WINE COOLER, 1825–35

Inscriptions:
Recto center top, in graphite: Wine Cooler
Recto lower left, in graphite: 23
Graphite on white wove paper 16½ x 10¾ in. (41.9 x 26.4 cm)
The Metropolitan Museum of Art, The Elisha Whittelsey Collection, The Elisha Whittelsey Fund, 1953 (53.652.25) Image © The Metropolitan Museum of Art

This graphite sketch for a wine cooler illuminates the creative process more clearly than do the finished drawings. Horizontal and vertical grid lines were used for layout or perhaps for transferring this sketch to another sheet. Erasures at the base indicate that it has been redrawn or refined. Although the coin molding on the plinth appears to have been made using a compass or a template, areas such as the handle, the wreath, the stem, and the overlapping leaves were executed freehand. Only the left-hand side of the wine cooler is rendered, suggesting that the right was to be a mirror image. The curly-hair head at the center appears to have erasures above and below. Although it now displays a bacchic air, it might originally have had two braids tied beneath the chin, in the manner of French ornamental mounts.[20]

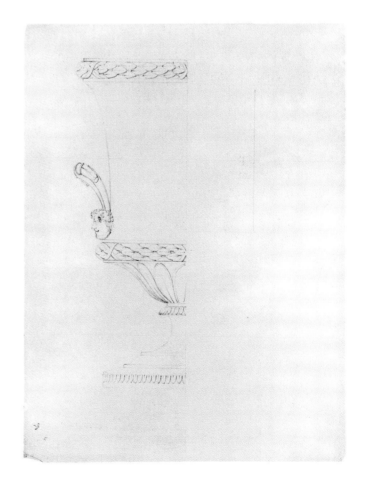

9. A COVERED DISH AND BOWL 1825–35

Inscription:

Lower left, in graphite: 6

Lower left, in graphite: See over for teapot

Lower left: METROPOLITAN / MUSEUM / OF ART / NEW YORK (encircled) / 53.652.12

Graphite on paper 15⅞ x 21¼ in. (40.3 x 54 cm)

The Metropolitan Museum of Art, The Elisha Whittelsey Collection, The Elisha Whittelsey Fund, 1953 (53.652.12) Image © The Metropolitan Museum of Art

Both the covered entrée dish, depicted in profile and plan on the right, and the two-handled tureen with cover, on the left, reflect the influence of fused silver plate on the design of nineteenth-century American dinnerwares. The carefully detailed border patterns and handles, as well as the volumetric shading, indicate a finished drawing. The bud finial on the tureen resembles that on the drawing for a coffee or hot water urn, and the double C-scroll handle on the entrée dish is similar to one illustrated in Drawing 6. Silver entrée or vegetable dishes of this type marked by Fletcher & Gardiner survive in some quantity.[21]

10. DRAWING FOR A WINE COOLER, 1825–35
Inscription:
Recto lower left, in graphite: 31
Pen and brown ink and brown wash on cream wove paper 17⅜ x 14⅛ in. (44 x 35.7 cm)
The Metropolitan Museum of Art, The Elisha Whittelsey Collection, The Elisha Whittelsey Fund, 1953 (53.652.26) Image © The Metropolitan Museum of Art

This lovely ink-and-wash presentation drawing can be dated to the years around 1830, consistent with a surviving silver wine cooler of this design (see F&G cat. no. 75). Based on the Greek calyx krater form, the wine cooler is encircled at the neck by a band of acorns and oak leaves and at the belly by a Dionysian garland of grapes and grape leaves. Acorns, which are found on ancient Greek vessels, appear again on the lip molding,

which is identical to the midband on the coffee urn in Drawing 11.[22] The same die-rolled echinus border was also used on both objects.

Antique inspiration for this drawing could have derived from objects that Thomas Fletcher encountered on travels in England and France or from illustrations in the catalogue of antiquities that he purchased while abroad. The design also recalls wine coolers produced by the London firm of Rundell, Bridge & Rundell, whose premises Fletcher had visited in June 1815. Among the patterns in production at Rundell's by 1808–9 was a wine cooler modeled on the Medici krater, which was illustrated in Piranesi's influential *Vasi, Candelabri, Cippi*, published in 1778. That volume, as well as sources such as Thomas Hope's *Household Furniture*, were available for consultation at the Library Company of Philadelphia early in the nineteenth century.[23]

11. DRAWING FOR A COFFEE URN, 1825–35
Inscriptions:
Recto center bottom, in brown ink: Coffee Urn wt 100 oz
Recto lower left, in graphite: 25
Verso lower right, embossed: JOHN PARSONS / (Royal Coat of Arms)
Graphite on white wove paper 16⁵⁄₁₆ x 10⅜ in. (41.4 x 26.4 cm)
Watermark: J WHATMAN / 1811
The Metropolitan Museum of Art, The Elisha Whittelsey Collection, The Elisha Whittelsey Fund, 1953 (53.652.28) Image © The Metropolitan Museum of Art

This highly finished drawing appears to be by the same hand that rendered the teapot in Drawing 3. It is executed on similar paper, watermarked J WHATMAN / 1811 along the bottom edge, and embossed with the John Parsons blind stamp. This sheet has also seen considerable wear. The brown ink inscription below the foot, "Coffee Urn wt 100 oz," indicates a sizeable vessel and, by extension, a costly one. That it did indeed require approximately 100 troy ounces of silver is confirmed by the survival of a coffee or hot water urn of this very design, now in a private collection (see F&G cat. no. 42). The extant urn, weighing 103 oz. 10 dwt., is ornamented in almost identical fashion, with egg-and-dart borders on the upper body and the top of the base; a midband of leaf, shell, and acorn pattern; and a leafy bud finial. Slight variations in the animal paw feet, loop handles, and die-rolled borders are among the few discrepancies. The finished urn was equipped with a spigot, which is not visible on the drawing. A hot water urn would have been an optional addition to a standard tea or coffee service, such as the similar set illustrated in F&G cat. no. 41.

12. DRAWING FOR A WINE COOLER, 1825–35
Inscription: none
Pen and brown ink and wash on cream wove paper 17⅝ x 13⅜ in. (44.8 x 34 cm)
The Metropolitan Museum of Art, The Elisha Whittelsey Collection, The Elisha Whittelsey Fund, 1953 (53.652.31) Image © The Metropolitan Museum of Art

The use of wash and shading on this unusual drawing, as well as the absence of pencil marks or pinholes, suggests that it was prepared for presentation. It is drawn on textured cream-color paper that has been cut down.

Silver and silver-gilt wine coolers of Greek calyx krater form were popular in England during the early decades of the nineteenth century. Some were copied from surviving vessels such as the Medici krater, adaptations of which were manufactured by Rundell, Bridge & Rundell in 1811/12. Antique calyx kraters were also illustrated in volumes such as Piranesi's *Vasi, Candelabri, Cippi* and Henry Moses's *Collection of Antique Vases*. The vase in this drawing is less ornate than most classical examples, and the fluting and shaped pedestal base are variations on the traditional design. The leaf-and-shell border at the lip is repeated on the foot, and the grapevine ornament around the belly is delicately drawn. What the overall design resembles most is a type of wine cooler produced in silver plate at Matthew Boulton's manufactory in Birmingham, England, around 1830, a pair of which is in the collection of the Metropolitan Museum of Art.[24]

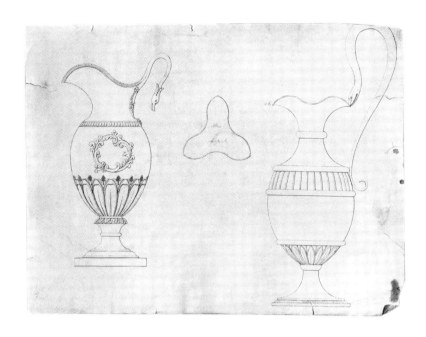

13. DRAWINGS FOR TWO PITCHERS (RECTO) AND A COVERED VASE (VERSO), 1827–35

Inscriptions:

Recto center, in black ink: Plan/of/Lip. A

Recto lower left, in graphite: 22

Recto: pen and fine brush and brown ink with graphite under drawing on cream wove paper

Verso: graphite on cream wove paper 15⅝ x 21 in. (39.7 x 53.3 cm)

The Metropolitan Museum of Art, The Elisha Whittelsey Collection, The Elisha Whittelsey Fund, 1953 (53.652.30) Image © The Metropolitan Museum of Art

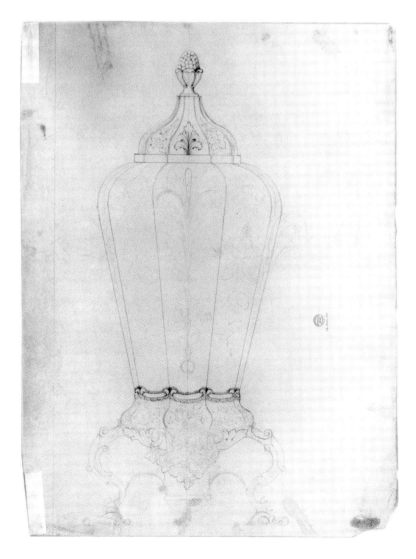

The drawing on the verso of this sheet depicts a tall, paneled, covered vessel on what appears to be a burner stand with scrolled legs and feet. Sketchily rendered foliate ornament covers much of the vessel, which is surmounted by a bud finial. Whatever its original intent, this drawing remains unfinished.

The recto illustrates two versions of a single-handled pitcher shaped like a Greek amphora. The model on the left is ornamented with leaf moldings, a calyx of overlapping leaves, and a vacant scrolled cartouche. The handle, fashioned as an open loop terminating in a bird's head, joins the body at an anthemion or palmette. An ancient source could possibly have served as inspiration for the terminal, since the use of a bird's head was common on the handles of Greek, Roman, and Etruscan ladles and strainers. A silver pitcher by Fletcher & Gardiner based on this design survives (see F&G cat. no. 77). It varies from the drawing mainly in the choice of moldings and the placement of the cartouche. The second pitcher, drawn with more geometric ornament, has a tri-lobed lip that is depicted from above in the center of the sheet. It is neatly labeled "Plan of Lip A," referring to a tiny script letter "A" inscribed to the left of the vessel's lip. Its handle takes the form of a sinuous serpent, attached to the lip at the mouth and to the body at the curved tail.[25] From the degree of foxing, stains, and tears, the present sheet has seen considerable use.

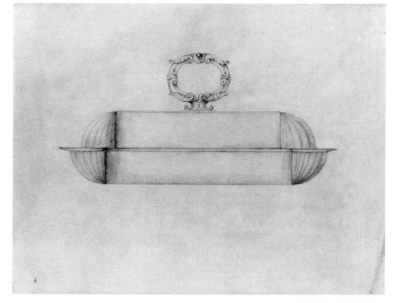

14. DRAWING FOR A PITCHER, 1827–35
Inscriptions:
Recto lower left, in graphite: 33
Recto center right, in graphite: 52^{oz} ea @ $2.50
Pen and ink on cream wove paper 19⅜ x 12½ in. (49.2 x 31.8 cm)
Watermark: J WHATMAN/[TURKEY MILL]
The Metropolitan Museum of Art, The Elisha Whittelsey Collection, The Elisha Whittelsey Fund, 1953 (53.652.35) Image © The Metropolitan Museum of Art

Although shown without a handle, the vessel depicted here was probably intended as a pitcher modeled like those in Drawing 13. The overall form has been drawn with a pen that created indented lines alongside the ink. The ornate bands of classical ornament, which include wave scroll, anthemia, and palmettes, were drawn freehand. A graphite inscription to the right of the foot reads "52^{oz} ea @ $2.50," indicating that a pitcher weighing 52 troy ounces would have been priced at $2.50 per ounce, or $130.00. This weight suggests a fairly large vessel. The sheet of paper has been cut down, as has its watermark, J WHATMAN. Below it, however, is evidence of a "T" between the "J" and the "W" and an "M" directly under the "M," most certainly for TURKEY MILL.[26]

15. DRAWING FOR A COVERED ENTRÉE DISH, 1830–40
Inscription:
Recto lower left, in graphite: 4
Graphite on tan wove paper 13 x 17⅛ in (33 x 43.5 cm)
The Metropolitan Museum of Art, The Elisha Whittelsey Collection, The Elisha Whittelsey Fund, 1953 (53.652.22) Image © The Metropolitan Museum of Art

The body of this covered dish was drawn with a ruler while the handle and shaded corners were executed freehand. The corners appear to have been shell-shape, as on the plan for a similar dish shown as Drawing 16. The double C-scroll handle is a type used elsewhere with variations and is common on contemporary English silver and silver-plated wares.[27] Central grid lines, both horizontal and vertical, appear to have been used as a guide. The paper was bleached at some point to minimize staining.

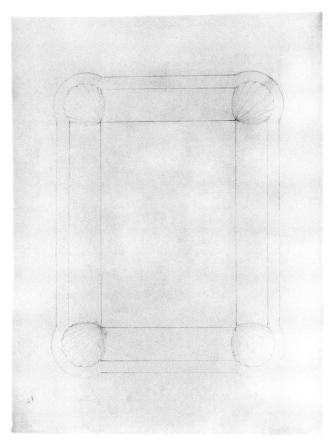

16. DRAWING FOR AN ENTRÉE DISH, 1830–40
Inscription:
Recto lower right, in graphite: 28 (sideways)
Graphite on tan wove paper 13 x 17⅛ in. (33 x 43.5 cm)
The Metropolitan Museum of Art, The Elisha Whittelsey
Collection, The Elisha Whittelsey Fund, 1953
(53.652.13) Image © The Metropolitan Museum of Art

This drawing appears to be a plan for the covered entrée
dish depicted in Drawing 15. Its straight lines were
drawn with a ruler, the corners with a compass or other
guide, and the shells at least partially freehand. Fine grid
lines are barely visible at one corner. Only one of the
shells is drawn with a tiny hinge.

**17. DRAWING FOR A CORNER DISH AND
COVER**, 1830–40
Inscriptions:
Recto center bottom, in graphite: Corner Dish & Cover
Recto lower left, in graphite: 29
Graphite on tan wove paper 16¾ x 12¹³⁄₁₆ in. (42.5 x 32.6 cm)
The Metropolitan Museum of Art, The Elisha Whittelsey
Collection, The Elisha Whittelsey Fund, 1953
(53.652.15) Image © The Metropolitan Museum of Art

"Corner Dish & Cover," written in graphite below this
heart-shape design, appears to be contemporary
although rendered in a more delicate hand than the
drawing. There are oil stains on the paper as well as
small metal inclusions. Two tiny pinholes at the upper
right and left, just inside the leaf-pattern outer border,
were probably made by calipers and indicate that the
drawing saw workshop use. No silver covered dishes of
this type survive among the Fletcher & Gardiner
oeuvre, nor is it a common form in silver. Related
models can be found in the kidney-shape porcelain
dessert dishes manufactured from the 1760s onward at
Worcester, Derby, Caughley, Wedgwood, and
elsewhere. The fan-shape thumbpiece at the top of this
design has parallels in early nineteenth-century
porcelain as well.[28]

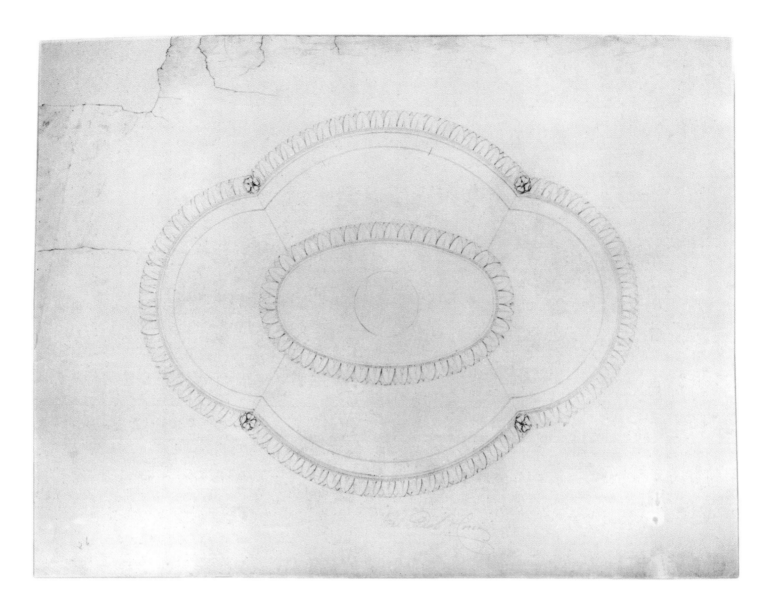

18. DRAWING FOR AN OVAL DISH AND COVER, 1830–40

Inscriptions:

Recto center right, in graphite: Oval Dish & Cover

Recto lower right, in graphite: 26

Recto lower left, in graphite: 26

Graphite on tan wove paper 17 x 12¾ in. (43.2 x 32.4 cm) The Metropolitan Museum of Art, The Elisha Whittelsey Collection, The Elisha Whittelsey Fund, 1953 (53.652.16) Image © The Metropolitan Museum of Art

This drawing is related in design and hand to the "Corner Dish & Cover" (Drawing 17) and is inscribed in a similar manner. The paper has been damaged in the upper left corner and has suffered oil stains. Pinholes at the center and at the outer edges of the inner oval again suggest the use of calipers or a compass. No covered silver dishes of this form are known to survive.

appears often in the drawings as well as in Fletcher & Gardiner's extant oeuvre. The leaf-wrapped handle is divided by two narrow horizontal bands similar to the ivory filets that were routinely used as insulators on coffee- and teapots. Designs for French Empire silver display a similar handle treatment. The leaf-capped paw foot is a formula also found repeatedly on the firm's manufactures.[29]

Three sketches for baluster-shape casters are drawn on the verso. The caster on the left is the most fully realized, with a paneled upper body, pierced cover, and rococo-revival ornament on the belly similar to that on the coffeepot in Drawing 31. Each of the casters has a vertical grid line through its center, and the design on the far left also displays a horizontal line at the narrow part of its neck.

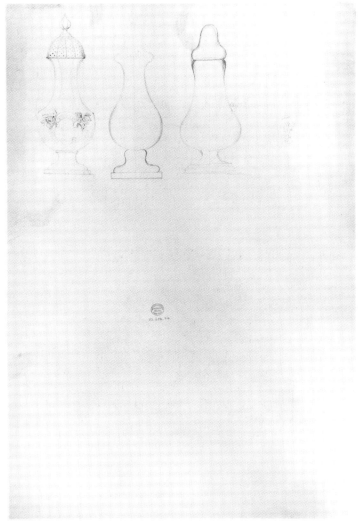

19. DRAWING FOR A PITCHER (RECTO) AND THREE CASTERS (VERSO), 1830–40

Inscription:
Recto lower left, in graphite: 34
Recto to right of base, in graphite: 55 (very faint)
Recto: pen and ink on cream wove paper. Verso: graphite on cream wove paper 19³⁄₁₆ x 13⁹⁄₁₆ in. (48.7 x 34.4 cm)
The Metropolitan Museum of Art, The Elisha Whittelsey Collection, The Elisha Whittelsey Fund, 1953 (53.652.34) Image © The Metropolitan Museum of Art

Characterized by a delicate hand, this careful rendering of a large-size pitcher is nearly identical to a surviving silver vessel (see F&G cat. no. 80). Several pinholes run vertically along the center. The faint pencil notation "55" inscribed to the right of the base probably refers to the anticipated weight of the finished pitcher in troy ounces; the silver example noted above weighs just an ounce and a half more at 56 ounces 10 pennyweight. The intricate border drawn on the shoulder is one that

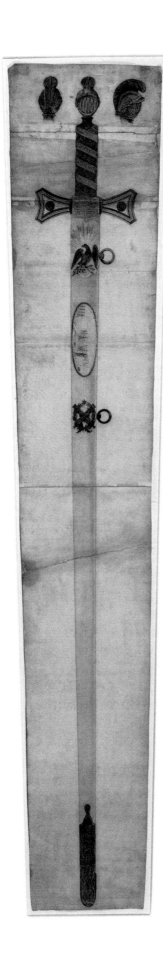

20. DRAWING FOR A SWORD, ca. 1834

Inscriptions:

Recto, on hilt of sword in escutcheon at cross guard: Presented to / Colⁿ Nathan Towson / by the / State of Maryland / in consideration of his / gallant services / during the War.

Recto, on grip: CALEDONIA / CHIPPEWA / BRIDGEWATER / FORT ERIE

Watercolor over graphite on cream wove paper 38¼ x 7³⁄₁₆ in. (97.2 x 18.3 cm) tapering to 5¼ in. (13.3 cm)

Maryland Historical Society, Gift of Joseph Katz, 1952.124.1

The cream wove paper on which this full-size design was drawn consists of two sheets joined horizontally at the center, now mounted on board. Despite several repaired tears and grime, it is a handsome watercolor rendering in a palette of green, brown, and salmon. Vertical and horizontal graphite lines intersect at the center of the cross guard, and there are numerous pinholes around the outermost edges.

According to the inscription on the cross guard, this sword was to be presented to Colonel Nathan Towson (1784–1854) by the State of Maryland in recognition of his distinguished service during the War of 1812. The names of four battles in which Towson triumphed are inscribed on the grip within diagonal bands, alternating with bands of stars. Ornament on the scabbard consists of an eagle on the throat mount; an oval vignette; a wreath enclosing crossed cannon at the center; and an arabesque-pattern mount at the tip. The pommel is fashioned as a knight's helmet with barred-and-plumed visor; back and profile views are depicted at either side to guide the silversmith. The finished sword survives (see F&G cat. no. 79). It is close in design aside from variations in the scabbard mounts and the battle site of Niagara, which has been changed to Fort Erie. An additional inscription was also engraved on the blade. The dating of this drawing is aided by an 1832 act of the Maryland General Assembly and by surviving correspondence with Thomas Fletcher. Among the Fletcher papers is an undated record of the material and labor costs involved in making this sword, totaling $605.16.[30]

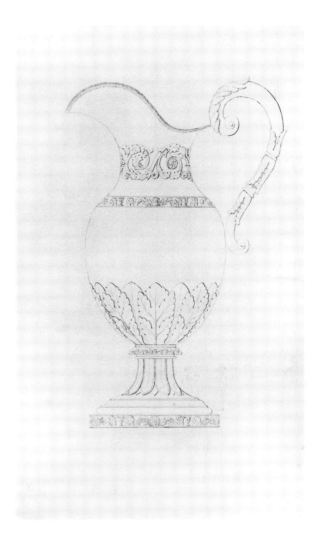

21. DRAWING FOR A PITCHER, ca. 1835

Inscriptions:

Recto lower left, in graphite: 11 (encircled)

Recto center right, in graphite: 45oz ea @ $2.50 chased

Recto center right, in graphite: 40oz ea @ $2.25 plain neck & foot

Recto right of bottom molding, above plinth, in graphite: − x omit This

Recto right of neck, in graphite:−x

Pen and brown ink on cream wove paper 19⅞ x 12 in. (50.5 x 30.5 cm)

Watermark: J WHATMAN / TURKEY MILL / [date cut off]

The Metropolitan Museum of Art, The Elisha Whittelsey Collection, The Elisha Whittelsey Fund, 1953 (53.652.20) Image © The Metropolitan Museum of Art

The date below the watermark has been trimmed off but would probably have been 1835, consistent with other papers in this group. The style of pitcher with its delicately drawn ornamental bands, calyx of overlapping leaves, and acanthus leaf-wrapped scrolled handle is characteristic of American silver of the 1830s. A compass hole on the belly of the pitcher at the center of the design suggests a carefully measured drawing. Graphite inscriptions to the right of the base itemize ornamental variations and their attendant costs. For instance, a chased version of the pitcher, weighing 45 troy ounces, would cost $2.50 per ounce, or $112.50. With a plain neck and foot, the weight dropped to 40 ounces and the cost to $2.00 per ounce, or $80.00.[31] Small "x" marks, indicating possible omissions, are placed beside the neck ornament, the chasing on the foot, and one of the steps on the foot above the plinth. These cryptic notes illuminate the process of manufacture: thicker silver was needed to accommodate the chasing; the neck and foot decoration was to be chased rather than cast and applied; and the narrow ornamental bands at the waist and on the plinth were presumably die-rolled.

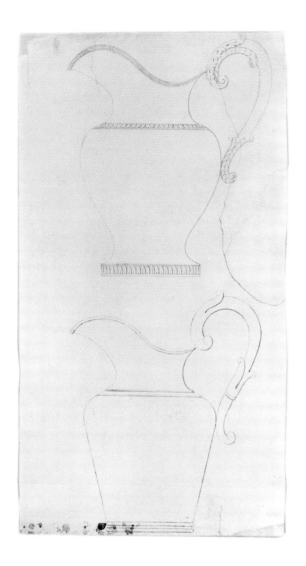

22. DRAWING FOR TWO PITCHERS, 1835–40

Inscriptions:

Recto lower left, in graphite: 21

Recto lower right, in graphite: W / M / 1835

Verso center left, in graphite: 250 / 225 / 1250 / 500 / 6250 (arranged vertically)

Pen and brown ink on cream wove paper 22⅟₁₆ x 12⅟₁₆ in. (56 x 30.6 cm)

Watermark: J WHATMAN / TURKEY MILL / 1835

The Metropolitan Museum of Art, The Elisha Whittelsey Collection, The Elisha Whittelsey Fund, 1953 (53.652.33) Image © The Metropolitan Museum of Art

Silver pitchers of baluster form were sometimes inspired by ceramic jugs imported from England, as in the example made for Commodore William Bainbridge (see F&G cat. no. 50). This rendering of two pitchers probably served as a pattern drawing after which silver vessels were modeled. The variations in form, and particularly in die-rolled ornament, would have translated into a difference in price. The meaning of the numbers listed in graphite on the verso is uncertain, but the watermark indicates that the drawing was produced no earlier than 1835.

23. DRAWING FOR A CHALICE AND PATEN, 1835–40

Inscriptions:

Recto lower left, in graphite: 15

Recto lower left, in graphite: For a Boston, Mass. / Church 1818. Park Street

Recto center right, in graphite: 8½ dia

Pen and fine brush and brown ink; also graphite on tan wove paper 20⅞ x 14¾ in. (53 x 37.5 cm)

The Metropolitan Museum of Art, The Elisha Whittelsey Collection, The Elisha Whittelsey Fund, 1953 (53.652.8) Image © The Metropolitan Museum of Art

Related in style and ornament to the flagon depicted in Drawing 24 and Drawing 25, this chalice and its accompanying paten display design elements of the 1830s. The chalice follows a centuries-old formula of inverted bell-shape bowl, spreading foot, and central knop.[32] As on the flagon, the sacred monogram IHS appears on the bowl of the chalice, set within the rays of glory. The ink line along the right side of the chalice is darker than that on the left, possibly indicating that the right side was drawn first, while the pen was still fresh with ink. The two borders drawn on a small section of the paten plan—one egg and dart, the other wave scroll —are identical to those below the lip of the flagon. There is a tiny hole at the center of the plan, caused by the compass point used to draw its circumference. Graphite shading is visible inside the wave scroll and on the inner border, and there are graphite guidelines at the center of the chalice and elevation of the paten. The sheet appears to have been cut down, evidenced by graphite lines on all four sides.

The later graphite inscription, "For a Boston, Mass. /

Church 1818. Park Street," suggests that these vessels were designed for the Park Street Church in Boston, which was founded in 1809. There is no record, however, that they were ever made or that the church ever owned silver of this design. Archival records, which survive at the Congregational Library in Boston, include no mention of this commission. That the firm received other orders for sacramental silver is, however, evident from extant examples (see F&G cat. nos. 2, 4, 39, 52).[33]

24. DRAWING FOR A FLAGON, 1835–40

Inscriptions:

Recto lower left, in graphite: For a Boston, Mass. / Church, 1818.

Recto center bottom, in graphite: W / M 1835

Recto lower left, in graphite: 17

Verso lower right, in graphite: Rudiments / of Grammar / Pho[?]mes / M.D. Lafourcade / Race St. opposite / Franklin Square

Verso lower left, in graphite: Rec^d Octob^r / Rudiments / Janotville / Janotsville

Pen and black ink on cream wove paper 20 x 13⅜ in. (50.8 x 34 cm)

Watermark: J WHATMAN / TURKEY MILL / 1835

The Metropolitan Museum of Art, The Elisha Whittelsey Collection, The Elisha Whittelsey Fund, 1953 (53.652.9)

Image © The Metropolitan Museum of Art

Although a later pencil inscription in the lower left corner reads "For a Boston, Mass./Church, 1818." this sheet of paper is watermarked 1835, a date more in keeping with the style of the flagon depicted. The bold acanthus leaves, foliate handle and finial, shell spout, and wave-scroll border suggest rococo-revival silver of the 1830s.[34] Drawn largely freehand in pen and black ink, this design appears to have been the model for the brown ink copy in Drawing 25. The tiny hole in the middle of the sacred monogram IHS suggests that a compass was used for measuring.

The fascinating array of sketches and inscriptions on the verso are evidently unrelated to the flagon but do correspond to some of the other drawings. An eagle with wings spread is nearly identical, although in reverse, to the ornamental design for the eagle in Drawing 1, and the column of soldiers shrouded in musket fire appears to be a sketch after the battle scene on the Jackson vase

(Drawing 5). The meaning of the inscription, "Rudiments / of Grammar / Phonemes / M.D. Lafourcade / Race St. opposite / Franklin Square" is unclear, but it could possibly refer to a Philadelphia bookseller and stationer called P. M. LaFourcade, whose shop was at the corner of Second and Race streets.[35]

25. DRAWING FOR A FLAGON, 1835–40

Inscriptions:

Recto lower left, in graphite: 18

Recto lower left, in graphite: Made for a Boston, Mass. Church, 1818

Pen and brown ink on cream wove paper 19⅜ x 13¾ in. (49.2 x 34.9 cm)

The Metropolitan Museum of Art, The Elisha Whittelsey Collection, The Elisha Whittelsey Fund, 1953 (53.652.10) Image © The Metropolitan Museum of Art

A graphite line running vertically down the center of this sheet may have been used for centering a tracing of the flagon depicted in Drawing 24. The two images are nearly identical, although this one is made in brown ink rather than black, and the execution is somewhat less fluid. The paper is also in better condition. In each example the draftsman has depicted the cover of the flagon as a separate unit, positioned above the body. A later inscription suggests that the flagon was designed in 1818 for a church in Boston, but its relationship to the drawing on paper watermarked 1835 indicates otherwise.[36]

26. DRAWING FOR A COVERED TUREEN, 1835–40

Inscription:

Recto lower left, in graphite: 20

Pen and brown ink on cream wove paper 14⅝ x 18³⁄₁₆ in. (37.1 x 46.2 cm)

The Metropolitan Museum of Art, The Elisha Whittelsey Collection, The Elisha Whittelsey Fund, 1953 (53.652.24) Image © The Metropolitan Museum of Art

This handsome line drawing is particularly well finished. Note the carefully drawn anthemion and flower ornament on the lower body and the tiny comma-like marks on each bead of the cover rim and finial, with give the effect of three-dimensionality. The bud finial is nearly identical to one on the design for a coffee urn (Drawing 11). A vertical centerline, now barely visible, appears to have been erased. That, along with the absence of pinholes, suggests that this was not a working drawing but rather a design model, perhaps a pattern drawing adaptable for reuse. No identical silver tureen marked by the firm is known, although parallels can be drawn with extant examples. The design also resembles ceramic tureens of the early nineteenth century, catalogues of which were circulated among designers, craftsmen, and fashionable consumers. [37]

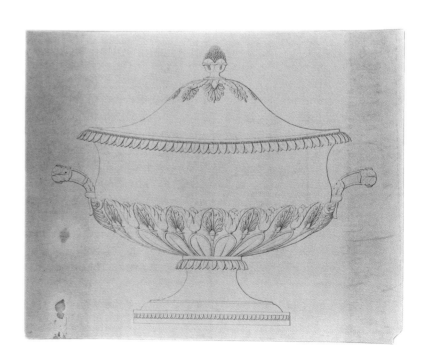

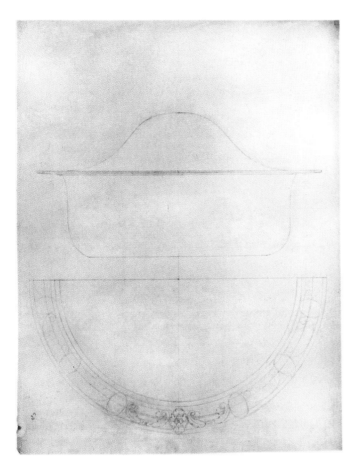

27. DRAWING FOR A COVERED DISH AND A BORDER DESIGN, 1835–40

Inscription:

Recto lower left, in graphite: 27

Graphite on tan wove paper 16¹³⁄₁₆ x 12¹⁵⁄₁₆ in. (42.7 x 32.9 cm)
The Metropolitan Museum of Art, The Elisha Whittelsey Collection, The Elisha Whittelsey Fund, 1953 (53.652.17) Image © The Metropolitan Museum of Art

This unfinished drawing depicts the elevation of a dish with domed cover as well as the plan of a border design ornamented with oval reserves and a central floral motif.[38] A graphite line bisects the entire drawing vertically, and there are several pinholes along its length. Another graphite line runs horizontally through the center of the drawing, which appears to have been either a simple workshop sketch or a design transferred to another sheet for completion. The wove paper is so soft that the imprint of the graphite lines can be read on the verso.

28. DRAWING FOR A WINE COOLER, 1835–40

Inscription:

Recto lower left, in graphite: 32

Pen and fine brush and brown ink, also graphite, on cream wove paper 15¹¹⁄₁₆ x 15¹¹⁄₁₆ in. (39.8 x 39.8 cm)
The Metropolitan Museum of Art, The Elisha Whittelsey Collection, The Elisha Whittelsey Fund, 1953 (53.652.27) Image © The Metropolitan Museum of Art

This design for a wine cooler combines some of the firm's most successful decorative elements. The twisted vine handles, for example, recall the massive "Warwick Vase" handles on the Clinton urns. The anthemion border on the lower body is nearly identical to that on the drawing for a covered tureen (Drawing 26), while the egg-and-dart borders appear on a number of different models. The ribbon-tied wreath of grapes and leaves is a variation on the usual banding of those motifs.[39] A graphite grid line running vertically through the center of the vase and another on the outer edge of the left-hand handle indicate workshop use. A variant border design featuring alternating acanthus and lotus motifs is drawn in pale graphite between two horizontal grid lines at the upper right.

29. DRAWING FOR A TEAPOT, SUGAR BOWL, AND CREAM JUG, 1835–40

Inscriptions:

Recto lower left, in graphite: 14 (encircled)

Recto lower left, in graphite: 13oz (partially erased)

Recto lower right, in graphite: 6½

Graphite on cream wove paper 20⅜ x 16 in. (51.8 x 40.6 cm)

Watermark: J WHATMAN / TURKEY MILL / 1835

The Metropolitan Museum of Art, The Elisha Whittelsey Collection, The Elisha Whittelsey Fund, 1953 (53.652.21) Image © The Metropolitan Museum of Art

Variations in shape and ornament suggest that these vessels were not intended as a set but rather as three design options. Their layout on the page, however, imitates contemporary Sheffield plate catalogues. The apple-shape teapot is the most completely drawn of the three, displaying die-rolled bands of flowers and foliage, floral chasing, a rococo-style spout, and a leaf-ornamented handle.[40] The handle was to be made in silver, with horizontal insulators held by pins. Even the cover hinge is carefully rendered. Although no identical teapot in this pattern is known, two very similar examples belong to a seven-piece tea and coffee service now in a private collection. A lightly sketched scheme of grapes and grape leaves is visible on the globular sugar bowl, as are bands of beading. Beading appears again at the rim of the cream jug, whose body is lightly ornamented with flowers. Pencil inscriptions probably indicate anticipated weights for the covered sugar bowl (13 ounces) and the cream jug (6½ ounces), although they seem rather light in comparison with extant objects.

30. DRAWING FOR A TEA SERVICE, 1835–40

Inscription:

Recto lower left, in graphite: 7 (encircled)

Pen and brown ink on cream wove paper 21¹³⁄₁₆ x 16¼ in. (55.4 x 41.3 cm)

Watermark: J WHATMAN / TURKEY MILL / 1835

The Metropolitan Museum of Art, The Elisha Whittelsey Collection, The Elisha Whittelsey Fund, 1953 (53.652.18) Image © The Metropolitan Museum of Art

The paper on which this three-piece tea service was drawn has been cut down on both vertical sides, indicated on the right by a pencil line and on the left by a wavy edge. The 1835 watermark at the top, upside down to the image, provides a *terminus post quem* for dating the drawing. These objects reflect the taste for melon-shape tea vessels, which were popular at that date in both England and America. A covered sugar bowl and cream jug modeled after this drawing survive in a private collection, and a tall ovoid teapot belonging to the Metropolitan Museum has a similar spout, although it differs in other respects. Additional tea services marked by the firm and other drawings in this group feature the same flower finials. The layout of these vessels on the page is reminiscent of contemporary Sheffield plate catalogues, such as T. Bradbury & Sons' illustration of ca. 1830 for "The Melon pattern Tea Service."[41]

31. DRAWING FOR A COFFEEPOT, 1835–40
Inscriptions:
Recto lower left, in graphite: 10
Recto in cartouche, in graphite: design to be finished further
Recto center right, in graphite: …ble foot [illegible]
Pen and brown ink on creamy wove paper 19⅜ x 12⅝ in. (49.2 x 32.1 cm)
Watermark: J WHATMAN / TURKEY MILL / [date cut off]
The Metropolitan Museum of Art, The Elisha Whittelsey Collection, The Elisha Whittelsey Fund, 1953 (53.652.19) Image © The Metropolitan Museum of Art

The inverted pear-shape body of the coffeepot is characteristic of rococo-revival styling, harking back to forms popular during the third quarter of the eighteenth century. This pen-and-ink drawing is inscribed indistinctly in graphite in the central cartouche, "design to be finished further," suggesting the option of personalized engraving.

A C-shape tear behind the leaf on the belly of the coffeepot has been repaired on the verso. The date that would normally appear below the J WHATMAN / TURKEY MILL watermark has been trimmed off, but we are able to approximate a date for the drawing on the basis of style and through comparison with dated examples.

Although the asymmetrical ornamental scheme of flowers, foliage, and C-scrolls around a central cartouche recalls fused silver-plate coffeepots manufactured in Sheffield during the 1760s and 1770s, this design is also of its moment.[42] For instance, the handle depicted here was to be manufactured in silver with thin ivory filets for insulation, whereas an eighteenth-century silver coffeepot would have had a wooden handle. The low domed cover with flower finial also displays an 1830s aesthetic, as seen on drawings for the melon-shape tea service in Drawing 30 and the Biddle service of ca. 1838 (Drawing 35). The melon-shape service is on paper watermarked 1835, helping to establish a date for this image.

32. DRAWING FOR A SWORD, 1835–36

Inscriptions:

Recto, on hilt of sword: FORT GEORGE / CHRYSLERS / CHIPPEWA / NIAGARA

Recto, on scabbard shield: LIEUT COL WORTH (white lettering on dark ground)

Recto upper right, in dark brown ink: ★outer lines. to be use [torn]

Recto, to left of grip in brown ink: 1⅜ inches wide

Watercolor, pen, black ink, and graphite on tan wove paper 23¾ x 9¾ in. (60.4 x 24.8 cm)

Maryland Historical Society, Gift of Joseph Katz, 1952.124.2

This partially unfinished drawing is stained overall and has numerous tears and losses. Horizontal and vertical graphite lines intersect at the center of the cross guard. Pinholes along the vertical line indicate that measurements were taken using calipers. There are also pinholes around the perimeter of the sheet.

The sword was designed for Lieutenant Colonel William Jenkins Worth (1794–1849) of New York, whose name is inscribed along the vine-pattern blade. Three alternate pommel designs are sketched in graphite at the upper right, one depicted in two views. A workshop notation beside the grip specifies its width at 1⅜ inches; another instructs the craftsman to use the outer lines marked by asterisks. The central escutcheon is ornamented with a wreath, and the entire cross guard is washed in yellow and orange watercolor to indicate gilding.

A lifelong soldier, Worth was commissioned as a first lieutenant in 1813 and served under Brigadier General Winfield Scott. Four of the battles in which he distinguished himself are inscribed in diagonal bands on the foliate grip. Eventually promoted to Brigadier General, Worth held the peacetime rank of Lieutenant Colonel. At his death from cholera in 1848 he commanded the departments of Texas and New Mexico. He was presented with three swords: one in 1838 by the State of New York; another in 1840 by Congress; and a

third by Hudson and Columbia counties, New York, in 1848. Which of those swords is represented here is uncertain.[43] An undated "list of plate & swords delivered to some of our military and naval heroes," however, indicates that Colonel Worth's sword, "paid for" by New York, cost $700.00.

33. DRAWING FOR A SWORD, 1837

Inscriptions:

Recto lower right, in brown ink: Length of Handle to Shield ... 5⅝ inches / " " Blade from hilt to point ... 28 in / Width of Blade at hilt ... 1 in / " " " 1 in from point ½ in / Length of Scabbord ... 29 in / Width of " at hilt ... 1¼ in / " " " point... ¾ " / Whole length of Sword including Handle 33⅝ in / " " " in Scabbord–34⅝ in / Fletcher & Ben[nett] [Phila –ᵃ] / 1837

Pen, black ink, and wash on tan wove paper, lined with tissue paper 20⅛ x 18¼ in. (51 x 46.2 cm)

Watermark: J B

The Metropolitan Museum of Art, Rogers Fund, 1995 (1995.38) Image © The Metropolitan Museum of Art

Probably the earlier of two nearly identical drawings for a post captain's sword, this design depicts on the far right an eagle-headed pommel with feathered grip and leaf-wrapped bow. The shield is ornamented with an eagle atop an anchor, surmounted by thirteen stars and flanked by flowering branches. The blade displays an anchor, a circle of stars, and oak leaves with acorns.[44] Decoration on the upper portion of the scabbard includes a shield encircled by stars and another anchor; below, a male head surmounts naval trophies and a palm frond. The inscription at the lower right itemizes measurements without the manufacturing details that appear on the other version (see Drawing 34).

The name *Fletcher & Ben[nett]* inscribed in the lower right suggests the styling of the firm at the time the drawing was made. In 1835 Fletcher had taken into partnership his nephew, Calvin W. Bennett, who left the firm by early January 1837.[45] By the time the later version was drawn, the name of Bennett had been omitted.

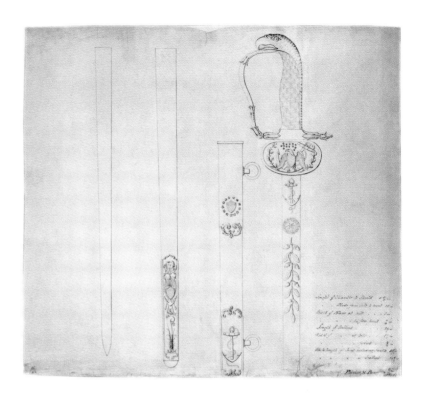

34. DRAWING FOR A SWORD, 1837

Inscriptions:
Recto lower right, in brown ink: Post Capt.[S] Swords. the Eagle Anchor / and Stars. to be silvered, others to be gilt. / The Blade to be of highly polished / Steel, and the ornaments on it to be etched. / Length of Handle to Shield…. 5¼ inches / " of Shield 3¼ in Width of do. 2 in / " of Blade from hilt to point 28 in / Width of " at hilt …. 1 in / " " " 1 inch from point ½ " / Length of Scabbord …. 29 in / Width of " at hilt … 1¼ in / " " " 1 inch from point ¾ " / Whole length of Sword includ-[g] handle 33⅜ in / " " " in Scabbord–34⅝ " / Tho=[S] Fletcher. / Phila–[a]1837
Pen, black ink, and wash on tan wove paper 18 x 22⅜ in. (45.7 x 56.7 cm)
Maryland Historical Society, Gift of Joseph Katz, 1952.124.2

Varying only slightly from Drawing 33, this design for an officer's sword is laid out in similar fashion, depicting, from right to left, the hilt and upper portion of the blade; the upper portion of the scabbard; the lower scabbard; and the lower blade. This version was probably a later step in the process of working out the sword's design. Minor changes include additional ornament alongside the upper suspension ring and the replacement of the floral bud terminal on the quillon by an acorn. The drawing is stained and has a number of tears. Pinholes are visible around the perimeter of the sheet.

An inscription at the lower right details materials, techniques, and measurements. We learn, for instance, that the eagle, anchor, and stars were to be silvered, "others to be gilt." The blade was "to be of highly polished Steel, and the ornaments on it to be etched." *Tho=[s] Fletcher. / Phila–[a]1837* is written in ink below the instructions. It is tempting to read this as the autograph of the draftsman, but the letters are rounder and more distinct than Fletcher's customary signature. It more likely represents the name of the firm, analogous to *Fletcher & Ben[nett]* inscribed on Drawing 33.

Richard Randall has noted the similarity between this drawing and the regulation design for an officer's sword adopted by the United States Navy in 1841. Although the final sword differs in certain respects, the firm most likely played an influential role in the design process.[46]

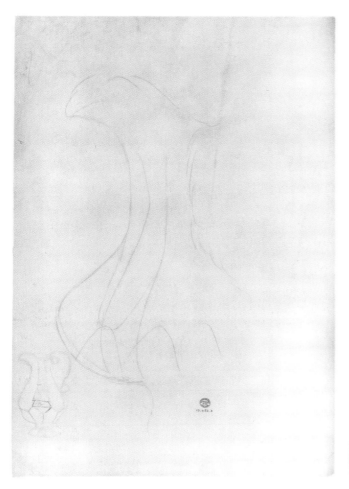

35. DRAWINGS FOR A TEA SERVICE (RECTO) AND TWO PITCHERS (VERSO), 1836–38

Inscriptions:

Recto lower left, in graphite: 8

Recto center bottom, in graphite: Nicholas Biddle tea service

Pen or fine brush and brown ink on cream wove paper. Verso: graphite on cream wove paper 21¾ x 15⅝ in. (55.2 x 39.7 cm)

The Metropolitan Museum of Art, The Elisha Whittelsey Collection, The Elisha Whittelsey Fund, 1953 (53.652.3) Image © The Metropolitan Museum of Art

This highly finished line drawing depicts three parts of a rococo-revival tea service designed for presentation to Nicholas Biddle (1786–1844), president of the Second Bank of the United States. A graphite inscription at the bottom of the sheet, although added later, correctly records it as such. The tea service was part of a much larger order, drawings for which are cited in surviving correspondence. In December 1836 Thomas Fletcher wrote to Daniel W. Coxe, advising him, as chairman of the committee that commissioned the plate, that "the designs and drawings of nearly all the service for Mr. Biddle have been prepared (some of which I beg leave to submit herewith for your inspection) and several of the Pieces are completed except the last polish which is omitted until the Cases are made." Fletcher goes on to suggest the vast extent of the service by mentioning plates, dishes, soup tureens, a large waiter, wine coolers, pitchers, sauce tureens, gravy boat, forks, and spoons.[47] Although the Biddle service was later melted down, a tea service modeled after this drawing survives (see F&G cat. no. 88). Since there is no physical evidence to indicate that this drawing was used during the manufacturing process, it is possible that it is one of the designs presented to Mr. Coxe and the committee for their inspection. The unfinished pencil sketches of two faceted pitchers on the verso do not appear to relate to the Biddle service.

36. DRAWING FOR A BASKET, 1836–38
Inscriptions:
Recto center bottom, in graphite: For Nicholas Biddle
(See over) Presented to him by United States Bank.
Recto lower left, in graphite: 9
Verso lower left, in graphite: S. Bonn & Sons / no. 304
HC (?)
Pen, ink and wash on cream wove paper 14⅞ x 19¹¹⁄₁₆ in.
(37.8 x 50 cm)
The Metropolitan Museum of Art, The Elisha Whittelsey
Collection, The Elisha Whittelsey Fund, 1953 (53.652.5)
Image © The Metropolitan Museum of Art

Part of the extensive silver service commissioned for
presentation to Nicholas Biddle by directors of the Second
Bank of the United States, this drawing for a pierced basket
represents a marriage of classical elements and rococo-
revival design. The border pattern of open and closed

palmettes or anthemia harks back to antique ornament,
while the asymmetrical cartouche surrounded by scrolls,
shells, and flowers is a nineteenth-century revival of a mid-
eighteenth-century motif. Even the drawing technique
varies. The repeating border is formally rendered while the
cartouche and flowers are drawn freehand. Note the
variation of plant forms on the body: a tulip is depicted on
the left and a rose on the right. The panels of pierced
diaperwork also recall silver baskets dating from the middle
decades of the eighteenth century.[48]

Although the Biddle service was melted down after
the failure of the Second Bank, a nearly identical basket
made for another client survives (F&G cat. no. 87). It sits
on a central pedestal foot rather than on the scrolled
acanthus-leaf feet depicted here. Its handle of classical
foliage and ribbon-bound reeding suggests what would
originally have been inserted into the two tubular
sockets depicted in the drawing.

Notes to the Catalogue

The objects discussed in the following entries have been selected from a substantial body of material with a view to presenting the best and most representative of Fletcher & Gardiner's work known to exist. However, the authors do acknowledge gaps. Several significant examples of the firm's War of 1812 and other presentation silver and gold have remained elusive, such as the vases for William Bainbridge and Charles Morris and services for Beverley Chew and Robert T. Spence. Twenty-four gold presentation swords are documented to the firm, the most notable being that for Don Cecilio Ayllon, governor of Matanzas, Cuba, in 1832–33. Judging from the written record, it was the most expensive sword the firm ever produced and must have been an impressive creation. Gold jewelry also proved to be elusive. The firm was called upon to make an extraordinary quantity throughout its history, but almost none is positively identifiable. We lament that more could not be located.

Catalogue entries are organized in date sequence. Objects that bear no specific date have been assigned a date span based on style and maker's mark. All known marks used by the firm are illustrated in Appendix 1. Stamped marks cited in each catalogue entry reference a representative example in the appendix and not necessarily the exact mark on the object. Presentation, household, and personal items can be found throughout the catalogue, providing readers with an insight into the dynamics between Fletcher and Gardiner and those who sought the firm's products.

With respect to the choice of terms, we have attempted to be true to the era under discussion. For instance, the words *urn* and *vase* were interchangeable during Fletcher and Gardiner's era, although the firm's correspondence favors "vase" more often after the War of 1812. Similarly, names of Greek and Roman gods, goddesses, and mythological figures, when cited, are in accordance with Fletcher and Gardiner's usage.

The partnership name "Fletcher & Gardiner," with the partners' preferential ampersand, is used throughout the catalogue. Thomas Fletcher continued working under that name for a time after Sidney Gardiner's death.

The troy weight in ounces and pennyweight, when known, is recorded for each object. When an object incorporates non-precious materials that cannot be separated from the precious, the weight is noted as gross. Dimensions are given in both inches and centimeters.

CATALOGUE ENTRIES

1. BRACELET, 1808–15

Inscription: *A.E. / E.D.S. / L.C.E.* engraved on underside of clasp

Mark: Appendix 1, fig. 1a, b stamped on both halves of clasp

Gold, hair, glass

L. 6⅜ in (16.2 cm), W. ¾ in (1.9 cm), D. ⅛ in (0.4 cm); Wt. 0.2 dwt. Troy (gross)

Collection of the Massachusetts Historical Society

On November 9, 1808, an advertisement appeared in the Boston newspaper the *Columbian Centinel*: "The subscribers have formed a connection in the business under the firm FLETCHER and GARDINER . . . Their principal attention will be directed to the manufacturing of Gold and Silver work of every description and particularly elastic HAIR WORK, for Bracelets, Necklaces, ear Rings and Watch Chains . . . They have on hand, for sale . . . newest patterns, fine gold mounted elastic hair Bar Hoops, Necklaces and Bracelets, in sets to match."

This bracelet is made of a braided band of brown hair, each end terminating with a plain red-gold band. A spring clasp is attached to one end with two loops. At the opposite end a circular red-gold oculus, centered with a domed colorless glass window, sits above a plait of light brown hair framed by a narrow band of ropework. The oculus is encircled with a tube of woven brown hair held in place with four ribbed thimbles. Fletcher and Gardiner stamped their surname initials and a federal spread eagle—the latter indicative of American manufacture—on both halves of the clasp.[1]

The tenor of the cited advertisement and many others by the firm indicates that Fletcher and Gardiner had a thriving business making jewelry, although little of their work in this area is identifiable today. Three sets of owners' initials are engraved in script on the back of the oculus, all apparently by the same hand at the same time. One belonged to Elizabeth Dwight Sedgwick (1791–1864) of Boston and Lenox, Massachusetts. For much of her adult life she was headmistress of the School for Girls at Lenox, where it has been noted that "of all the private schools in Berkshire [Massachusetts] . . . none could surpass the general excellence of Mrs. Charles Sedgwick's."[2] It is reasonable to presume that she wore this bracelet during her tenure there.

2. CUP, 1808–12

Inscription: *Presented / by a / Member & Friend / to the / First Church / Plymouth* engraved on side

Mark: Appendix 1, fig. 2a stamped on underside

Silver

H. 5³/₁₆ in (13.2 cm), Diam. 3⅝ in (9.2 cm); Wt. 9 oz. 18 dwt. Troy

Loan to Pilgrim Hall, First Church Plymouth Collection

The First Church traces its founding to the earliest Separatist community in Plymouth, Massachusetts; it is one of the country's oldest congregations. New England's protestant churches offered communion wine in a variety of vessels such as two-handled cups, beakers, mugs, and tankards. Several of these vessel types were also used for domestic beverage consumption; the activity rather than overall shape distinguished sacred from secular function.

Churches accrued communion silver over long periods of time, and donors might instruct a silversmith to make new silver according to the latest taste, or instead, to match existing vessels. The Plymouth church had at least four silver communion beakers (cups without handles) and three tankards made before 1800. Two of the beakers had a bellied body on a low foot. When Fletcher & Gardiner created this two-handled cup, they updated a familiar Boston ecclesiastical silver form by placing a bellied cup with a molded upper lip over a stepped pedestal foot. Generously looped handles, made by pulling the silver through a draw plate and then shaping it over a stake, facilitate the passing of a full cup between hands.[1]

Engraved inscriptions on communion silver often cite the church and/or donor's names, although plain vessels were not atypical. The Plymouth cup's prominent inscription fills most of one side, but the donor's name and date are absent. Church records preserve evidence of an order for new silver close to the time this cup was made: "Voted, That the pastor & Deacons be a Committee to exchange a Tankard bequeathed by the Wid. Desire Mathews to this Chh [church], & another piece of old plate belonging to the Chh, for such vessel or vessels as they think proper for the use of the Communion table."[2] Congregations were not averse to melting older silver to be refashioned into vessels suiting current needs and tastes.

3. FIVE-PIECE TEA AND COFFEE SET, 1811–12

Inscription: *Anne Dover / and Moses Thomas Oct. 10th 1811 / Ellen Thomas / and / Morton McMichael Jr. Nov. 25, 1857. / Anne McMichael / and / Henry Martyn Hoyt Jr. Jan. 31, 1883.* engraved on side of coffeepot
Mark: Appendix 1, fig. 2a, b stamped on underside of slop bowl; fig. 2a on underside of creamer
Silver, wood
H. 7¾ in (19.7 cm), L. 12½ in (31.8 cm), D. 5¾ in (14.6 cm); Wt. 43 oz. 10 dwt. Troy (coffeepot, gross)
H. 7¼ in (18.4 cm), L. 11 in (27.9 cm), D. 5 in (12.7 cm); Wt. 36 oz. Troy (teapot, gross)
H. 6¾ in (17.2 cm), L. 7⅛ in (18.1 cm), D. 4⅝ in (11.7 cm); Wt. 30 oz. 10 dwt. Troy (sugar bowl)
H. 5¼ in (13.3 cm), L. 5⅞ in (14.9 cm), D. 3⅛ in (7.9 cm); Wt. 13 oz. Troy (cream pot)
H. 4⅝ in (11.7 cm), L. 7⅞ in (20 cm), W. 5⅜ in (13.6 cm); Wt. 26 oz. Troy (slop bowl)
Private collection

On October 6, 1810, Fletcher & Gardiner announced in the *Columbian Centinel* that they "have removed their place of business from No. 43 Marlboro' Street to No. 59 Cornhill . . . where they are now opening a very complete assortment of Rich Jewellery, Plated Ware, Watches, Fine Cutlery, and Fancy Goods [as well as] Silver and Plated Goods [consisting of] Silver Setts containing Coffee and Tea Pots, Sugar Basons, Cream Pots and Slop Bowls with rich borders *in relievo* and some engraved."

This tea set, designed in what the partners described as the oblong style, was the height of fashion at the time, not only for the shape of the vessels but also for the die-rolled borders of ornament in relief and the cast, sculpted appendages, which in this instance consist of eagle-head spouts, lion-paw feet, acorn finials, and human mask handles (detail). All these features allude to an appreciation of ancient Greek and Roman design motifs and their appropriateness for American sensibilities.

Fletcher & Gardiner sold this set, which may have been made in their Boston shop, to Philadelphia bookseller Moses Thomas and his wife, Anne, about the time of their marriage on October 10, 1811. Thomas's bookstore was located at 52 Chesnut, later 108 Chesnut, Street in Philadelphia. He was deeply immersed in the city's literary culture as an associate of Washington Irving in the publication of *Analectic Magazine*; he also published *Select Reviews and the Spirit of the Magazines*.[1] As such, he undoubtedly knew Fletcher, also a lettered man, outside a business context. Thomas's bookstore ultimately closed, and he became a prosperous auctioneer. He and his wife apparently kept this tea and coffee set through good times and bad and passed it on to their daughter, Ellen, at the time of her marriage. She in turn gave it to her daughter, Anne, when she married.

4. PAIR OF CUPS, 1811–13

Inscription: *Pres[e]nted / by Elizabeth Phelps to the / Church of Christ in Hadley / Feby. 1813* (marked cup misspelled) engraved on side

Mark: Appendix 1, fig. 2a (one cup unmarked) stamped on underside

Silver

H. 5¼ in (13.3 cm); Wt. 9 oz. 16 dwt. Troy (marked cup); 9 oz. 6 dwt. Troy

First Congregational Church, U.C.C., Hadley, Massachusetts

The enduring form of a two-handled silver cup for use during the communion service was perpetuated by many Boston silversmiths during the eighteenth and early nineteenth centuries. Fletcher & Gardiner produced this pair for a congregation located about 100 miles west of Boston, in Hadley, Massachusetts, but the overall proportions, bellied bodies, and drawn-strap handles are similar to cups they made for the First Church in Plymouth and Boston's Second Baptist Church. Ecclesiastical silver was a tiny category of the firm's silver production, but congregations desiring new communion furnishings sought their work throughout several decades.[1]

Elizabeth Phelps (1747–1817) was approximately sixty-six years of age, and her husband Charles Phelps, Jr. (1743–1814) was about seventy when she donated these cups. They resided at "Forty-Acres," a homestead of several hundred acres near Hadley. The Phelps family, and in particular Elizabeth, financially, spiritually, and socially supported the Church of Christ in its mission in their community.[2] The specific occasion for this gift of cups, however, is elusive. Women typically donated silver to a church upon the death of a husband, or by leaving their own bequest. The engraved date upon these cups, February 1813, and Elizabeth's name (but not her husband's), presumably were written while both Phelpses were still living.

The family had social and business ties to Boston, and their son Moses "Charles" Porter Phelps settled in the city after 1800. Although the Fletcher & Gardiner firm moved to Philadelphia late in 1811, they continued producing silver for Boston patrons. These cups were possibly created in Boston and engraved later or produced after the workshop relocated to Philadelphia.

5. FIVE-PIECE TEA AND COFFEE SET, 1812–20

Inscription: *WAS* engraved in script on the side of each; *Presented to / William Sheepshanks / and / Ann Spencer / on their marriage / May 3, 1804* engraved on opposite side of each

Mark: Appendix 1, fig. 2a, b stamped on underside of each

Silver, wood

H. 10¾ in (27.3 cm), W. 13 in (33 cm), D. 6¼ in (15.9 cm); Wt. 51 oz. Troy (coffeepot, gross)

H. 8½ in (21.6 cm), W. 11 in (27.9 cm), D. 4¼ in (10.8 cm); Wt. 42 oz. Troy (teapot, gross)

H. 8 in (20.3 cm), W. 6¼ in (15.9 cm), D. 4½ in (11.4 cm); Wt. 30 oz. 10 dwt. Troy (sugar bowl)

H. 6¾ in (17.2 cm), W. 4¾ in (12.1 cm), D. 3¾ in (9.5 cm); Wt. 16 oz. Troy (cream pot)

H. 5¾ in (14.6 cm), W. 7½ in (19.1 cm), D. 5½ in (14 cm); Wt. 24 oz. 10 dwt. Troy (slop bowl)

Collection of the Newark Museum, Purchase 1968 Sophronia Anderson Bequest Fund, 1968.192a–e

The drinking of tea and coffee has been a popular pastime in America since the introduction of the beverages in the early eighteenth century. In a book authored on the subject in 1825, a professional butler by the name of Samuel Adams described the proper procedure for taking both. He dictated that "when the ladies have retired from the dining-room and the drawing-room bell rings for coffee, the footman enters with the tray . . . of coffee . . . Tea is announced to the gentlemen by the footman and the gentlemen having joined the ladies, the tea and coffee is handed round by the butler."[1]

This set, bearing the monogram of William Sheepshanks (d. 1837), a Philadelphia textile merchant, and his wife, Ann, was likely used in the drawing room of their house at 15 Palmyra Row. It was the height of fashion at the time it was made and is described in an advertisement by Boston merchant John C. Dyer that listed silver hollowware with "plain and rich engraved borders [in the] new oblong style."[2] This new style refers to the bodies of this set, which are slightly boat shaped and rectangular in plan with rounded corners.

Somewhat later, Fletcher & Gardiner advertised silver tea and coffee sets "with rich borders *in relievo.*" They were referring to die-rolled borders like those encircling the base, shoulder, and lip of each of the illustrated vessels. These are complemented by the eagle heads adorning the spouts of the two pots and cream pot handle. While they likely address American patriotic sentiment, the female masks that serve as handles on the sugar bowl and slop bowl have direct Parisian counterparts and speak to the strength of Franco-American bonds immediately following the War of 1812.[3]

6. PAIR OF SERVICE PLATES, 1812–15

Inscription: a coat of arms (argent and in chief azure 3 hawks belled); a crest (a hawk belled); and a motto *VIRTUS, LIBERTAS ET PATRIA* in a banner, engraved on the front of both
Mark: Appendix 1, fig. 2a, b stamped on back of brim on both
Silver
H. 1 in (2.5 cm), Diam. 10 in (25.4 cm); Wt. 17 oz. Troy each
Private collection

These plates, originally part of a set, served as part of individual settings on a table; they were place holders for ceramic plates on which the first course of a meal was served. Food was not eaten directly from them. Service plates like these were considered an essential part of formally set tables in the United States during the nineteenth century and were usually made in sets of no fewer than twelve at the time these were fashioned. By the late nineteenth century, sets contained as many as thirty-six or forty-eight.

They are wrought of heavy gauge metal and have a gadrooned border, made in a "gadroon mill," soldered around the perimeter.[1] In keeping with the sophisticated social context in which these plates were used, their owner had his coat of arms engraved at the center of each, signaling to all that his lineage was as impressive as his wealth.

The arms belonged to William Wetmore (1749–1830), Harvard graduate and Boston jurist. He commissioned the plates from Fletcher and Gardiner shortly after they set up shop in Philadelphia. He undoubtedly did so because he had likely done business with their firm when it was located in Boston, between 1808 and 1811.

The plates passed to his son William S. Wetmore (1801–62), also a Harvard graduate, who is perhaps best known for building the first of the great Victorian-era "cottages," *Chateau-sur-Mer*, in Newport, Rhode Island, in 1852. They subsequently passed to his son George Peabody Wetmore (1846–1921), governor of Rhode Island, and then to his two maiden daughters, Edith and Maude. During the last three generations of ownership in the Wetmore family, the plates were used regularly on the dining table at *Chateau-sur-Mer*.[2]

7. TANKARD, 1815–20

Inscription: a coat of arms (argent, a bugle-horn gules, stringed or, and in chief of the second 3 stars of the first); a crest (on a mount vert, a talbot sejant or, collared and lined gu., the line fastened by a bowknot to a halberd erect, the staff of the second, the blade arg., all over a trophy of musical instruments and crossed boughs), engraved on the side
Mark: Appendix 1, fig. 5 stamped on underside
Silver
H. 10⅝ in (27 cm), W. 7½ in (19.1 cm), Diam. 5⅛ in (13 cm); Wt. 43 oz. Troy
Private collection

This capacious three-pint tankard is an anomaly for its time. The hand-wrought bellied body, circular stepped foot, and hinged domed lid recall tankards made in Philadelphia and other East Coast metropolitan centers a half-century earlier.[1] It has, however, been given currency via the die-rolled borders at the lip and base, the acorn finial encircled by a mantle of oak leaves, and its dramatic eagle-head handle.

While the ornamental features that constitute the finial and upper end of the handle relate stylistically to then-current motifs on the most fashionable French and English silver, they also resonated for American patriotic sensibilities, as illustrated by closely related imagery on United States coinage and medallic art.

The coat of arms and crest engraved on the barrel opposite the handle belong to the surname Hunt (detail). Tradition records that Fletcher & Gardiner made it for Trenton, New Jersey, merchant Abraham Hunt, who commissioned it for his son, Theodore Hunt (1788–1832). The younger Hunt entered service in the United States Navy at the age of fifteen, whereupon he was assigned to the frigate *Philadelphia* under the command of Captain William Bainbridge. Following a tour of duty in the Mediterranean, where Hunt was captured and held for a period of time by pirates, he returned to Trenton before moving to St. Louis, Missouri, in 1813.

In St. Louis he married the only daughter of Judge John B.C. Lucas, one of the largest landholders in the area. At the same time, he purchased and operated the tan yards of William C. Carr & Company and opened a general merchandise store, both of which he operated until his death. In 1824 President James Monroe appointed him United States Recorder of Land Titles, a position he held to the end of his life.[2]

8. THREE-PIECE TEA SET, 1812–20

Inscription: a crest (a demi-Pegasus within crossed boughs) engraved on side of each
Mark: Appendix 1, fig. 3 stamped on bottom of each
Silver, wood
H. 9⅜ in (23.8 cm), W. 10¾ in (27.3 cm), Diam. 5¾ in (14.6 cm); Wt. 38 oz. 10 dwt. Troy (teapot, gross)
H. 9¼ in (23.5 cm), W. 6¾ in (17.1 cm), Diam. 5 in (12.7 cm); Wt. 31 oz. Troy (sugar bowl)
H. 7 in (17.8 cm), W. 5⅝ in (14.3 cm), Diam. 3⅜ in (8.6 cm); Wt. 12 oz. Troy (cream pot)
Private collection

The circular bodies of this teapot, sugar bowl, and cream pot are in what was called the round style, which was popular from the 1790s to about the time this set was made. Each vessel was wrought to shape in the traditional manner, whereas the ornament was created using a combination of casting and die rolling. The acorn finials, eagle-head spout on the teapot, related handle on the cream pot, cornucopia-handle sockets on the teapot, female mask handles on the sugar bowl, and ball-and-claw feet were all cast in sand flasks. The narrow rope borders, wider rose borders, and even wider imbricated leaf borders on all three were die rolled. These ornamental features and the manner in which they were incorporated into the design of these objects follow the dictates of the then-current fashion that emulated ancient Roman and Greek cultures through the study and interpretation of antiquarians, connoisseurs, architects, and designers.[1]

Tea sets were among the most sought–after products of silversmiths during the nineteenth century, driven not only by the popularity of tea as a beverage but also because the ceremony of taking tea was a fashionable way of socializing. This set was the smallest in number that one might buy. If a consumer wished to be more extravagant, a hot water pot, a coffeepot, a slop bowl, and even a hot water urn could be added.

The engraved crest on these three belongs to the surname Bond (detail). Though the individual who commissioned this set from Fletcher & Gardiner is not presently known, it might have been Joshua B. Bond, who was recorded as a gentleman living at 92 South 8th Street in Philadelphia at the time this set was made.

9. PITCHER, 1811–13

Inscription: OZIAS GOODWIN / Presented by the / *N.E.M. Insurance* / COMPANY / 1811 engraved on side opposite handle

Mark: Appendix 1, fig. 2a, b stamped on underside

Silver

H. 7¼ in (18.4 cm), L. 7¾ in (19.7 cm), Diam. 4⅛ in (10.6 cm); Wt. 24 oz. 2 dwt. Troy

Ruth J. Nutt Collection of American Silver

Maritime trade around the Atlantic carried the steep financial risk of cargo lost to fierce weather or threats from privateers. Grateful passengers and insurance companies traditionally rewarded a captain's heroism and service with money or gifts of silver. This pitcher was commissioned during the time of intense risk for American maritime commerce that culminated with the War of 1812.

The New England Marine Insurance Company (incorporated 1803) presented the pitcher to Ozias Goodwin, the given name of multiple generations of New England seafarers. Captain Ozias Goodwin (1755–1819) settled in Boston and joined the Boston Marine Society. In 1813 he was one of many witnesses to give a deposition attesting to the impressment of American seamen by the British Navy. He described himself thusly: "I, Ozias Goodwin, of Boston, merchant, do depose and say–that I was master of a vessel about eighteen years from the port of Boston, until the year 1799–and since that time have been concerned in commerce and navigation." The occasion prompting this presentation pitcher, dated 1811, is not known.[1]

Hooped barrel forms appear in American late eighteenth- and early nineteenth-century silver, particularly in New England.[2] Some pitchers of this design were entirely hand wrought, but Fletcher & Gardiner fabricated the body into a cylinder from a sheet of flattened silver. It was seamed up the side, with a circular bottom, spout, molded ribbing, and handle all soldered in place.

Goodwin's pitcher is one of the earliest known presentation pieces made by the firm. The mark on the base indicates it was completed in Philadelphia, although the order may have first come to their Boston store. The contrast with the urn presented to Isaac Hull just one or two years later could not be more marked in design and ornament, technical skills used by the workshop, and amount of money invested by patrons.

10. URN, 1813

Inscription: The Citizens of Philadelphia, at a meeting convened on the 5th of Septr. 1812, voted / this Urn, to be presented in their name to CAPTAIN ISAAC HULL, Commander of the / United States Frigate CONSTITUTION, as a testimonial of their sense of his distinguished / gallantry and conduct, in bringing to action, and subduing the British Frigate GUERRIERE, / on the 19th day of August 1812, and of the eminent service he has rendered to his / Country, by achieving, in the first naval conflict of the war, a most signal and decisive / victory, over a foe that had till then challenged an unrivalled superiority on the / ocean, and thus establishing a claim of our Navy to the affection and confidence / of the Nation; Engraved by W. Hooker
Mark: Appendix 1, fig. 14
Silver
H. 29½ in (74.9 cm), W. 22 in (55.9 cm), Diam. 12 in (30.5 cm); Wt. 561 oz. 10 dwt. Troy[1]
Private collection

Isaac Hull (1773–1843) led the crew of the frigate *Constitution* as captain in the dismasting and ultimate sinking of Britain's *Guerrière* off the coast of Newfoundland on August 19, 1812. News of this first decisive American naval victory rippled throughout the nation, and within a few weeks citizens in Philadelphia subscribed to a list funding "a splendid piece of Plate to be presented to Captain Hull." Fletcher & Gardiner won the commission and matched the public outpouring of enthusiasm for Hull by creating the heaviest, tallest, and most complex work in silver ever produced in North America. The unprecedented, staggering

size of this urn testified to not only the importance of Hull's victory but also the skill of Philadelphia's artisans, who matched European silver in monumentality as well as artistry. The powerful national eagle on the lid clasping a spiral thunderbolt stood for the triumphant nation and new emperor of the seas.[2]

The urn's design has no known contemporary model. Fletcher & Gardiner's inspiration included judiciously selected ornament from engravings of antiquities as well as from European goldsmiths' work. They particularly looked to French designers Charles Percier and Pierre-François-Léonard Fontaine. Elements of the Hull urn resemble an engraving of a tureen-on-stand designed for Empress Josephine, which was produced and exhibited by Martin-Guillaume Biennais in 1806 (see chap. 4, fig. 10). Likewise, ram's-head handles and overlapping leaf chasing on the bowl of a vase designed by Giovanni-Battista Piranesi and republished by Henry Moses in London bear a similarity to the Hull urn (see chap. 4, fig. 11).[3]

Fletcher & Gardiner's ambitious design employed nearly every technique practiced by the silversmith's craft. Complex, layered ornament creates an interplay of sculptural, cast rams' heads; entwined dolphins; and hairy-paw feet with a low-relief, die-rolled, scallop-shell border;

chased and applied figures of Fame and History; bosses of Neptune (one chased, three cast); richly textured surfaces of overlapping leaves and acroterion corners; and the smooth planes of the bowl. A naval battle featuring the *Constitution*'s triumph is chased in repoussé into the wrought upper section, as are oak boughs and beribboned laurel wreathes and flowers beneath handles. The opposite side bears the lengthy dedication signed by engraver William Hooker (active 1804–46). Inside, a fitted, removable basin lines the bowl.

When the urn was complete, Thomas Fletcher wrote with pride to his father in Massachusetts: "We have had thousands to view it, and it is allowed to be the most elegant piece of workmanship in this country." He continued, "We have plenty of work in hand–The Philadelphians don't like to see the Yankees get above them so."[4] Fletcher & Gardiner's engraved name and the Latin verb *fecerunt* (made this) appear prominently on the pedestal, permanently connecting them to this historic monument. The Hull urn launched the workshop's national reputation, and new orders for presentation silver quickly followed. Fittingly, an engraved rendition of the Hull urn served as the firm's trade card for two decades (see chap. 3, figs. 5–7).

---

11. PITCHER, 1815–20
Inscription: none
Mark: Appendix 1, fig. 5 stamped on underside
Silver
H. 15¾ in (40 cm), W. 10¼ in (26 cm), D. 6¾ in (17.1 cm); Wt. 76 oz. 6 dwt. Troy
Winterthur Museum, 1969.16

Large silver pitchers, though rarely made by eighteenth-century American silversmiths, became a staple production item during the nineteenth century. Customers commissioned Fletcher & Gardiner to make them throughout the firm's existence, both for household use and presentation. The rise in popularity of the pitcher during the early nineteenth century was influenced greatly by "ancient examples dug from underground [at sites of antique civilization in Italy and Greece], or otherwise found and preserved in the cabinets of the curious."[1]

This large, hinged-lid pitcher employs sculpted animal features as its appendages in the form of lion-paw feet, a

serpent, a dog head (possibly one of the three belonging to the mythical Cerberus), and a dolphin, all of which figured importantly in classical art. Here they lend an aggressive muscular stance to the vessel that accords with design precepts of the era. The serpent's body is interrupted with a segment of bundled reeding. That feature, which English furnituremaker Thomas Sheraton (1751–1806) claimed was "much preferable to fluting or cabling in point of strength and in look," may reference ancient Egyptian columnar design.[2]

The modified vase-shape body and pedestal are additionally ornamented with borders and panels of vegetal decoration, the most prominent of which were hammered out of the metal. Fletcher & Gardiner incorporated these hand-made borders into this pitcher in keeping with the vogue for architecture and its dependant arts, including silver. For the most part, such borders consisted of stylized renderings of plants that flourished around the Mediterranean basin, including acanthus, olive, honeysuckle, and lotus.

12. URN, 1814

Inscription: *To Lieut.¹ James Biddle U.S.N. / From the early Friends and Companions / of his Youth, who, while their Country / rewards his public services, present / this testimonial of their esteem for / his private worth. Philad.ᵃ 1813* engraved on side

Mark: none

Silver

H. 15½ in (39.4 cm), W. 11¹¹⁄₁₆ in (29.8 cm); Wt. 94 oz. 16 dwt. Troy

United States Naval Academy Museum Collection

In 1812, serving under Captain Jacob Jones on the *Wasp*, James Biddle (1783–1848) helped capture and then command the British sloop *Frolic*. In a dramatic twist, the *Frolic* was reclaimed a few hours later and her intrepid new commander Biddle temporarily taken prisoner. Fletcher & Gardiner received an order for this urn from Biddle's friends late in 1813. Its battle scene illustrates the first capture of the *Frolic*, but the inscription emphasizes Biddle's character and personal virtues rather than that heroic exploit.

The donors published an open letter in city newspapers declaring their esteem for Biddle and their gift of a silver urn. At least one paper also printed his modest response: "Such a testimonial of esteem from gentlemen with whom I have long been associated in habits of intimacy, is in the highest degree flattering to me, and has excited all my sensibilities; whilst I cannot but be aware, that the partiality of your feelings toward me has greatly overvalued my services on the occasion alluded to in your communication."[1]

Biddle's friends funded an urn smaller in stature than the public's gift to Isaac Hull but one richly ornamented with cast elements and multi-layered leaf chasing. Although seemingly composed of several sections, the entire bowl is wrought from one billet and joined to the pedestal base. Fletcher & Gardiner acquired patterns or sources for cast elements, such as the exquisite eagle and handles combining heads of Neptune and dolphins, which exemplify the workshop's artistic standards. An engraved dedication fills one side; the other bears the *Wasp* and *Frolic*'s encounter chased on a separate tablet and soldered in place between engraved oak-leaf branches. Subsequent losses and repairs to the eagle and finial have compromised its stance, but its naval symbolism gives national character to this private award.

13. URN, 1814

Inscription: *Presented to Capt. Jacob Jones, Commander of the U.S. Sloop of War, / the Wasp, by the Legislature of the State of Delaware, as a / testimony of the / high sense of gallantry, intrepidity, and skill displayed by him on the 18th, of October 1812, in the capture of the British Sloop of / War the Frolic, a vessel of superior force, after an action of 43 minutes; / By which brilliant achievement he has reflected high honor upon the / arms of his Country, fixed on an imperishable basis his own fame, / and entitled himself to the admiration and gratitude of his Native State* engraved on bowl

Mark: none, R55455 etched on bottom

Silver

H. 17 in (43.2 cm), W. 13½ in (34.3 cm), Diam. 8½ in (21.6 cm); Wt. 101 oz. 10 dwt. Troy

Historical Society of Delaware Collection, Bequest of the Estate of Frank C. Jones, Jr., 1952.021.001

Shortly after his ship the *Wasp* captured the *Frolic*, Jacob Jones's name joined those of other officers in the poetry and songs celebrating American naval triumphs. One song triumphantly declared:

> Our DECATUR, our HULL, & our JONES, on the sea
> Have prov'd to Old Nep. that his fav'rites they be,
> And the jolly old dog their birth-right to maintain,
> His trident gave up, and bade them rule the main."

A distinguished War of 1812 naval hero, Jones received many awards, including a gold medal funded by Congress and two weighty silver urns. His native state, Delaware, resolved to offer Jones "a handsome piece of PLATE, with appropriate emblematic engravings thereon, as a testimonial of the high esteem in which his services are held by the General Assembly" to cost up to $500.[1]

Fletcher & Gardiner interpreted the request for emblems as ornament possessing symbolic national character, such as the sculptural eagle and anchor finial, or antiquity-inspired emblems, such as the ram's-head handles and lush repoussé layers of leaves and egg-and-dart borders. They personalized the award to a specific moment in American history with a pictorial panel of the *Wasp*'s encounter, hand chased on one side, and the Delaware State seal engraved on the other. Figures, most likely personifications of Fame and History, were cut and chased from thin sheets of silver and applied on either side of the battle scene (such as those on Isaac Hull's urn) but are now missing. A lengthy inscription permanently testifies to Jones's service.

The urn's current condition is not indicative of the bold presence it commanded when given to Jones. The lid's eagle has collapsed, and trophy elements are missing; the entire finial was once cut out and resoldered in place. On either side of the *Wasp* and *Frolic* one sees burnished, untextured areas and plugged holes, giving evidence of missing supporting figures. Additionally, the bowl and pedestal foot were once separated and then reattached with two circular silver disks for reinforcement. The pedestal remains slightly collapsed just below the bowl. The urn is unmarked, but its overall design, ornament, and troy weight identify it as a Fletcher & Gardiner naval award.

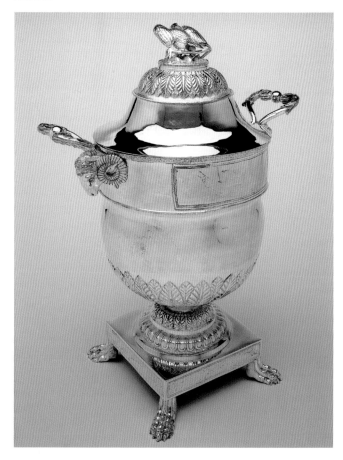

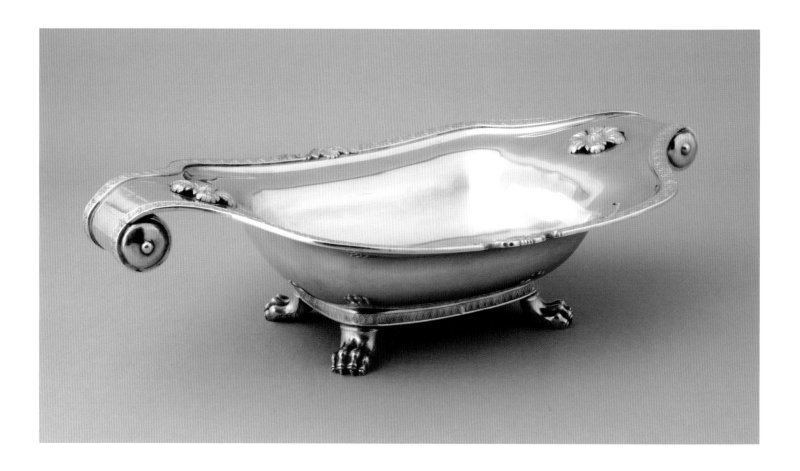

14. CAKE BASKET, 1814

Inscription: *From the Citizens / of Philadelphia to / Commodore William Bainbridge; Constitution, K, 9, W, 25, Java, 60, 101* engraved on handles

Mark: Appendix 1, fig. 2a, b stamped on underside

Silver

H. 4½ in (10.8 cm), L. 16 in (40.6 cm), W. 9½ in (24.1 cm); Wt. 50 oz. 18 dwt. Troy

Ruth J. Nutt Collection of American Silver

One report of the death of William Bainbridge (1774–1833) recalled: "The event of his life . . . which has most familiarized our readers to his name, was his gallant achievement of the capture of the Frigate Java . . . being the third of those victories which established the character of the American Navy." Bainbridge, a naval officer seasoned by battles off Algiers, commanded the *Constitution* when she captured the massive British frigate *Java* in December 1812. Jubilation in this national triumph led to parades, dinners, and in Philadelphia, a public call for contributions to fund an award. Philadelphia's subscription advertisement for "an elegant piece of plate, to be presented to Com. Bainbridge, in testimony of the high sense entertained of his gallantry .

. . opened this day at the Coffee House" was printed in papers from Maine to Maryland.[1]

Historian Benson Lossing's sketch of the monumental urn Fletcher & Gardiner created for Bainbridge is the only presently known image.[2] The table service he received is evidenced by this silver basket, which incorporates decorative motifs used on the firm's household wares, such as the die-rolled, rose-and-leaf border and cast patera flowers soldered on the handles. The basket functioned as an elegant dish to serve fruit or cake, but its long volute handles also served as a permanent memorial for Bainbridge's victory. The inscription tallies the killed (K) and wounded (W) from both sides of this important battle.

Fletcher & Gardiner offered several basket forms in their table services, but round volute handles soldered in place were technically challenging and atypical in American and European baskets.[3] Their inspiration mostly likely sprang from classical architecture: when viewed from the side, the profile of Bainbridge's basket suggests the volutes of an Ionic capital. They also resemble rounded crest rails and armrests on the then-very-fashionable "Grecian" couches made on both sides of the Atlantic.

15. URN, 1814
Inscription: HIS FELLOW CITIZENS OF NEW PORT TO / OLIVER H. PERRY / A MEMORIAL TO THE SENSE OF HIS SIGNAL / MERITS IN ACHIEVING THE VICTORY OF THE / 10th SEPT 1813, ON LAKE ERIE
Marks: Appendix 1, figs. 2a, b (impressed twice); fig. 15 stamped on underside; Kearny DEL.T and Hooker SC engraved on side
Silver
H. 15½ in (39.4 cm), W. 14¼ in (36.2 cm); Wt. 123 oz. 18 dwt. Troy
United States Naval Academy Museum Collection

Oliver Perry (1785–1819) commanded naval forces on Lake Erie during a critical triumph over British Commander Robert H. Barclay's squadron. Shortly thereafter newspaper items, engraved pictures, and diagrams

recounted each stage of the battle that helped protect the nation's northern border. Amid the flood of awards bestowed upon Perry, a committee from his hometown in Rhode Island applied to Fletcher & Gardiner for a suitable monument. The resulting urn is engraved with the "First View of Com. Perry's Victory," depicting his momentous mid-battle journey in a cutter from the battered *Lawrence* to command the *Niagara* and break the British line.[1] The urn's overall elliptic bowl likely was designed to best feature William Hooker's wide pictorial image.

Hooker's engraving and the dedication on the opposite side were directly worked on a section of flatted silver that was seamed vertically and joined to the lower bowl. The lid, composed of three elliptic sections, has textured repoussé work simulating rocky ground beneath the eagle finial and densely layered acanthus-leaf ornament. Masterfully cast-and-chased handles feature Neptune's head and dolphin mounts. The letter "P" (for Perry) encircled by a heroic laurel wreath and boughs decorates each side of the base. Although restrained overall, the leaf ornament and jewel-like burnished border on the pedestal enrich this costly urn.

Cost concerned the Newport committee, and documents indicate that Fletcher & Gardiner asked for $150 more than the original $500 commission. Perry's letter of thanks declared: "Among the testimonies of respect I have received from my countrymen for the part I bore in the action on Lake Erie, – none has given me more satisfaction than the very flattering expressions of regard which accompany the present of a superb piece of plate from my fellow Townsmen. The convincing proof of esteem shown me by those with whom I have passed my happiest days, and among whom my strongest affections are placed, is a source from whence I have always derived the greatest pleasure."[2]

16. PITCHER, 1815

Inscription: *Lady Houstoun presents this Pitcher to / Colonel Johnston with her grateful Thanks / for his attention in settling the Estates of / Sir Patrick and Sir George Houstoun* engraved on side opposite handle

Mark: Appendix 1, figs. 2b, 3 stamped on underside

Silver

Overall H. 13½ in (34.3 cm), L. 10⅛ in (25.7 cm), D. 6½ in (16.5 cm); Wt. 53 oz. Troy

The Museum of Fine Arts Houston, The Bayou Bend Collection, Gift of Mrs. James P. Houstoun, Jr. in memory of Mr. James P. Houstoun, Jr., B77.16

Wealthy and titled women in England bestowed significant gifts of silver in private presentation, but the custom had infrequent practice among women in North America. The South Carolina urn given to Andrew Jackson in 1816 was an unusual presentation commission; more often women willed silver to family members or donated it to their churches. In this case, a member of a family with significant landholdings in Georgia and descended from a Scottish titled family requested a heavy, suitable pitcher from Fletcher & Gardiner.

Ann M. Moodie Houstoun, the widow of Sir George Houstoun (seventh baronet) and sister-in-law of Georgia's two-term Governor John Houstoun, waited twenty years for family property claims to be instated after the Revolutionary War. Lady Houstoun was responsible for settling the estate of her husband and his elder brother, loyalist Sir Patrick Houstoun. In this she relied on her son-in-law Colonel James Johnston, Jr. of Savannah for assistance. This pitcher from the nation's leading silver workshop testifies to her gratitude. The surviving bill indicates Lady Houstoun sent "old Silver" and coins to be credited against the costs of "1 Silver Pitcher, round on square pedestal & claw feet / chased leaves on the body & lid, with dolphin top} $150.00" and a coffeepot engraved with a coat of arms she ordered at the same time.[1]

Fletcher & Gardiner's reputation reached most corners of the United States via word of mouth, newspaper descriptions of presentation awards, and household silver shipped to major seaports. The commission from Savannah is an indication of the firm's reach. Johnston's covered pitcher features an eagle handle and elements, such as a square base supported by hairy-paw feet, used for the firm's War of 1812 presentation awards. The die-rolled border of stars at the lip and an imbricated water-leaf pattern at the shoulder also appear in other contemporary silversmiths' work.[2]

17. FISH SERVER, 1815–25

Inscription: a crest (an eagle displayed with two heads, grasping a bough in each talon) engraved on back of blade
Mark: Appendix 1, fig. 4a, c, d stamped on back of blade
Silver, ivory
L. 13¼ in (33.7 cm), W. 3¾ in (9.5 cm); Wt. 8 oz. Troy (gross)
Private collection

Silver fish servers, alternately called fish knives or fish slices, first appeared on English dining tables about 1740; American householders followed suit about twenty years thereafter. They remained a popular accoutrement on stylish dining tables until about the 1880s. Their purpose was to enable the host or butler to cut and serve the fish course at the table. During their century-long presence on American dining tables, several different types of fish servers were used, identified by their blade shape. They have been categorized as trowel, scimitar, oval, oblong, acorn, fork, and double bladed. One additional category, exemplified by the pictured example, is kidney.[1] Most have silver handles, although wood, bone, horn, mother of pearl, and ivory were also used.

The blades are invariably pierced, sometimes with a simple pattern of circles, diamonds, or rectangles, but more often the piercing assumes elaborate, even florid patterns of geometric, naturalistic, or fanciful shapes that vastly increase their visual drama. Sometimes the piercing is so extensive that the blade assumes a gossamer spider web character. Frequently, the piercing is augmented with complementary engraving. In this instance, the kidney-shape blade is pierced and engraved with a swimming dolphin, alluding to the utensil's purpose. Here the dolphin assumes a fierce aspect in contrast to most of its counterparts, which are benign. It is surrounded with a pencil-thin border of rouletted ornament. The back edge has been reinforced with a die-rolled border of leaf tips, and the blade is held to its handle via a die-stamped scallop shell of the type Fletcher & Gardiner used on their shell-and-thread spoons and forks. This latter feature nicely reinforces the marine theme so appropriate for a table utensil such as this.

The crest engraved on the back of the blade probably belongs to a member of the Bibby family of New York or the Rhodes family of Pennsylvania (detail).

18. PAIR OF PINT TANKARDS, 1815–20

Inscription: *EW* engraved within crossed laurel boughs on side of both; *N.W.S.* engraved on underside of one
Mark: Appendix 1, figs. 2b, 3 stamped on underside of both
Silver
H. 4¾ in (12.1 cm), W. 5½ in (14 cm), Diam. 3⅞ in (9.8 cm); Wt. 18 oz. 15 dwt. Troy each
Winterthur Museum, Gift of Denison and Louise Hatch, 2001.2.22.1, .2

This charming diminutive pair of tankards, each of one-pint capacity, was made at a time when the form was in decline in America as a household drinking vessel. Examples in silver had been widely made from the mid-seventeenth through the end of the eighteenth century. However, lidless drinking vessels eclipsed them after that. Even so, tankards were occasionally ordered from silversmiths during the early nineteenth century.

This pair is an attractive variant of a type that seems to have been made in Philadelphia but infrequently elsewhere in America. Typical examples have their barrels encircled with two clustered bands of reeds and are fitted with flat lids and angular handles. Their style derived from fashionable London-made examples, while their planar character resulted from the advent of flattening silver into sheets by passing it between paired iron rollers. Such vessels were more easily and quickly made by cutting, bending, and soldering the edges of a piece of sheet silver than by the more traditional method of hammering the body to shape from a billet.

The barrels of these tankards, of rolled sheet silver seamed vertically on the handle side, are encircled by two applied borders of roses and leaves instead of reeds.[1] These and the narrower borders of anthemia at the lip and base, made in a device similar to that used to roll sheet silver, distinguish these tankards from the norm. Also distinctive are the hinged lids, which are domed rather than flat, and the graceful S-shape handles with voluted terminals and conforming acanthus leaf that eschew typical angular design in favor of mid-eighteenth-century prototypes.

19. CREAM OR MILK POT, 1815–25

Inscription: a coat of arms (lion rampant and in chief an etoile between 2 torteaux); a crest (a sword in pale entwined with a vine, all over crossed boughs, an open book and sword) engraved on side

Mark: Appendix 1, fig. 2a, b stamped on bottom

Silver

H. 7 in (17.8 cm), W. 6⅜ in (16.2 cm), D. 4⅛ in (10.5 cm); Wt. 20 oz. 10 dwt. Troy

Private collection

On February 11, 1837, Thomas Fletcher wrote to Samuel Smith (1752–1839) of Baltimore that "I received your favor of the 28 ult . . . and have had sketches made of . . . 4 patt[ern]s of silver tea setts . . . A tea sett of either pattern no 1 or 2 to weigh from 220 to 230 oz will cost from $600 to $690 the set. A tea sett of like weights will cost from $675 to $700. A sett of patt[er]n no 4 of same weight will cost from $550 to $600. By the term sett I mean the pieces which you have enumerated namely: 1 each coffee, tea, water, sugar, slop and cream. The sketches which I send are of our newest and most richly wrought patt[er]ns."[1]

Like the sketches, this cream pot is of the newest and most richly wrought pattern, but from the 1815 to 1825 era. The pot bears the engraved Smith coat of arms and crest and employs a die-rolled rose border on its pedestal, a similarly made imbricated leaf-and-bead border at its shoulder, and a border of eight-pointed stars at its lip, all of which were in vogue on silver made by Fletcher & Gardiner during the 1810s.[2]

The makers also used two examples of dramatic cast ornament on this pot, a ram's head directly below the handle and cloven hoof feet to support the base. Both these features ultimately derive from antique Roman design as interpreted through late eighteenth- and early nineteenth-century French designers, metalworkers, and porcelain makers. These elements may have entered the firm's inventory of design elements when Fletcher was on a buying trip in Paris in 1815, at which time he purchased a "catalogue of antiques, engravings [and] models" for a total of $216.50.[3]

20. PUNCH BOWL, TRAY, BEAKERS, AND LADLE, 1816

Inscription: *Presented by* a number of *the Citizens of Baltimore / to / Lieut. Colonel /* GEORGE ARMISTEAD */ for his* Gallant *and* Successful *defense of / Fort McHenry / during the bombardment of a large British Force, / on the 12th and 13th September 1814 / when upwards of 1500 shells were thrown, / 400 of which fell within the area of the Fort / and some of them of the diameter of this / VASE.* engraved on bowl

Mark: Appendix 1, figs. 2b, 5, 16 (Baltimore 1816 assay on beakers, A.E.W. and Baltimore 1816 assay on ladle)

Silver

H. 15⅜ in (38.7 cm), Diam. 12½ in (13.8 cm)

National Museum of American History, Smithsonian Institution, Behring Center, #66427

A curious anomaly amid Fletcher & Gardiner's urn-shape presentation vessels is this punch service awarded to George Armistead (1780–1818) by Baltimore's grateful citizens. The spherical design is novel in American silver and is directly connected to commanding officer Armistead's heroic actions at Fort McHenry in September 1814. Armistead and his men withstood relentless bombardment by a British fleet throughout the night of September 12, defending the fort and sparing the city of Baltimore. This powerful siege gave the Star Spangled Banner its fame. As specified by the award committee, Armistead's spherical silver bowl closely replicates the dimensions and details of the largest British bombs (thirteen-inch "shells") fired on the fort.

Fletcher & Gardiner collaborated with several artists to create this impressive award. Thomas Fletcher, the firm's primary designer, was in Europe from 1815 to 1816, and an English painter in Philadelphia, George Bridport (d. 1819), provided initial drawings for the punch bowl. Sidney Gardiner's workshop met the challenging design of a wrought sphere and fitted lid supported by magnificent cast-and-chased eagles on the pedestal. The pictorial view of Fort McHenry's bombardment wreathed by oak leaves flanked by war trophies was engraved on one side by an unidentified artist.[1] Baltimore silversmith Andrew Ellicott Warner (1786–1870) completed the service by supplying one dozen barrel-shape beakers, with shapes reminiscent of powder kegs, and a ladle.

When George Armistead received the punch service in May 1816, a published account of the outdoor ceremony at Fort McHenry credited the entire award to Fletcher & Gardiner. The firm's name is prominently engraved on the punch bowl base. Warner's initials and the Baltimore 1816 assay marks appear on his work. Although the expansive tray is unmarked, its scale, cast winged talon feet, and die-rolled, rose-and-leaf border connect it to Fletcher & Gardiner's workshop.[2]

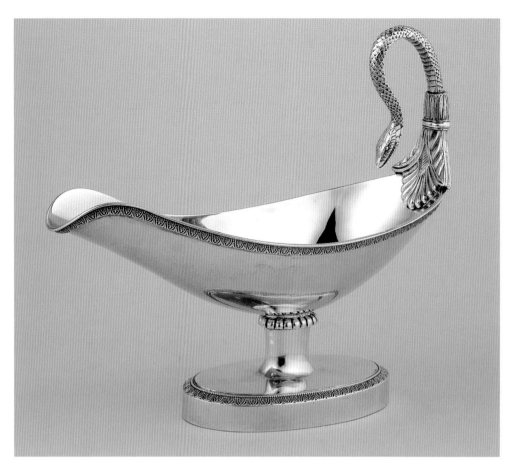

21. SAUCEBOAT, 1812–20

Inscription: none
Mark: Appendix 1, fig. 2a, b stamped under base
Silver
H. 8¼ in (21 cm), L. 10 in (25.4 cm), W. 4½ in (11.4 cm);
Wt. 23 oz. 10 dwt. Troy
Private collection

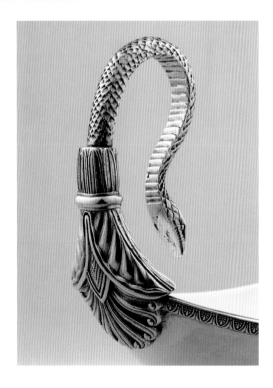

The serpent has been an object of fascination and revulsion since the fabled Garden of Eden. It is rife with symbolic meaning, the most widely accepted of which in Judeo-Christian tradition is the personification of evil, but it also refers to fertility, wisdom, and the power to heal. It has long been a mainstay in the work of artists and artisans, particularly during the late eighteenth and early nineteenth centuries. Its popularity then was directly associated with the rise of interest in the art of ancient Greece and Rome, which was filled with images of serpents.

French and English silver made between 1780 and 1820 frequently incorporated serpents as handles, not only for symbolic imagery but also because their long sinuous bodies suited the aesthetic character of stylish design at that time. Tureens, presentation vases, teapots, cream jugs, sauceboats, and other fashionable silver incorporated them as handles.[1] American silversmiths, attuned to current style in European fashion centers, also used them in this way. Thomas Fletcher and Sidney Gardiner were among the most accomplished practitioners of this genre, as seen in this serpent-form handle that realistically springs from clustered anthemia and arches over the sauceboat.

Fletcher traveled to England and France in 1815 and 1816, then again in 1825. He may have seen inspirational examples during either or both of those trips. However, the partners could just as easily have seen serpent handles on sauceboats made by French émigrés in Philadelphia, since a pair virtually identical to this bearing the mark of Jean Simon Chaudron (1758–1846) exists.[2]

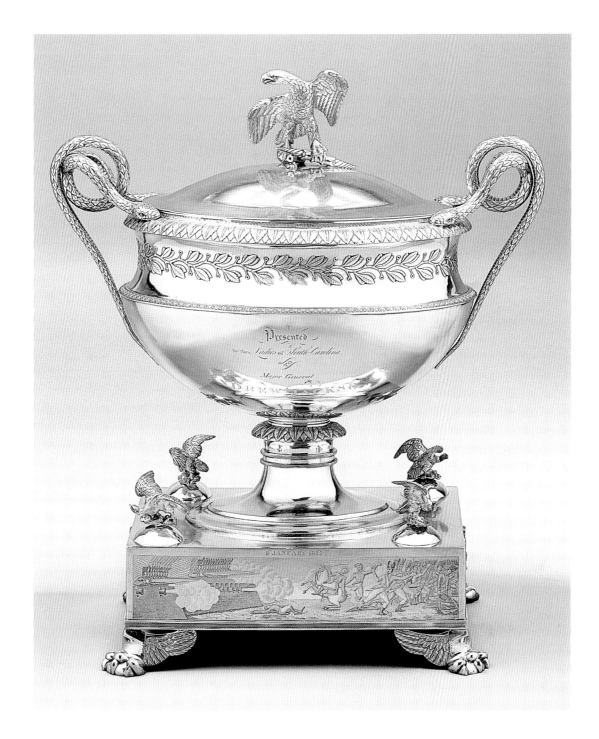

22. URN, 1816

Inscription: Presented / by the *Ladies of South-Carolina.* / TO / *Major General* / ANDREW JACKSON; engraved on side; added ca. 1845: PRESENTED BY / GEN.L ANDREW JACKSON / TO / Wm. B. STANLEY / PRESIDENT OF THE PALMETTO ASSOCIATION IN TRUST FOR THE / LAST SURVIVOR; South Carolina state seal and motto; engraved on base: 8th JANUARY 1815

Mark: Appendix 1, figs. 5, 2b, 17 stamped on underside

Silver

H. 18 in (45.7 cm), W. 16 in (40.6 cm), Diam. 9½ in (34.1 cm); Wt. 178[1] oz. Troy

Collection of the South Carolina State Museum, Columbia

In a tour de force of sculptural animation—powerful eagle finial, entwined snake handles, and massive winged feet—this urn for Andrew Jackson (1767–1845) heralds Fletcher & Gardiner's mature neoclassical design. Fletcher's exposure to French and English silver during travels in 1815 and 1816 inspired new ideas that pressed the workshop's innovations. Sinuous lines of the snake handles and a concave middle register with repoussé laurel leaves reflect a fresh interpretation of urn ornament, as do the varied cast, chased, and textured elements. Four eagles in "frosted silver" once perched on each corner of the plinth base.[2] An engraved depiction of the Battle of New Orleans transforms one side of the base into a pictorial surface. The other three sides hold eagles perched on spiral thunderbolts.

An uncommon aspect of Fletcher & Gardiner's patronage is preserved by the dedication from "the Ladies of South-Carolina." Jackson's award is an expression of a women's public initiative sparked by his post–War of 1812 victory over Major General Packenham's forces. Honoring their hero, women in Charleston organized a statewide campaign, raising $500 to commission this urn. A letter written by a gentleman who called on Fletcher & Gardiner's workshop assured them Jackson's urn would be worthy of their efforts:

> There appears to be every anxiety on the part of Messrs. Fletcher & Gardiner . . . to gratify us to the utmost extent of our wishes. They have laid aside every other work, to enable them to employ their whole force, both in taste and execution, upon the one in question. I have no hesitation to declare that I believe when the vase shall be exhibited in Charleston, it will excel by far any thing ever exhibited there. I am warranted in this belief, from having seen with admiration, the pieces executed by them for other heroes of our late glorious war.[3]

A description published when the vase was completed confirmed earlier hopes: "The beauty of this elegant piece of workmanship, consists, not only in the minute perfection of its parts – but in the general and striking effect produced upon the beholders from the harmony of the whole. The polish of the work is such, that all its ornaments are *multiplied by reflection*–and gives it a richness beyond description . . . The design and execution do honor to the artist, and the object for which it is intended by the enlightened *fair* of South Carolina, must be as gratifying to our state, as it can be to the *hero* for whose honor it was designed."[4]

longer needed . . . Membership was . . . hereditary from father to eldest son [and eventually included] French military officers who were colonels or higher and naval officers who ranked as captains or higher."[1]

Scott most likely commissioned this badge, the society's insignia, for himself shortly after he was accorded honorary membership. Though the badge is unmarked, he probably had Fletcher & Gardiner make it since Scott extolled their work as being "executed with superior taste and workmanship [inspired by] a great variety of antique models from which [they] compose the ornaments of their work."[2]

He was not the only member of the Society to possess badges made by Fletcher & Gardiner, as recorded in the firm's business records. On June 9, 1830, Fletcher wrote to Eustis Prescott of New York City that he had sent with Baldwin Gardiner "the gold Cincinnati Badge which you did me the favor to order." Again, on December 12, 1834, Fletcher wrote to General Nathan Towson that "Col. McKenney has been so kind as to offer to take your gilt sword to Washington [DC] for me. He has also taken with him the gold badge you did me the favor to order."[3] Although neither Prescott's nor Towson's badges are known to exist, this extraordinary large, exquisitely designed and richly detailed example testifies to the quality of goldsmithing work that emanated from Fletcher & Gardiner's establishment.

23. THE SOCIETY OF THE CINCINNATI BADGE, 1815–20
Inscription: *SOCIETAS CINCINNATORUM INSTITUTA AD 1783* chased around enamel plaque on which is painted *VIRTUTIS, PRAEMIUM* and *ESTO PERPETUA* on reverse; *OMNIA RELIQUIT SERVARE REPUBLICAM* chased around enamel plaque on obverse
Mark: none
Gold, enamel, ruby
H. 2¾ in (7 cm), W. 1⅜ in (4.1 cm), D. ⁵⁄₁₆ in (1.2 cm); Wt. 1 oz. 10 dwt. Troy (gross)
West Point Museum Collection, United States Military Academy

Winfield Scott (1786–1866), a general in the American army, distinguished himself fighting against the British during the War of 1812. In recognition of his heroism he was elected to The Society of the Cincinnati in 1815. This organization, founded in 1783, encompassed "all Continental [American] officers in service at the end of the [Revolutionary] war, all who had served three years honorably during the war, and those who had been . . . dismissed during the war when their services were no

24. PORTION OF A TABLE SERVICE, 1817

Inscription on each object: *Presented by the / Citizens of Baltimore to / Com. John Rodgers / in testimony of their Sense of / the important aid afforded by him / in the defence of Baltimore on / the 12th & 13th of Sept.¹ 1814* (line breaks vary per object; variation in inscription: cake basket *deffence*) engraved on underside of each

Mark: Appendix 1, fig. 6a, b stamped on underside

Silver

H. 11⅞ in (30.2 cm), W. 9½ in (24.1 cm), Diam. 6¼ in (15.9 cm); Wt. 59 oz. 16 dwt. Troy (pitcher)

H. 2 in (5.1 cm), L. 22¾ in (57.8 cm), W. 17¾ in (45.1 cm); Wt. 100 oz. 6 dwt. Troy (dish)

H. 6¼ in (15.9 cm), L. 9½ in (24.1 cm), W. 4⅜ in (11.1 cm); Wt. 25 oz. 12 dwt. Troy (sauceboat)

H. 8¼ in (21 cm), W. 10½ in (26.7 cm), Diam. 8½ in (21.6 cm); Wt. 46 oz. 7 dwt. Troy (vegetable tureen)

H. 5¼ in (13.3 cm), L. 14 in (35.6 cm), W. 9½ in (24.1 cm); Wt. 42 oz. 10 dwt. Troy (cake basket)

The Maryland Historical Society, Gift of William Ledyard Brewster, 1935.35.4 (pitcher), 1935.35.1 (dish), 1935.35.2b (sauceboat); Gift of the Macomb heirs, 1935.34.3 (vegetable tureen), 1935.34.5 (cake basket)

TUREEN (one of two), 1817

Inscription: Same as above, variation: Commodore, engraved

Mark: Appendix 1, figs. 5 (impressed thrice), 6a, b stamped on underside

Silver

H. 15¼ in (38.7 cm), L. 15¼ in (38.7 cm), W. 10½ in (26.7 cm); wt. [?] oz. Troy

The Saint Louis Art Museum, Funds given by the Decorative Arts Society and the Eliza McMillan Trust, 15:1974

On the third anniversary of the British bombardment of Fort McHenry, the citizens of Baltimore recognized John Rodgers (1773–1838) for his role in defending the city. Rather than a silver bombshell like Armistead's, the committee invested $4,000 in a table service of approximately fifty items, with monumental serving pieces.¹ Only the engraved dedications on the bottom of each piece signified their purpose. Although individual pieces were grand in scale, the cumulative effect of so much silver for one man's dining table and sideboard was a truly lavish show.

When the service was completed, Baltimore citizens

arranged a public display for several days in Fielding Lucas's store. Newspapers carried details around the country. In Baltimore: "It is a most superb service of plate . . . all of the most substantial workmanship, and reflecting on the artists, Messrs. Fletcher and Gardiner, of Philadelphia, the highest degree of credit . . . It is splendidly 'ornamented with borderings and embossed figures after the manner of the Egyptian and Grecian sculpturings,' and it is universally admired." In Norfolk: "This is the true way to reward public men, either as meritorious Soldiers, Statesmen, or Citizens—A dinner passes away, and is no more thought of; but a splendid present like the one we now speak of, is a monument ever present to the receiver, and descends to his posterity, exciting future generations to heroic deeds in the service of their country."[2]

The Rodgers service required Fletcher & Gardiner to refine and expand their tableware forms, which they did by looking to French interpretations of antiquity. Using antique vessels and borders as inspiration, the Rodgers silver features smooth reflective surfaces and judiciously placed ornament. Tureens claimed pride of place on the dining table or sideboard, and the massive pair in this set indicated their owner's eminence. A band of winged human and animal heads encircles the body with grotesque ornament similar to passages on tureens made

by contemporary French silversmiths. The weighty fruited finial, eagle-handle terminals, star bosses, and massive winged feet mix Greco-Roman with Egyptian ornament.[3]

Pitchers with water-leaf borders and winged feet also give an "Egyptian" sensibility to the service. Each pitcher's upper section was formed from flatted sheet silver seamed vertically on one side with stylized leaf borders chased directly on the raised body. Four sizes of dishes, a deep cake basket with cone-shell handles, multiple serving pieces, and heavy flatware rounded out the table service.[4]

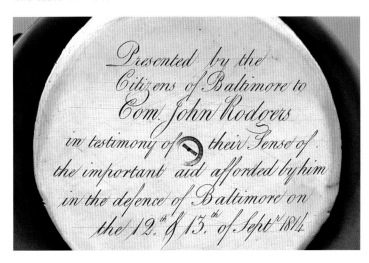

Presented by the Citizens of Baltimore to Com. John Rodgers in testimony of ⬭ their Sense of the important aid afforded by him in the defence of Baltimore on the 12.th & 13.th of Sept.r 1814

25. PITCHER, 1815–25
Inscription: none
Mark: Appendix 1, fig. 6a, b stamped on underside
Silver
H. 9¹³⁄₁₆ in (25 cm), W. 6⅝ in (16.8 cm), Diam. 5⅜ in (13.7 cm); Wt. 17 oz. 17 dwt. Troy
Private collection

Pitchers were used occasionally on American dining tables during the eighteenth century but came to be a standard feature during meals in the nineteenth century. American silversmiths were commissioned to make them in considerable numbers, in part because the form was seen as a fashionable, yet usable reference to ancient Greek and Roman vases that had captured the imagination of all those fascinated with antique cultures. This is perhaps nowhere better documented than in the large numbers of silver pitchers made by American silversmiths during the first half of the nineteenth century for presentation to individuals to commemorate a heroic action or significant event.[1]

This example is one of many that Fletcher and Gardiner made throughout their respective careers. Although it bears no date, the pitcher does employ a number of features that indicate it was made early in the firm's history, probably before 1825. Its body is rather bulbous in outline; their later pitchers were more slender and vertical in design. The two upper ornamental borders are die rolled while the lower two are flat chased; later examples used a larger proportion of die-rolled borders. The handle is designed as three separate motifs—an eagle head, a reeded section, and a bifurcated leaf with cornucopia—that are dramatic in appearance but not fully integrated visually (detail). Handles on the firm's pitchers made at a later date more fully address the design challenge of visually organizing disparate motifs into an integrated whole.

The prominent sculpted presence of the eagle head and cornucopia strongly suggest the designer of this pitcher sought to infuse it with a symbolic sense of America. Both these motifs were used frequently by image makers and others catering to Americans' post–War of 1812 heightened sense of patriotism.[2]

26. PITCHER, 1815–25

Inscription: none
Mark: Appendix 1, fig. 6a, b stamped on underside
Silver
H. 12⅝ in (32.1 cm), W. 10 in (25.4 cm), Diam. 5½ in (14 cm); Wt. 55 oz. Troy
Private collection

This large pitcher is one of many that Fletcher & Gardiner were called upon to make for customers throughout the United States, including Coleman R. Jacobs of New York, Nicholas Biddle of Philadelphia, William Norvell of Lynchburg, Virginia, and J. Curice Duncan of New Orleans, Louisiana. Pitchers of silver, pewter, glass, and porcelain—at the time called ewers or jugs—were widely used in American dining rooms during the early nineteenth century for wine, cider, beer, water, and other potables.[1] They were typically of large capacity, holding from one to four quarts.

This example was hand wrought to shape, the body being of several parts. The portion of the pedestal above the ornamental features is one; the vase-shape body is a second; and the third is the neck and spout. All have been planished and polished to a brilliant smooth and reflective surface. The makers contrasted these mirror-like sections with a number of highly articulated and differing ornamental components; a narrow die-rolled border of flowers is soldered to the lip, and another wider die-rolled border has been soldered into the shoulder of the body. It employs a meandering vine of grape leaves and clusters. A third border, soldered around the four sides of the base, was die rolled in the form of a marine shell flanked by acanthus leaves.

The remaining parts were cast. The four paw feet with acanthus-leaf brackets were each cast as a single piece. They are thick walled and sufficiently substantial to support the pitcher and its contents. The handle was cast vertically in two halves, which were soldered together before being soldered to the pitcher. Its prominently placed eagle head with panels of reeding in the form of an overlapping collar, inspired by French interpretation of an Egyptian prototype, was designed to appeal to American patriotic sensibilities.[2]

27. PLATE, 1820–30

Inscription: a coat of arms (a lobster in bend in bordure);
a crest (a helm affronty under a lobster in pale within
wings conjoined, within a leafy mantle) engraved on
front; a monogram (*JFG* in feathered script within
bound laurel boughs) engraved on back
Mark: Appendix 1, fig. 6a, b stamped on back
Silver
H. ⅝ in (1.5 cm), Diam. 9⅜ in (23.8 cm); Wt. 14 oz. 18
dwt. Troy
Ruth J. Nutt Collection of American Silver

This plate, possibly part of a set, is unusual for the leaves,
flowers, and berries chased around the brim. Although
the coat of arms engraved on the obverse has not been
positively identified, it may belong to a member of the
Gorham family of Barnstable, Massachusetts, as suggested
by the initials "*JFG*" engraved on the reverse.

On August 21, 1830, Thomas Fletcher wrote to
Benjamin Gorham: "Your letter enclosing the sketch of
an article of silver plate came to hand this morning. I
will have the work put in hand as soon as possible." On
October 26 Fletcher again wrote to Gorham that "I
regret that it was not in my power to complete the set of
Plate you did me the favor to order, but I assure you that
I am anxious to get it out of my hands as Mrs. G can be
impatient to receive it."[1] Though Gorham's letter
prompting this apology is not known to exist, one can
imagine from the tenor of Fletcher's reply that he was
upset at not having received his silver. Fletcher went on
to say that he hoped to complete the work and send it
in two weeks.

He apparently met that deadline and satisfied Gorham,
for the latter placed an order for more. Record of it
exists in another letter Fletcher wrote to him on June
10, 1831: "I very much regret that the delay has taken
place respecting your plate but it has been utterly out of
my power to prevent it. If the Arms & Cypher had been
left with me, this delay would not have happened, but
when the drawing was sent back the Engraver was
engaged on a piece of work which he stated he could
not leave if I were to give him fifty dollars. No other
engraver in this city would undertake to engrave the set
who could do it well enough to give satisfaction."[2]

28. SALVER (one of a pair), 1820–25

Inscription: none

Mark: Appendix 1, fig. 6a, b stamped on back of each

Silver

H. 1½ in (3.9 cm), Diam. 8 in (30.2 cm); Wt. 16 oz. 10 dwt. Troy each

Yale University Art Gallery, Gift of Mr. Frederick C. Kossack, 1986.102.108.1

Salvers, on a central pedestal, three or four feet arranged around the perimeter, or with no support at all, have been used in American households since the seventeenth century. Their purpose varies depending on size, but Curice Duncan of New Orleans stipulated when he wrote to Fletcher in 1841 that he wanted "two handsome plated waiters, small size, for handing a tumbler of water on."[1]

Silversmiths supplied them frequently to customers throughout the eighteenth century. Though considerable variation exists, salvers made by eighteenth-century American silversmiths were typically wrought and had scroll and scallop-shell borders that were cast in sections

and soldered around the perimeter. They were infrequently made in pairs, averaged about six to ten inches in diameter, and stood on three short cabriole legs with pad or ball-and-claw feet.[2]

This salver and its mate, made in Fletcher & Gardiner's manufactory, follow that model. Each is eight inches in diameter. They are wrought, but the ornamental reinforcing around the edge in the form of scrolled leaves was die stamped, not cast, of thin sheet silver. Eleven individually stamped elements, each filled with silver solder, were soldered in place, end to end, around the perimeter of each salver. Though die-stamped borders like these were cheaper and faster to make than cast borders, care had to be taken in the cutting of the iron dies, as noted in a letter written by Fletcher to the "American merchants" in Birmingham, Joseph Goddard and George Bibby. On October 7, 1829, he wrote that the goods they had shipped him were largely satisfactory, except "in some few instances the silver dyes were so thin as to show the solder through," rendering them useless.[3] The three muscular, hairy-paw feet on each salver were cast, chased, and soldered in place.

29. PITCHER, 1820–25

Inscription: *Presented / By friends of National Industry in Philadelphia / to M* Eleazer Lord; / as a mark of sincere approbation / of the / Zeal, talents, and intelligence / he displayed at Washington. / in support of American Manufacturers, / during the first session / of the sixteenth Congress.* engraved on side opposite handle
Mark: Appendix 1, fig. 6a, b stamped on underside
Silver
H. 11½ in (29.2 cm), W. 9½ in (24.1 cm), Diam. 5⅝ in (14.3 cm); Wt. 39 oz. Troy
Private collection

In the nineteenth century, civic presentation awards often took the form of a silver pitcher. With expansive mirror-like surfaces, classical proportions, dynamic sculptural elements, and useful purpose, pitchers prominently brought style to dining experiences. Fletcher & Gardiner fashioned scores of pitchers, recombining varieties of die-rolled and chased ornament on different body shapes. This example features the eagle-head handle designed for the Rodgers service pitchers, but proportions, borders, and the base differ. A grape-leaf border was a recurring motif, not only on silver but also on Chinese export dinner services as well as printed or woven textiles used in America early in the nineteenth century.[1]

The Sixteenth Congress of the United States sat from 1819 to 1821. After four years of petitions from numerous states urging that the interests of domestic industry be addressed, Congress established a separate Committee on Manufacturers in the first session of 1819. States disagreed about import tariffs, some called for higher duties on materials and goods (such as metalwork and textiles); others pleaded the opposite. Eleazer (Eleazar) Lord (1788–1871) was ordained as a preacher but later worked in New York City in many professional vocations.[2] Lord repeatedly lobbied Congress for higher tariffs to protect American manufacturers, drawing commendations from New York and Philadelphia merchants. In 1820 he helped found the National Institution for the Promotion of Industry, later serving as president.

Fletcher & Gardiner's business interest in the tariff question might appear mixed; they manufactured silver and jewelry but retailed significant amounts of imported goods. Staunch patriots, both Thomas Fletcher and Sidney Gardiner actively supported domestic manufacturing interests. In 1819 Fletcher directly petitioned Congress for higher duties on imported English screws to benefit his firm's short-lived venture into wood screw manufacturing. It is not surprising that citizens in Philadelphia turned to Fletcher & Gardiner for a presentation pitcher to reward Lord's lobbying efforts.[3]

---

30. GOBLET, 1817–30

Inscription: *Presented / by the Members of the / Southwark Hose Company / in testimony of their / individual respect / for their late / President / Wm E. Bowen* engraved on side; *FA* (flanking a fire hydrant and hose) chased on opposite side

Mark: Appendix 1, fig. 6a, b stamped on underside

Silver

H. 7⅞ in (18.9 cm), Diam. 4⅛ in (10.5 cm); Wt. 13 oz. 10 dwt. Troy

Private collection

Goblets are some of many vessels made in the United States between 1810 and 1840 that derive from the calyx krater, an ancient Greek pottery form used to mix wine and water for everyday drinking. Some served as wine coolers, presentation vases, or, as illustrated here, vessels for dining table use. The last of these, however, appear to have been infrequently purchased by householders; they preferred more modestly priced beakers, which survive in far greater numbers.[1]

This goblet was commissioned for presentation to William E. Bowen, a Philadelphia merchant, who like all men of his profession was particularly sensitive to the danger of fire. He addressed that concern through membership in the Southwark Hose Company and must have served well as its president, judging from the testimonial engraved on this vessel. The company was located not far from his house at the south end of Cedar Street. "The fire department [of which his company was part] is very energetic and efficient, but forms a dangerous body of men. They are very numerous, are influenced by an esprit de corps, act together, and being composed of the young and hardy of the lower classes have the power to do a great deal of mischief."[2] Nevertheless, this testimonial in silver suggests altruism and a measure of sensitivity and refinement in the members of the Southwark Hose Company.

Although Fletcher & Gardiner modeled this vessel on ancient prototypes, the fire hydrant and hose flanked with the initials *FA* worked in repoussé below the lip derive from more immediate inspiration. The design is a miniature replica of cast-iron fire insurance marks hung on the façades of commercial and private buildings throughout Philadelphia. These marks were made at local iron foundries for a number of volunteer fire companies that amalgamated as the Fire Association of Philadelphia in 1817.[3] They were placed on buildings belonging to fire insurance subscribers as evidence they were entitled to the services of member fire companies.

31. TWO TABLE FORKS, 1820–25

Inscription: *JMS* and a crest (a lion's head erased) engraved on handle backs

Mark: Appendix 1, fig. 4a, c, d stamped on backs of handles

Silver

L. 8⅛ in (20.6 cm), W. 1⅛ in (2.8 cm); Wt. 3 oz. Troy each

Private collection

John Morin Scott (1789–1858) was born in New York City, grew up in Philadelphia, attended school at Princeton, and subsequently entered law practice, specializing in insurance and commercial law. Although he did not actively seek public service, he served in that realm for much of his adult life, including several terms as a member of the House of Representatives of Pennsylvania, a member of the Common Council of Philadelphia, and three terms as mayor of Philadelphia. He was described as "among the most eminent members of the Philadelphia Bar."[1]

In 1824 Scott served on a six-person committee to help plan the highly anticipated visit of the Marquis de Lafayette to Philadelphia. Such activities were among the many social obligations in which Scott participated in the community. Central among them was entertaining, which frequently took place while dining. For that purpose Scott needed silver forks of excellent quality and the most current fashion, exemplified by the illustrated pair from a surviving set of ten. In response to orders like his, Fletcher typically stated that thread-and-shell pattern forks "are plain backs and . . . may be burnished to suit just as well as polished [since] no one [seems] to notice the burnished spoons from the polished forks." Though the price of the silver used to make forks like these varied according to current economic conditions, a contemporary of Scott's "bought of Thomas Fletcher 3 doz table forks polished double threaded @ [$] 1.87½ pr oz [plus] engraving crest & cypher @ [$] .25" on January 6, 1830.[2]

---

32. SALVER, 1820–30

Inscription: a coat of arms (gules, a chevron ermine between three talbots' heads erased); a crest (a talbot's head erased within a laurel wreath) engraved on front

Mark: Appendix 1, fig. 6a, b stamped on underside

Silver

H. 1½ in (3.8 cm), Diam. 15¼ (38.7 cm); Wt. 57 oz. Troy

Private collection

On August 19, 1812, two months after the United States declared war on Great Britain, Isaac Hull (1773–1843) commander of the frigate *Constitution*, wrested a decisive victory over the British frigate *Guerrière* in a fierce and closely fought battle in the Atlantic, east of Boston. In recognition of his valor, the citizens of Philadelphia contributed more than two thousand dollars to fund "a piece of plate of the most elegant workmanship" for presentation to him.[1] Fletcher and Gardiner, newly arrived in the city, were selected to design and make the gift. In response, the partners created one of the most grandiose presentation objects in the history of American silver to that date (cat. no. 10).

That vase was one of many that the Fletcher & Gardiner

firm made for national heroes. Virtually all recipients were pleased, as expressed by DeWitt Clinton, who stated, "I receive these splendid fabrics with the highest gratification. In the design and the execution, they reflect honor on the taste, skill and ingenuity of our artists." Many of these men, impressed with the quality of Fletcher & Gardiner's work, subsequently returned to order objects in silver. Hull did so in a letter he wrote to Fletcher on December 7, 1829: "Sir–I have determined

not to have the <u>bason</u> belonging to the <u>urn</u> made over at present, & will be greatly obliged if you will have the urn & the <u>sett of plate</u> sent on as soon as possible."[2]

This salver, engraved with Hull's coat of arms, was made in Fletcher & Gardiner's manufactory following such an order. It stands on three cast, powerfully articulated animal-paw feet flanked by leafy spandrels and employs a gadrooned border at its edge that encloses and highlights the coat of arms (details).

33. SAUCEBOAT, 1820–27

Inscription: *JNW* engraved on one side
Mark: Appendix 1, figs. 2b, 3 stamped on underside
Silver
H. 5⅝ in (14.3 cm), L. 7½ in (19 cm), W. 5⅜ in (13.7 cm);
Wt. 17 oz. Troy
Private collection

Silver sauceboats first began to appear on American dining tables during the second decade of the eighteenth century. The earliest were elliptic in shape with a spout at each end and a handle on each side; they stood on a footrim. By the mid-1720s this type evolved into an oval shape with a pouring spout at the narrow end and handle at the opposite end. This variant typically stood on a central foot or sometimes four short legs but by the 1740s was usually supported on three short legs only. That model remained basically unchanged for the ensuing fifty years or so, although the stylistic attributes of any given example reflected the fashion of the era in which it was made.

Those made during the third quarter of the eighteenth century typically have slightly bulbous, elliptic bodies with a flaring scrolled lip and arched pouring spout. Their handles consist of multiple opposed and graduated scrolls, the upper one of which, often ornamented with an acanthus leaf, arches above and over the vessel. These sauceboats stand on three short, scrolled legs with modified scallop shells for feet and also at their upper ends. Sauceboats of this design fully represent the naturalistic style that held sway at the time.[1]

Sauceboats made after that evolved with changing taste. Although their basic body design remained the same, ornamental components are quite different. By about 1810 these vessels employed die-rolled decorative borders in addition to feet, handles, and sometimes spouts in the form of animal, human, or mythological creatures recalling ancient Greek and Roman design.[2] By the 1820s that style had begun to lose its preeminence, and a revived naturalistic interpretation proved to be the most compelling, as exemplified by this sauceboat. Its makers most likely referred to one or more examples made in Philadelphia fifty years or so earlier prior to undertaking this well-conceived and executed interpretation.

34. TANKARD, 1820–30

Inscription: none
Mark: Appendix 1, fig. 6a, b stamped on underside
Silver
H. 7⅛ in (18.1 cm), W. 6⅞ in (17.5 cm), Diam. 4½ in (11.4 cm); Wt. 32 oz. 10 dwt. Troy
Private collection

The barrel of this tankard consists of silver that was flattened into a sheet in a rolling mill. The sheet was bent into a cylindrical shape and the edges butted vertically on the handle side and soldered to form an almost invisible joint. A flat, circular piece was subsequently soldered into the bottom end. This method of fabrication for tankards replaced the traditional method of hammering the form to shape from a thick disk of metal.

Following fabrication, the barrel was decorated with four strips of die-rolled ornament of three differing patterns that were cut to length, bent to shape, and soldered into place. Just as the tankard body was made using an efficient, semi-mechanized, proto-industrial technique, so too were the decorative bands. These were made in a hand-powered rolling mill that Thomas Fletcher purchased in Sheffield, England, in 1815. This mill was designed to interchangeably accommodate rollers that the partners acquired as they changed or expanded their offerings of silver.

Each of those rollers had a design cut into its perimeter by a specialist engraver, called a die sinker. Although these specialists were expensive, the engraved rolls were capable of generating large quantities of decorative strips cheaply. This allowed Fletcher & Gardiner to decorate the barrels of tankards, edges of cake baskets, footrims of pitchers, bodies of teapots, and many other vessels attractively, easily, and inexpensively.

35. SNUFF BOX, 1820–27
Inscription: a coat of arms (gules a lion rampant or within a bordure of the last); a crest (a pelican in her piety) engraved on lid
Mark: Appendix 1, fig. 6a, b stamped on bottom
Silver
H. ½ in (1.3 cm), Diam. 3⅜ in (8.6 cm); Wt. 2 oz. 5 dwt. Troy
Winterthur Museum, Gift of Mrs. George L. Batchelder, 1972.75

Tobacco was among the most heralded discoveries when European explorers arrived in the New World. Little time elapsed before its use became widespread among European settlers in America and also throughout Europe. The tobacco leaf was cut up for smoking, chopped for chewing, and powdered for snuff. All needed to be kept in boxes, not only for ready availability but also to maintain their moisture content. Consequently, snuff boxes were a staple of many artisans' work. Though snuff takers could satisfactorily transport and store snuff in wood, horn, painted sheet iron, tortoise shell, papier-mâché, and other inexpensive boxes, many chose silver. Their willingness to underwrite the expense was succinctly noted as follows, "Snuff and snuffing are things we can love, because they are always with us; and we can season them with a little vanity if we possess a snuff box of silver or gold."[1]

James Lloyd III (1769–1831) commissioned this silver snuff box from Fletcher & Gardiner. Lloyd, born in Massachusetts, traced his ancestry there back several generations and appears to have been proud of his heritage, as evidenced by the Lloyd family coat of arms he had engraved on the cover of the box. Lloyd had a distinguished career, serving as United States Senator from Massachusetts from 1808 to 1813 and again between 1822 and 1826.

In spite of his deep roots in Massachusetts, Lloyd did cement a Philadelphia connection when he married Anna Breck in 1809, and he retired in Philadelphia following his second term in the Senate. Lloyd also had another connection with Philadelphia through Fletcher and Gardiner, from whom he purchased silver. Fletcher acknowledged their cordial business relationship when he wrote, "I have the pleasure to acknowledge the receipt of your kind favour . . . I feel obliged by the friendly note taken by you of the plate recently executed in my establishment . . . To merit the approbation of those who favour me with their orders, is always to me the most valuable part of the compensation."[2]

36. CASTER AND CRUET FRAME, 1820–27

Inscription: none
Mark: Appendix 1, fig. 6a, b stamped on underside
Silver, glass
H. 11¼ in (28.3 cm), Diam. 11½ in (29.2 cm); Wt. 61 oz.
Troy (frame)
Private collection

Condiments and flavorings of many varieties have long been desirable adjuncts at the dining table. They have been kept in and dispensed from ceramic, metal, and glass bottles called cruets (for liquids) and casters (for powdered, granular, or flaked substances). When several condiments are used at the table, the bottles are normally placed in frames designed to keep them together, in good order, and safe from breakage, spilling, or loss.

Soy or cruet frames could hold from two to as many as ten bottles. This elegant example relates to the "Cruet frames, 5, 6, 7 and 8 glasses, richly cut engraved borders" that Fletcher & Gardiner advertised in the October 6,

1810, issue of the Boston *Columbian Centinel*. It was designed to hold seven glass bottles. Four have glass stoppers and held liquids; three, with silver caps, held powders. Though the bottles do not identify their contents, they most likely contained oil, vinegar, soy, mustard, lemon, tarragon, and cayenne pepper.[1]

Fletcher & Gardiner fashioned this cruet frame using a combination of traditional methods, such as hammering the circular platform to shape and casting the applied border around the edge and feet soldered to the underside. They used the more modern technique of die rolling the rings that hold the bottles in place and die stamping the centrally located foliate ring handle and the short, shell-decorated legs that support the ring cluster. They obtained the bottles from a glass house. Though that glass supplier is unidentified, it was probably one of several that mass produced such bottles for silver and silver-plated cruet frames in Birmingham and Sheffield that Fletcher visited when he traveled to England in 1815 and 1816.[2]

37. TRAY, 1820–30
Inscription: none
Mark: Appendix 1, fig. 6a, b stamped three times on underside
Silver
H. 2¼ in (5.7 cm), L. 34½ in (87.6 cm), W. 21 in (53.3 cm); Wt. 251oz. 11 dwt. Troy
Private collection

This large oblong tray, hammered to shape from a billet of silver, was a challenging form to make even though it might appear an easy task to the casual observer. Only the most experienced and capable silversmiths were able to fashion trays like this successfully. Although it is substantially made, its large size required reinforcing so that it would not flex, bend, and crack when used. This was accomplished by adding a thick ornamental edge around the perimeter. In this instance, the edge consists of a die-stamped scallop shell flanked by enfolding acanthus leaves. This unit is about 3¼ inches long and was stamped to shape out of a thin strip of silver in a gravity-operated downfall press. After removal from the press it

was filled with silver solder to give it rigidity and then soldered to the edge of the tray. Twenty-two of these stamped-and-filled units have been soldered end to end to form the entire border that both strengthens and decorates the tray. The two handles and four feet were cast and soldered in place.

This tray has another labor-intensive feature in the broad expanse of flat chasing on the upper surface. Similar in appearance to engraving and taking its stylistic cue from the motifs in the die-stamped border, this chasing was accomplished by first embedding the tray in pitch after which the chaser "selects his punches and indents the outline on the surface of the tray by tapping home the various lines and curves . . . afterwards carefully matting over with specially delicate punches the finer details of the pattern, such as the veins of leaves, petals of flowers, etc."[1]

Silver objects of this weight and amount of labor were by definition expensive. Americans rarely commissioned them prior to about 1850. Instead, they normally purchased imported English silver-plated trays, which were cheaper.

38. THE SOCIETY OF THE CINCINNATI BADGE,
ca. 1821
Inscription: *SOCIETAS CINCINATORUM INSTITUTS A D 1783* cast on reverse; *OMNIA RELINQUIT . SERVARE REMPUBLICAM* cast on obverse
Mark: none
Silver gilt
H. 2⅟₁₆ in (5.2 cm), W. 1³⁄₁₆ in (3 cm), D. ⁵⁄₁₆ in (0.8 cm); Wt. 0.32 oz. Troy
Collection of Gary E. Young

As documented by Minor Myers, Jr. in *The Insignia of The Society of the Cincinnati*, the Rhode Island chapter of that organization "commissioned a new issue of eagles from an unidentified Philadelphia firm, and in June 1821, 32 were delivered. Two of them were solid gold at $20 each. The rest were coin silver, double plated in gold at $10 each. Thirty [of them] had been distributed [to members] by 1827 . . . Like the early French [Cincinnati medals], the bodies [of each eagle] were prepared as a separate casting with a hollow center, thus saving valuable silver or gold. The medallions were then attached [to each side] over the hole in the center."[1]

Myers further noted that the Rhode Island chapter ordered these insignia in response to being "approached by an entrepreneurial Philadelphia goldsmith who sought to produce new eagles." This same goldsmith solicited the Massachusetts chapter, which declined ordering any insignia. The author lamented that the records of both chapters omit to name the person who approached them. Even so, it is reasonable to presume that the unnamed individual was Thomas Fletcher, who with his partner Sidney Gardiner, advertised that "their principal attention will be directed to the manufacturing of Gold and Silver of every description and particularly . . . GOLD JEWELRY."[2]

In that regard on November 4, 1835, an employee of Fletcher's, William S. Peirce, wrote to William H. McCarer of Philadelphia, "In reply to your note, we can state that for 25 medals of Jeweller's Gold the price will be $3-each complete. For 25 do of fine gold the price will be $3.75 each. For 50 do of each the price will be the same. If you honour us with your order, we will pledge ourselves to have them executed in the best possible manner."[3] Though positive evidence is lacking, McCarer may have requested a quote for Cincinnati badges.

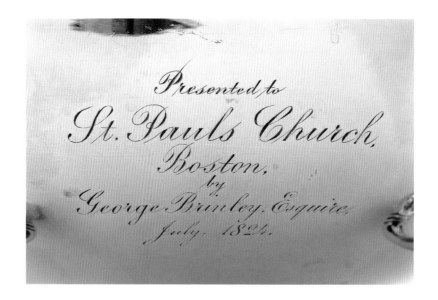

39. BAPTISMAL BASIN, 1824

Inscription: *Presented to / St. Pauls Church, / Boston, / by / George Brinley, Esquire, / July 1824* engraved on side
Mark: Appendix 1, fig. 6a, b stamped on underside
Silver
H. 3¾ in (9.5 cm), Diam. 11¼ in (28.6 cm); Wt. 39 oz. 10 dwt. Troy
Cathedral Church of St. Paul (Episcopal), Boston, Massachusetts

On April 19, 1819, a small group of Bostonians met to plan the funding of a new Episcopal church. Called St. Paul's Church, its cornerstone was laid in September 1819. Construction on the Greek Revival stone building was completed by June 1820, when the building was consecrated and services commenced.[1]

The church purchased "a pair of chalices, patens, flagons, alms dishes and 1 large paten" from London silversmith William Burwash in 1821.[2] However, it did not acquire a baptismal basin. That oversight was rectified shortly thereafter when George Brinley commissioned the basin seen here and presented it to the church in 1824.

Brinley (1774–1857) was a member of the congregation. For many years he owned and operated a drug store at 3 & 4 Old Market, where he sold "drugs, medicines, dye stuffs, painters' colours, surgeons' instruments, &c, &c," which had earned him a

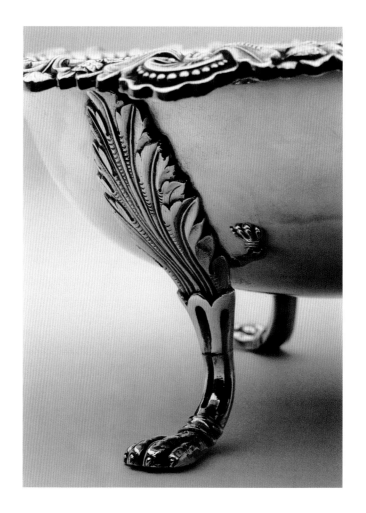

considerable fortune.³ Consequently, he was wealthy enough to seek the services of Fletcher & Gardiner—then America's most prestigious silversmithing firm—to make this basin.

In filling the commission, Fletcher & Gardiner chose to fashion a dramatic and stylish interpretation. The hemispherical bowl has a die-stamped border of scallop shells and acanthus leaves that repeat in a regular pattern.

The partners created and used this border on silver tea sets that were the height of fashion during the 1820s. Instead of the more traditional circular stepped-pedestal base, the partners chose to support the basin on three sinuous cast legs, each with a paw foot at the lower end and a handsomely detailed acanthus leaf where it joins the bowl. They used this same acanthus-leaf casting on their sugar tongs (cat. no. 41).

40. FRUIT OR CAKE BASKET, 1820–25

Inscription: *R. F. Stockton* engraved on side of base

Mark: Appendix 1, fig. 6a, b stamped on underside

Silver

H. 6⅝ in (16.9 cm), L. 17 in (43.2 cm), W. 11⅝ in (29.6 cm); Wt. 66 oz. 10 dwt. Troy

The Baltimore Museum of Art, BMA 1993.2

On November 9, 1808, Thomas Fletcher and Sidney Gardiner placed an advertisement in the *Columbian Centinel* stating that they had just formed a partnership and that they had "taken the Shop No. 43 Marlboro Street, where . . . their principal attention will be directed to the manufacturing of Gold and Silver work of every description . . . [where they] have on hand, for sale . . . cake and fruit baskets" in addition to an extensive assortment of other silver and jewelry as well as imported silverplate.

The silverplate that Fletcher & Gardiner imported from manufacturers in Sheffield and Birmingham, England, may have provided the stylistic inspiration for both the upswept oblong shape and sculpted ornament of this basket, including the cornucopia-shape handles. The cornucopia has long been a symbolic component in Western culture, extending back to Greek mythology as the attribute of Demeter, goddess of agriculture. Because of this tradition, Americans often incorporated it into imagery and artifacts.[1] Many associated it symbolically with increasingly productive agricultural activity, from which by extension they reasoned that the United States was blessed and destined to be a land of plenty.

Hence, the cornucopia was exploited in all manner of media, including furniture, textiles, prints, glass, and silver. Those that form the handles of this basket are particularly striking when considered in context with the apples, pears, melons, grapes, and other fruit the basket held on the dining table.[2]

The original owner of this basket, Robert Field Stockton (1795–1866) of Princeton, New Jersey, served in the United States Navy from 1811 until 1850, at which time he campaigned for, and was elected to, the United States Senate.

41. SIX-PIECE TEA SET, 1820–30

Inscription: none

Mark: Appendix 1, fig. 6a, b stamped on underside of two teapots, sugar bowl, cream pot, and slop bowl; fig. 4a, c, d stamped inside arm of sugar tongs

Silver, wood

H. 9½ in (24.1 cm), W. 11⅝ in (29.5 cm), Diam. 6¼ in (15.9 cm); Wt. 40 oz. 5 dwt. Troy (teapot, gross)

H. 9⅝ in (24.4 cm), W. 11⅝ in (29.5 cm), Diam. 6⅜ in (16.2 cm); Wt. 37 oz. 3 dwt. Troy (teapot, gross)

H. 9 in (22.9 cm), W. 7¼ in (18.4 cm), Diam. 6¼ in (15.9 cm); Wt. 36 oz. 5 dwt. Troy (sugar bowl)

H. 6⅜ in (16.2 cm), W. 5⅝ in (14.3 cm), Diam. 4 in (10.1 cm); Wt. 13 oz. 5 dwt. Troy (cream pot)

H. 5¼ in (13.3 cm), Diam. 9⅜ in (23.8 cm); Wt. 25 oz. Troy (slop bowl)

L. 7 in (17.8 cm), W. 1⅛ in (2.8 cm), D. 1½ in (3.8 cm); Wt. 3 oz. Troy (sugar tongs)

Philadelphia Museum of Art, P1933–65–1a-f, Bequest of Clara Norris

When Abbé Claude C. Robin visited the United States in 1781, he recorded that Americans "use much tea . . . the greatest mark of civility and welcome they can show you, is to invite you to drink it with them."[1]

This six-piece set is an impressive example of Fletcher & Gardiner's work for a client who chose to entertain on a lavish scale. In addition to the standard three-piece unit, this set includes a second pot of the type described by Fletcher as "a smaller teapot for water to match," and a slop bowl used for dregs and to empty cold tea from one's cup before refilling as well as a pair of sugar tongs.[2]

The bodies of all are wrought in the traditional manner. The primary ornamental borders encircling the bodies were executed using a gravity-operated downfall press. Each border consists of several stamped elements designed in the form of a scallop shell enfolded within a pair of acanthus leaves and flanked by a segment of another acanthus leaf. These components are visually tied by a row of beading above, which is an undulating wave pattern. When these stamped elements are joined end to end, they form a continuous border that can easily be soldered to vessels of varying shapes and circumference. Used in this manner, such borders provide drama and visually unify the set.[3]

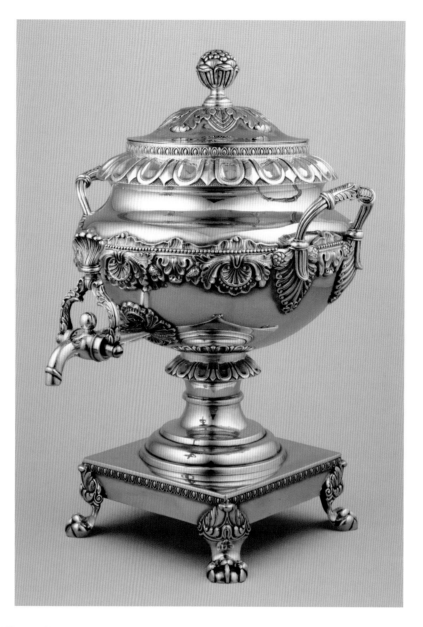

42. HOT WATER URN, 1820–30

Inscription: none
Mark: Appendix 1, fig. 6a, b stamped on underside
Silver
H. 13¾ in (34.9 cm), W. 10 in (25.4 cm), D. 11¼ in (28.6 cm); Wt. 103 oz. 10 dwt. Troy
Private collection

With the growing popularity of tea and coffee during the mid-eighteenth century, American silversmiths were increasingly called on to make silver teapots and coffeepots. They sometimes made companion vessels for cream and sugar, but rarely en suite. As tea and coffee became more widespread by the late eighteenth century, the number of vessels in a typical silver set grew and became more unified stylistically.[1]

Fletcher and Gardiner's manufactory made large numbers of tea and coffee sets, and each often had many pieces. Furthermore, their sets typically had capacious bodies, and every vessel was associated stylistically with every other one in the group. The partners, and later Fletcher alone, supplied sets, typically billed as "a set of plate," for customers throughout the United States. They listed a representative instance in a bill to Mrs. Richard Ashhurst of Philadelphia on January 27, 1836, identified as "a tea and coffee sett [consisting of] 1 coffee pot 50 [oz] 10 [dwt] 1 tea pot 48 [oz] 1 water pot 45 [oz] 05 [dwt] 1 sugar bowl 38 [oz] 05 [dwt] 1 slop bowl 24 [oz] 15 [dwt] 1 cream pot 20 [oz] 10 [dwt] 227 [oz] 04 [dwt] @ $2.31 [totaling] $524.83."[2]

To a set like this might be added a hot water urn of the type illustrated.[3] An expensive option, it provided a supply of hot water for refilling cups as needed during a gathering over tea. Its modified vase-shape body is garnished with a multitude of ornamental borders made using various techniques. The echinus border on the square base is die rolled; the shell-and-leaf border encircling the body is die stamped; and the egg-and-dart border encircling the neck is hand chased.

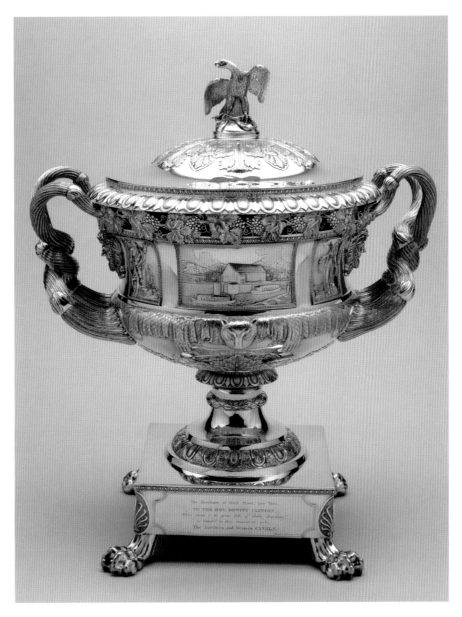

43. VASE (one of pair), 1824
Inscription: The Merchants of Pearl Street, New York. / TO THE HON. DEWITT CLINTON, / *Whose claim to the proud Title of "Public Benefactor," / is founded on those magnificent works, /* The Northern and Western CANALS. engraved on base
Mark: Appendix 1, figs. 7a, b, 6a, b (two impressions) stamped on underside; fig.18 and *Philad.a December 1824* engraved on base
Silver
H. 23½ in (59.7 cm), W. 20 in (50.8 cm), D. 14½ in (36.8 cm); Wt. 410 oz. 6 dwt. Troy[1]
The Metropolitan Museum of Art, Purchase, Louis V. Bell and Rogers Funds; Anonymous and Robert G. Goelet Gifts; and Gifts of Fenton L. B. Brown and of the grandchildren of Mrs. Ransom Spaford Hooker, in her memory, by exchange, 1982 (1982.4ab) Image © 2002 The Metropolitan Museum of Art

VASE (two of pair), 1825
Inscription: TO THE HON. DEWITT CLINTON, /

Who has developed the resources of the State of New York. / AND ENNOBLED HER CHARACTER, / The Merchants of Pearl Street offer this testimony of their / GRATITUDE AND RESPECT. engraved on base
Mark: Appendix 1, figs. 7a, b, 6a, b (two impressions) stamped on underside; fig.18 and *Philad.a February 1825* engraved on base
Silver
H. 23¾ in (60.4 cm), W. 20¾ in (52.7 cm), D. 14¾ in (37.5 cm); Wt. 401 oz. 2 dwt. Troy
The Metropolitan Museum of Art, Gift of the Erving and Joyce Wolf Foundation, 1988 (1988.199) Image © 2002 The Metropolitan Museum of Art

In March 1825, one year after winning the design contest for a pair of vases sponsored by a committee of merchants in New York City, Fletcher & Gardiner unveiled two magnificent monuments dedicated to Governor DeWitt Clinton and the Northern and Western Canals (Erie Canal). These vases quickly

became the nation's most celebrated works in silver.[2] Their grandeur and meaningful symbols embodied a conviction of national triumph, from the eagle perched upon the globe to the layers of ornament fusing classical references with New York's industrial accomplishments.

Thomas Fletcher, with committee secretary Isaac S. Hone, composed a "Description of the Vases" that was printed as a broadsheet and carried by newspapers (see Appendix 3). It begins:

> The form of these vases is copied from the celebrated antique vase, found among the ruins of the Villa of Adrian, and now in the possession of the Earl of Warwick. The handles and some of the ornaments are also similar to those upon that beautiful specimen of ancient art; but all the tablets and figures in *bas relief* are different, and exhibit scenes upon the Grand Canal, or allegorical illustrations of the progress of the arts and sciences.

Fletcher drew inspiration from one of the era's most famous antiquities, an enormous marble vase constructed from fragments excavated from a lake at Hadrian's villa at Tivoli and installed in the late 1770s at Warwick Castle (see chap. 4, fig. 15). He had also admired silver-gilt wine coolers of the "Warwick" design sold by the London firm Rundell, Bridge & Rundell (see chap. 4, fig. 16).[3] Although the Clinton vases retain similar molding, entwined grape-stalk handles, and the motif of animal skins chased into the lower bowl, the iconography transformed and multiplied Fletcher's design into a panoramic celebration of New York's new canal scenery framed by meaningful mythological and allegorical figures.

A frieze of classical figures on the reverse of each base illustrates themes that Fletcher described as "intended to represent the progress of the Arts and Sciences from their rude origin to their present improvement."[4] The progress motif aptly characterizes overall layers of ornament on the vases by linking the achievements of New York investors, politicians, and engineers to the foundations established by the ancients.

Bas-relief chased tablets identified as Mercury, Ceres, Minerva, and Hercules on the vase dated December 1824, and allegorical figures of Fame, History, Plenty, and a Native American man on the February 1825 vase are bolted to the concave sides. They are paired to flank rectangular tablets of canalscapes based upon engravings of the engineering wonders. The 1824 vase features locks near Albany and the astonishing Rochester aqueduct, the beginning and end of the enormous canal projects. The 1825 vase illustrates two impressively bridged sections of falls (Cohoes and Little Falls) near the mouth of the Mohawk River. Draped skins and diminutive animals in the lower bowl depict wild North American fauna.[5] Heads of Neptune with entwined dolphins are mounted under each handle, and cartouches of a reclining male river deity bolted to the base extend the water theme.

The combined spectacle of both vases represents a supreme effort in artistic synthesis, diverse craft techniques, and tremendous investment of labor. Perhaps reflecting this achievement, Fletcher & Gardiner created a special Z-shape banner mark specifically for this commission. Public awareness of the so-called Clinton vases was revived three years later at Clinton's death. Newspapers reported that "the splendid vases" were rescued from public auction by a Masonic lodge in Troy, New York, which purchased them for return to the family.[6]

44. FRAME FOR MINIATURE PORTRAIT, 1825
Inscription: FRANCES K. HUGER / *Presented to* / GEN[L] LAFAYETTE / *by the* / *City of Charleston* / *through SAML PRIOLEAU* / *Intendant* / *1825.* engraved on back
Mark: Appendix 1, fig. 19 engraved on back
Gold, ivory, paint, glass
H. 6¼ in (16 cm), W. 5 in (12.7 cm), D. ⅝ in (1.6 cm); Wt. 10 oz. 16 dwt. Troy (gross)
The Metropolitan Museum of Art, Harris Brisbane Dick Fund (38.165.33) Image © The Metropolitan Museum of Art

This remarkable frame encloses a portrait miniature on ivory of Francis Kinlock Huger (1773–1855) executed by Charles Fraser (1782–1860), both of Charleston, South Carolina. As recorded on the reverse, the portrait and frame were made as a gift for the Marquis de Lafayette when he visited Charleston. It served as a memento of the friendship between Huger and Lafayette that resulted from the former's involvement in freeing the latter from prison in the Austrian fortress of Olmutz in 1797, for which Huger was imprisoned for eight months.

The generous amount of gold and artistry expended on this frame tangibly records the significance of the gift

and importance of the recipient in the minds of those who commissioned it.[1] In response to that mandate Fletcher & Gardiner designed and executed an extraordinary *tour de force* that must rank as among the most ambitious and exquisite of such creations made in America to that date.

The presentation side of the frame consists of a cast rectangle with a separate narrow inner frame of leaf tips. Within it is a third frame that holds the miniature and its protective glass in place. This innermost frame appears to be removable, allowing access to the miniature, since the back of the entire construct is covered with a sheet of red gold soldered permanently in place.

Virtually the entire front of this frame has been ornamented, the outermost component cast of yellow gold with a finely stippled surface. Soldered to it is a meandering composition of leaves, tendrils, and flowers in red, white, and green gold, each chased in minute genus-specific detail.[2] The leaf-tip border of yellow gold that it encloses has been chased to an equal level of precision in which each separate leaf is rendered in detail. The third border, of yellow gold, with red, white, and green appliqués, repeats the composition of the first in a simpler but no less detailed design.

The yellow-gold, barrel-shape hanger supported on paired opposed scrolls is covered with a bouquet of red, white, and green flowers, and the engraved presentation inscription on the back of the frame is enclosed with a multi-colored floral border soldered in place.

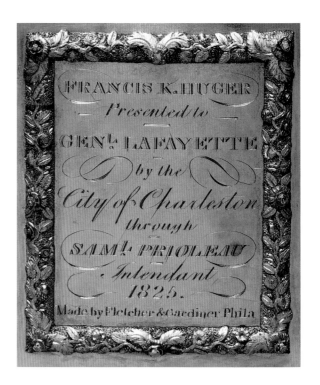

45. PAIR OF COMPOTES, 1825–30
Inscription: none
Mark: Appendix 1, fig. 6a, b stamped on bottom of each
Silver
H. 4¼ in (10.8 cm), Diam. 10¾ in (27.3 cm), W. 13 in (33 cm); Wt. 35 oz. Troy each
Private collection

The pedestals and bowls of this graceful pair were wrought to shape; the narrow borders encircling the base and collar of the pedestal were die rolled, and the handles at the edge and floral boss at the center of the bowl were cast. The meandering vine with handsomely articulated overlapping leaves and grape clusters was die stamped of thin strips of silver about six-and-a-half inches long. These were subsequently filled with silver solder and attached end to end around the perimeter of each compote.

When Thomas Fletcher visited the great English industrial cities of Sheffield and Birmingham in 1815, he noted that silver and silverplate manufacturers there

"dyed up [ornament like this] by a downfall the weight of which does not exceed 150 lbs. It is placed between two posts & a wheel about 2 feet dia[meter] is fixed above over which the band is passed which raises the blocks, by which the workman is enabled to raise it with one hand & strike up whatever he wishes with great facility–the [ornaments] are all struck up & filled with solder."[1]

Fletcher realized the advantage that machinery like this offered in creating dramatic and stylish ornamental features of many kinds quickly, in quantity, and inexpensively. He resolved to equip the manufactory in Philadelphia with machinery of this type. On July 2, 1815, he acquired the necessary equipment. He purchased a pair of ten-inch rolls fitted into a frame with gear train as well as two smaller rolling mills and a drop press for slightly more than £48 from Sheffield machinery manufacturers John and Samuel Darwin. With it he enabled his workmen to make a grapevine border more quickly and cheaply than cast counterparts by competitors.[2]

46. FIVE-PIECE TEA SET, 1820–30

Inscription: *EWC* engraved on side of each
Mark: Appendix 1, fig. 6a, b stamped on bottom of each, except coffeepot, which is unmarked; *OLD SILVER 141* stamped on underside of each
Silver, ivory
H. 10¾ in (27.3 cm), W. 11¼ in (28.6 cm), Diam. 5¾ in (14.6 cm); Wt. 43 oz. Troy (teapot, gross)
H. 10⅝ in (27 cm), W. 10½ in (26.7 cm), Diam. 5⅜ in (13.7 cm); Wt. 41 oz. 10 dwt. Troy (teapot, gross)
H. 10 in (25.4 cm), W. 7¾ in (19.7 cm), Diam. 5 in (12.7 cm); Wt. 37 oz. Troy (sugar bowl)
H. 5½ in (14 cm), Diam. 8½ in (21.6 cm); Wt. 29 oz. Troy (slop bowl)
H. 7 in (17.8 cm), W. 5⅞ in (14.9 cm), Diam. 3½ in (8.9 cm); Wt. 16 oz. 10 dwt. Troy (cream pot)
Private collection

On January 19, 1829, Charles Fletcher wrote to his brother Thomas from Baltimore that a local silversmith "Mr. [Hugh] Gelston keeps but little silver plate but wishes to make an arrangement with someone to supply him with new and handsome patterns." Charles probably had silver like this tea set in mind. He traveled widely throughout the United States for the firm looking to make commercial connections whereby they could sell their silver. To that end Charles went to Washington, D.C., the following month and again wrote to Thomas that "I sent two sugar dishes up to General Jackson's apartment" as samples in competition for supplying a silver tea and coffee set to the White House.[1]

Tea and coffee sets were the single most popular "article" that customers in Washington and other American cities wanted at the time, except for spoons. This set records the appearance of fashionable silver during the 1820s, an era when the look of silver was evolving from formal classical to more naturalistic rococo. All five components of the set stand on a plinth. The body of each is shaped like a vase, which in conjunction with the footed plinths conceptually derives from ancient Greek and Roman design. By contrast, the principal ornamental border, prominently encircling the bodies of the two pots, the sugar bowl, and the cream pot and at the lip of the slop bowl, relates to organic plant forms that dominated American silver design during the mid-eighteenth century.[2]

47. HOT WATER URN, 1820–30

Inscription: *SNK* engraved above petcock; *JR* engraved on back
Mark: Appendix 1, fig. 6a, b stamped on underside
Silver
H. 16 in (40.6 cm), W. 10 in (25.4 cm), D. 10 in (25.4 cm); Wt. 101 oz. 10 dwt. Troy
Private collection

In 1788 Ann Warder of Philadelphia wrote in her journal that she purchased a new silver hot water urn that she placed on the pembroke table in her best parlor. She recorded that "our new urn [is] a piece of furniture much admired & for this country particularly convenient, coffee being mostly used . . . [my uncle has] requested us to order one for each of his Daughters exactly like it."[1] Her enthusiasm was understandable, for as noted by authors on the subject, hot water, coffee, or tea urns held a respected place in the parlors and dining rooms of fashionable and well-to-do householders from about the middle of the eighteenth century until well after this example was made.

These urns typically held from two to three quarts of

water, which was kept hot by various means. The earliest was with an iron slug that was heated and placed in a central compartment. Alternatively, water could be kept hot by means of a small charcoal fire, like those used in braziers. Although these worked well, care had to be taken because of the carbon monoxide that charcoal fires produced. However, "tea urns with lamps and burners [as illustrated here] are by far the most satisfactory in use" because they burn clean and are easy to maintain.[2] The fuel reservoir was always placed directly under the water container. It had a separate lid pierced with a small

diameter tube that held a woven strip of fabric, which burned as a wick. The reservoir, being small, was removable so that it could be refilled without disturbing the water supply. These burners were fueled with alcohol or spirits of wine.

This urn has a removable lid so that it can be refilled when needed, and two loop handles facilitate its being carried from one location to another. It is ornamented largely with stylized leaves, the most dramatic of which is the die-stamped asymmetrically scrolled acanthus border that prominently encircles the body.

48. PAIR OF SAUCEBOATS AND STANDS, 1827–35

Inscription: *B* engraved on both sides of sauceboats
Mark: Appendix 1, fig. 9a stamped on underside of sauceboats and stands
Silver
H. 6 in (15.2 cm), L. 9½ in (24.1 cm), W. 4⅛ in (10.5 cm); Wt. 18 oz. 11 dwt. Troy (sauceboats)
H. ½ in (1.2 cm), L. 10¼ in (26 cm), W. 6 in (15.2 cm); Wt. 13 oz. 11 dwt. Troy (stands)
Ruth J. Nutt Collection of American Silver

Mrs. Richard Ashhurst, wife of a successful silk and dry goods merchant in Philadelphia, purchased a considerable amount of silver from Fletcher & Gardiner during the 1820s and 1830s. Among the many stylish household objects was a six-piece set, comprising a coffeepot, teapot and hot water pot, sugar bowl, slop bowl, and cream ewer. The bill for this set noted that the maker included "3 pair ivory tenons for handles of tea pots."[1] These became necessary when silver handles began to replace wood handles on tea- and coffeepots about 1820. Whereas

wood handles remained cool to the touch, those of silver did not. This was remedied by the insertion of ivory tenons or ferrules, which acted as insulators.

Previously she had purchased "1 pair sauceboats, silver, wt. 42.10 [oz] @ $2.25 = $95.12." Those sauceboats may have looked like this pair with silver handles designed and fabricated as if they had ivory tenons in them like those that held silver handles to fashionable tea- and coffeepots.[2]

Sauceboats such as these were a popular accoutrement on fashionable American dining tables. While some householders owned single examples, many preferred them in pairs. This pair rests on accompanying stands with centers that have been dished to fit the base of each. These stands were typically made en suite; they facilitated passing from diner to diner and caught errant drippings.

The lip and foot of each sauceboat, as well as the edge of their stands, have been reinforced with die-rolled ornamental borders. In addition, both sides of each sauceboat have a leafy wreath hammered in repoussé, enclosing the owner's initial, *B*.[3]

---

49. SIX-PIECE TEA AND COFFEE SET, 1827–35

Inscription: a coat of arms (ermine, on a fess sable three crescents argent); a crest (a chevalier on horseback, his spear in bend); and motto, *VIVE DEO UT VITAS* engraved on side of coffeepot and cream pot
Mark: Appendix 1, fig. 9a stamped on underside of each
Silver, ivory

H. 12¾ in (32.4 cm), W. 8¾ in (22.2 cm), Diam. 5 in (12.7 cm); Wt. 53 oz. Troy (coffeepot, gross)
H. 9 in (22.9 cm), W. 10⅝ in (27 cm), Diam. 6¼ in (15.9 cm); Wt. 41 oz. 10 dwt. Troy (teapot, gross)
H. 9 in (22.9 cm), W. 11⅝ in (29.5 cm), Diam. 6⅜ in (16.2 cm); Wt. 41 oz. 14 dwt. Troy (teapot, gross)
H. 9⅛ in (23.2 cm), W. 7¼ in (18.4 cm), Diam. 6⅛ in (15.6

cm); Wt. 32 oz. 14 dwt. Troy (sugar bowl)
H. 6⅞ in (17.5 cm), W. 6⅝ in (16.8 cm), Diam. 3⅞ in (9.8 cm); Wt. 13 oz. 5 dwt. Troy (cream pot)
H. 6 in (15.2 cm), Diam. 7¼ in (18.4 cm); Wt. 26 oz. 10 dwt. Troy (slop bowl)
Philadelphia Museum of Art, Promised gift of Cordelia Biddle Dietrich, Mr. and Mrs. H. Richard Dietrich III, and Christian Braun Dietrich in memory of Livingston L. Biddle, Jr. and in honor of Cordelia Frances Biddle 120-1991-1-6

The craftsmen in Thomas Fletcher's silversmithing establishment made this set in response to the longstanding and widespread popularity of tea and coffee in America. Tea and coffee sets could be made of porcelain, earthenware, pewter, or fused plate, but silver proved to be a favored choice because of the social status its value bestowed. The coffeepot and cream pot are engraved with the coat of arms of a member of the Craig family of Philadelphia, probably James Craig (born 1787) or his brother, John C. Craig (1802–40), both of whom were recorded as gentlemen living in the city at the time this set was made.[1]

The makers fashioned the bodies of the two teapots, sugar bowl, cream pot, and slop bowl into modified vase shapes popular at the time. They could have done a larger version of the same for the coffeepot but chose instead to design it after tall, double-bellied examples made by Philadelphia silversmiths fifty to eighty years earlier. The handle, though silver instead of wood, and handle sockets also recall eighteenth-century Philadelphia design. The spout is an even closer interpretation, seemingly an identical copy of those used by Joseph and Nathaniel Richardson between 1777 and 1790.[2]

All the bodies of these vessels are enriched with a meander of grape leaves and clusters encircling their outermost diameter. Fletcher & Gardiner began to incorporate this ornamental feature into their work during the mid-1820s, and it appears to have received a popular response judging from the frequency of its use through the mid-1830s. Illustrative is a letter Fletcher wrote to John B. Jones in Boston on September 25, 1829, in which he noted, "I have a set of plate consisting of coffee pot, tea, sugar & cream weighing oz 113 at [$] 1.85 wholesale with large grape leaves on the body. Shall I send it to you?"[3]

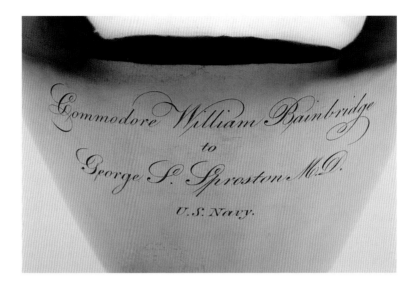

50. JUG, 1828–33
Inscription: *Commodore William Bainbridge / to / George S. Sproston M.D. / U.S. Navy* engraved under spout
Mark: Appendix 1, fig. 11a, b stamped on underside
Silver
H. 7½ in (19 cm), W. 8½ in (21.6 cm), Diam. 6 in. (15.2 cm); Wt. 28 oz. Troy
Private collection

Immediately following the War of 1812, British potters began making creamware jugs with transfer-printed images of American naval heroes to send to the United States, where they were enthusiastically purchased. Their jugs vary in design, but the example seen here was one of the most popular shapes—a broad inverted baluster with short cylindrical neck, arched spout, and C-shape handle.

"The first American hero to be shown [on these jugs] is *Commodore William Bainbridge* named above his bust and surrounded by naval symbols." This must have been very gratifying to Bainbridge (1774–1833), who was vain and proud of his successful but somewhat checkered naval career.[1] Perhaps his most glorious deed occurred on December 29, 1812, when as commander of the *Constitution* off the coast of Brazil he engaged and sank the British frigate *Java*. This event, during which he was twice wounded, spurred English creamware manufacturers to memorialize him on their jugs.

Undoubtedly, both Bainbridge and Fletcher were familiar with imported creamware jugs when the former commissioned this example from the latter.[2] Except for small differences in the design of the handle, the base, and the application of two patterns of borders, this jug is closely related to creamware examples.

Bainbridge spent time in Philadelphia during his career and was assigned command of the Philadelphia Navy Yard from 1828 until 1832, when he was reassigned to the Boston Navy Yard. He held that post for only one year and returned to Philadelphia. During his later years he was in declining health and required doctors' care regularly. This silver jug was a gift to George S. Sproston (d. 1842), a naval physician who attended him.

51. VASE, 1829

Inscription: *Presented to Hugh Maxwell, Esq.', by the Merchants of the City of New York in testimony of / their high opinion of the* ABILITY, FIRMNESS, INDUSTRY, PERSEVERENCE, & PUBLIC-SPIRIT / *exhibited by him in the discharge of his duties as District Attorney. AD 1829* engraved on plinth; later inscriptions: *I give to the President of the Law Institute of the City of New York and to his successors in office my silver / vase given as a mark of regard for professional services as District Attorney by the Merchants of the City of / New York while acting as such under the appointment of Governors Tompkins and Clinton I also / give to the said Institute the portraits of Kent and Emmett my honored friends; and EXTRACT FROM THE LAST / WILL AND TESTAMENT / OF / Hugh Maxwell / WHO DIED / March 31, 1873.* engraved on ends and back of plinth
Mark: Appendix 1, fig. 25a, b
Silver and iron
H. 24¼ in (61.6 cm), W. 20½ in (52.1 cm), D. 17¾ in (45.1 cm); Wt. 356 oz. 15 dwt. Troy
Collection of The New-York Historical Society, L.1959.5

Public enthusiasm for rewarding merit extended from military successes to legal conflicts, as with this vase given to Hugh Maxwell (1787–1873) shortly after his retirement as a New York district attorney. When investor Henry Eckford became embroiled in bailing out the failing Life and Fire Insurance Company directed by Jacob Barker, Maxwell prosecuted Barker for fraud during the so-called conspiracy cases. Both Eckford and Maxwell received splendid silver vases from their supporters following the bitter battles. The vases were announced in the press and emblematically reinforced public opinion of each man's character. One paper remarked about the Maxwell vase: "It is, indeed not only a well merited compliment to an excellent officer, that must be gratifying to him, but it displays a disposition and spirit on the part of our citizens to rally around and support the administration of justice, that we cannot too highly applaud."[1]

A conspiratorial aspect of these vases was the role undertaken by Baldwin Gardiner, Sidney's brother and owner of the store in New York to which both commissions came. Baldwin directed Eckford's vase to local silversmiths and secretly wrote Thomas Fletcher to arrange for Maxwell's. His letter to Fletcher reveals the competitive silver trade between cities: "None of the silversmiths here know that I have the order, as several of them wd. drop the hammer for me, if they knew I sent to Philad."[2] In response, Fletcher designed a magnificent, soaring centerpiece that cleverly supports a Warwick-style bowl on the tails of reposing sphinxes.

Regal in scale, Maxwell's vase reflects Fletcher's talent for drawing inspiration from European and classical silver design and recombining elements for an overall sumptuous effect. New chased border-and-leaf designs, new patterns for handles based loosely on the Warwick vase, and cascading foliate and paw feet as well as an ingeniously masked support for the heavy bowl indicate a significant investment of workshop artistry and labor.

The sphinx figures draw upon familiar Egyptian motifs but are an unusual blend of Egyptian male torsos with wings more typical of female Greek sphinxes.[3] The sphinx, a symbol of eternal wisdom, echoed currents of archaeological interest in the arts but also might allude to Maxwell's professional discernment.

52. FLAGON, 1829

Inscription: *Trinity Church Pittsburgh: Incorporated A.D. 1805*; triangle enclosing Hebrew letters engraved on side

Marks: Appendix 1, fig. 6a, b; scratched inside foot: 352.4 dwt

Silver

H. 13½ in.; Wt. 52 oz. 8 dwt. Troy

Episcopal Diocese of Pittsburgh, Trinity Cathedral Collection

Shortly after his installment as priest of Trinity parish in Pittsburgh in 1825, Reverend John H. Hopkins (1792–1868) designed and oversaw construction of the new Trinity Church, down to the last details of ordering communion silver. In 1829 he requested this statuesque wine flagon as well as a paten, two chalices, and a scalloped plate from Fletcher & Gardiner, instructing them to be made "as handsome & rich in their aspect as those of St. Stephen's Church, and light enough not to exceed the price limited $300." This flagon with a grape cluster finial draws upon French pitcher designs and reflects the firm's penchant for smooth expanses of silver relieved by concentrated passages of ornament. It is not surprising that the firm used this same overall design for a household pitcher, a practice in keeping with interchangeable domestic and ecclesiastical forms in colonial America.[1]

A common theme in Thomas Fletcher's letters to patrons is the defense of higher-than-expected cost due to the weight or gauge of silver the workshop deemed appropriate for vessels. In his explanation enclosed with the silver for Reverend Hopkins, Fletcher wrote: "I hope [the silver] will meet your approbation. The amount is greater than you wished but the articles could not be made lighter without reducing their size or making them too thin for durability either of which would be objectionable."[2] The flagon cost approximately $100.

Reverend Hopkins's commission occurred during an epoch of religious fervor known as the Second Great Awakening. As informal revivals were sweeping less-urban regions, Pittsburgh's Trinity parish established itself and gave rise to the current cathedral. Revealing a deliberate sense of historicism, this flagon is engraved with the date of the parish's founding, 1805, as well as the Hebrew letters for the sacred name of God, inside a triangle.

53. SWORD and SCABBARD, 1829

Blade inscription: PRESENTED BY THE STATE OF
MARYLAND TO / Lieut.t Henry E. Ballard. MARCH
1828. as the / reward of Patriotism and Valor etched on
side; verso: E Pluribus / Unum; and Constitution/Cyane
& Levant etched on opposite side
Mark: Appendix 1, fig. 29a stamped incuse on blade
Sword: gold, steel; scabbard: leather, gold, brass
L. 32½ in (82.6 cm), W. 5 in (12.7 cm)
Ruth J. Nutt Collection of American Silver

Although firepower and shorter blades for combat
displaced the cut-and-thrust sword, its lean elegant form,
fine steel blade, and figural pommel remained resplendent
parts of an officer's military dress.[1] The cast-and-chased
gold hilt, etched blade decoration, and gold scabbard
mounts of this presentation sword represent superlative
work by several artisans. Fletcher & Gardiner designed the
whole, created the gold elements, and collaborated with
cutlers William Rose & Sons and etcher John Meer (d.
1834) for the blade. Bald eagles (one on the pommel,
three on the counter guard, and one the blade) blend
patriotic iconography with naval and mythological images
on the hilt and blade. This synthesis of ornament and style
reflects a high point for the firm's sword designs.

Henry Ballard's was one of three swords requested
from Fletcher & Gardiner in 1828 by the state of
Maryland. Letters between Governor Daniel Martin's
secretary and Thomas Fletcher describe this sword,

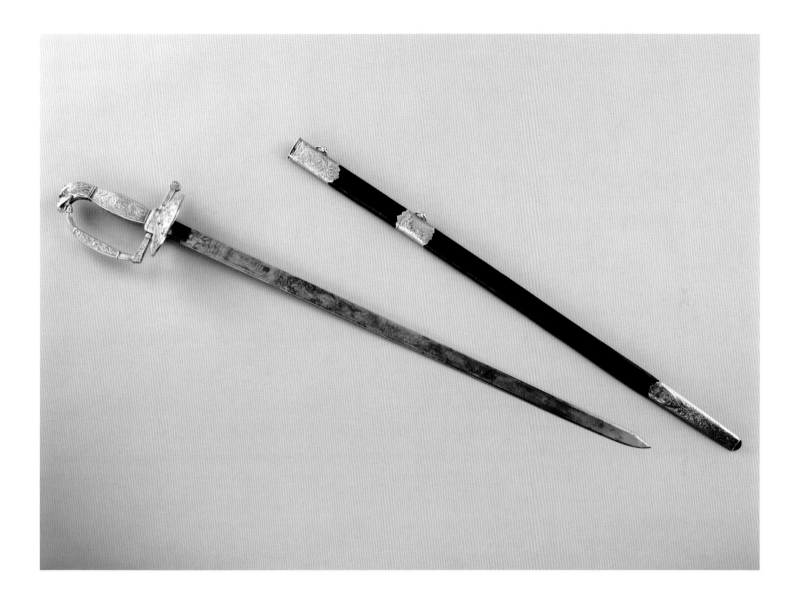

which recognizes Ballard's service on the *Constitution*.[2] Ballard served under Captain Charles Stewart in February 1815, when they challenged two British vessels in a twilight chase off the coast of Portugal. Stewart placed Ballard as captain on the *Levant*, which he commanded until recaptured.

Ballard received this sword fourteen years later in the Annapolis council chambers. Governor Martin declared: "On you sir, is bestowed the richest reward the patriot asks, the gratitude and applause of his countrymen, of which this sword is intended to be the testimonial." Henry Ballard responded: "It will be a source of lasting gratification to reflect that for an achievement in which I bore an humble part (and in which many of the brave sons of Maryland participated,) the legislature of my native state, has bestowed upon me, a vote of thanks and this sword. I accept and shall preserve it, as the most valued gift of my generous country men."[3]

54. PORTION OF TABLE SERVICE, 1825–40

Inscription: a coat of arms (argent, a cross crosslet sable and in chief gules a lion passant guardant or); a crest (on a helm out of a ducal coronet a griffin's head between wings, and a vacant banner), all engraved on both sides of soup tureen, under spout of sauceboat, both sides of sauce tureen, and twice on brim of dish

Mark: Appendix 1, fig. 9a stamped on underside of soup tureen, on underside of sauceboat and stand, on underside of sauce tureen, on underside of dish; figs. 11a, b stamped on underside of sauce tureen stand, on underside of oblong vegetable dish; fig. 10 stamped twice on underside of elliptic vegetable dish brim; figs. 6a, b stamped on underside of lidded bowl

Silver

H. 13 in (33 cm), L. 14⅞ in (37.8 cm), D. 8⅝ in (21.9 cm); Wt. 112 oz. Troy (soup tureen)

H. 7⅞ in (20 cm), L. 8 in (20.3 cm), W. 4⅛ in (10.5 cm); Wt. 27 oz. 10 dwt. Troy, (sauceboat)

L. 9¼ in (23.5 cm), W. 5⅜ in (13.6 cm), H. ½ in (1.2 cm); Wt. 11 oz. Troy (sauceboat stand)

H. 7½ in (19 cm), L. 8⅛ in (20.6 cm), W. 4⅜ in (11.1 cm); Wt. 28 oz. Troy, (sauce tureen)

L. 9¼ in (23.5 cm), W. 5⅜ in (13.6 cm), H. ½ in (1.2 cm); Wt. 13 oz. Troy (sauce tureen stand)

H. 5⅛ in (13 cm), L. 11¾ in (29.8 cm), W. 9¼ in (23.5 cm); Wt. 74 oz. Troy (oblong vegetable dish)

H. 5½ in (14 cm), L. 12⅝ in (32.1 cm), W. 9 in (22.9 cm); Wt. 70 oz. 10 dwt. Troy (elliptic vegetable dish)

L. 22¼ in (56.5 cm), W. 15 in (38.1 cm), H. 1½ in (3.8 cm); Wt. 110 oz. Troy (elliptic dish)

H. 8¼ in (21 cm), W. 13½ in (34.3 cm), Diam. 10⅜ in (26.4 cm); Wt. 81 oz. Troy (lidded bowl)

The Athenaeum of Philadelphia, Gift of Mary Radclyffe Furness Savage in Memory of Natalie Chauncey Pierrepont

The objects seen here are part of a large and impressive table service consisting of two soup tureens, two sauceboats and stands, two sauce tureens and stands, four lidded oblong vegetable dishes, two lidded elliptic vegetable dishes, a

lidded bowl, two large elliptic dishes, two medium dishes, and a footed circular salver, all made in Fletcher & Gardiner's establishment. A pair of monteiths by French silversmith Jean-Baptiste-Claude Odiot accompanies them.

All were owned by Charles Chauncey (1777–1849) whose coat of arms is engraved on most of the pieces.[1] Chauncey lived at 87 Walnut Street in Philadelphia and was a lawyer by profession. Thomas Fletcher and Sidney Gardiner were among his many clients. He provided the partners with valuable advice and representation in several legal matters during the 1820s and 1830s.

As indicated by the size and cost of this service, determined by weight, Chauncey was eminently successful and entertained on a lavish scale. A large table would have been needed to accommodate this service in conjunction with plates, flatware, glasses, and centerpiece. An insight into the appearance of Chauncey's dining table set with Fletcher & Gardiner's silver might be gained through the survival of a pencil sketch of the table of his contemporary, Dr. James Rush, who lived at 1914 Chesnut Street. Rush's cloth-draped pedestal table is densely set with a multitude of stylish and useful accoutrements. This service remained in use in the Chauncy family through several generations until it was given in 1993 to the Athenaeum of Philadelphia, of which Chauncey was a founding member.[2]

---

55. TWO TABLE FORKS, 1829–35

Inscription: a crest (a boot with a spur) engraved on handle backs
Mark: Appendix 1, fig. 10 stamped on back of each
Silver
L. 8¼ in (21 cm), W. 1⅛ in (2.8 cm); Wt. 3 oz. 10 dwt. Troy each
Private collection

Spoons and forks with so-called fiddle handles with a double-thread outline and scallop-shell tip appeared in France during the mid-eighteenth century. The design found its way into English silversmiths' work by about 1800. By 1820 thread-and-shell flatware was being made in Philadelphia and New York.[1]

Of the spoons and forks in this pattern made in the United States prior to 1840, Fletcher & Gardiner's are the most beautifully designed and executed, as illustrated by this massive pair from a surviving group of eleven made for George Archibald McCall (1802–68). The quality of the firm's flatware was recognized and acknowledged at the time, evidenced by the surviving number of examples bearing their mark. Charles W. Short of Lexington, Kentucky, was among those who felt that Fletcher & Gardiner's flatware was the best to be had. On August 14, 1833, he had an intermediary write, "My friend C. W. Short asks and desires me to obtain from you 1 Doz Silver tablespoons [and] 1 Doz Ditto Tea Ditto of the above pattern."[2] The pattern carefully and precisely drawn at the head of the letter is a thread-and-shell spoon.

Fletcher invariably answered such inquiries quickly and in detail. Typical is a letter he penned to Richard S. Smith of Philadelphia, which reads "I have had sketches made of 2 patt[ern]s of silver forks . . . I subjoin a list of forks, spoons &c. The prices of plain thread and thread and shell patt[er]n are the same to wit:

table forks and spoons at $70 per doz
dessert   "   50   "

All the articles are die hardened, as we term it, which renders the silver as firm and elastick as the finest hardened steel. If you honor me with your order you may depend on receiving silver ware of a superior quality and of the finest workmanship."[3] Solicitous correspondence such as this, in addition to the objects themselves, clearly indicates that Fletcher took great pride in the quality of the spoons and forks made in his establishment.

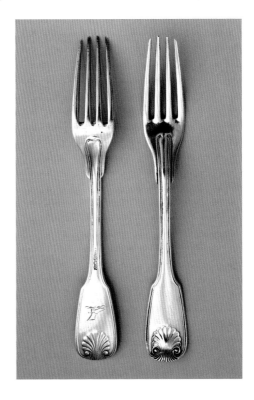

56. VASE, 1830

Inscription: *Presented by the Stockholders / of the late bank of the United States to / JAMES C. FISHER, ESQ. / in testimony of his faithful and / judicious administration / as one of the Trustees. / March 1, 1830.* engraved

Mark: Appendix 1, figs. 6a, 10 (four impressions) stamped on underside

Silver

H. 21½ in (54.6 cm), W. 13 in (33 cm); Wt. 153 oz. 2 dwt. Troy

The Historical Society of Pennsylvania, Atwater Kent Museum, Miss Edith S. Fisher and Mrs. Cyril Fisher Morand, 1928

Following the War of 1812, Philadelphia's business community perpetuated the impulse for civic celebration in silver recognizing feats of engineering and business leadership. Wing-footed Mercury (minus his caduceus and bag of money), the Greco-Roman deity associated with merchants, gold, and travel, appropriately tops a covered vase awarded by the stockholders of the old First Bank of the United States to James C. Fisher (1754–1840). Fisher served as one of the founding directors from 1791. The bank building (completed 1797) was one of Philadelphia's earliest neoclassical marble façades and is depicted on three sides of the base in oval cartouches surrounded by floral swags and a basket of flowers.[1]

Fisher and eleven other trustees were recognized by stockholders in 1830 with a choice between $500 or a silver award costing that amount. Fisher opted for silver

and chose the Fletcher & Gardiner firm to make the presentation vase. The resulting new design became an unofficial standard for civic presentation vases in Philadelphia for the next few years.[2]

Fisher's vase incorporates chased egg-and-dart molding, entwined grape-stalk handles with die-stamped grapevines encircling the body, and a square platform base mounted on paw feet—all elements related to the Clinton vases (see cat. no. 43). The overall scale is shorter and lighter with a vertical emphasis; however, the echo of Clinton's vases is seen in ornament as well as the subsequent creation of a mate to this vase. Fisher had been instrumental in directing the Chesapeake and Delaware Canal project, and the award of a nearly identical vase within the same year as this one from the First Bank prompts speculation about his wish for a pair of vases not unlike the more famous pair.

191

57. VASE, 1830

Inscription: *Presented by the Proprietors / of the Chesapeake and Delaware Canal to /* JAMES C. FISHER, ESQ. */ in testimony of his faithful and / useful Services / as President of the Company / June 7, 1830.* engraved
Mark: Appendix 1, figs. 6a, b, 10 stamped on underside
Silver
H. 21 in (53.3 cm), W. 12¼ in (31.1 cm); Wt. 144 oz. 15 dwt. Troy
Yale University Art Gallery, Gift of Joseph B. Brenauer, 1942.245

A committee of investors in the long-awaited canal connecting the Delaware River to the Chesapeake Bay recognized outgoing company president James Fisher (1754–1840) with an award of plate. Overall this vase is nearly identical to the award given to Fisher by the First Bank of the United States in the same year (see cat. no. 56). The dimensions, wrought bowls, chased acanthus and water-leaf ornament, stamped grape leaves, handles, and borders are remarkably close, but the lid sports a cast figure of Neptune (minus his trident), and the base has a view of the canal and a reclining river deity in an elliptic cartouche bolted to the sides. Appropriately, Neptune and the river deity symbolize the canal project's intended mastery over the flow of water for commercial benefit.[1]

These weighty vases given to Fisher by two separate committees provide insight to the interaction between the Fletcher & Gardiner workshop and an award recipient. Local patrons conducted business in person, thus this communication rarely survives. A copy of a letter from Thomas Fletcher to Fisher indicates that the canal committee appropriated only $350 toward this award. Fletcher wrote to Fisher asking whether he would supply the remaining balance ($150) personally to settle the bill.[2] It is probable that Fisher desired a pair of equal weight vases rather than a second one of smaller scale. His personal opinion and financial contribution influenced the resulting vase.

Fletcher did not engrave the firm's name on either of the vases for Fisher. Instead, they bear recently created "hallmarks" featuring his initials in addition to the round Fletcher & Gardiner mark. Although his deceased partner's name remained on the storefront, Fletcher began using his name alone to guarantee the workshop's silver.

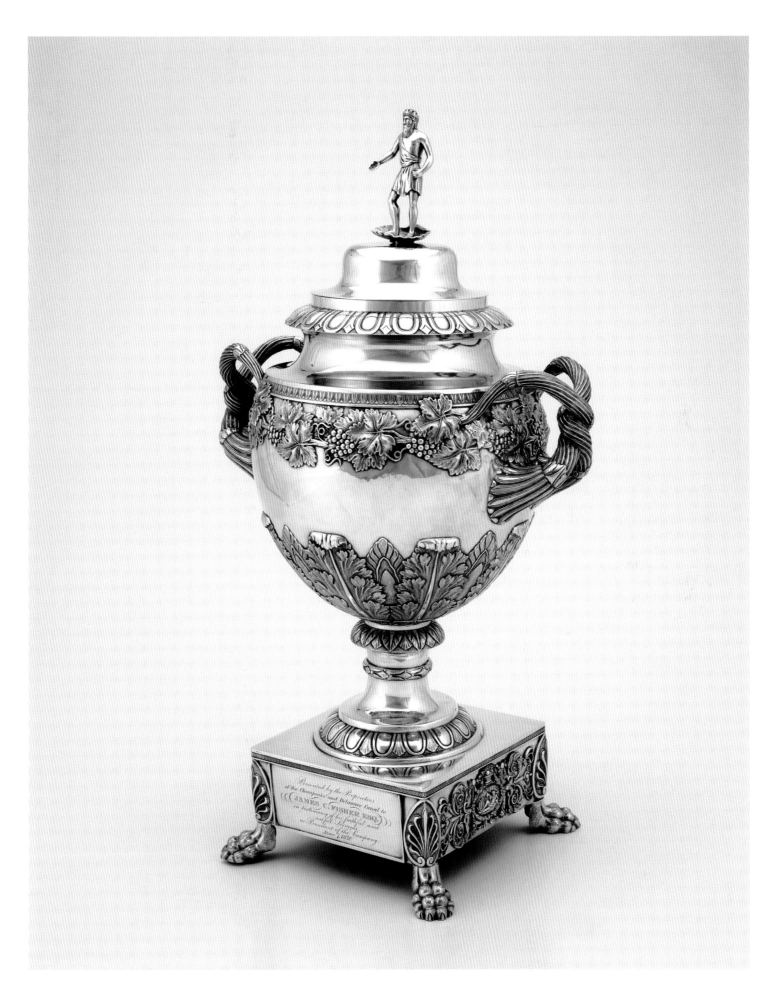

58. VASE, 1830

Inscription: *Presented / by the Stockholders of the /* SCHUYLKILL NAVIGATION COMPANY / to / CADWALADER EVANS, ESQ., / *their late President.*; and *In testimony of / their respect and gratitude for his long continued / faithful and laborious services in that capacity / as well as for the valuable support and aid / he has at all times given to this great /* PUBLIC WORK engraved on side
Mark: Appendix 1, fig. 10 (four impressions) stamped on underside
Silver
H. 21¼ in (54 cm), W. 13 in (33 cm); Wt. 160 oz. 8 dwt. Troy
The Historical Society of Pennsylvania, Atwater Kent Museum, Mrs. J. de Forest and Mrs. H.V.C. Ogden, 1939

Canal fever, energized by the opening of the Erie Canal, manifested itself in Baltimore and Philadelphia as a possible answer to widespread commercial depression in the 1820s. Seeking water-borne connections to Philadelphia for inland agricultural and natural resources, Schuylkill Navigation Company stockholders financed canals connected to the Schuylkill River. Cadwalader Evans, Jr. (1762–1841) served as the company's first president, and he received this presentation vase in 1830, the year he retired.[1]

Evans, like James Fisher, was an influential participant in the region's financial networks, and his vase followed quickly on the heels of Fisher's awards (see cat. nos. 56, 57). Variations in design distinguish the vases, but Thomas Fletcher clearly created an overall form that appealed to the city's business leaders. Just three years later, in 1833, the Schuylkill Navigation Company commissioned five identical vases to present to their retiring officers (see cat. no. 70).

Representing fertile agricultural markets, the allegorical figure atop this vase, Plenty, holds a cornucopia next to an overturned water vessel. Both upper sides of the wrought bowl are engraved with

dedications to Evans, freeing all sides of the platform base for chased pictorial ornament. These softly rendered, naturalistic panels bolted to the base add an element of the picturesque to a decidedly neoclassical vase.

The waterscapes were directly connected to Evans's canal legacy and juxtapose American scenery with antique references on the vase. The Upper Ferry's covered bridge and an aqueduct, if not all four panels (two views of falls), closely resemble lithographs created by Philadelphia artist George Lehman (d. 1870) published in 1829. They also reflect Fletcher's connections with Philadelphia's thriving print industry. He subscribed to the *Views of Philadelphia and Its Environs* project published by Cephas Childs in 1830; Childs's partner for a time in the 1830s was George Lehman.

59. SILVER-HILT SWORD, 1830–40

Inscription: none
Mark: Appendix 1, fig. 11a, b stamped on underside of quillon
Silver, steel, wood
L. 31⅝ in (80.3 cm), W. 3¾ in (9.5 cm), D. 1⅛ in (2.9 cm); wt. unknown
Collection of Robert Jackson/Ann Gillooly, Inc.

Silver-hilt swords had been the provenance of gentlemen and military officers in Europe since the fifteenth century. That tradition came to America with the first European settlers, though the sword largely disappeared as an item of dress for gentlemen in America by 1800. Conversely, the tradition was strongly perpetuated with the advent of several American military branches following independence. Swords, sometimes identified as sabers if with a curved blade, remained a significant part of American military equipment, both practical and ceremonial, until their use was abolished in 1942.

The hilt of this sword, employing a twisted, wire-wrapped black wooden grip, strap-like knuckle guard and quillon with simple voluted terminal, and dramatically defined eagle-head pommel, accords generally with federal regulations governing the design of officers' edged weapons between 1813 and 1841 and specifically with weapons made in Philadelphia during that time. It could be an artillery officer's or, alternately, a naval officer's sword, but it is difficult to state with certainty since "officers had to purchase their swords from outside the government. Thus their choice could only be directed through the passing of regulations. Prior to 1840 these regulations . . . were very general in their wording [and] there was a tendency among many officers to ignore the regulations and carry the sword of their own choice."[1]

Fletcher & Gardiner manufactured a large number of gold-hilt presentation swords given to heroes of the War of 1812 by state governments. The fame that accrued the firm because of these commissions encouraged military officers to seek them out for silver-hilt examples as well. Fletcher and Gardiner actively cultivated this aspect of the business, as recorded in an advertisement that states they "offer a general assortment of GOODS in their line on the most reasonable terms wholesale and retail–viz – . . . Best Gilt and plate Cut and Thrust Swords with eagle heads, ivory grips and blue and gilt blades."[2]

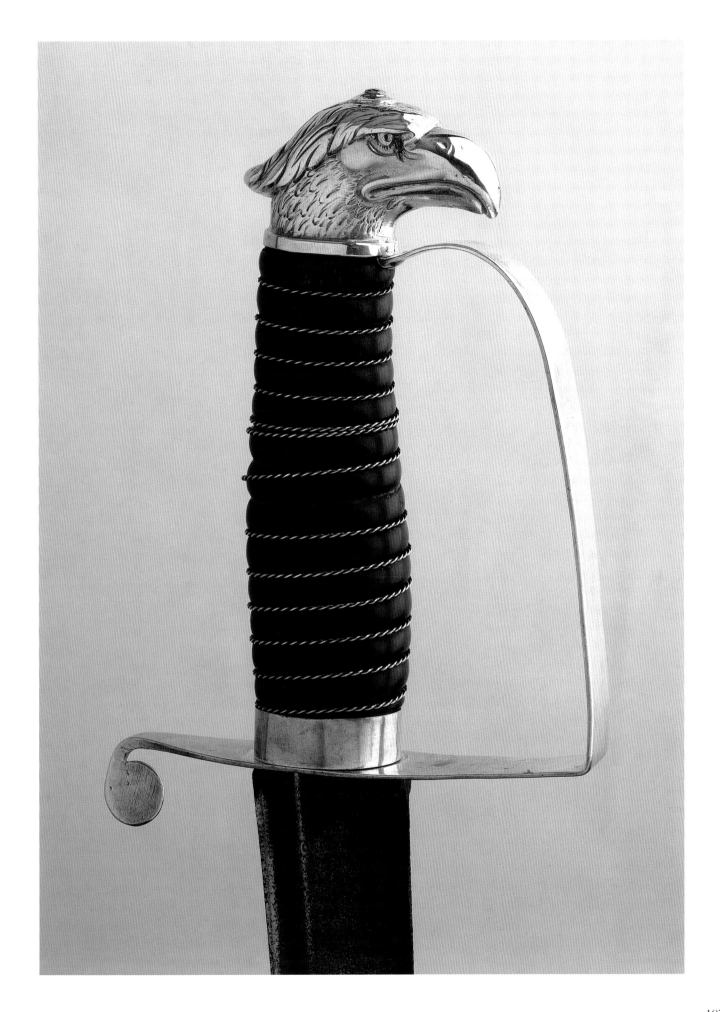

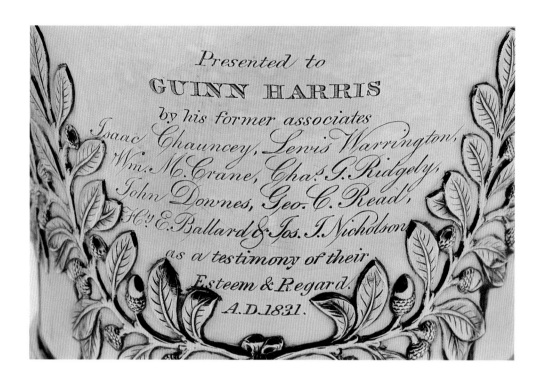

60. VASE, 1831

Inscription: *Presented to / GUINN HARRIS / by his former associates / Isaac Chauncey, Lewis Warrington, / Wm. M. Crane, Chas. G. Ridgeley, / John Downes, Geo. C. Read, / Hy. E. Ballard & Jos. J. Nicholson / as a testimony of their / Esteem & Regard. / A.D. 1831.* engraved on side
Mark: Appendix 1, fig. 6a, b stamped on underside
Silver
H. 12¼ in (31.1 cm), W. 8½ in (21.6 cm); Wt. 58 oz. 14 dwt. Troy
The Maryland Historical Society, Bequest of Mrs. Mattie M. Key, 1942.10.36

In addition to public subscription or state-legislated commissions, Fletcher & Gardiner fashioned silver as gifts between military colleagues, such as the vase (or wine cooler) awarded to Gwinn Harris of Maryland in 1831. Harris served as a naval purser from April 25, 1812, until September 29, 1830. Eight of his colleagues, all distinguished War of 1812 officers, united their names with his in the inscription, which likely reflects Harris's retirement. The donors knew of Fletcher & Gardiner's presentation vases, and several of these men conducted other business with the firm.[1]

Alternating passages of hand-chased and die-rolled borders visually punctuate the smooth surfaces of this vase. The encircling repoussé acorn and oak-leaf swags allude to the mighty oak-like strength of the navy. A tiny oak-and-acorn, die-rolled border echoes this motif on the base. The oak swags and layers of waterleaf and acanthus encircling the bowl indicate the investment in talented hand-chasing artistry and labor. The body is composed of two primary sections with a horizontal seam at the waist, and the pedestal foot is formed from three separate parts.

Thomas Fletcher's letters from this era reveal difficulties in finding engravers and chasers to work for the manufactory. This vase for Harris evidences a rare lapse in the firm's attentiveness by the misspelling of his name. Fletcher's solicitous letter to Henry Ballard explained the mishap: "Since the Vase has been finished it has been discovered that the second letter of Mr. Harris's name should be W instead of U–I send you the original manuscript Inscription enclosed, which appears to be as the engraving, if there is a mistake I regret it, & would have corrected it but for the impossibility of so doing without producing a blemish more conspicuous than the mistake itself. It may be done at some future time, when the vase may require refinishing."[2]

Presented to
GUINN HARRIS
by his former associates
James Chauncey, Lewis Warrington,
Wm M. Crane, Chas G. Ridgely,
John Downes, Geo. C. Read,
... Ballard & Jos. A. Nicholson,
as a testimony of their
Esteem & Regard.
A.D. 1831

199

61. WINE COOLER, 1832–33

Inscription: none
Mark: Appendix 1, fig. 10 stamped on side of base
Silver
H. 11 in (27.9 cm), W. 9¼ in (23.5 cm), Diam. 9 in (22.9 cm); Wt. 108 oz. 10 dwt. Troy
Private collection

Richard Singleton (1776–1852), who lived near Statesburg in Sumpter County, South Carolina, was enamored of thoroughbred horses and deeply committed to racing. His plantation, called Home Place, later Singleton Hall, supported an extensive stable of finely bred horses from which he took the best to Charleston every year to compete in the Jockey Club races. Singleton also raced regularly at Saratoga, New York. He enjoyed a large measure of success in these competitions throughout the 1820s and 1830s, with many winning horses.

His most successful effort occurred in 1827. In February of that year his horses Red Gauntlet, Ariel, and Kosciusko won every day at the five-day Jockey Club meet in Charleston. This remarkable feat was achieved by only two others in the annals of American horseracing history, Wade Hampton and James Richardson. Silver

trophies and/or monetary purses were presented to the winners of these events, a tradition that continues to this day. No trophy is recorded in association with Singleton's sweep at Charleston in 1827, indicating he probably received a large monetary purse. If so, he may have used a portion of it to purchase this wine cooler and a now-lost mate from Thomas Fletcher.[1]

This wine cooler consists of four parts, the principal one being the extensively decorated calyx krater-form vase. It is fitted with a removable lip with a broad egg-and-dart molding on the upper surface. With the lip removed, the vase will accept the third part, a plain cylindrical insert, the lower end of which is held in alignment by a shallow-lip pan bolted inside the bottom of the body (detail). Water poured into the vase keeps a wine bottle in the insert cold. When the removable lip is put in place, it holds the upper end of the insert firmly in place and provides a finished appearance.

Both sides of the vase between and slightly above the reeded loop handles have a large elliptic reserve encircled by an engraved oak branch and wheat sheaf bound together. While one of these reserves is vacant, the other, in accordance with popular tradition, depicts two racehorses at full gallop being spurred on by their jockeys.

62. SOUP TUREEN, 1830–40

Inscription: none
Mark: Appendix 1, fig. 10 stamped on outside edge
Silver
H. 11 in (27.9 cm), W. 12⅞ in (32.7 cm), Diam. 10 in
(25.4 cm); Wt. 105 oz. Troy
Private collection

With the growing popularity of soup as a fashionable course on European dining tables during the eighteenth century, soup tureens became increasingly necessary; many were made of silver. They were typically made in pairs or larger numbers. The tradition of the soup course as a distinct part of fashionable dining quickly transferred to America, with the result that numbers of American silversmiths supplied tureens to their customers, though very few are known to date from the eighteenth century. By the beginning of the nineteenth century, American silversmiths were being called upon increasingly to supply them, none more than Fletcher and Gardiner.[1]

On June 18, 1830, Fletcher wrote to John Linton in New Orleans that "The service of plate which you were pleased to order in October last to be presented to Beverly Chew Esq is now on board the Ship Chester to sail tomorrow for your port . . . The soup tureens weigh about 22 oz more than the estimate & I have reduced the price to $1.93½ pr oz so that the charge for workmanship remains the same." Again on May 24, 1834, Fletcher wrote to Linton that "Enclosed I hand you a Bill of Lading and invoice of one box containing [another] pair of silver soup tureens being part of your esteemed order."[2]

This tureen, one of a pair bearing Fletcher's mark, follows French design precedent in its squat body on pedestal, austere decoration, and strongly upswept lid with stylized cauliflower-like finial atop a plateau.[3] Fletcher may have seen a drawing for such a tureen or an actual example in French silver during one of his two business trips to Paris, one in 1815 and the other in 1825.

63. TRAY, 1830–33

Inscription: a coat of arms (a fess humettée gules between 3 ravens rising); a crest (a raven rising); and motto *DEUS MIHI SOL* on banner, all engraved on the center front; *Mary Peirce 1820 / Anne R.P. Burroughs 1838 / Sarah C. Kennard & Robert C. Peirce 1877 / Elizabeth W. Macmahon 1916 / Llora C. Bortman 1945 / Jane B. Larus 1994* engraved on back

Mark: Appendix 1, fig. 9a stamped on back

Silver

L. 21¼ in (54 cm), W. 13½ in (34.3 cm), H. 1 in (2.5 cm); Wt. 88 oz Troy

Private collection

American silver trays of this intermediate size are rare. The form was difficult to hammer perfectly flat from a billet, and English silver-plated examples, which look exactly the same, could be imported cheaply. Nevertheless, some Americans chose to pay the considerable cost of having large trays made by American silversmiths.[1] Mark Wentworth Peirce (Pierce, Pearse) (1787–1846) of Portsmouth, New Hampshire, was among them.

Peirce received a letter from Thomas Fletcher on May 13, 1833, that informed him, "I have shipped the Plate specified in the two fore going bills . . . I hope it will arrive safely & meet your approbation." In response, on June 4 Peirce wrote, "The package of plate was received on the 1st and was opened yesterday and found to agree with your bills and gave I believe entire satisfaction."[2]

Although the bills specifying exactly what objects were made and sent do not survive, this tray, with the Peirce family coat of arms engraved at its center, might be presumed to have been among them.

The body of the tray is completely wrought and stands on four low hemispherical feet. The gadrooned scrolls alternating with scallop shells that make up the border were stamped thinly in a downfall press, filled with silver solder, and soldered in place to decorate and reinforce the edge. Substantial borders like this kept trays of all shapes and sizes rigid, thus preventing them from bending when in use. This is particularly important on a tray of this scale when it was used to support a tea and coffee set of three or possibly four pieces. The handles on each end, designed as a composition of flowers, leaves, and scrolls, were cast and soldered in place.

64. VEGETABLE DISH, 1829–40

Inscription: none
Mark: Appendix 1, fig. 10 stamped on underside; the number 4 stamped incuse on end of lid and base; and number 1 on underside of removable handle
Silver
H. 5¾ in (14.6 cm), L. 11¼ in (28.5 cm), W. 8½ in (21.6 cm); Wt. 88 oz. Troy
Ruth J. Nutt Collection of American Silver

It has been noted that "the most important articles for table use in the olden days were undoubtedly entrée dishes, . . . their varieties and forms were innumerable [and] they were described as 'double dishes,' 'steak dishes,' and 'hash dishes.'" These might be octagonal, elliptic, rectangular, or serpentine in shape, with or without feet and applied ornamental borders, but they always had a handle affixed to the center of the removable lid. The illustrated example is representative of the basic model in fashion during the second quarter of the nineteenth century. The rectangular shape with rounded corners was referred to as the oblong style at the time. The ornamental borders are die rolled, but the floral corner elements were "all struck up [in a downfall press] & filled with solder" and then soldered in place.[1]

Whereas silver and silverplate manufacturers in Birmingham and Sheffield, England, used presses that "weighed 10 <u>tons</u> to strike up vegetable dishes at a blow," Fletcher & Gardiner hand hammered the lid and bottom of this example to shape.[2] The leafy decorated

handle at the center of the lid can be twisted ninety degrees to remove it, thereby allowing the lid to be inverted so it can serve as a second dish, if needed.

English manufacturers of vegetable dishes and other silverplated wares, such as Watson & Bradbury of Sheffield, and Spooner, Painter & Co. of Birmingham, exported their goods to the United States.[3] These wares proved to be influential on American silver makers. Indeed, Fletcher & Gardiner imported considerable quantities of English silverplate through the above-identified firms, including vegetable dishes that undoubtedly served as the model for this and other examples bearing their mark. When the firm was asked to make a dinner service for Nicholas Biddle of Philadelphia in 1836, "6 vegetable dishes & covers," at a cost of $558, were among the many fashionable tabletop forms in the order.

65. FRUIT OR CAKE BASKET, 1830–33

Inscription: a coat of arms (a fess humettée gules between 3 ravens rising); a crest (a raven rising); and motto *DEUS MIHI SOL* on banner all engraved on one end; *Mary Peirce* engraved on inside edge of foot
Mark: Appendix 1, fig. 9a stamped on bottom
Silver
H. 4⅞ in (12.4 cm), L. 16⅞ in (42.9 cm), W. 9⅜ in (23.9 cm); Wt. 49 oz. 10 dwt. Troy
Private collection

American silver fruit baskets, also called cake baskets, first appeared on dining tables about 1750. They continued in popularity for slightly more than one hundred years, eventually waning from fashion about 1870. Their office was to display and dispense fancy cakes and related baked goods, including marchpane, seedcakes, macaroons, naples biscuits, almond puffs, meringues, queen cakes, jumbles, savoy cakes, and gingerbread.[1]

Throughout their century-long presence on American tables, cake baskets evolved through several styles. This basket, boat shape in profile and rectangular with rounded corners in plan, was described as being in the oblong style.[2] Judging from the numbers that were made by silversmiths in most major American urban centers, oblong cake baskets were widely popular.

Fletcher & Gardiner produced an impressive number of cake baskets in this style for customers within and outside Philadelphia. They made the illustrated example at the request of Mark Wentworth Peirce (Pierce, Pearse) (1787–1846) of Portsmouth, New Hampshire, whose coat of arms is engraved on one end. After receiving a shipment of silver from Fletcher & Gardiner in 1833,

Peirce wrote that everything "gave entire satisfaction [but] the cream bottle, sugar ladle & sugar tongs & the engraving the crest on them belong to Mrs. Pierce's [Margaret] bill. Will you have the goodness to send me bills so altered . . . and [I] wish the receipt on Mrs. Pierce's bill to state the amo[un]t being received by my hand."[3]

Mary Peirce, whose name is engraved in script inside the footrim, may have been the niece, born in 1833, of Mark and Margaret Peirce, although there were several women of that name living in New Hampshire at the time.

206

66. FOUR SAUCEBOATS AND STANDS, 1830–35

Inscription: a crest (a dove rising and olive branch) engraved under spout of sauceboats and on top of stands; *S.C.P. / 1877 / to / A.B.P. / 1895* engraved under crest on one stand and under crest on one sauceboat

Mark: Appendix 1, fig. 9a stamped on underside of each sauceboat; figs. 11a, b stamped on underside of each stand

Silver

H. 8½ in (21.6 cm), L. 9¾ in (24.8 cm), W. 3⅞ in (9.9 cm); Wt. 26 oz. 10 dwt. Troy (sauceboats)

H. 1¼ in (3.2 cm), L. 11 in (27.9 cm), W. 6¼ in (15.9 cm); Wt. 15 oz. 16 dwt. Troy (stands)

Ruth J. Nutt Collection of American Silver;
Private collection

Thomas Fletcher wrote to Mark Wentworth Peirce, of Portsmouth, New Hampshire, on May 13, 1833, that he had sent him silver itemized in two separate bills and that "I hope it will arrive safely & meet your approbation . . . your further consideration will meet prompt attention."[1]

Peirce purchased a considerable amount of silver from Fletcher & Gardiner during the 1820s and 1830s. Consequently, it is not known if the illustrated sauceboats were among the group Fletcher sent on May 13, 1833. Regardless, these are certainly the most handsome productions of the form to have emanated from the firm. While the oval bodies with upswept spouts follow the norm at the time in terms of neoclassical design, the pendant bud-shape handle has no prototype; it appears to have sprung solely from the imagination of its designer, most likely Thomas Fletcher.

That coupled with the arrangement of acanthus leaves in repoussé around the body and the stand that is oval in plan infuse a visual drama into these sauceboats that places them at the forefront of innovative and dramatic design for their era.

Peirce and his wife, Margaret, owned these sauceboats until their deaths, at which time they passed to their niece, Sarah Coffin Peirce. She bequeathed them to Anne Burroughs Peirce, as recorded via engraved inscriptions on one of the sauceboats and stands. Following that, the four sauceboats were separated, for they appear sporadically and individually in twentieth-century literature on antique silver.[2]

67. VASE, 1831–32

Inscription: *To* / DR. PHILIP SYNG PHYSICK / *This tribute of gratitude for* / *restored health offered by* / *J. Marshall.* / *Philadelphia* / *November 19th 1831*; and FRUITUR FAMA engraved on opposite sides

Mark: Appendix 1, fig. 9a stamped on underside

Silver

H. 11⅛ in (28 cm), W. 6¾ in (17.1 cm), Diam. 7⅜ in (19 cm); Wt. 61 oz. Troy

Pennsylvania Hospital, on loan to the Philadelphia Society for the Preservation of Landmarks

Philip Syng Physick (1768–1837), lauded as the father of American surgery, was a grandson of Philadelphia silversmith Philip Syng, Jr. and no stranger to silver for display and use. This handsomely chased vase mounted on a low, footed platform is one of several silver gifts grateful patients presented to Dr. Physick. The shape is based upon a Greek calyx krater, a visual reference to antiquity also employed by Fletcher & Gardiner in their household silver. The Latin inscription on one side, "FRUITUR FAMA" (he enjoyed a well-deserved reputation), was a tribute from a judge to a physician—men who both used Latin professionally.

The vase triumphantly memorialized a surgery Dr. Physick conducted on Chief Justice John Marshall (1755–1835). In October 1831, when Marshall was seventy-six years of age, Dr. Physick agreed to perform the operation "which proved to be one of the most difficult, and resulted in one of the most brilliant successes of his life." A description by Dr. Physick's son-in-law, who assisted him, recounted details of the successful lithotomy removing approximately 1,000 *calculi* (gallstones) from John Marshall.[1] Dr. Physick's surgical dexterity as well as inventive improvements to medical tools drew complicated cases and high-profile persons to his practice. Marshall, the Virginia-born champion of the constitution, served as Supreme Court Chief Justice from 1801 to 1835. An unusual personal element on this presentation vase is the simulation of Marshall's signature engraved under the dedication.

The vase's generously bellied, wrought bowl is richly chased with stylized leaves and flowers evocative of those painted on ancient Greek ceramic vessels. Dynamically spiraling inverted-anthemion (honeysuckle) handle mounts give sculptural dimension to the sides. Similar cast handles also appear on dinner service items fashioned by the Fletcher & Gardiner workshop in the early 1830s.

68. VASE, 1832

Inscription: *Extract from the will of / Major Thos. Biddle / U.S. Army / 25th. August 1831. / "I request that / my beloved wife will / present to each of my / brothers & sisters a silver / vase, as a testimony / of my affection"* engraved on side
Mark: Appendix 1, fig. 9a stamped on underside
Silver
H. 8½ in (21.6 cm); Wt. 21 oz. 15 dwt. Troy
Private collection

In the era of the young republic, silver awards visually represented the testimony of an historic event or belief held by the donor. The patron of this richly ornamented vase (or cup) wished to leave it as a permanent sign of his love for his closest relations. It was originally one of ten ordered from Fletcher & Gardiner in 1832, and the memorial documents the exchange of silver vases between individuals. The donor, Thomas Biddle (1790–1831) died in St. Louis, but his widow, Ann, directed his request to the nation's leading silversmith firm in Philadelphia.[1]

Thomas Fletcher's ever-fruitful genius for design combined the traditional form of a two-handled cup with the proportions of a Greek calyx krater to create a fashionable and distinctive vase for Major Biddle's family. The bowl and upper section are wrought in two parts ornamented with hand-chased leaf ornamentation, die-rolled anthemion and leaf-tip borders, and cast sculptural handles. References to timeless motifs such as the Greco-Roman acanthus leaves and dolphins, and Egyptian-style water leaves on the bowl and pedestal foot, reinforce the memorial character. Rather than crisp, classical acanthus leaves chased in high relief, the sides of the vase hold elongated, softly curving acanthus arches formed by crossed-leaf tips. The leaves seemingly bow their heads, evocative of the ubiquitous memorial symbol of a weeping willow tree, or perhaps a martyr's palm leaves. Interlaced tails on the dolphin handles echo the crossed-leaf tips.

Biddle's posthumous gifts do not appear to have been published, although accounts of his duel with Missouri Congressman Spenser D. Pettis (1802–31) were sensationalized in newspapers from St. Louis to New York and Vermont. Thomas Biddle, U.S. Army paymaster, objected to Pettis's political attacks on his brother, U.S. Bank president Nicholas Biddle, and on their family reputation. According to contemporary accounts, Thomas Biddle printed anonymous rebuttals against Pettis and then resorted to physically whipping him, whereupon Pettis challenged him to a duel.[2] Both men were mortally wounded.

The engraving on the urn reads:

*Extract from the will of
Major Thos. Biddle
U.S. Army
25th August 1831
"I request that
my beloved wife will
present to each of my
brothers & sisters a silver
vase, as a testimony
of my affection."*

69. BOWL, 1830–34

Inscription: Engraved, base front: United Bowmen / of / PHILADELPHIA; back: INSTITUTED, / *September 3, 1828. / This Bowl is the absolute Property of the United Bowmen.*; right side: Founders of the Club with six names; Associate & Honorary Members with 5 names; left side: club symbols and 15 names; bowl interior: Members of Club of United Bowmen with names from 1828 to 1855; attached to rim: 23 medallions engraved with name of annual prize shooting winner and date from 1834 to 1856
Mark: Appendix 1, fig. 11 (four impressions) stamped on underside; fig. 21 (Th[S] Fletcher Maker and W.G. Mason sc[1] engraved on base front)
Silver
Overall H. 13½ in (34.3 cm), Diam. 14 in (35.6 cm); Wt. 175 oz. Troy
The Historical Society of Pennsylvania, Atwater Kent Museum, HSP.X–181

The current state of this elegant vase, or "bowl," with fourteen acanthus leaves bolted around the bowl and four encircling the side, is best understood through its history. Nearly all of its surfaces preserve records of the nation's first archery club, the United Bowmen, founded in 1828 in Philadelphia by Franklin Peale, Titian R. Peale, Robert E. Griffith, Samuel P. Griffitts, Jr., Jacob G. Morris, and Thomas Sully. The club adopted regulations and symbolic names, held practice on an eighty-yard target range (often concluding with convivial dinners), and hosted annual prize meetings beginning in 1829.[2]

The shooting contests in September evolved into semi-public spectacles with club members donning uniforms and inviting guests via printed cards. A newspaper description of the 1835 meeting estimates 1,200 guests and mentions that during the competition "when ever an arrow struck the centre or gold spot, the band gave a flourish with their trumpet." This silver bowl was displayed on a table with other trophies, and the highest point winner took it home for one year. According to regulations, each winner added an ornament of value and design prescribed by the club.[3]

Thus, every year a cast silver acanthus leaf was bolted around the wrought bowl. Eventually, truncated leaves began encircling the side. From 1834 to 1856 the winner's name and year were engraved on a medallion attached to the die-rolled, leaf-tip rim. Founders' names and their symbols were engraved on the base; three were later erased. The use of individual mottoes, marks, and colors were steady elements of the club's inventive heraldry. In the late 1880s the club engraved founders' and successive members' names inside the upper rim of the bowl.[4] Artistically, the bowl appears incomplete in resolution, but it is replete as a historic document.

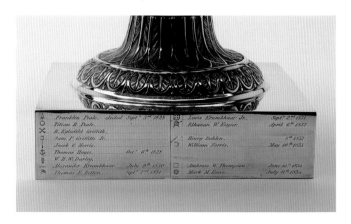

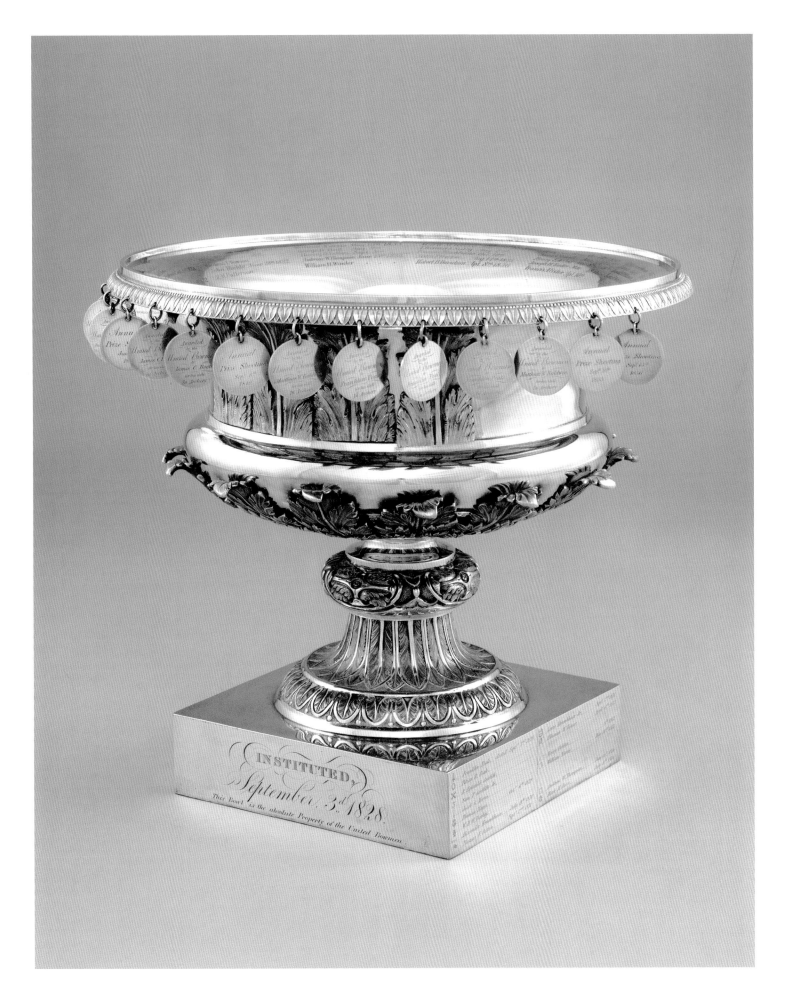

70. VASE, 1833

Inscription: Engraved, front: *Presented / by the Stockholders of the /* SCHUYLKILL NAVIGATION COMPANY / – to – / THOMAS FIRTH, ESQ., / *under a resolution of the 7. of January 1833*; back: In testimony / of their sense of his long continued, faithful / and disinterested / service as a MANAGER in conducting / their concerns, under circumstances often / of great discouragement, / and bringing them at length to an / eminently prosperous condition.

Mark: Appendix 1, figs. 9a, 6b stamped on underside

Silver

H. 20⅛ in (51.1 cm), W. 13 in (33 cm); Wt. 145 oz. Troy

Philadelphia Museum of Art, Purchased with the Richardson Fund, the John D. McIlhenny Fund, and the American Art Revolving Fund, 1985–89–1

Within one week of a resolution passed by the board of directors for the Philadelphia-based Schuylkill Navigation Company, Thomas Fletcher heard from several members about the order for five more presentation vases. The request was for "vases of the same form and size as that made for C. Evans, Esq." This vase for Thomas Firth was one of the five, and it closely resembles Cadwalader Evans's of three years earlier, with only subtle changes to molding ornament (see cat. no. 58). Thomas Firth, Manuel Eyre, Dr. Jonas Preston, Joshua Lippencott, and Lindzey Nicholson all served for more than seven years as company officers during challenging times for canal projects. Fletcher & Gardiner's vase design with Schuylkill River waterscapes enhancing the base was fashioned for all five managers. Two vases are known today.[1]

A company report notified the public of these awards: "Five pieces of plate of the value of five hundred dollars each, were by their directions manufactured by Mr. Thomas Fletcher, in a manner entirely satisfactory to the Committee, and very creditable to Mr. Fletcher's taste and skill. One of them was, on the 23rd day of November last, delivered to each of the five following named gentlemen."[2]

Their statement conveys high regard for the design of the vase, as does the testimony of the repeated production of this form. Beginning with James Fisher's two vases, the six Schuylkill Navigation Company awards, and a hot water urn in the same form, the silver workshop produced this design at least nine times. Vases like Firth's are the first known instance of Fletcher & Gardiner's workshop fashioning multiples of a monumental award for members of a group. Each presentation vase no longer represented individual characteristics; instead, five identical vases with similar inscriptions celebrated their corporate unity.

71. SAUCEBOAT, 1830–40

Inscription: none

Mark: Appendix 1, fig. 11a, b stamped on underside

Silver

H. 8 in (20.3 cm), L. 8 in (20.3 cm), W. 3½ in (8.9 cm); Wt. 15 oz. Troy

Ruth J. Nutt Collection of American Silver

On March 15, 1815, Thomas Fletcher wrote to his father that he had made preparations to travel to England and France, possibly Germany and Switzerland, as well, for business, which he anticipated would last "about a year." Fletcher was in Paris by September, during which time he busied himself meeting and transacting business with silversmiths, glass makers, leather workers, and makers of anything in the fancy hardware line that he felt would sell well in the United States. While there he received a letter from the shipping firm of Welles, Williams & Green in Harve, France, stating "Your esteemed favors of 29 & 30 [September] and 2 [October] have been received in due course and the goods therein alluded have been regularly shipped in conformity with your instructions . . . 12 cases . . . consigned to Messrs Fletcher & Gardiner of Philadelphia."[1]

Fletcher & Gardiner maintained commercial connections with their Parisian suppliers in the succeeding years, and Fletcher returned to Paris in 1825. As before, the goods he acquired were sold at a profit and used as design inspiration for the silver made in his Philadelphia manufactory. This striking sauceboat is an exemplary instance of the latter. Its spare, sweepingly curved body stands on a severe, plain elliptic foot. Both are ornamented with a narrow, simple border consisting of an alternating leaf and berry. The most dramatic feature is the upwardly curved handle ornamented with precisely defined palmettes and anthemia and terminating with a female mask, possibly a Sabine. All these features have direct parallels in Parisian silver made at the time. There can be little doubt that Fletcher had this example modeled from one or more he saw during the course of his business trip there.[2]

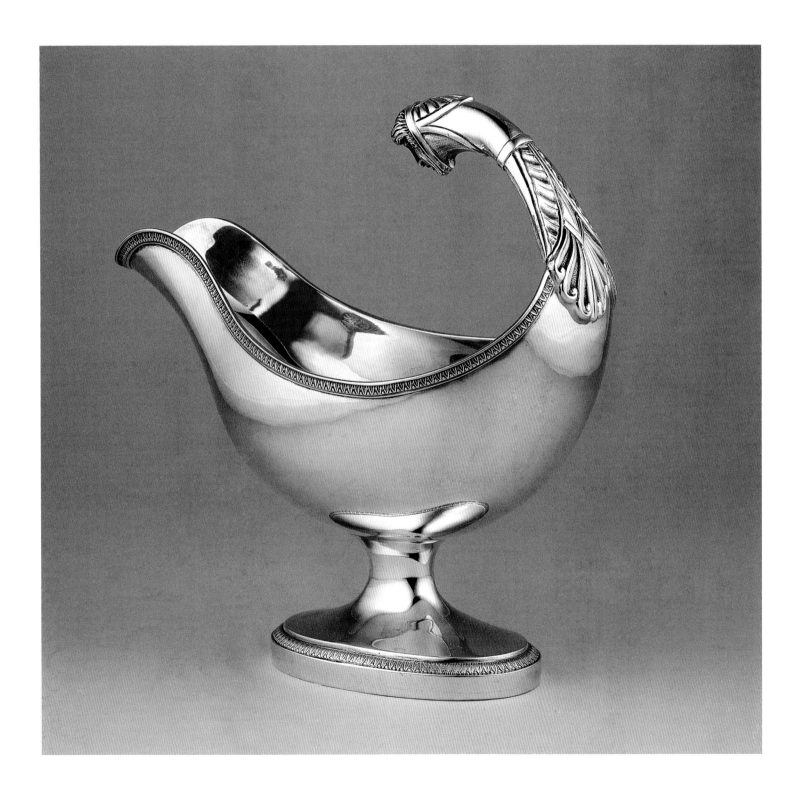

72. PITCHER, 1827–40
Inscription: *JRJ* engraved on side of body
Mark: Appendix 1, fig. 9a stamped under base
Silver
H. 8½ in (21.6 cm), W. 5⅞ in (15 cm), Diam. 3½ in (8.9 cm); Wt. 17 oz. Troy
Brooklyn Museum, 76.6H, Randolph Lever Fund

Thomas Fletcher visited Paris twice during his working career, once in 1815 and again in 1825. Both times he sought to make mercantile connections for the supply of fashionable goods—gold jewelry, watches, music boxes, clocks, vases, chimney pieces, swords, and the like—that he could sell in his Chesnut Street establishment as well as through stores with which he had business and personal ties in New York; Lexington, Kentucky; and New Orleans.

At the same time, Fletcher was not insensitive to the character and influence of French design in the arts. Consequently, he made time to visit museums, purchase design books and engravings of antiques, and draw objects and decorative details he saw that might be useful in designing silver. The pitcher illustrated here documents the impact of his time in Paris, for it is French in character, as evidenced by the proportion—a moderately tall, narrow body on a small, bell-shape pedestal. Comparable French pitchers employ this same ratio, in contrast to typical English examples. Fletcher also used cast and applied mounts, a ram's head under the handle, and a human mask under the spout. This, too, follows French prototypes closely.[1]

A third feature that Fletcher incorporated into this pitcher, the mantle of imbricated leaves that encircles the pedestal, suggests another influential source that he may have encountered in Paris. In contrast to the accurately rendered acanthus leaves on the body, these leaves are highly stylized in their veining and simplified in their outline. Abstracted images of such leaves were a prominent part of dynastic Egyptian design, as seen on the capitals of the temple columns recorded in *Voyage dans la Basse et Haute Égypte,* published in Paris in 1802.[2] As such, they are a tangible instance of Franco-Egyptian design in American silver.

73. HOT WATER URN, 1830–35

Inscription: *JHS* engraved on side opposite petcock
Mark: Appendix 1, fig. 9a stamped on underside; fig. 11a, b stamped on back of base; the words *OLD SILVER* stamped incuse on underside of base
Silver, ivory
H. 17¾ in (45.1 cm), W. 11¾ in (29.9 cm), D. 11¼ in (28.6 cm); Wt. 142 oz. Troy
Ruth J. Nutt Collection of American Silver

When hosting a tea party, well-to-do and style-conscious early nineteenth-century householders would have needed a silver teapot, hot water pot, cream pot, sugar bowl and slop bowl as well as sugar tongs and teaspoons. With money no object, a capacious hot water urn like the illustrated example would have been essential. This grand amenity for tea not only supplied a constant supply of hot water, it unequivocally stated the owner's wealth and taste.

The wrought vase-shape body is enriched with a plethora of ornament, all ultimately inspired by ancient Greco-Roman design. During a business trip to England and France in 1815 and 1816, Thomas Fletcher recorded in his notebook evidence of his inspiration for the design of this and similar vessels made in his establishment. After visiting the shop of London's foremost silversmithing manufactory, Rundell, Bridge & Rundell, on June 14, 1815, he wrote that he had studied elaborately decorated silver of a type he had never seen before, particularly a vase copied from a large Roman marble one in the possession of the Earl of Warwick. He noted that it was slightly smaller than the one he and Gardiner made for Isaac Hull and that the "handles are grape stalks and a vine runs all around covered with leaves & clusters of grapes."[1]

As evidenced by this and similarly decorated vessels made in Fletcher & Gardiner's shop—the most significant being a pair of monumental vases presented to DeWitt Clinton, governor of New York State, in 1825—the Rundell, Bridge & Rundell vase had a profound effect on Fletcher's design sensibilities. This influence can be seen on wine coolers, coffeepots, compotes, and this urn.[2]

74. PAIR OF SAUCE TUREENS, 1830–40

Inscription: *WSJ* engraved on side

Mark: Appendix 1, fig. 9a stamped on underside of both

Silver

H. 8½ in (21.6 cm), Diam. 7⅝ in (19.4 cm); Wt. 36 oz. 18 dwt. Troy

Ruth J. Nutt Collection of American Silver

Sauces have long been a desirable adjunct to meals. They complement the flavor of virtually all meats, vegetables, and desserts. So important are sauces in the minds of cooks that one nineteenth-century authority on cooking and food wrote, "The difference between good and bad cookery can scarcely be more strikingly shown than in the manner in which sauces are prepared and served." This is dramatically underscored by another author who listed no fewer than seventy-eight different sauces in his cookbook, *Ketter's Book of the Table*.[1]

This pair of small tureens with lids stood on the table to dispense sauces of the type identified in Ketter's book. They have been fashioned into the shape of a

calyx, a cup with a comparatively shallow bowl and high foot used by the ancient Greeks for drinking wine.[2] The bodies and pedestals are wrought, while the lids, of relatively thin gauge and lacking deep hammer marks like those visible on the inside of the bodies and underside of the pedestals, were probably made of silver flattened into a sheet in a rolling mill and subsequently hammered or possibly stamped to their domed contour. These components contrast with a die-rolled border of acorns and oak leaves encircling the base, another of flowers and leaves just under the body, and a third of leaf tips and beading at the lip. A collar of acanthus leaves in repoussé encircles the cast berry finial.

Sauce tureens, like their larger companions soup tureens, normally had accompanying ladles. Frequently, but not always, both sauce and soup tureen lids could be closed over the ladle handles via a small semi-circular or square cutout in the edge, but that is not the case here. These tureens, being circular in plan, are unusual; most made at that time were elliptic.

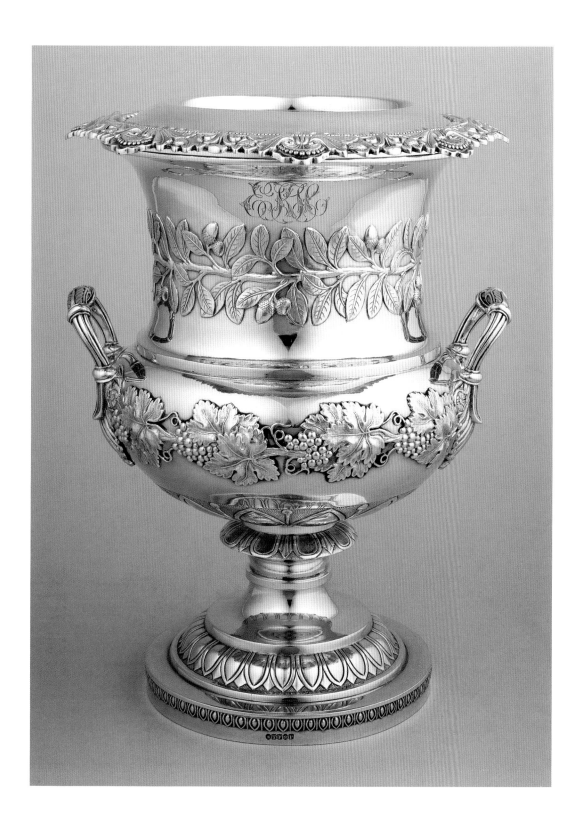

75. WINE COOLER, 1830–40

Inscription: *EKH* engraved on side under lip; *From A.E.A. / J.W.A. / J.De.K.A. / F.O.P.A. / OCT. 1903* engraved under base

Mark: Appendix 1, fig. 10 stamped on side of base

Silver

H. 12¼ in (31.1 cm), W. 9¼ in (23.5 cm), Diam. 8⅛ in (20.6 cm); Wt. 103 oz. 10 dwt. Troy

Private collection

The krater was one of many pottery vessels widely used by ancient Greeks. It occurred in several forms, one of which was the calyx krater, so named because the body was fashioned in the shape of the calyx of a flower. The vessel typically had a circular pedestal, with bulbous lower body and tall flaring neck; two loop handles were usually affixed to the bulbous lower section. Ancient Greeks used it to mix wine and water for drinking.[1] The calyx krater became a favored form in silver and silverplate in France, England, and, to a lesser extent in the United States, in the early nineteenth century when it was adapted for other purposes, including household and presentation.

Thomas Fletcher positioned himself to contribute to this phenomenon when he traveled to England and France in 1815, for he recorded in his letterbook on August 12 of that year that he purchased a "Catalogue of Antiques [and] antique engravings," which probably illustrated examples of the form. He also may have seen actual ancient Greek examples that had been collected by English connoisseurs or English silver adaptations of the form when he visited the London showrooms of Rundell, Bridge & Rundell, where he noted encountering a vase on which "a vine runs all around covered with leaves & clusters of grapes."[2] The ongoing influence the calyx krater had on Fletcher is manifest in this wine cooler and a carefully rendered drawing associated with his firm (see chap. 6, drawing 10).

---

76. CANDELABRUM, 1834–40

Inscription: none
Mark: Appendix 1, fig. 9a stamped four times on underside
Silver
H. 24¼ in (61.6 cm), Diam. 16 in (40.7 cm); Wt. 192 oz. Troy
Ruth J. Nutt Collection of American Silver

This candelabrum is remarkable for its grand size. Additionally, the elaborate, seven-branch design has no counterpart in the work of other eighteenth- and early nineteenth-century American silversmiths. Indeed, it anticipates comparable examples by Tiffany and Gorham by almost half a century.[1]

Prior to the beginning of the nineteenth century, American silversmiths were occasionally asked to make candlesticks, but such commissions were infrequent because stylish English silver and silver-plated candlesticks and candelabra could be imported much more cheaply. Consequently, American silversmiths often advertised that they supplied English silverplate lighting. Fletcher and Gardiner's firm was fully engaged in this trade. On November 9, 1808, the firm advertised that it had "on hand, for sale . . . Best Sheffield Plated Candlesticks, all sizes (some very elegant) and Branches," and again on April 20, 1811, the advertisement noted the partners "have received by the late arrivals [from England] a part of their SPRING SUPPLY, and now offer a general assortment of GOODS in their line on the most reasonable terms wholesale and retail–viz ... Candlesticks, all sizes, 2, 3, and 5 light Branches."[2]

In addition to fused plate, the partners also offered their customers gilt brass fixtures. On March 10, 1832, Fletcher billed George Cadwalader for "1 7lt cand[lestic]k for center table, Triumph of Bacchus, Mosaic Gold," an ormolu fixture he had imported from England or France, priced at $250. Two years later Fletcher wrote to a correspondent who inquired about having a silver candelabrum made that "a pair of three light branches I think would cost, although I have never made any, from $180 to 250, according to size, weight & pattern."[3] It is not known if his correspondent decided to have the pair of three-light branches made, but this example proves his manufactory was capable of supplying a fixture equal in size and elaboration to those he imported from across the Atlantic.

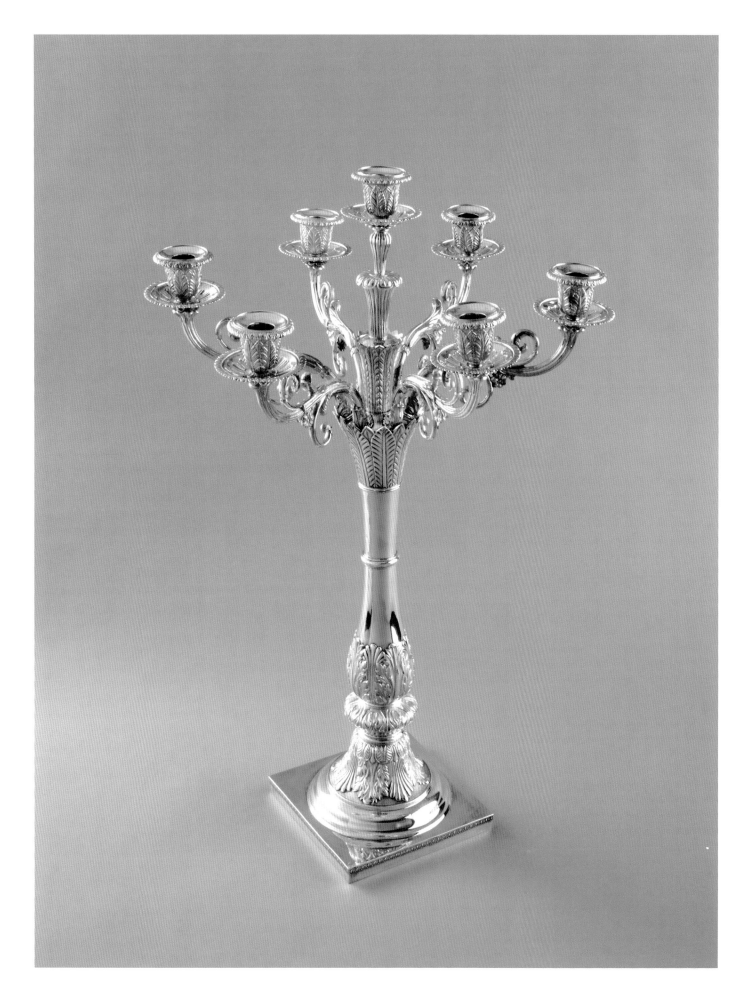

77. PITCHER, 1830–42
Inscription: none
Mark: Appendix 1, fig. 11a, b stamped on underside
Silver
H. 10 in (25.4 cm), W. 6⅝ in (16.8 cm), Diam. 4⅜ in. (11.1 cm); Wt. 18 oz. Troy
Private collection

Thomas Fletcher was trained as a merchant, whereas Sidney Gardiner was trained as a silversmith. When they formed their partnership in 1808, they brought together complementary talents that were necessary to the success of their silversmithing business. The silver designed and produced in their manufactory generated widespread admiration and caused observers like the New York City diarist Philip Hone (1780–1851) to record that "nobody in this 'world' of ours hereabouts can compete with them in this kind of work."[1]

A third talent possessed by the partnership was artistic sensitivity and an ability to incorporate original elements of style into the manufactory's work. This graceful creation and its design (see chap. 6, drawing 13) are representative. The tall, slender stance is punctuated with a series of five discrete horizontal borders that contrast with and complement the broad passages of brilliantly reflective surface. Each border is tailored in width and imagery to its location, hence a very narrow border with a tiny repeat at the lip contrasts with a wide border composed of large elements encircling the lower portion of the body. Like the vase-shape body on circular pedestal, these borders allude to French interpretation of ancient Greek design.

Perhaps the most compelling ornamental passage of this pitcher is the handle, which springs from an anthemion punctuated with flowers and arches upward and outward, ending in a pendant bird head. Although the Fletcher & Gardiner firm produced numerous pitchers, this is the only example known with the handle configured in this manner. It underscores the versatile approach to design fostered by the partners.[2]

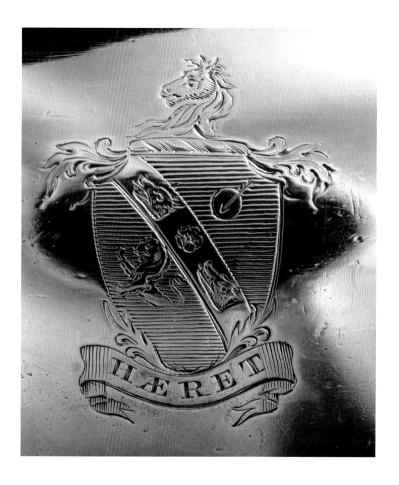

78. SOUP TUREEN, circa 1833

Inscription: *Daniel Webster* engraved on one side; a coat of arms (azure on a bend argent between a plate pierced by an arrow bend sinisterways and a demi-lion, a rose bet 2 boars' heads couped); a crest (a horse's head couped), and a banner with the word *HÆRET* engraved on opposite side
Mark: Appendix 1, fig. 9a stamped on underside
Silver
H. 14 in (35.5 cm), L. 14 in (35.5 cm), W. 11½ in (29.2 cm); Wt. 122 oz. Troy
Ruth J. Nutt Collection of American Silver

Following studies at Dartmouth College, Daniel Webster (1782–1852) went on to a brilliant career as a lawyer, politician, and orator. Through innate talent as well as advantageous social and political connections, he forged an impressive national reputation as an advocate in state and federal courts prior to his election to the House of Representatives in Washington in 1812.

In the 1830s he became embroiled in the struggle over renewal of the charter of the United States Bank by the federal government. He served as a lawyer on retainer for the bank, no doubt because of his legal oratorical skill but also because he was a close friend of bank president Nicholas Biddle (1786–1844), for whom Thomas Fletcher made silver.

A second personal matter in Webster's life that undoubtedly impinges on the illustrated soup tureen was his marriage to Grace Fletcher, Thomas's third cousin, in 1808.[1] These factors cemented a relationship between Webster and Fletcher, though they would most likely have been aware of each other since both had acquired prominence in their respective endeavors.

It comes as no surprise, therefore, that Fletcher wrote to Webster on April 17, 1833, informing him he had just sent one box containing two soup tureens at a cost of $685.25.[2] This tureen and its mate (unlocated), the subject of that letter, represent the best of Fletcher's work at the time. It stands on massive paw feet that support an unusual elliptic pedestal with a lobe above each paw. The remainder of the ornament, including the die-rolled borders and wrought acanthus leaves on the body and cast finial, accords with Greek and Roman antecedents. An intriguing variant is the four eagle heads supporting the loop handles, which employ leafy mantles akin to those used in dynastic Egypt.

79. SWORD and SCABBARD, 1834

Inscriptions: Engraved, hilt lancet: Presented to / Col. Nathan Towson / by the / State of Maryland / (his native State) / In consideration of his / gallant services during the / late war with Great Britain; chased in relief, hilt grip: CALEDONIA CHIPPEWA BRIDGEWATER FORT ERIE; etched on both sides, blade: Black Rock March 1813 / Fort George Stoney Creek / Forty Mile Creek Queenstown September 1813 / Chippawa [sic] October 1814

Mark: Appendix 1, figs. 22, 29b ROSE inverted on *ricasso*; T. FLETCHER / —Maker—/ Philadelphia engraved on back of upper scabbard mount

Sword: yellow gold and steel[1]

Overall L. 37 in (94 cm), W. 5 in (12.7 cm); blade: L. 31 in (78.7 cm), W. 1⅛ in (2.9 cm)

Scabbard: mercury gilded silver, red and yellow gold L. 31¼ in (79.4 cm), W. 1½ in (3.8 cm)

Collection of the Maryland State Archives

Nathan Towson (1784–1854), recognized for his leadership in the artillery battles of the War of 1812, was brevetted brigadier-general in 1834. That same year his native state memorialized his earlier successes with a helmet-pommel presentation sword. The design of the hilt spirals the names of Towson's decisive battles in banners alternating with a band of stars around the grip.[2] An engraved escutcheon on the langet keeps Towson's name and the dedication visible even when the sword is sheathed. Six more battle names were etched above and below the fuller on one side of the steel blade, and two gold scabbard mounts depict his engagements; thus, this sword is a condensed chronicle of his entire War of 1812 career.

The Maryland General Assembly's desire for richly ornamented gold swords to present to veterans was tempered only by the high cost of each. Towson's was the tenth sword they ordered from Fletcher & Gardiner, and the governor requested a sword for John Gallagher at the same time. He encouraged Fletcher to create Towson's sword in excess of $500 if necessary. It was necessary; the total cost was approximately $700 when complete. Presumably to save cost, the scabbard was fashioned in silver and gilded for an impressive luster, with four yellow- and red-gold mounts and tip. The uppermost mount incorporates designs from the state's seal created by Maryland-born artist Charles Willson Peale in 1794. A rare surviving drawing depicts a preliminary stage of this sword with the eagle of the 1817 Maryland state seal placed at the top of the scabbard (see chap. 6, drawing 20).[3] In its final resolution, the scabbard featured Peale's emblems, which prompts speculation of the donors' deliberate choice for historicism or perhaps a decision to unify the words, images, and overall design with a seal apropos of the time of Towson's battles.

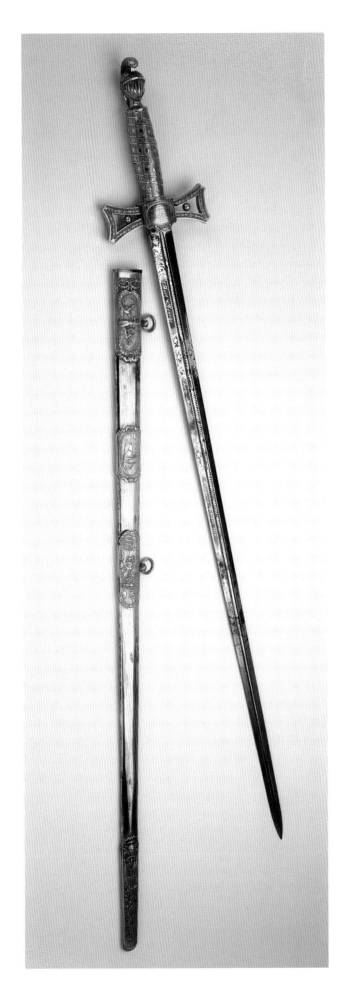
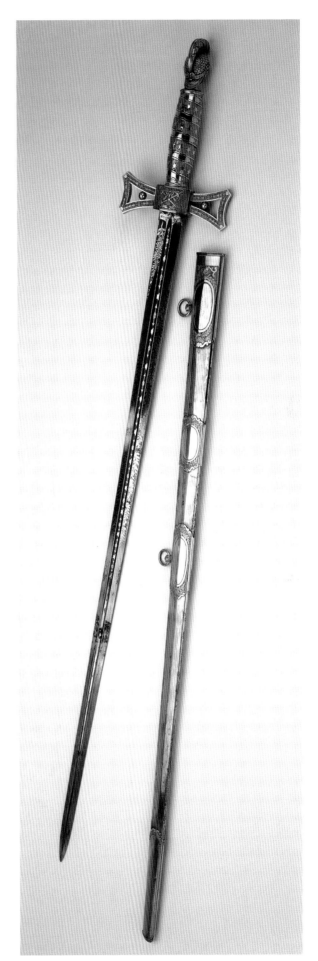

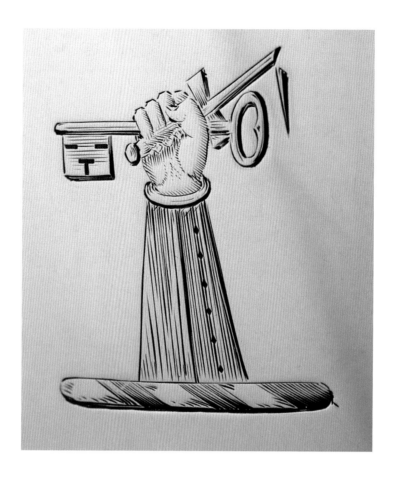

80. PITCHER, 1830–40

Inscription: a crest (a dexter arm in armor holding in the hand a broken dagger, the point falling down, and a key) engraved under spout; *Lee Wood Gorham March 29, 1910* engraved on side of base

Mark: Appendix 1, fig. 11a, b stamped on underside of base

Silver

H. 14⅜ in (36.5 cm), W. 9⅛ in (23.2 cm), Diam. 5¾ in. (14.6 cm); Wt. 56 oz. 10 dwt. Troy

The Metropolitan Museum of Art, Purchase, William Cullen Bryant Fellows Gift, 2007 (2007.25)

This pitcher, for which there exists a closely related design (see chap. 6, drawing 19), typifies the late work of Thomas Fletcher's firm. It is tall and slender with a substantial quantity of floral and leafy imagery arranged on the body and pedestal in horizontal bands and incorporated into the handle. The wide border of acanthus alternating with water leaves encircling the lower portion of the body has been hammered out in repoussé, a labor-intensive campaign of decorating directed exclusively and solely to this object.

Conversely, the narrower but more florid border above

it consists of short die-stamped sections arranged end to end. Die stampings, in this instance multiple replications of a decorative element, allowed the Fletcher & Gardiner manufactory to mass produce ornamental components that could be quickly tailored to a variety of uses much more cheaply than repoussé work, illustrated by this pitcher, the tray in cat. no. 37, the basin in cat. no. 39, the tea set in cat. no. 41, and the hot water urn in cat. no. 42, all of which use identical stampings.

Flexibility and adaptability in workshop production are also evident in the cast handle, which, like that on the flagon in cat. no. 52, is the same pattern as those on the tankard in cat. no. 34 and jug in cat. no. 50, but enriched with three lotus buds.

As with much of Fletcher & Gardiner's silver, the original owner asked that his crest be engraved on the object as proof of ownership. Although the use of heraldic emblemata such as this was rigorously controlled in Europe and England, Americans were more lax and adopted imagery without authority. Hence, the owner of this crest is not known. However, it might have been a member of the Montgomery family of Maryland or the King family of Pennsylvania.

81. PAIR OF TABLE FORKS, 1831–39

Inscription: a crest (a demi-lion rampant) engraved on handle backs

Mark: Appendix 1, fig. 11a stamped on handle back of both

Silver

L. 6⅞ in (17.5 cm), W. ⅞ in (2.2 cm); Wt. 2 oz Troy each

Winterthur Museum, Bequest of Henry Francis du Pont, 1965.3066, 1970.1323.1

The swelled, curvilinear profile of the handles on these forks is outlined with leaf-embellished molding flanking a scallop shell at the tip and a small waisted cartouche, often described as an hourglass, at the lower ends. This is a design formula that originated in France during the mid-eighteenth century. English silversmiths began to make flatware in this pattern by the first decade of the nineteenth century, and Americans followed suit by the time the illustrated examples were made. A closely related design called the King's Pattern, in which the waisted cartouche was replaced with a double-ended anthemion, appeared in England about 1815 and in the United States about 1830.[1]

Spoons and forks in these patterns were very much the vogue on American tables through the mid-nineteenth century. They were stamped up in iron dies, representing a striking advance in the incorporation and replication of currently fashionable ornamental motifs on flatware when compared to eighteenth-century hand-wrought counterparts. Fletcher & Gardiner were at the forefront of making tableware like this, as recorded in correspondence between their firm and that of Robert and Andrew Campbell, importers and silver dealers in Baltimore, Maryland. On April 20, 1831, Robert Campbell requested that Fletcher make him "of dollar silver . . . 3 dozen of large sised forks & 3 do small sised forks." Sometime later Fletcher responded, "I did not understand your order for forks. You say 'let them be of the King's pattern & burnished'–If you mean the pattern which Whartenby makes, I have not the dies, if the

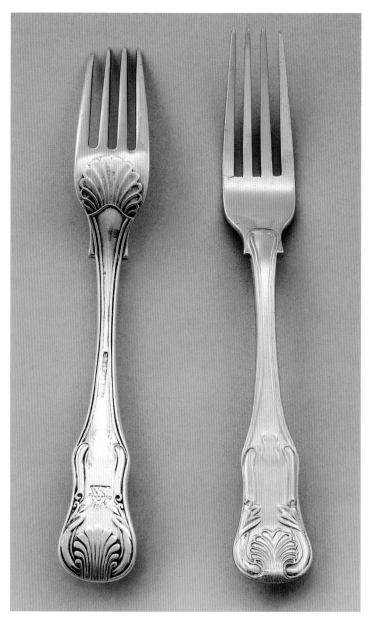

double thread & shell, I have them."[2]

These forks, engraved with the crest of the Cuthbert family of Philadelphia, document that Fletcher, seeing potential demand for these elaborate patterns, lost no time having dies engraved so that he could supply them. They are of heavy weight and are as sophisticated an interpretation of the so-called "hourglass" pattern as was available in the United States at the time.[3]

82. TWO SALTS FROM A SET OF FOUR, 1835–38

Inscription: a crest (a cross pattée fitché or) engraved on side of each

Mark: Appendix 1, fig. 9a, c, d, e stamped on underside of each

Silver

H. 1⅞ in (4.8 cm), Diam. 3¾ in (9.5 cm); Wt. 5 oz. 2 dwt. Troy each

Private collection

On October 28, 1831, Rezin D. Shepherd, Boston merchant, wrote to Thomas Fletcher that "the Box of Plate ordered by me for my daughter has been safely received, and it all gives satisfaction except the salts which are without exception in the worse taste and more out of proportion than anything I ever saw. I therefore loose no time in sending them back to you in order that so great a mistake may be corrected . . . [Make] . . . an entire new set . . . leaving off all ornament but . . . a wreath on each side, for the Cypher, and by no means forget to wash or plate the inner sides & rim with gold."[1]

Shepherd was no more specific regarding the appearance of the salts made in Fletcher's manufactory, so one cannot be certain of their appearance. However, they may have looked like this pair, with low-bellied bodies extensively worked with repoussé flowers and leaves below egg-and-dart rims. Each stands on three feet cast in the form of a lion-head monopod.[2]

The inspiration for the design of these salts is traceable to the work of mid-eighteenth-century London silversmiths, some of whom fashioned examples that differ little, if at all, from these in appearance. Fletcher may have encountered such antique salts among the "old plate &c lying about the floor" during a business trip to the London silversmithing manufacturer Rundell, Bridge & Rundell in 1815. However, he more likely saw an example by famed silversmith Paul Storr (1771–1844), who was associated with Rundell, Bridge & Rundell during much of his career.[3]

83. TUREEN (one of two), 1836
Inscription: THE CHESAPEAKE AND DELAWARE
CANAL COMPANY / —to— / *Robert M. Lewis /
many years their President. / As a testimony of his efficient
and assiduous services. /* June 6th 1836 engraved on side; 2
stamped incuse on lid, handle, and tureen
Mark: Appendix 1, fig. 9a stamped on underside
Silver
H. 13 in (33 cm), L. 14½ in (36.8 cm), W. 10 in (26 cm);
Wt. 100 oz. Troy
Private collection

Tureens held pride of place in formal dining
arrangements, proliferating in ceramics and appearing in
silver in early nineteenth-century homes on both sides
of the Atlantic. Demonstrating a sophisticated ability
particular to silver, this tureen's lid doubles as a serving
dish when it is inverted with the twist-off handle
removed.

Although retaining a classical sensibility with broad
expanses of smooth silver, the tureen is enriched for its
presentation purpose with chased and die-stamped
ornament. Individually stamped and applied anthemion-
and-feather ornaments encircle the lid.[1] Stylized pointed
leaves evocative of Egyptian ornament are chased into
the wrought bowl. Fletcher & Gardiner unified the
overall visual richness by repeating dense, leaf-tip die-
rolled borders on the lid and pedestal foot. Cast
sculptural features include the foliate lid handle and
tureen handles with spiraling anthemion terminals.

Outgoing president Robert M. Lewis (1786–1855)
received two tureens from the Chesapeake and Delaware
Canal Company, the same organization that

commissioned a vase from Fletcher & Gardiner for James
Fisher in 1830. Philadelphians led the management of
this tri-state canal project and, after the federal
government, were the major financiers. The C&D Canal
opened in 1829 and operated with increased success
despite financial and physical challenges, including
managing water levels along its 13.63 miles. Lewis was
president when the Pennsylvania legislature voted to
increase funds toward the canal's operation in 1835.[2]

Fletcher & Gardiner not only made silver for canal
company officers but also took advantage of the canal for
swifter deliveries. Isaac Hull, writing from Washington
just after the canal opened, directed Fletcher: "I will be
greatly obliged if you will have the urn & the sett [sic]
of plate sent on as soon as possible. I believe there is
water conveyance through the canal to this place &
should suppose that the best mode of sending it on."[3]

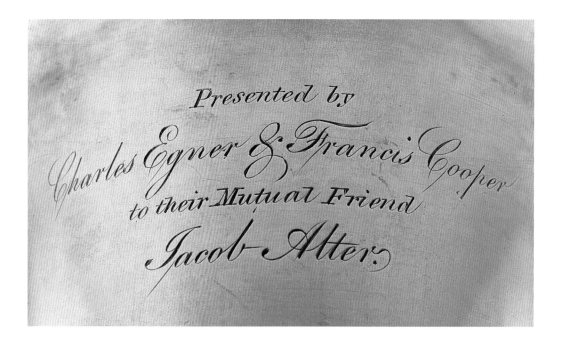

84. TWO-HANDLED VASE, 1830–40

Inscription: *Presented by / Charles Egner & Francis Cooper / to their Mutual Friend / Jacob Alter*; verso: PIGNUS GRATIA engraved on opposite sides

Mark: Appendix 1, fig. 9a stamped on underside

Silver

H. 8¾ in (22.2 cm), Diam. 8⅛ in (13 cm); Wt. 23 oz. Troy

Ruth J. Nutt Collection of American Silver

Newspapers in the 1820s and 1830s often announced awards of silver to national heroes under the heading "A Tribute of Merit." A silver urn or vase (somewhat interchangeable terms in the time) served as an international visual evocation of the antique world.[1] A vase might symbolize any of several interwoven and intangible qualities such as virtue, heroism, fame, or even eternity. Following the War of 1812, this form in silver enjoyed a growing practice of exchange between business associates as private awards for recognizing merit.

This vase, deceptively diminutive in scale, is an example of the antique forms and motifs Fletcher & Gardiner favored for presentation silver. The firm adapted a Greek vase form (krater) with a flaring neck, two cast handles, and a pedestal foot to create an award in the spare manner of the *goût grec* (Greek taste). The body is wrought in three parts with solder joints at the waist and at the top of the foot pedestal. Die-rolled borders in three patterns—guilloche, leaf-tip, and a foliated design—enliven the smooth body. Loop handles with punched grounds and highly burnished outlines of stylized leaves contribute dark and light contrast to the sides.

The donors, purveyors of grocery dry goods and possibly tobacco in Philadelphia, dedicated this vase to a mutual colleague, Jacob Alters, as a pledge of their friendship (*pignus gratia*). The donors' choice of a Latin motto suits the character of this classically inspired vase, but the surrounding boughs of wheat are an appropriate emblem for their grocery trade. Alters is listed as a grocer with a business on High Street, an extension of Philadelphia's busy Market Street, and he had a partial interest in the wine and liquor business Alters, Taylor & Dewey at the same address.[2] The specific occasion prompting this award is unknown.

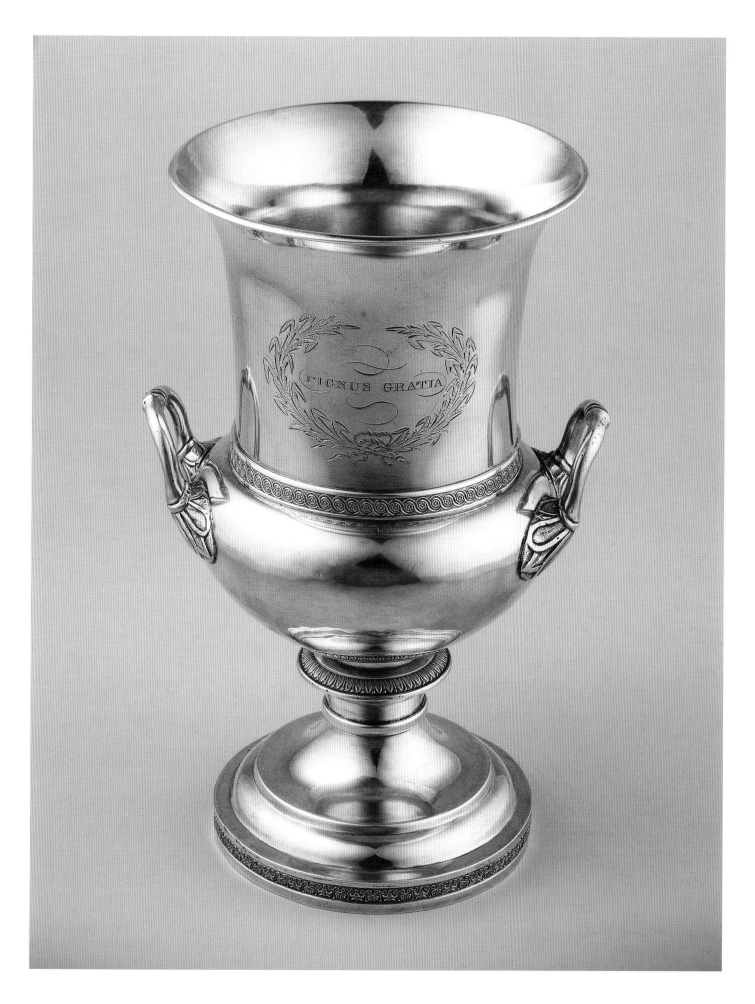

85. SWORD and SCABBARD, 1837

Inscription: Blade: PRESENTED TO / EDMUND P. KENNEDY / OF THE UNITED STATES NAVY / BY HIS NATIVE STATE MARYLAND / FOR HIS GALLANT SERVICES OFF TRIPOLI IN 1804. etched on side

Mark: Appendix 1, fig. 29b ROSE stamped incuse inverted on *ricasso*

Sword: yellow gold, red gold, steel[1]

Overall L. 34½ in (87.6 cm), W. 5¼ in (13.3 cm)

Scabbard: leather, gold mounts

Overall L. 28½ in (72.4 cm), W. 1¾ in (4.4 cm)

The Maryland Historical Society, Gift of Mrs. M. Trippe Kennedy, 1886.4.1

More than thirty years after participating in the naval blockade of Tripoli, Edmund Kennedy (d. 1844) received a gold-hilt sword from the State of Maryland to memorialize his service. Helmets, eagles, and laurels remained favored emblems of valor for presentation swords celebrating battles long-since concluded. Kennedy's sword has a helmet pommel facing in profile to one side. On the grip, an eagle suspends a framed oval wreathed by laurels in its beak above a military trophy. The elliptic guard features an eagle grasping a flaming brand

and a spiral thunderbolt in its talons, before a sunburst and encircling billowing clouds. One note of austerity is the angular cross-guard design, but even this is enlivened with yellow-gold surfaces bordered in red gold.[2]

Edmund Kennedy's name is etched prominently on the blade with flowering garlands surrounding the dedication. Most of the opposite side is etched with a naval battle scene and bell flowers, oak branches with acorns, and a stylized leaf. The overall foliate decoration is a departure from detailed pictorial scenes etched on Fletcher & Gardiner's earlier swords. Gold mounts on the black leather scabbard depict emblems from the 1794 Maryland seal, a coastal battle off Tripoli, and, on the tip, Neptune's head above a naval trophy with flowers.

In 1836 the new governor, Thomas Veazey, remarked about Kennedy's sword: "The Artist engaged is a first rate workman, the same who made the swords for Genl. Towson & Capt. Gallagher, that were presented last winter & I have no doubt of its being executed in the best manner."[3] Veazey may have penned these words in defense of the firm because the sword was ordered in October 1835 but not delivered until the summer of 1837. Fletcher had difficulties finding and keeping highly skilled goldsmiths and rarely made much profit on $500 swords like Kennedy's.

  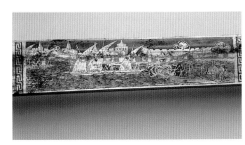

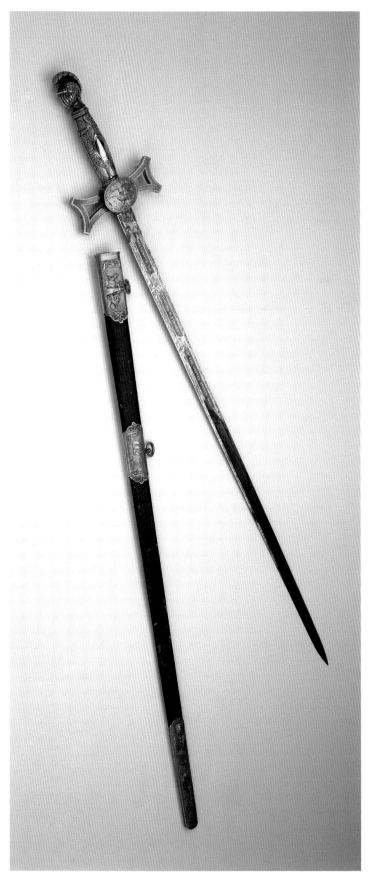

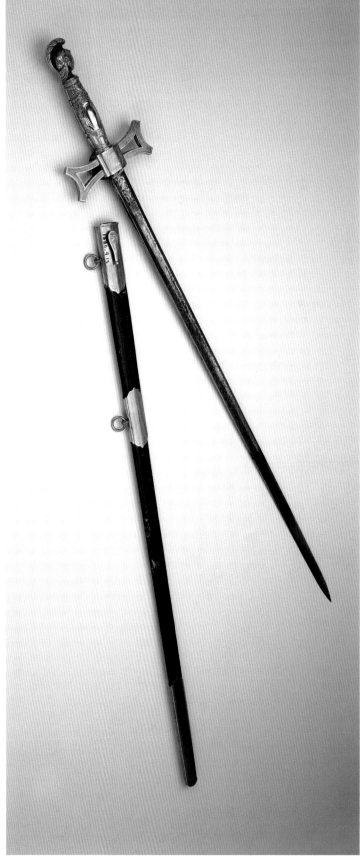

86. PARTIAL TABLE SERVICE, 1836–37

Inscription: *NJB* engraved on handles of carving knife, carving fork, and teaspoon; *B* in a circle engraved on handles of fish knife, tablespoon, dessert spoon, table knife, dinner fork, and luncheon fork

Mark: Appendix 1, fig. 10 stamped on fish knife, dessert spoon, and teaspoon; fig. 11a, b on table fork, luncheon fork, and tablespoon

Silver, steel, pitch

L. 14½ in (36.8 cm), W. 3¼ in (8.2 cm); Wt. 10 oz. Troy (fish knife)

L. 11½ in (29.2 cm); Wt. 4 oz. Troy (carving knife, gross)

L. 10¼ in (26.1 cm); Wt. 4 oz. Troy (carving fork, gross)

L. 10¼ in (26.1 cm); Wt. 4 oz. Troy (table knife, gross)

L. 8 in (20.3 cm); Wt. 3 oz. Troy (table fork)

L. 7 in (17.8 cm); Wt. 2 oz. Troy (luncheon fork)

L. 9 in (22.9 cm), Wt. 4 oz. Troy (tablespoon)

L. 7½ in (19 cm); Wt. 3 oz. Troy (dessert spoon)

L. 6⅛ in (15.5 cm); Wt. 1 oz. Troy (teaspoon)

Property of the Andalusia Foundation

Nicholas Biddle (1786–1844) was elected president of the Second Bank of the United States in 1822. During his fourteen-year tenure he sought to use the bank as an instrument of national monetary policy that would spur economic growth and foster financial stability. Toward that end he was spectacularly successful until the monetary policy of the government changed. Biddle, as the figurehead of the bank, clashed with government officials led by President Andrew Jackson, who believed its existence violated the Constitution.

In gratitude for Biddle's successful tenure at the bank,

the board of directors decided to commission and present him (and his wife, Jane) with a large silver service. They chose Thomas Fletcher's firm to make the silver, which consisted in part of "2 oval soup tureens & stands, 2 wine coolers richly chased, 6 casseroles & covers, 4 butter tubs, covers, tops & stands, 4 gravy boats & stands, 4 sauce tureens & stands, 6 vegetable dishes & covers, 6 meat dishes polished, 24 round plates polished . . . 2 pitchers . . . 1 30-inch waiter . . . 3 10-inch waiters [and] 72 table forks."[1]

In addition, Fletcher's manufactory made ladles and other flat silver, some of which is pictured, as part of the service. On December 10, 1836, Fletcher wrote Daniel

W. Coxe, chairman of the committee charged with procuring the silver, that "the [handles] of the forks & spoons will shortly be completed from new dies designed expressly for this order." Those iron dies were cut to stamp handles that highlight one of the most ubiquitous and popular ornamental motifs in America during the early nineteenth century, the anthemion—a stylized interpretation of the honeysuckle flower that was first used by the ancient Greeks. In spite of the widespread use of the anthemion at the time, Fletcher's interpretation is strikingly original, as is the profile of the handles on which it is stamped.[2]

87. FRUIT OR CAKE BASKET, 1836–40
Inscription: none
Mark: Appendix 1, fig. 11a, b stamped on underside
Silver
H. 10½ in (26.6 cm), L. 14¼ in (36.2 cm), W. 10¾ in (27.3 cm); Wt. 54 oz. 10 dwt. Troy
Private collection

This cake basket is a masterful example of the design aesthetic under Thomas Fletcher's aegis and stands as a record of his ability to use ornamental motifs to capture the essence of a style, even as that style was evolving. For most of his professional career, Fletcher oversaw the creation of silver in the neoclassical idiom; as such, he adaptively used design motifs that had been developed to a high degree of sophistication by ancient Greek and Roman cultures. These included plant forms such as anthemia, palmettes, and water leaves; animals including goats, lions, and dolphins; and mythological figures such as Zeus, Neptune, and Ceres. Furthermore, he organized these features into balanced symmetrical compositions, contrasting highly sculpted passages with brilliantly reflective unadorned areas, which he frequently incorporated onto vase-shape bodies.[1]

This cake basket, dating toward the end of Fletcher's career, contrasts markedly with his earlier designs. Although it features several neoclassical motifs, most notably the alternating acanthus and anthemion border around the lip, it relates strongly to the antithesis of the neoclassical—the rococo. It is conceptually derived from English and American pierced cake baskets dating to the middle of the eighteenth century.[2] It documents the adaptability of one of America's most adept proponents of the neoclassical style just as it waned during the 1830s in favor of more naturalistic design.

Although this basket is not dated, it was likely made shortly after another like it emanated from Fletcher's manufactory for presentation to Nicholas Biddle, president of the United States Bank in Philadelphia in 1836. That basket and the service of which it was a part (see chap. 6, drawings 35, 36) was highly influential, as alluded by Sidney George Fisher, who on attending a ball at Biddle's noted, "The women looked . . . remarkably handsome, Mrs. Blight, Mrs. Wm. Ashhurst . . . A part of the splendid service of plate presented by the stockholders of the Bank was displayed on the supper tables."[3]

88. SIX-PIECE TEA AND COFFEE SET, 1836–42

Inscription: none

Mark: Appendix 1, fig. 9a stamped on underside of each

Silver, ivory

H. 12 in. (30.4 cm), W. 11⅝ in. (29.5 cm), Diam. 6⅛ in. (15.5 cm); Wt. 53 oz. 10 dwt Troy (coffeepot, gross)

H. 11 in (27.9 cm), W. 11 in (27.9 cm), Diam. 5⅞ in (15 cm); Wt. 47 oz. Troy (teapot, gross)

H. 10½ in (26.7 cm), W. 10⅞ in. (27.6 cm), Diam. 5⅝ in. (14.3 cm); Wt. 45 oz. Troy (teapot, gross)

H. 10⅛ in (25.7 cm), W. 7 in. (17.8 cm), Diam. 5⅝ in. (14.3 cm); Wt. 34 oz. 10 dwt Troy (sugar bowl)

H. 7¾ in (19.7 cm), W. 6⅛ in (15.5 cm), Diam. 4 in. (10.1 cm); Wt. 14 oz. Troy (cream pot)

H. 6¾ in (17.1 cm), Diam. 6¼ in. (15.9 cm); Wt. 21oz. 10 dwt. Troy (slop bowl)

Hartman Rare Art

In 1836 the directors of the Second Bank of the United States, located on Chesnut Street next to Thomas Fletcher's silver manufactory, ordered from Fletcher a large and lavish service of silver for the president of the bank, Nicholas Biddle. On December 10, 1836, Fletcher wrote to Daniel W. Coxe, chairman of the committee overseeing the commission with "a report of the condition and progress of the work on the plate ordered [for which he noted that] some time was spent in the study & examination of various designs . . . The designs and drawings for nearly all the service for Mr. Biddle have been prepared . . . and several of the pieces are completed."[1]

The service was immense, consisting of dozens of pieces weighing a total of 3,400 troy ounces at a cost of $7,985.50. On February 14, 1838, diarist Philip Hone recorded seeing it when he noted, "I was shown this

afternoon, at the shop of Messrs. Fletcher & Co., in Chesnut street, the most superb service of plate I ever saw, to be presented by the directors of the old Bank of the United States to Mr. Nicholas Biddle."[2]

As expected, a tea and coffee set was part of this service; the drawings for the teapot, sugar bowl, and cream pot survive (see chap. 6, drawing 35). They picture vessels virtually identical to the illustrated set. The Biddle service was short-lived; historical circumstance dictated that it be melted for bullion when the Second Bank of the United States was not rechartered by the federal government. Fortunately, however, as noted by Hone and others, it was highly influential during its short life. Fletcher was asked to make imitative sets. This set, with bodies that Fletcher described as in the new "fluted" style and covered with repoussé ornament, is one example.

Endnotes

Chapter 1

1. Cathy Matson, "The Permeable Boundaries of Commerce: Stephen Girard's Transnationalism during War and Revolution," paper delivered at a conference in honor of Jack Greene, Brown University, April 21, 2005; Thomas Doerflinger, *A Vigorous Spirit of Enterprise: Merchants and Economic Development in Revolutionary Philadelphia* (New York: W. W. Norton, 1987), pp. 112–14, 123–25; Arthur Jensen, *The Maritime Commerce of Colonial Philadelphia* (Madison: University of Wisconsin, 1963), pp. 7–8; Alice Hanson Jones, "Wealth Estimates for the American Middle Colonies, 1774," *Economic Development and Cultural Change* 18 (July 1970): 1–182; Marc Egnal, "The Changing Structure of Philadelphia's Trade with the British West Indies," *Pennsylvania Magazine of History and Biography* (hereafter *PMHB*) 99 (April 1975): 156–79; Glenn Porter and Harold C. Livesay, *Merchants and Manufacturers: Studies in the Changing Structure of Nineteenth-Century Marketing* (Baltimore: Johns Hopkins University Press, 1971), chap. 1; Cathy Matson, "Capitalizing Hope: Economic Thought and the Early National Economy," in *The Wages of Independence: Capitalism in the Early American Republic*, ed. Paul Gilje (Madison, Wis.: Madison House, 1997), pp. 117–36.

2. In addition to n. 1, see Jonathan Goldstein, *Philadelphia and the China Trade, 1682–1846* (University Park, Pa.: Penn State University Press, 1978).

3. Matson, "Permeable Boundaries of Commerce"; Louis M. Sears, "Philadelphia and the Embargo, 1808," *Annual Report of the AHA for the Year 1920* (Washington, D.C.: Government Printing Office, 1925).

4. In addition to notes above, see Diane Lindstrom, *Economic Development in the Philadelphia Region, 1810–1850* (New York: Columbia University Press, 1978); and Donald R. Adams Jr., "Wage Rates in the Early National Period: Philadelphia, 1785–1830," *Journal of Economic History* 28 (1968): 404–26; Gary Nash, *Forging Freedom: The Formation of Philadelphia's Black Community, 1720–1840* (Boston: Harvard University Press, 1988), pp. 71–72, 74–78, 144–58; Herman Krooss and Martin Blyn, *A History of Financial Intermediaries* (New York: Random House, 1971), pp. 12–17.

5. Simeon Crowther, "The Shipbuilding Industry and the Economic Development of the Delaware Valley, 1681–1776" (Ph.D. diss., University of Pennsylvania, 1970), pp. 6–15, 180–82; Peter Mancall, *Valley of Opportunity: Economic Culture along the Upper Susquehanna, 1700–1800* (Ithaca: Cornell University Press, 1991); Martha Gandy Fales, *Joseph Richardson and Family: Philadelphia Silversmiths* (Middletown, Conn.: Wesleyan University Press, 1974); John L. Bishop, *A History of American Manufactures from 1608 to 1860*, 3 vols. (Philadelphia, 1868), II:73; Philadelphia Trade Directory, 1800, Historical Society of Pennsylvania (hereafter HSP); Ledgers of the Bank of North America, 1800, HSP.

6. Billy G. Smith, "Material Lives of Laboring Philadelphians," *William and Mary Quarterly*, 3d ser., 38

(1981): 181–200. Cathy Matson and Peter Onuf, *A Union of Interests: Political and Economic Thought in Revolutionary America* (Lawrence: University of Kansas Press, 1990); "Report of the Committee for American Manufactures," *American Museum* 4 (November 1788), p. 305; *Pennsylvania Gazette*, March 19, 1788; March 31, 1790; June 12, 1791; Eugene Ferguson, *Oliver Evans: Inventive Genius of the American Industrial Revolution* (Greenville, Del.: Hagley Museum, 1980); Pennsylvania Society for the Encouragement of Manufactures and the Useful Arts, Minutes, 2 vols., HSP, esp. December 21, 1787, and January 22, 1788; Cynthia J. Shelton, *The Mills of Manayunk: Industrialization and Social Conflict in the Philadelphia Region, 1787–1837* (Baltimore: Johns Hopkins University Press, 1986), pp. 26–30, 46–48.

7. Tench Coxe, *A View of the United States of America* (Philadelphia, 1794); Richard Vernier, "The Fortunes of Orthodoxy: The Political Economy of Public Debt in England and America during the 1780s," in *Articulating America: Fashioning a National Political Culture in Early America, Essays in Honor of J. R. Pole*, ed. Rebecca Starr (Madison, Wis.: Madison House, 2000), pp. 93–130; Shawn Kimmel, "Sentimental Police: Struggles for 'Sound Policy and Economy' amidst the Torpor of Philanthropy in Mathew Carey's Philadelphia," *Early American Studies* 3 (Spring 2005): 164–226.

8. Donald R. Adams, Jr., "Wage Rates in the Early National Period: Philadelphia, 1785–1830," *Journal of Economic History* 28 (1968): 404–26; Nash, *Forging Freedom*, pp. 144–58; Edwin T. Freedley, *Philadelphia and Its Manufactures: A Hand-book* (Philadelphia: Edward Young, 1859); Shelton, *Mills of Manayunk*, p. 41; Philip Scranton, *Proprietary Capitalism: The Textile Manufacture at Philadelphia, 1800–1885* (New York: Cambridge University Press, 1983), pp. 42–44; and Lindstrom, *Economic Development*, chap. 1; Bruce Laurie, *The Working People of Philadelphia, 1800–1840* (Philadelphia: Temple University Press, 1980), pp. 11–13; Stuart M. Blumin, *The Emergence of the Middle Class: Social Experience in the American City, 1760–1900* (New York: Cambridge University Press, 1989); Sam Bass Warner, *The Private City: Philadelphia in Three Periods of Growth* (Philadelphia: University of Pennsylvania Press, 1968); and Nash, *Forging Freedom*, pp. 71–72, 74–78, 161–62.

9. For this and the next two paragraphs, see Douglass North, *The Economic Growth of the United States, 1790–1860* (Englewood Cliffs, N.J.: Prentice-Hall, 1961), pp. 43, 78–80, 177–78, 228; on the significance of re-exports, see David T. Gilchrist, ed., *The Growth of Seaport Cities, 1790–1825* (Charlottesville: University Press of Virginia, 1967), pp. 134–35; *Pennsylvania Gazette*, March 5, 1828; William Sullivan, *The Industrial Worker in Pennsylvania, 1800–1840* (Harrisburg, Pa.: Pennsylvania Historical and Museum Commission, 1955), p. 51; Mathew Carey, *Addresses of the Philadelphia Society for the Promotion of National Industry* (1819; reprint, Philadelphia, 1822); and Mathew Carey, *A View of the Ruinous Consequences of a Dependence on Foreign Markets* (Philadelphia, 1820). On the origins and unfolding of the

Panic, see George Dangerfield, *The Awakening of American Nationalism, 1815–1828* (New York: Harper & Row, 1965), pp. 13–16; Murray Rothbard, *The Panic of 1819: Reactions and Policies* (New York: Columbia University Press, 1962), pp. 3–4, 7, 11–13; *Independent Balance* (Philadelphia), August 18, 1819; *General Advertiser* (Philadelphia), August 28, 1819; J. David Lehman, "Explaining Hard Times: Political Economy and the Panic of 1819 in Philadelphia" (Ph.D. diss., UCLA, 1992); on the Second Bank, see Bray Hammond, *Banks and Politics in America: From the Revolution to the Civil War* (Princeton: Princeton University Press, 1957), esp. pp. 253–54; Leon M. Schur, "The Second Bank of the United States and the Inflation after the War of 1812," *Journal of Political Economy* 68 (February 1960): 119; Laurie, *Working People of Philadelphia*, pp. 11–13; Mathew Carey, *Essays on Political Economy; or, The Most Certain Means of Promoting the Wealth, Power, Resources, and Happiness of States: Applied Particularly to the United States* (Philadelphia, 1822), pp. 9–11. On social conditions, see Larry Peskin, *Manufacturing Revolution: The Intellectual Origins of Early American Industry* (Baltimore: Johns Hopkins University Press, 2003); Priscilla F. Clement, "The Philadelphia Welfare Crisis of the 1820s," *PMHB* 105 (1981): 150–53; Shelton, *Mills of Manayunk*, pp. 59–60, 95–98; Laurie, *Working People*, chap. 1; and Michael Meranze, *Laboratories of Virtue: Punishment, Revolution, and Authority in Philadelphia, 1760–1835* (Chapel Hill: University of North Carolina Press, 1996), pp. 229–30, 235–42. On the debate over the pacing of economic growth in the first half of the nineteenth century, including cities such as Philadelphia, see Robert Gallman, "Economic Growth," in *Encyclopedia of American Economic History*, ed. Glenn Porter, 3 vols. (New York: Scribner, 1980), I:133–50; and Thomas Weiss, "Economic Growth before 1860: Revised Conjectures," in *American Economic Development in Historical Perspective*, ed. Thomas Weiss and Donald Schaefer (Stanford, Calif.: Stanford University Press, 1994), pp. 11–27.

10. Matson, "Permeable Boundaries"; Lindstrom, *Economic Development*, chap. 4.

11. James W. Livingood, *The Philadelphia-Baltimore Trade Rivalry* (Harrisburg, Pa.: Pennsylvania Historical and Museum Commission, 1947); Lindstrom, *Economic Development*, pp. 32–35; John Majewski, *A House Dividing: Economic Development in Pennsylvania and Virginia before the Civil War* (Cambridge, Eng.: Cambridge University Press, 2000), pp. 151–53, chap. 6; Gilchrist, *Growth of Seaport Cities*, pp. 50, 87; Philip Scranton, *Proprietary Capitalism: The Textile Manufacture at Philadelphia, 1800–1885* (New York: Cambridge University Press, 1983), pp. 49–51, 70–72.

12. *Hazard's Register* 8 (1831): 65; *Hazard's Register* 1 (1828): 28; *Hazard's Register* 2 (1828): 30; Scranton, *Proprietary Capitalism*, pp. 95–103, 110–13, 115;. For 1824, see Thomas J. Scharf, *History of Philadelphia, 1609–1884* (Philadelphia: Everts Publishers, 1884), pp. 2234–5; for the late-decade recession, see Sullivan, *Industrial Worker*, p. 52; *Hazard's Register* 3 (1829): 224; and *Hazard's Register* 4 (1829): 336. For Manayunk, see Shelton, *Mills of Manayunk*, pp. 54–58, 86–88. On immigration and

manufactures, see Scranton, *Proprietary Capitalism*, pp. 177–95; Shelton, *Mills of Manayunk*, pp. 33–35; and Majewski, *House Dividing*, pp. 154–58.

13. "House of Refuge," *Mechanic's Free Press*, October 18, 1828; Negley K. Teeters, "The Early Days of the Philadelphia House of Refuge," *Pennsylvania History* 27 (1960): 165–97; Dennis Clark, "Babes in Bondage: Indentured Irish Children in Philadelphia in the Nineteenth Century," *PMHB* 101 (1977): 480–81; Meranze, *Laboratories of Virtue*, p. 283; Hammond, *Banks and Politics in America*, pp. 457–99.

Chapter 2

1. Wares made from silver alloy were called "plate," from the Spanish *plata* (silver). This essay is based in part on materials presented in my Ph.D. dissertation, "The Workmanship of an American Artist": Philadelphia's Precious Metals Trades and Craftsmen, 1788–1832 (University of Delaware, 1981), directed by Dr. John A. Munroe. As a member of the Winterthur Library staff while I undertook the research leading to the dissertation, I benefited from the wise counsel of the late Ian M. G. Quimby, Louise C. Belden, Dr. Frank H. Sommer, and my WPEAC classmate Donald L. Fennimore. Jack L. Lindsey, *Worldly Goods: The Arts of Early Pennsylvania, 1680–1758* (Philadelphia: Philadelphia Museum of Art, 1999), pp. 176–83. James Mease, *The Picture of Philadelphia* (Philadelphia: B.&T. Kite, 1811), p. 74.

2. Tench Coxe, *A Statement of the Arts and Manufactures of the United States of America* (Philadelphia: A. Cornman, Junr., 1814), pp. xxiv–xxxv; Coxe's figures may be distorted, as only three states (Massachusetts, Pennsylvania, and Virginia) reported manufactures of gold and silverwork and jewelry; see Coxe, *Statement*, pp. 14, 37.

3. For the impact of the classical world on aspects of American life, see Wendy A. Cooper, *Classical Taste in America, 1800–1840* (New York: Abbeville, 1993), pp. 8–13. On gentility, see Richard L. Bushman, *The Refinement of America: Persons, Houses, Cities* (New York: Alfred A. Knopf, 1992), pp. 74–78, 409–13.

4. For the Soho Manufactory's "Catalogue of Silverware," see Heather Jane McCormick et al., *Vasemania: Neoclassical Form and Ornament In Europe, Selections from The Metropolitan Museum of Art* (New Haven: Yale University Press, 2004), cat. nos. 46–49, pp. 104–7; Beatrice B. Garvan, *Federal Philadelphia, 1785–1825: The Athens of the Western World* (Philadelphia: Philadelphia Museum of Art, 1987), frontispiece, pp. 18–19, 26–27, 50, 59, 74, 89. Abraham Dubois ventured to Boston in 1805 and secured an order from silversmiths Rufus and Henry Farnam for holloware to be fabricated by his son (Abraham Jr.). Dubois stressed the ready availability of a set or an individual piece of plate of "the urn fashion" that could be forwarded by the first conveyance. Abraham Dubois Letterbook, 1803–1807, Eleutherian Mills Historical Library, Wilmington, Del. (hereafter Eleutherian Mills).

5. Whitfield J. Bell, Jr., ed., *Francis Hopkinson's Account of the Grand Federal Procession Philadelphia 1788* (Boston: Old South Association, 1962), pp. 24–25.

6. As early as 1733, a mill was listed in the estate inventory of Philadelphia silversmith Cesar Ghiselin of Philadelphia

(1670–1733). Joseph Richardson, Sr. (1711–84) used a model imported from England for which he ordered a set of rollers in 1760. The rollers arrived in such rusty condition as to be unacceptable. At the turn of the eighteenth century, refiner Charles Gilchrist advertised "Silver,&c. flatted" for those craftsmen without their own mills; Harrold E. Gillingham, "Cesar Ghiselin," *Pennsylvania Magazine of History and Biography* (hereafter *PMHB*) 57 (July 1933): 248–49; Martha Gandy Fales, *Joseph Richardson and Family: Philadelphia Silversmiths.* (Middletown, Conn.: Wesleyan University Press, 1974), pp. 282–83, n. 23; *Aurora*, December 14, 1797. Silversmith Abraham Dubois procured a cast-steel flatting mill with five-inch rollers, "just the size of my own," from jeweler and hardware merchant John Carrell in 1805 and shipped it to Bedford and Morton of Baltimore. When silversmith John Owen of Callowhill Street near Second Street died in September 1828, his shop contained a rolling mill valued at $15.00. Owen also owned a $20.00 turning lathe, a draw bench and tongs worth $6.00 for the preparation of silver wire and moldings, and an array of stakes, hammers, turning tools, flatware punches, vices, files and scrapers, burnishers, chasing tools to ornament finished articles, shears, pliers, saws, steel and iron binding wire, a soldering lamp, forge tools, a bellows, and scotch and pumice stone for polishing. The value of his tools comprised more than one-third of the total value of his estate; see Philadelphia Register of Wills, Administration 1828, #226. Abraham Dubois Letterbook, 1803–1807, Eleutherian Mills; *Poulson's American Daily Advertiser*, February 7, 1817; March 12, 1817; October 29, 1831; *Relf's Philadelphia Gazette and Daily Advertiser*, January 2, 1812. Advertisement of Matthew George, fall and screw press manufactory, *Mechanics' Free Press*, August 14, 1830.

7. U.S. Bureau of the Census, Third Census, 1810; population schedules, Philadelphia City, National Archives microfilm M–252, Roll 55.

8. Fales, *Richardson*, p. 159; John Fanning Watson, *Annals of Philadelphia*, 3 vols. (Philadelphia: Edwin S. Stuart, 1887), 1:220–21; Bruce Laurie, *Working People of Philadelphia, 1800–1850* (Philadelphia: Temple University Press, 1980), pp. 4–5, 24–27. For an examination of the inner workings of the goldsmith's craft in Boston a century earlier than the present study, see Barbara McLean Ward, "Boston Goldsmiths, 1690–1730," in *The Craftsman in Early America*, ed. Ian M. G. Quimby (New York: W. W. Norton, 1984), pp. 126–57. For one New York City craftsman's experience in the 1794–1820 period, see Deborah Dependahl Waters, "Taste, Trade, and Industry: Making and Marketing New York Silver, 1700–1900," in *Elegant Plate: Three Centuries of Precious Metals in New York City*, ed. Deborah Dependahl Waters, 2 vols. (New York: Museum of the City of New York, 2000), 1:47–48.

9. "This evening a few minutes after Eight O'clock, Father Lownes departed aged about 63 years" (Isaac Harvey Diary, I, June 1820–1824, Historical Society of Pennsylvania (hereafter HSP), entry for December 16, 1820); Philadelphia Register of Wills, Administration 1821, #4; *Poulson's American Daily Advertiser*, January 22, 1821; Philadelphia Monthly Meeting Southern District Minutes, 1781–93, p. 149, March 29, 1786; Negley K. Teeters, "What is Known from Fact and Fiction concerning Hugh and Jane Stretch Lownes," typescript, Department of Sociology, Temple University, 1957, pp. 2–3; Philadelphia Monthly Meeting Minutes, 1782–1789, p. 224, November 25, 1785;

p. 239, January 27, 1786; John Beale's Bond and Judgment, July 16, 1785, 68x28.5, Joseph Downs Collection of Manuscripts and Printed Ephemera, Winterthur Library (hereafter Downs Collection, Winterthur Library).

10. Pennsylvania Abolition Society Papers, vol. I, folder 3, character references for blacks, 1787, Joseph Lownes certificate on behalf of Negro apprentice Joseph Head, October 16, 1787, HSP; Ellen Beasley, "Samuel Williamson: Philadelphia Silversmith, 1794–1813" (Master's thesis, University of Delaware, 1964), p. 4; *Federal Gazette*, April 2, 1792; Philadelphia Register of Wills, Will 1792, #182; *Pennsylvania Packet*, December 18, 1798. Josiah Hewes Lownes was first listed in city directories as a partner in the firm Joseph and Josiah H. Lownes in 1816. James Robinson, ed., *Philadelphia Directory for 1816* (Philadelphia, 1816); Isaac Harvey, Jr. Diary, I, October 22, 1821, HSP; Philadelphia Deed Registry IW 8–257; IW 8–367; Philadelphia Deed Registry, IC 22–257, 262, August 29, 1812; Philadelphia Register of Wills, Will 1823, #154. Philadelphia Register of Wills, Will 1807, #78; Philadelphia Deed Registry, EF 23–698; IW 1–302; IW 8–266, 268; EF 5–139; IC 22–257, 261, 262; IC 25–632; IC 27–451; IW 10–135; Joseph Lownes holder of bonds of Jas. Wilson Esq., July 13, 1795, 68x28.6, Downs Collection, Winterthur Library; Card Index to "Old Loan" Ledger of the Bureau of The Public Debt 1790–1836, National Archives Microfilm Publication 521, Roll 8; Harrold E. Gillingham, "The Cost of Old Silver," *PMHB* 54, no. 1 (1930): 50–51; Philadelphia Deed Registry, D 72–290, Indenture between John David and Susanna his wife and Joseph Lownes, July 18, 1798.

11. Robinson, *Philadelphia Directory for 1816*; James Robinson, ed., *Robinson's Original Annual Directory for 1817* (Philadelphia, 1817); Philadelphia Register of Wills, Will 1834, #138. *Poulson's American Daily Advertiser*, September 6, 1819; May 1, 1821. Bruce Sinclair, *Philadelphia's Philosopher Mechanics: A History of The Franklin Institute, 1824–1865* (Baltimore: Johns Hopkins University Press, 1974), pp. 4–5, 31; Franklin Institute membership roll, 1824.

12. Both the 1817 and 1828 pitchers were part of the collection of the Historical Society of Pennsylvania in 1973; see *Classical America* (Newark: Newark Museum, 1963), no. 96, pp. 91, 101; and File 73.3572, Decorative Arts Photographic Collection, Winterthur Library. Like the 1827 Physick ewer, the 1817 pitcher has both the E.LOWNES in rectangle mark and an accompanying fleur-de-lis (with the name mark struck four times, and the fleur-de-lis struck five times on the underside). The fleur-de-lis may indicate that the alloy used was equivalent in composition to that of French crowns.

13. Philadelphia Deed Registry EF 3–388, 392; Philadelphia City Archives, County Tax Assessment Ledgers, Dock Ward, 1802, p. 11; Philadelphia City Archives, Indentures, II, p. 189, August 27, 1804; Joseph Richardson, Jr. Ledger 1796–1831, AM 92404, f 256–257, HSP; Beasley, "Samuel Williamson," p. 28; Contributionship Insurance Company of Philadelphia, Survey #3424, and Survey #3908, August 4, 1818; *United States Gazette*, May 1, 1817; *Poulson's American Daily Advertiser*, January 13, 1831; November 1, 1832.

14. Harvey Lewis bill to J. Skerrett, June 19, 1823, Loudoun

Papers, Box 34, HSP; Harvey Lewis bill to Chas. Wister, January 22, 1824, Charles Wister Papers, 71x103.737, Downs Collection, Winterthur Library; Harvey Lewis receipt to Reverend Dr. Samuel F. Jarvis, July 1, 1821, 75x139, Downs Collection, Winterthur Library; Wendy A. Cooper, *In Praise of America* (New York: Alfred A. Knopf, 1980), no. 104, pp. 84–85, 87, 269 n. 11. Vase presented to Frederick Graff, HSP, gift of Miss Henrietta Graff, 1906; Beatrice B. Garvan et al., *Philadelphia: Three Centuries of American Art* (Philadelphia: Philadelphia Museum of Art, 1976), no. 219a, pp. 262–63; Henry Simpson, *The Lives of Eminent Philadelphians, Now Deceased* (Philadelphia: William Brotherhead, 1859), p. 435; The Sellers Family Association, *Descendants of Samuel Sellers* (Ardmore, Pa., 1962), p. 40; Eugene S. Ferguson, *Early Engineering Reminiscences (1815–1840) of George Escol Sellers* (Washington, D.C.: Smithsonian Institution Press, 1965), p. xix.

15. At the time of his death in 1834, Edward Lownes owed Harvey Lewis ten thousand dollars plus interest and employed Lewis's former shop clerk. *Poulson's American Daily Advertiser*, August 7, 1827; September 9, 1835; "Sixteenth Quarterly Report, 17 January 1828," *The Franklin Journal and American Mechanics' Magazine* 5, no. 2 (February 1828): 75; Diary of John Sellers, Jr., B/P–31–32d & 32c, American Philosophical Society; Philadelphia Deed Registry GWR 32–211, May 23, 1829; "The Sellers Homes," *Proceedings of the Fourth and Fifth General Meetings of The Sellers Family Association Held in the Years 1916 and 1920*, p. 18; Philadelphia Register of Wills, Will 1834, #238: Morris Family Papers, Elliston Perot Morris Section, Box 24, Ann Morris Receipts, 1830–1858, receipts, Isaac D. Griffith for Edw. Lownes, June 14, 1832, HSP; Philadelphia Register of Wills, Will 1835, #150.

16. Samuel Hildeburn to Nathaniel Munroe, March 16, 1818; Samuel Hildeburn to Charles W. Scott, March 11, 1817; Samuel Hildeburn to Williams & Victor, March 29, 1817; Hildeburn & Woolworths to Jehu Scott, November 15, 1817; Hildeburn & Woolworths to Mr. Jordan, November 18, 1817; Hildeburn & Woolworths to R. Jordan, February 5, 1818; Hildeburn & Woolworths to J. W. Woodbridge, August 9, 1817, in Hildeburn and Woolworths Letterbook 1815–1818, Am 9321, HSP.

17. Joseph Jackson, *Encyclopedia of Philadelphia* (Harrisburg, 1931), II:528–30; *Pennsylvania Packet,* July 8, 1795; *Federal Gazette*, August 22, 1795; Norris Manuscripts, Philadelphia and Other Counties volume, Folio 70, broadside "Whereas Joseph Cooke ... August 15, 1796," HSP; Martin P. Snyder, *City of Independence: Views of Philadelphia before 1800* (New York: Praeger Publishers, 1975), no. 205, fig. 143, pl. 14.

18. Samuel Williamson Daybooks 1803–1809 and 1810–1813, 89x35, Downs Collection, Winterthur Library; Rachel E. C. Layton, "Samuel Williamson's Presentation Silver: Important New Discoveries," *Silver* 25, no. 1 (January–February 1992): 8–13; Waters, *Elegant Plate*, II:403–5.

19. Beasley, "Samuel Williamson," pp. 8–16; *Poulson's American Daily Advertiser*, August 29, 1815.

20. Frank and Dixie Orum Stollenwerck, *The Stollenwerck, Chaudron & Billon Families in America* (Privately printed, 1948), pp. 1–10, 13–15, 19, 26. Norman Mack, *Missouri's Silver Age: Silversmiths of the 1800s* (Carbondale: Southern Illinois University Press, 2005), pp. 20–21, gives Billon's

wedding date as May 12, 1797, based on the Clara Billon Journal, 1876–91, at the Missouri Historical Society, St. Louis. Stollenwerck, *Stollenwerck*, pp. 25–26, 56, 59; *Aurora*, March 22, 1797; *Aurora*, January 2, 1801; Davida Tenebaum Deutsch, "Washington Memorial Prints," *The Magazine Antiques* 111, no. 2 (February 1977): 329, fig. 12; S. Chaudron billhead dated December 9, 1803, Stauffer collection, vol. 18, #1308, HSP.

21. *Aurora*, November 9, 1810; January 4, 1811; March 28, 1811; Donald L. Fennimore, "Chaudron's & Rasch Tea and Coffee Set," *Silver* 17, no. 3 (May–October 1984): 20–22; Ian M. G. Quimby, *American Silver at Winterthur* (Winterthur, Del.: Henry Francis du Pont Winterthur Museum, 1995), pp. 339–45.

22. *Relf's Philadelphia Gazette and Daily Advertiser,* November 19, 1813; *Relf's*, October 20, 1813.

23. *Relf's Philadelphia Gazette and Daily Advertiser*, March 23, 1814.

24. Stollenwerck, *Stollenwerck*, pp. 21, 47, 53, 59–60; Garvan, *Three Centuries of American Art*, pp. 226–27.

25. *Crescent City Silver* (New Orleans: Historic New Orleans Collection, 1980), p. 76; WPA typescript, Index to Records of Aliens' Declarations of Intention and/or Oaths of Allegiance 1789–1880, vol. 9; *Poulson's American Daily Advertiser*, August 4, 1817; November 22, 1817; July 14, 1819; July 16, 1819; August 6, 1819.

26. *Poulson's American Daily Advertiser*, September 9, 1819; September 23, 1819; January 24, 1820; January 31, 1820; April 14, 1820; *Relf's Philadelphia Gazette and Daily Advertiser*, July 15, 1819. Judith B. Gura, "The Anthony Rasch Sauceboats: A High Point of American Neoclassical Style," Part I, *Silver* 31, no. 2 (March/April 1997): 28–33; Part II, *Silver* 31, no. 3 (May/June 1997): 28–32.

27. Delgado Art Museum WPA project typescript, *Louisiana Gazette* (New Orleans), January 21, 1820; July 25, 1820; *Crescent City Silver*, p. 76.

28. U.S. Bureau of the Census, Fourth Census, 1820. Pennsylvania Manufactures, Eastern District (part): Philadelphia, Returns #528, 532, 542, 548. *Philadelphia in 1824; or, A Brief Account of The Various Institutions and Public Objects in This Metropolis* (Philadelphia: H. C. Carey and I. Lea, 1824), pp. 36–40. Carey and Lea noted that directories included only master workmen, householders, and shopkeepers. More recent scholars have confirmed that journeymen of all trades were systematically excluded; see Stuart Blumin, "Mobility and Change in Ante-bellum Philadelphia," in *Nineteenth-Century Cities*, ed. Stephen Thernstrom and Richard Sennett (New Haven: Yale University Press, 1969), pp. 170, 207, n. 8.

29. Deborah Dependahl Waters, "Of Pure Coin: The Manufacture of American Silver Flatware 1800–1860," in *Winterthur Portfolio 12*, ed. Ian M. G. Quimby (Winterthur, Del.: Henry Francis du Pont Winterthur Museum, 1977), pp. 19–20; Robert Wilson Administration, Philadelphia Register of Wills, Administration 1824, #386; *Poulson's American Daily Advertiser*, December 12, 1824; April 8, 1826; January 6, 1827; October 17, 1826; *The United States Gazette*, January 2, 1829; *Pennsylvania Inquirer and Daily Courier*,

June 9, 1834; August 23, 1834.

30. *Poulson's American Daily Advertiser*, February 14, 1832; February 17, 1832; February 20, 1832; February 22, 1832; February 24, 1832; March 13, 1832; Nicholas B. Wainwright, *Philadelphia in the Romantic Age of Lithography* (Philadelphia: Historical Society of Pennsylvania, 1958), no. 380, pp. 24, 215. One student of Philadelphia's working people pinpoints jewelry manufacture as an example of a skilled craft in which laboring traditions and skills remained intact in the 1820s and whose practitioners continued to command high wages and more prestige than those artisans employed in such occupations as tailoring and shoemaking; see Bruce Gordon Laurie, "The Working People of Philadelphia, 1827–1853" (Ph.D. diss., University of Pittsburgh, 1971), p. 12.

31. Diane Lindstrom, *Economic Development in the Philadelphia Region, 1810–1850* (New York: Columbia University Press, 1978), pp. 42–43, 49–51, tab. 2.6, 2.8; George Rogers Taylor, ed., "'Philadelphia in Slices' by George G. Foster," *PMHB* 93 (January 1969): 29.

Chapter 3

1. An anonymous handwritten record of Thomas Fletcher's family genealogy and a portion of a typed but unpublished Fletcher family genealogy assembled by Henry Fletcher in 1950, entitled *Descendants of Robert Fletcher: The First Six Generations,* can be found in the Winterthur Library. A published account of the Fletcher family genealogy assembled by Edward H. Fletcher is entitled *Fletcher Genealogy: An Account of the Descendants of Robert Fletcher, of Concord, Mass.* (Boston: Alfred Mudge & Son, 1871). Sidney Gardiner's family genealogy is detailed in Curtiss C. Gardiner, *Lion Gardiner and His Descendants* (St. Louis: A. Whipple, 1890).

2. Sidney, being the oldest surviving son of a medical doctor, may have had the opportunity to enter that profession, but he did not pursue this.

3. Until the identity of Sidney Gardiner's master is documented, Samuel S. Greene can be considered a likely candidate, among other goldsmiths working at the time in the immediate vicinity, including Nathaniel Austin, Joseph Foster, William Homes, Joseph Loring, Ebenezer Moulton, Samuel Belknap, Epes Ellery, and Ebenezer Brown.

4. Letter, James Fosdick Fletcher to Thomas Fletcher, March 26, 1808, Thomas Fletcher Papers, Collection 39, The Athenaeum of Philadelphia (hereafter Fletcher Papers, Athenaeum).

5. Eddy died in 1804; see *Boston Gazette*, October 14, 1805. The move was announced in the March 3, 1806, issue of *The Repertory*.

6. See Dyer and Eddy advertisement, *Boston Gazette*, June 20, 1803, and Joseph C. Dyer advertisements, *Boston Gazette*, July 21, 1806, and *New England Palladium*, November 21, 1806. Joseph C. Dyer advertisement, *The Repertory*, February 27, 1807.

7. *The Repertory*, June 19, 1807. The address of the sale, number 49 Marlboro Street, is an apparent misprint, since Dyer moved from that location to 48 Marlboro Street in 1806.

8. *Columbian Centinel*, April 20, 1808.

9. *Columbian Centinel*, September 21, 1808.

10. Letter, Thomas Fletcher to James Fosdick Fletcher, December 10, 1808, Fletcher Papers, Athenaeum.

11. This same advertisement repeats in several issues of the newspapers until mid-December.

12. Letter, Thomas Fletcher to John Gardiner, April 21, 1809, Fletcher Papers, Athenaeum.

13. *Columbian Centinel*, December 28, 1808; January 3, 1810; January 10, 1810. *Columbian Centinel*, June 30, 1810; August 18, 1810.

14. Letter, Thomas Fletcher to John Dyer, October 20, 1810, Fletcher Papers, Athenaeum. Of the workmen in their manufactory at this time, the full names of five apprentices are known: Daniel H. Dodge, Ezra Dodge, William D. King, Samuel Wittington, and Benjamin Frobisher. In addition, the given names of two other apprentices are known: John and Douglas. Daniel H. Dodge went on to become foreman of Fletcher and Gardiner's shop, but his career ended abruptly when he stole from them, as recorded in the August 9, 1822, issue of the *Baltimore Patriot* and the February 21, 1823, issue of the *New Bedford Mercury*.

15. Letter, Thomas Fletcher to Joseph Dyer, April 17, 1810, Thomas Fletcher Papers, Collection 1343, Historical Society of Pennsylvania (hereafter Fletcher Papers, HSP).

16. Letter, Thomas Fletcher to John Gardiner, October 18, 1808, Fletcher Papers, Athenaeum.

17. Letter, Thomas Fletcher to John Gardiner, April 21, 1809, Fletcher Papers, Athenaeum.

18. Fletcher to Gardiner, Fletcher Papers, Athenaeum.

19. Letter, Thomas Fletcher to Timothy Fletcher, November 21, 1809, Fletcher Papers, Athenaeum.

20. Letter, Thomas Fletcher to unknown recipient, May 17, 1811, Fletcher Papers, HSP. Letter, Thomas Fletcher to Timothy Fletcher, February 4, 1811, Fletcher Papers, Athenaeum. A billhead from this short-lived partnership survives among the William Stearns papers at Peabody Essex Museum Library, Salem, Massachusetts.

21. Letter, Thomas Fletcher to unknown recipient, May 7, 1811; Letter, Thomas Fletcher to James Fosdick Fletcher, September 13, 1811, Fletcher Papers, HSP.

22. Letter, Thomas Fletcher to James Fosdick Fletcher, October 10, 1811, Fletcher Papers, HSP.

23. Letter, Sidney Gardiner to Thomas Fletcher, April 4, 1810, Fletcher Papers, Athenaeum.

24. Letter, Thomas Fletcher to Timothy Fletcher, October 11, 1811, Fletcher Papers, HSP. Letter, Thomas Fletcher to Timothy Fletcher, December 16, 1811, Fletcher Papers, Athenaeum.

25. Elizabeth Ingerman Wood, "Thomas Fletcher: A Philadelphia Entrepreneur of Presentation Silver," in *Winterthur Portfolio III*, ed. Milo M. Naeve (Winterthur, Del.: Henry Francis du Pont Winterthur Museum, 1967), p. 138.

26. Letter, Thomas Fletcher to Timothy Fletcher, December 19, 1813, Fletcher Papers, Athenaeum. Fletcher's celebratory letter stated: "Since Mr. G [ardiner] and myself removed to this city we have enjoyed a patronage beyond our expectations and, should it be continued, will soon place us in an elevated situation & enable us to be of service to our friends" (Letter, Thomas Fletcher to James Fosdick Fletcher, October 4, 1814, Fletcher Papers, Athenaeum).

27. Nathan Miller, *The U.S. Navy: An Illustrated History* (New York: American Heritage Publishing Company, 1977), pp. 85, 86.

28. Miller, *U.S. Navy*, pp. 96, 100, 101.

29. Isaac Hull subscription list, September 3, 1812, Miscellaneous Collection, Subscription Lists, box 5-C, Historical Society of Pennsylvania. Lieutenant Charles Morris served under Hull on the *Constitution* during its engagement with the *Guerrière*; *Aurora General Advertiser*, September 17, 1812.

30. Letter, Thomas Fletcher to Timothy Fletcher, December 19, 1813; Letter, Thomas Fletcher to James Fosdick Fletcher, January 19, 1814, Fletcher Papers, Athenaeum.

31. *Niles' Weekly Register*, November 6, 1813.

32. Letter, Charles Fletcher to Thomas Fletcher, July 8, 1815, Fletcher Papers, Athenaeum.

33. Letter, Thomas Fletcher to James Fosdick Fletcher, October 5, 1814, Fletcher Papers, Athenaeum.

34. Letter, Thomas Fletcher to Timothy Fletcher, March 15, 1815; Letter, Thomas Fletcher to Asa Peabody, March 19, 1815; Letter, Thomas Fletcher to Timothy Fletcher, May 25, 1815, Fletcher Papers, Athenaeum.

35. *Relf's Philadelphia Gazette and Daily Advertiser*, September 23, 1815.

36. For an excellent discourse on the invention and early history of fused plate, see Frederick Bradbury, *A History of Old Sheffield Plate* (London: Macmillan and Company, 1912), pp. 40, 75–132.

37. These purchases are recorded in a letter from Samuel Dalton to Thomas Fletcher, June 10, 1815, Fletcher Papers, HSP.

38. Letter, Thomas Fletcher to Baldwin Gardiner, June 7, 1815; Letter, Thomas Fletcher to Sidney Gardiner, May 27, 1815, Fletcher Papers, Athenaeum.

39. Although Baldwin Gardiner began his career apprenticing in Fletcher and Gardiner's shop and manufactory, he soon began exploring business on his own under the aegis of F&G. By 1814 he recorded himself in the Philadelphia city directories as a jeweler working first at the southwest corner of Chesnut and Third streets and subsequently at the northeast corner of the same intersection, both addresses just a few doors from Fletcher and Gardiner's shop at the southeast corner of Chesnut and Fourth.

40. *Poulson's American Daily Advertiser*, October 19, 1820. A modified and expanded version of the illustration in the Gardiner and Veron advertisement was used by Lewis Veron after he and Baldwin Gardiner separated in 1826; see 74x388, Joseph Downs Collection of Manuscripts and Printed Ephemera, Winterthur Library. Letter, Thomas Fletcher to Thomas Cox and Company, October, 28, 1833, Thomas Fletcher Papers, Collection 278, Winterthur Library (hereafter Fletcher Papers, Winterthur Library). For an example of such a lamp with Baldwin Gardiner's label, see Donald L. Fennimore, *Metalwork in Early America* (Winterthur, Del.: Henry Francis du Pont Winterthur Museum, 1996), p. 259, fig. 168. Insight into the considerable size of the lamp business for Lewis Veron is found in invoices from Messenger and Sons to Veron among the United States Custom House Papers, Philadelphia, 1790–1869, microfilm 2808–2811, University of Delaware Library.

41. Letter, Thomas Fletcher to Timothy Fletcher, August 25, 1815; Letter, Thomas Fletcher to Charles Fletcher, August 31, 1815; Thomas Fletcher letterbook, Fletcher Papers, Athenaeum.

42. Thomas Fletcher journal, Fletcher Papers, Athenaeum. For more on Denière and Matelin, see Pierre Verlet, *Les Bronzes Dorés Français* (Paris: Grands Manuels Picard, 1987), p. 344; see also Betty C. Monkman, *The White House: Its Historic Furnishings and First Families* (New Tork: Abbeville, 2000), pp. 65, 272.

43. Thomas Fletcher letterbook, Fletcher Papers, Athenaeum.

44. Letter, Sidney Gardiner to Thomas Fletcher, December 15, 1815, Fletcher Papers, Athenaeum.

45. Thomas Fletcher letterbook, Fletcher Papers, Athenaeum. A downfall press of the type described is illustrated in Bradbury, *History of Old Sheffield Plate,* p. 104; a hand-powered rolling mill related to the type described is illustrated on p. 109.

46. Letter, Thomas Fletcher to Sidney Gardiner, May 15, 1815, Fletcher Papers, Athenaeum.

47. Thomas Fletcher letterbook; Letter, Mark Tyzack to Thomas Fletcher, February 6, 1816, Fletcher Papers, Athenaeum.

48. Letter, Thomas Fletcher to William Pelham, April 25, 1818, Fletcher Papers, Athenaeum.

49. Letter, Charles Fletcher to Thomas Fletcher, October 24, 1815, Fletcher Papers, HSP. Felix, Francis, and Frederick Thibault were goldsmiths and jewelers in Philadelphia.

50. The information regarding these buildings is contained in fire insurance surveys done on the property by the Philadelphia Contributionship in 1818; see

www.philadelphiabuildings.org , records CONTRIB-S03796, CONTRIB-S03797, and CONTRIB-S03798.

51. Letter, Charles Fletcher to Thomas Fletcher, July 2, 1815; Letter, Thomas Fletcher to Melina Fletcher, September 24, 1828, Fletcher Papers, Athenaeum.

52. Indenture of apprenticeship, Samuel Wittington to Fletcher and Gardiner, December 16, 1809, Fletcher Papers, Athenaeum.

53. United States Bureau of the Census, Fourth Census, 1820, Pennsylvania Manufactures, Eastern District (part): Philadelphia, Return 532, Record Group 28, National Archives, Washington, D.C.; see also Deborah D. Waters, "The Workmanship of an American Artist: Philadelphia's Precious Metals Trades and Craftsmen, 1788–1832" (Ph.D. diss., University of Delaware, 1981), pp. 129–30.

54. United States Bureau of the Census, Fourth Census, 1820, Pennsylvania Manufactures, Eastern District (part): Philadelphia, Return 532, Record Group 28, National Archives, Washington, D.C. Aurora General Advertiser, November 1, 1822; see also Carroll Wirth Pursell, Early Stationary Steam Engines in America (Washington, D.C.: Smithsonian Institution Press, 1969), pp. 72, 73, 87, 113, 114. Letter, Thomas Fletcher to Baldwin Gardiner, July 20, 1831, Fletcher Papers, Winterthur Library. One of Fletcher's engineers was probably Matthias W. Baldwin, who later founded the Baldwin Locomotive Works.

55. Letter, Charles Fletcher to Thomas Fletcher, January 18, 1829, Fletcher Papers, HSP.

56. Aurora General Advertiser, April 30, 1823.

57. Letter, Charles Fletcher to Thomas Fletcher, May 15, 1828; January 18, 1829; January 19, 1829, Fletcher Papers, HSP.

58. Letter, Charles Fletcher to Thomas Fletcher, February 28, 1829, Fletcher Papers, Athenaeum.

59. Letter, William Pelham to Sidney Gardiner, April 23, 1815, Fletcher Papers, HSP.

60. Letter, Thomas Fletcher to Henry Fletcher, October 3, 1829, Fletcher Papers, Winterthur Library.

61. Noble W. and Lucy F. Hiatt, The Silversmiths of Kentucky, 1785–1850 (Louisville: Standard Publishing Company, 1954), p. 30; see also Marquis Boultinghouse, Silversmiths, Jewelers, Clock and Watch Makers of Kentucky, 1785–1900 (Lexington: By the author, 1980), pp. 61, 62, 119, 120; This Fletcher & Bennett firm is not to be confused with another partnership of the same name, which was between Thomas Fletcher and his nephew Calvin W. Bennett in Philadelphia from 1835 to 1837.

62. Letter, James Fosdick Fletcher to Thomas Fletcher, April 9, 1810, Fletcher Papers, Athenaeum. Letter, Thomas Fletcher to James Fosdick Fletcher, June 11, 1810, Fletcher Papers, HSP.

63. For an illustration and discussion of this medal, see wikipedia.org/Mexican_Imperial_Orders.

64. Letter, Sidney Gardiner to Thomas Fletcher, November 26, 1822, Fletcher Papers, HSP.

65. Letter, Sidney Gardiner to Thomas Fletcher, January 9, 1823; November 26, 1822, Fletcher Papers, HSP. In a subsequent letter, Gardiner noted, "From all that I have seen & learnt, I have not brought half nor even a quarter enough goods with me—goods properly selected for this country will pay from 50 to 100 percent proffit after deducting all expenses which are very high." Letter, Timothy Veron to Thomas Fletcher, February 8, 1824, Fletcher Papers, Athenaeum.

66. Village Record, West Chester, Pa., June 20, 1827. The inventory and appraisal of Sidney Gardiner's estate is at Philadelphia City Hall, Register of Wills, 1828, no. 128, admin. No. N, p. 194.

67. Printed petition, John Stoddard, Thomas Fletcher, Sidney Gardiner, and Richard T. Leech, Philadelphia, November 27, 1819, Fletcher Papers, Athenaeum. William Elliot, The Patentee's Manual (Washington, D.C.: Printed by S.A. Elliot, 1830), p. 82.

68. Undated balance sheet of indebtedness of John O. Stoddard, Fletcher Papers, HSP. Relf's Philadelphia Gazette, August 28, 1820.

69. Letter, George Newbold to Watson & Bradbury, April 7, 1821, BR 173-126, Sheffield City Libraries, Sheffield, England.

70. Letter, Thomas Fletcher to Thomas M. Jolly, January 13, 1834, Fletcher Papers, Winterthur Library. About 1829, John C. Standbridge asked Fletcher to obtain spinning machines through American merchants in Birmingham, Goddard and Bibby. Dyer's improvement was on a bobbin and flyer for spinning cotton patented by Charles Danforth of Ramapo, New York, on September 2, 1828. Letter, Thomas Fletcher to Joseph C. Dyer, September 23, 1832, Fletcher Papers, Winterthur Library.

71. Letter, Samuel Jaudon to Thomas Fletcher, January 14, 1820, Fletcher Papers, Athenaeum.

72. Bruce Sinclair, Philadelphia's Philosopher Mechanics: A History of the Franklin Institute, 1824–1865 (Baltimore: Johns Hopkins University Press, 1974), pp. ix, x, 31. This announcement is in the National Gazette and Literary Register, February 2, 1824.

73. Franklin Institute, Annual Report of the Exhibition (1825), section VI, p. 19. Franklin Institute, Annual Report of the Exhibition (1836), p. 321.

74. Journal of the Franklin Institute 53, no. 1 (January 1867): 69.

75. Letter, Calvin Durand to Thomas Fletcher, June 26, 1832; Letter, John A. Grace to Thomas Fletcher, July 23, 1832, Fletcher Papers, HSP.

76. Letter, Thomas Fletcher to John A. Grace, September 22, 1832, Fletcher Papers, Winterthur Library.

77. Letter, Thomas Fletcher to John A. Grace, April 24, 1833, Fletcher Papers, Winterthur Library.

78. Letter, Thomas Fletcher to John Linton, May 24, 1834; Letter, Thomas Fletcher to Levi Fletcher, May 6, 1834, Fletcher Papers, Winterthur Library.

79. Letter, Thomas Fletcher to Francis Grillet, July 11, 1836; Letter, Thomas Fletcher to Richard Singleton, June 12, 1835, Fletcher Papers, Winterthur Library.

80. Letter, Thomas Fletcher to Samuel Jaudon, August 30, 1834, Fletcher Papers, Winterthur Library. A representative instance is recorded in a letter from William Dubs to Thomas Fletcher, September 11, 1826, Fletcher Papers, Athenaeum. For more on the countermarking of coins, see Ralph C. Gordon, West Indies Countermarked Gold Coins (Erik Press, 1987).

81. Letter, Thomas Fletcher to Veron Fletcher, June 17, 1842, Fletcher Papers, Athenaeum.

82. Letter, Thomas Fletcher to Charles Fletcher, September 6, 1850, Fletcher Papers, Athenaeum. Letter, Thomas Fletcher to Timothy Fletcher, January 18, 1852, Fletcher Papers, Winterthur Library.

83. Letter, Thomas Fletcher to Isaac Otis, November 13, 1852; Letter, Thomas Fletcher to Timothy Fletcher, January 11, 1858; Letter, Thomas Fletcher to Henry Fletcher, December 21, 1857, Fletcher Papers, Winterthur Library. The inventory and appraisal of Thomas Fletcher's estate is on file at the Burlington County Court House, Mount Holly, New Jersey, Register of Wills, Surrogate Office, book 1, p. 174, blocks 3, 4.

Chapter 4

1. Letter, Thomas Fletcher to James Fletcher, October 5, 1814, Thomas Fletcher Papers, Collection 39, The Athenaeum of Philadelphia (hereafter Fletcher Papers, Athenaeum). Thomas Fletcher also placed orders in England and France for his brother James, of Fletcher & Whiting in New Orleans; Letter, James Fletcher to Thomas Fletcher, May 17, 1815, Fletcher Papers, Athenaeum. By 1815 the path to artist Benjamin West's London studio had been well worn by American-born painters (John Trumbull, Gilbert Stuart, Thomas Sully, etc.), but we know of few retail merchants who crossed the Atlantic. William H. Webb (1773–1868), a brass founder in Maine, did travel to Birmingham in 1803–5 to study the brass industry; see Donald L. Fennimore, Metalwork in Early America (Winterthur, Del.: Henry Francis du Pont Winterthur Museum, 1996), p. 248, cat. no 158. Thomas Fletcher letterbook, March 25, 1815, Fletcher Papers, Athenaeum. Fletcher's return voyage departed Liverpool on March 16, 1816, and arrived in Boston on April 28, 1816; certificate of departure and letter, Thomas Fletcher to James F. Fletcher, June 11, 1816, Fletcher Papers, Athenaeum.

2. Letter, Thomas Fletcher to Asa Peabody, Boston, March 19, 1815, "Saml Williams Esq.r will be my friend and banker in London" (Fletcher Papers, Athenaeum). Williams remained a friend, assisting Fletcher & Gardiner again with credit arrangements in 1825, when Fletcher returned to London. On Williams, see Carrie Rebora Barratt and Ellen G. Miles, Gilbert Stuart (New Haven: Yale University Press, 2004), p. 135. We are grateful for Ellen Miles and Margaret Christman for this identification of Williams.

3. Letterbook, June 14, 1815, p. 144, Fletcher Papers, Athenaeum. At that time, Benjamin West was president of

the Royal Academy, London. Letter, Thomas Fletcher to Sidney Gardiner, May 25, 1815, Fletcher Papers, Athenaeum.

4. The artistic responses to eighteenth-century archaeological excavations of Herculaneum and Pompeii, as well as writings extolling arts from ancient Greece and the circulation of motifs in northern Europe and America, are extensively addressed by other texts. For an early work on art history, see Hugh Honour, *Neo-Classicsm* (Baltimore: Penguin Books, 1968). For a recent treatment of decorative arts, see Heather Jane McCormick et al., *Vasemania: Neoclassical Form and Ornament in Europe, Selections from the Metropolitan Museum of Art* (New Haven: Yale University Press, 2004).

5. Dominique-Vivant Denon, *Voyage dans la Basse et la Haute Égypte*, 2 vols. (Paris: Imprimerie de P. Didot l'Aîne, 1802); also *Description de l'Egypte ou recueil des observations et des recherches qui ont été faites en Egypte pendant l'Expédition de l'Armée Française* (Paris: L'Imprimerie Imperiale & L'Imprimerie Royale, 1809–13). As director-general of museums from 1804 until 1815, Denon advised Napoleon with additions to, and management of, his collection of antiquities; see also Timothy Wilson-Smith, *Napoleon and His Artists* (London: Constable, 1996).

6. Recent studies of the subject include Anthony Phillips and Jeanne Sloane, *Antiquity Revisited: English and French Silver-Gilt from the Collection of Audrey Love* (London: Christie's, 1997); Christopher Hartop, *Royal Goldsmiths: The Art of Rundell & Bridge, 1797–1843* (Cambridge, Eng.: John Adamson, 2005); and McCormick, *Vasemania*.

7. Fletcher's entry in his notebook titled "Expenses in Paris" for August 12, 1815, lists purchases of $50.00 for engravings and $1.50 for a catalogue of antiques under the heading of "private" purpose. On September 28, 1815, he listed $165.00 spent for "models," presumably for silver ornament (Fletcher Papers, Athenaeum); Letter, Charles Fletcher to Thomas Fletcher, July 8, 1815, Fletcher Papers, Athenaeum.

8. Fletcher & Gardiner received commissions for gold jewelry from Emperor Iturbide and Spanish aristocrats in Mexico, and a sword from Cuba in the 1820s and 1830s, but the majority of their patrons were not titled or of the level of wealth that patronized Rundell, Bridge & Rundell; Hartop, *Royal Goldsmiths*.

9. Leslie Southwick, "The Silver Vases Awarded by the Patriotic Fund," *Silver Society Journal* (Winter 1990): 27–49.

10. Charles Percier and Pierre-François-Léonard Fontaine, *Recueil des décorations intérieures* (Paris: Chez les Auteurs, 1812). For more on French influence, see Beatrice B. Garvan, *Federal Philadelphia, 1785–1825: The Athens of the Western World* (Philadelphia: Philadelphia Museum of Art, 1987).

11. Elizabeth I. Wood first identified this similarity in "Thomas Fletcher: A Philadelphia Entrepreneur of Presentation Silver," in *Winterthur Portfolio III*, ed. Milo M. Naeve (Winterthur, Del.: Henry Francis du Pont Winterthur Museum, 1967), pp. 138–40. Biennais's tureen is illustrated in Henri Bouilhet, *L'Orfèvrerie Française aux XVIIIe et XIXe siècles* (Paris: H. Laurens,

1910), p. 96; see also Chaudet's design for Empress Marie-Louise Bonaparte in Jean-Marie Pinçon and Olivier Gaube du Gers, *Odiot l'Orfèvre* (Paris: Sous le Vent, 1990), p. 91.

12. Henry Moses, *A Collection of Antique Vases, Altars, Paterae, Tripods, Candelabra, Sarcophagi, &c.* (London: H. G. Bohn, 1814), pl. 34. Giovanni-Battista Piranesi (1720–78) was a draftsman, engraver, and architect whose published designs were widely imitated and collected in northern Europe. Joseph Russell, of the firm Russell and LaFarge, expressed similar selectivity in a letter to President Monroe in 1818, as the firm sought gilded brass mantel clocks in Paris that did not feature nude figures; see Betty C. Monkman, *The White House: Its Historic Furnishings and First Families* (New York: Abbeville, 2000), p. 62.

13. See Moses, *Collection of Antique Vases*; Charles Heathcote Tatham, *Designs for Ornamental Plate, Many of Which Have Been Executed in Silver, from Original Drawings* (London: Printed by Thomas Gardiner for John Barfield, 1806). Rudolph Ackermann, *Repository of Arts* (London: By the author, 1817–19). Sidney Gardiner's executors listed 30 volumes in his estate; see City of Philadelphia Register of Wills, Admin. files, 1828, file k28, book N, p. 194. When Thomas Fletcher died in 1866, his single most valuable possession other than jewelry and debts owed him was his library. The Denière & Matelin partnership in Paris provided Fletcher with models; Notebook, "Expenses in Paris," August and September 1815, Fletcher Papers, Athenaeum. Thomas Fletcher bought chasing tools and some prints in London; see Letterbook, June 14, 1815, p. 144, Fletcher Papers, Athenaeum.

14. Donald Fennimore, "Thomas Fletcher and Sidney Gardiner: The Stylistic Development of Their Domestic Silver," *The Magazine Antiques* 102, no. 4 (October 1972): 642–49.

15. For the Rodgers service, see French *légumier* and *écuelle à bouillon* forms such as one illustrated in Véronique Alemany-Dessaint, *Orfèvrerie Française* (Paris: Editions de l'Illustration Baschet, 1988), p. 121, fig. 1. Winged paw feet on the sauceboats and cake basket appear in contemporary Philadelphia silver but also in Odiot's work and in Charles Percier designs. The winged feet on both Rodgers tureens and Jackson vase and mantled eagle-handle terminals of Rodgers's pitchers and vegetable tureens reflect Egyptian motifs. For Jackson vase designs, see Chap. 6, Drawing 5. The comment about Jackson's vase was printed in the *Boston Gazette*, September 26, 1816; *Salem Gazette*, September 27, 1816; *Newburyport Herald*, September 27, 1816; and *The Providence Gazette*, September 28, 1816. For the Rodgers service, see *Niles' Weekly Register*, June 14, 1817, p. 245. See also a design for an Odiot service for Empress Marie-Louise pictured in Pinçon and du Gers, *Odiot l'Orfèvre*, p. 91. Letter, Thomas Fletcher to Charles Fletcher, August 31, 1815, Fletcher Papers, Athenaeum.

16. "The Fine Arts," *The American Beacon and Commercial Diary*, November 28, 1816, p. 3.

17. See Nicholas M. Penzer, *Paul Storr: The Last of the Goldsmiths* (London: B. T. Batsford, 1954), p. 27.

18. Letterbook, June 14, 1815, p. 144, Fletcher Papers, Athenaeum.

19. Books of architecture and antiquities in the Library Company of Philadelphia included Alexander Adam, *Roman Antiquities*, 5th ed. (London, 1801); P. Bouillon, *Musée des Antiquités, Dessine at Grave* (Paris); Francisco Gorius, *Antiquitates Etruscae* (Norimb, 1770); Basil Kennett, *The Antiquities of Rome* (Philadelphia, 1822); James Stuart and Nicholas Revett, *The Antiquities of Athens, Measured and Delineated* (London, 1762); and Andrea Palladio, *First Book of Architecture* (1676); see *Catalogue of the Books* (Philadelphia: C. Sherman and Co., 1837).

20. Benjamin H. Latrobe, *Anniversary Oration Pronounced before the Society of Artists of the United States, by Appointment of The Society, On the Eighth of May, 1811*, Winterthur Library.

Chapter 5

1. Thomas Hope, *Household Furniture and Interior Decoration* (London: Printed by T. Bensley for Longman, Hurst, Rees & Orme, 1807), p. 1.

2. *Columbian Centinel*, November 9, 1808; October 6, 1810; January 5, 1811; March 13, 1811.

3. Wendell Garrett, "*Novus Ordo Seclorum*: A New Order of the Ages," in *Neo-Classicism in America* (New York: Hirschl & Adler Galleries, 1991), pp. 10, 11.

4. *Niles' Weekly Register*, June 14, 1817, p. 245.

5. Bayard Tuckerman, *The Diary of Philip Hone, 1828–1851*, 2 vols. (New York: Dodd, Mead, 1889), 1:289. Letter, Charles Fletcher to Thomas Fletcher, July 8, 1815, Thomas Fletcher Papers, Collection 39, The Athenaeum of Philadelphia (hereafter Fletcher Papers, Athenaeum). For a survey of the partners' household silver, see Donald L. Fennimore, "Thomas Fletcher and Sidney Gardiner: The Stylistic Development of their Domestic Silver," *Antiques* 102, no. 4 (October 1972): 642–49.

6. *Baltimore Patriot*, October 11, 1823. Platina is another name for platinum. *The Union*, Washington, Kentucky, August 2, 1816. Letter, Fletcher & Bennett to A. Girard & Company, December 28, 1835, Thomas Fletcher Papers, Collection 278, Joseph Downs Collection of Manuscripts and Printed Ephemera, Winterthur Library (hereafter Fletcher Papers, Winterthur Library). Clare Le Corbeiller, "The Construction of Some Empire Silver," *Metropolitan Museum Journal* 16 (1982): 195–98; Anthony Phillips and Jeanne Sloane, *Antiquity Revisited: English and French Silver-Gilt from the Collection of Audrey Love* (London: Christie's, 1997), p. 136.

7. Letter, Thomas Fletcher to Baldwin Gardiner, March 8, 1831, Fletcher Papers, Winterthur Library.

8. The dozens of die-rolled ornamental borders on early nineteenth-century American silver offer rich potential for research. The only signed examples presently recorded bear the name of Moritz Furst (b. 1782), a die sinker who emigrated from Germany to Philadelphia and later New York. A few ornamental rolled borders and stamped panels made with dies he cut, which he marked *Furst F*[ecit], appear in tea sets and pitchers marked by New York and Philadelphia silversmiths.

9. Letter, Baldwin Gardiner to Thomas Fletcher, August 29, 1828, Fletcher Papers, Athenaeum.

10. *Niles' Weekly Register*, October 3, 1829, p. 90. Letter, Robert & Andrew Campbell to Thomas Fletcher, June 8, 1831, Thomas Fletcher Papers, Collection 1343, Historical Society of Pennsylvania (hereafter Fletcher Papers, HSP). Letter, Thomas Fletcher to Alfred Welles, September 18, 1832, Fletcher Papers, Winterthur Library.

11. An additional instance, wherein silverware made in Fletcher and Gardiner's manufactory bears the mark of Washington, D.C. jeweler and watchmaker Seraphim Masi, is discussed in Jean Taylor Federico, "An Unfinished Tale of Three Cities," *Washington Antiques Show Catalogue* (1980), pp. 87–90. Fletcher & Gardiner were not the only silver manufacturers to supply others in the trade. This little-studied aspect of the trade seems to have been fairly widespread during the early nineteenth century and deserves further scrutiny.

12. Specialist artisans in the manufactory included engraver George Fletcher and watchmaker Jeremiah Tolman. Independent jobbers were engravers William and John Warr and William Hooker; die sinkers John McPherson and Mark Tyzack, the latter in Sheffield, England; sword-blade maker William Rose; and decorators John Meer and William Tucker. Many others remain anonymous, such as spoon makers in Fletcher's employ and chasers to whom he jobbed work.

13. Letter, John Linton to Thomas Fletcher, August 11, 1830, Fletcher Papers, HSP.

Chapter 6

1. The drawings for hollowware were acquired by the Metropolitan Museum of Art in 1953 from the Old Print Shop in New York. Nothing is known of their earlier provenance. A typed list of the drawings, dated 2/28/52 and presumably created by the dealer, is numbered 1 through 36, corresponding to the numerals written in graphite on each drawing; curatorial files, The Metropolitan Museum of Art. Of the sword drawings, three belong to the Maryland Historical Society in Baltimore (the gifts of individual donors), and the fourth was purchased by the Metropolitan Museum in 1995.

2. Philippa Glanville, *Silver in England* (London: Unwin Hyman, 1987), p. 248; see also Martha Gandy Fales, *Early American Silver for the Cautious Collector* (New York: Funk & Wagnalls, 1970), p. 115. The term *pattern drawing* was introduced to me by Michael Snodin at the Victoria & Albert Museum, London, to whom I offer many thanks for his insightful observations.

3. For information on watermarks, see Thomas L. Gravell and George Miller, *American Watermarks, 1690–1835* (New Castle, Del.: Oak Knoll Press, 2002); and Thomas L. Gravell and George Miller, *A Catalogue of Foreign Watermarks Found on Paper Used in America, 1700–1835* (New York: Garland Publishing, 1983). English-made Whatman papers were exported widely to Europe and North America; see Theresa Fairbanks Harris and Scott Wilcox, *Papermaking and the Art of Watercolor in Eighteenth-Century Britain* (New Haven: Yale University Press, 2006), p. 63. On excise duties, see Harris and Wilcox,

Papermaking and the Art of Watercolor, p. 134. I am grateful to Peter Bower for confirming the meaning of the blind stamps; see Peter Bower, *Turner's Later Papers: A Study of the Manufacture, Selection, and Use of His Drawing Papers, 1820–1851* (New Castle, Del.: Oak Knoll Press, 1999), nos. 49, 68, 70.

4. Letter, Thomas Fletcher to his wife, Melina, March 12, 1825; Letter, Thomas Fletcher to J. A. Grace, September 18, 1832, Thomas Fletcher Papers, Collection 39, The Athenaeum of Philadelphia (hereafter Fletcher Papers, Athenaeum). Letter, Thomas Fletcher to Thomas Smith, February 11, 1837, Fletcher Papers, Athenaeum.

5. Glanville, *Silver in England*, p. 171.

6. Letter, Charles Fletcher to Thomas Fletcher, July 2, 1815; Letter, Thomas Fletcher to Charles Fletcher, August 31, 1815, Fletcher Papers, Athenaeum; see also cat. no. 20. On the Bridports, see James F. O'Gorman et al., *Drawing toward Building: Philadelphia Architectural Graphics, 1732–1986* (Philadelphia: Pennsylvania Academy of the Fine Arts, 1986), p. 65; and Alexandra Alevizatos Kirtley, "George Bridport," and "The Painted Furniture of Philadelphia: A Reappraisal," *The Magazine Antiques* 169, no. 5 (May 2006): 76–79, 138–39. Advertisements for the Bridports' Academy for Drawing appeared in the press, e.g. *Poulson's American Daily Advertiser*, January 29, 1817, p. 4, and February 27, 1817, p. 4. The Clinton watercolor is in the collection of the Metropolitan Museum, acc. no. 53.652.2; see Catherine Hoover Voorsanger and John K. Howat, eds., *Art and the Empire City, New York, 1825–1861* (New York: Metropolitan Museum of Art, 2000), p. 356, fig. 290. On the Franklin Institute, see Bruce Sinclair, *Philadelphia's Philosopher Mechanics: A History of the Franklin Institute, 1824–1865* (Baltimore: Johns Hopkins University Press, 1974); and Henry Butler Allen, "The Franklin Institute of the State of Pennsylvania," *Transactions of the American Philosophical Society*, n.s. 43 (1953): 275–79.

7. On design drawings, see Charles Oman, "A Problem of Artistic Responsibility: The Firm of Rundell, Bridge & Rundell," *Apollo* 83 (March 1966): 174–83; Michael Snodin, "J. J. Boileau, A Forgotten Designer of Silver," *Connoisseur* 198 (June 1978): 124–33; Michael Snodin, "Some Designs for English Gold and Silver," in *The V&A Album 4* (London: Associates of the V&A, 1985), pp. 147–53; Hilary Young, "Sir William Chambers and John Yenn: Designs for Silver," *Burlington Magazine* 128 (January 1986): 30–35; Hilary Young, "Neo-Classical Silversmiths' Drawings at the Victoria and Albert Museum," *Apollo* 129 (June 1989): 384–88; and Artemis Group, *Valadier, Three Generations of Roman Goldsmiths: An Exhibition of Drawings and Works of Art* (London: David Carritt Limited, 1991). For more on the Rundell, Bridge & Rundell firm, see Christopher Hartop, *Royal Goldsmiths: The Art of Rundell & Bridge, 1797–1843* (Cambridge, Eng.: John Adamson, 2005). Exceptionally complete records survive—albeit without the names of individual draftsmen—for the eighteenth-century London partnership of John Parker and Edward Wakelin. The Parker and Wakelin ledgers detail the extent to which the firm contracted with refiners, gilders, engravers, piercers, jewelers, and specialist silversmiths to serve its many clients; see Helen Clifford, *Silver in London: The Parker and Wakelin Partnership, 1760–1776* (New Haven: Yale University Press, 2004), pp. 208–9.

8. Letter, Sidney Gardiner to Thomas Fletcher, April 4, 1810, Fletcher Papers, Athenaeum. The pair of Chaudron sauceboats was sold at Sotheby's New York, January 18, 2001, lot 280.

9. The Faris drawings are illustrated in Mark B. Letzer and Jean B. Russo, eds., *The Diary of William Faris: The Daily Life of an Annapolis Silversmith* (Baltimore: Maryland Historical Society, 2003), pp. 429–50; the full set of drawings was also published in J. Hall Pleasants and Howard Sill, *Maryland Silversmiths, 1715–1830* (Baltimore: Lord Baltimore Press, 1930), pls. 48–67. Among the reference books available by this date at the Library Company of Philadelphia were Thomas Hope, *Household Furniture and Interior Decoration* (London: Printed by T. Bensley for Longman, Hurst, Rees, and Orme, 1807) and G. B. Piranesi, *Vasi, Candelabri, Cippi, Sarcophagi, tripodi Lucerne et ornamenti antichi* (Rome, 1778).

10. There is no indication that these handwritten letters relate in any other way to the drawing. Margaret Lawson noted the use of similar pin pricks as guidelines on medieval manuscripts.

11. *Portsmouth Oracle*, October 31, 1807, p. 2. Selected references to Dobel's sea journeys appear in early American newspapers, e.g. *The Carolina Gazette*, July 17, 1800, p. 1; *American Citizen and General Advertiser*, August 1, 1801, p. 2; and *New-York Gazette & General Advertiser*, February 12, 1807, p. 3. Canton factory records indicate that the *Asia* arrived in Canton on September 11, 1807, from Philadelphia with Captain Williamson and a crew of 32 men aboard; see Rhys Richards, "United States Trade with China, 1784–1814," *The American Neptune*, special supp. to vol. 54 (1994): 51. I am most grateful to Wendy Schnur, Reference Manager, G. W. Blunt White Library, Mystic Seaport, for this reference. For other references to Captain Williamson as master of the *Asia*, see Richards, "United States Trade," pp. 49, 57; *Poulson's American Daily Advertiser*, May 6, 1807, p. 1; and *Mercantile Advertiser*, May 17, 1810, p. 2. On marine insurance, see Dalit Baranoff, "Fire Insurance in the United States," *EH Net Encyclopedia*, October 1, 2004, http://eh.net/encyclopedia/article/Baranoff.Fire.final.

12. Regarding Chaudron, Sidney Gardiner wrote to Thomas Fletcher on April 4, 1810, "I have made A bargain with him to let us have silver goods & pay A part in our work" (Fletcher Papers, Athenaeum). There is also evidence that the two firms retailed related goods, for instance the sauceboat of 1812–20 (see cat. no. 21). A similar pair is marked by Chaudron; see Sotheby's New York, January 18, 2001, lot. 280.

13. Thomas Amies bought the mill, which had been owned by Conrad Schütz, in 1798. Originally from Switzerland, Amies is identified in Philadelphia city directories from 1791 to 1807 as a "cordwainer" or "shoemaker" and in the 1809 directory as a "paper manufacturer"; see Gravell and Miller, *American Watermarks*, p. 236. The configuration of the marks on these sheets suggests that the paper dates from about 1804; Gravell and Miller, *American Watermarks*, p. 12, figs. 57–58.

14. See *Relf's Philadelphia Gazette and Daily Advertiser*, August 10, 1810, p. 3 (my thanks to Richard Lindberg,

Genealogy and Local History Librarian at the State Library of Pennsylvania for supplying a photocopy of the *Relf's* notice); *Mercantile Advertiser*, August 13, 1810, p. 2; *The Evening Post*, August 16, 1810, p. 3; and *Boston Gazette*, August 16, 1810, p. 2. For an Italian silver comparison, see Giovacchino Belli's silver-gilt bowl and cover at the Metropolitan Museum, acc. no. 1981.204.1, illustrated in *Notable Acquisitions, 1981–1982* (New York: Metropolitan Museum of Art, 1983), p. 30.

15. The same stamp appears on Drawing 11. My thanks to Peter Bower for his comments on these stamps and to Jean Stirk and Harry Dagnall of the British Association of Paper Historians for their helpful guidance.

16. A teapot in the collection of the Sterling and Francine Clark Art Institute in Williamstown, Massachusetts, marked by Fletcher & Gardiner (acc. no. 2003.4.262), is of related design, particularly the cover and spout, although the bird's head is slightly different. The pot sits on a circular base, and the handle sockets are of cornucopia design.

17. The four cast eagles on the base of the Jackson vase are documented replacements of the early twentieth century (see cat. no. 22). I am indebted to Michael Snodin for his observations on this drawing and its similarity to Boileau's designs. Boileau came to London around 1787 to work at Carlton House under the direction of Henry Holland; see Snodin, "J. J. Boileau," pp. 124–33, in particular figs. 11, 12; see also Hilary Young, "A Further Note on J. J. Boileau, 'a Forgotten designer of Silver,'" *Apollo* 124 (October 1986): 334–37. Coiled snake handles also appear on antique vases; see, for example, a marble vase illustrated in Piranesi's *Vasi, Candelabri, Cippi*, reproduced in John Wilton-Ely, *Giovanni Battista Piranesi: The Complete Etchings*, vol. 2 (San Francisco: Alan Wofsy Fine Arts, 1994), pl. 963. For paw feet, see Boileau's sketches in Arthur Grimwade, "New Light on Canadian Treasure: The Royal Communion Service of Quebec," *Country Life* 31 (January 1985): 272, fig. 8; see also Thomas Hope, *Household Furniture and Interior Decoration* (1807; reprint, New York: Dover, 1971), pls. 11, no. 1, and pls. 33–36. Jackson described this moment in a letter to the secretary at war, published in the press: "I cannot speak sufficiently in praise of the firmness and deliberation with which my whole line received their approach" (*The National Advocate*, February 10, 1815, p. 2). A sketch related to the regimented line of American soldiers appears on the verso of Drawing 24. The precise source for this scene has not been identified, but the battle prompted the production of a large number of prints and at least one painting; see John Carbonell, "Prints of the Battle of New Orleans," in *Prints of the American West: Papers Presented at the Ninth Annual North American Print Conference*, ed. Ron Tyler (Fort Worth: Amon Carter Museum, 1983), pp. 1–12; and Carl W. Drepperd, "Three Battles of New Orleans," *The Magazine Antiques* 14, no. 2 (August 1928): 129–31.

18. See cat. no. 20.

19. Compare the design of a tureen of 1800–1809 by Henri Auguste, illustrated in Heather Jane McCormick et al., *Vasemania: Neoclassical Form and Ornament in Europe, Selections from The Metropolitan Museum of Art* (New Haven: Yale University Press, 2004), cat. no. 67. For

English silver plate, see Frederick Bradbury, *History of Old Sheffield Plate* (London: Macmillan and Co., 1912), pp. 265, 285, 417, 419. The sketch appears in pocket notebook, Fletcher Papers, Athenaeum. For similar handles on other drawings, see Drawings 9 and 15. See cat. no. 83 for the Lewis tureens, Ches. & Del. Canal Co.

20. Drawings for silver wine coolers by the French designer J. J. Boileau include such heads; see Snodin, "J. J. Boileau," figs. 10, 11; see also fig. 12 for a silver-gilt wine cooler marked by Paul Storr in 1803/4 with similar cast and applied mounts.

21. This drawing was accessioned in 1953 but cannot be located in the Metropolitan Museum's Department of Drawings and Prints; only a photograph of the verso is on file. For a discussion of the importation of silver-plated wares by the firm of Fletcher & Gardiner, see Chap. 3. For a similar entrée dish as it appeared in an 1818 Watson & Bradbury catalogue, see Bradbury, *History of Old Sheffield Plate*, p. 417; the entrée dish follows English design prototypes, but the tureen is more French in style; see Bradbury, *History of Old Sheffield Plate*, pp. 284–85, 164. For the bud finial, see Drawing 11. There are three vegetable dishes in the collection of the New-York Historical Society (acc. nos. 1951.285a-f) and one in a private collection (see cat. no 64); see also those supplied to Charles Chauncey as part of an extensive dinner service that included four oblong covered dishes (see cat. no. 54).

22. The species of oak seen here appears to be the Holm or Holly Oak, native to the Mediterranean and the south and west of Britain. The shape and veining of the leaves and the long acorn cups are similar to those drawn here; I am grateful to Dorrie Rosen at the New York Botanical Garden for this suggestion. Donald Fennimore has also noted the resemblance of these leaves to the Laurel Oak, which grows in Pennsylvania. In either case, it is as likely that the draftsman's source was a published illustration or a silver object rather than an actual oak leaf and acorn. Similar leaves and acorns appear on a vase presented to Guinn Harris in 1831 (see cat. no. 60). Acorns can be seen on a gold phiale (libation bowl) from the 4th century BC at The Metropolitan Museum of Art, acc. no. 62.11.1. I am grateful to Joan Mertens for making this connection.

23. One of the sketches that Fletcher made in his pocket notebook depicts a krater vase, but with gadrooning above the foot, egg-and-dart at the lip, and without handles; Fletcher Papers, Athenaeum. The Medici krater is illustrated in Wilton-Ely, *Giovanni Battista Piranesi*, p. 1017, pl. 939; a design by J. J. Boileau for Rundell's wine cooler is published in Young, "Further Note on J. J. Boileau," fig. 7; for silver-gilt models of the vase, see Hartop, *Royal Goldsmiths*, p. 100, fig. 91; p. 150, cat. no. 23. Piranesi's *Vasi* entered the Library Company of Philadelphia's collection in 1803; Hope's *Household Furniture* did so about the time of its publication in 1807. My thanks to Cornelia S. King, Reference Librarian at the Library Company, for confirming acquisition dates of these volumes.

24. For Rundell's use of the krater form, see Hartop, *Royal Goldsmiths*, p. 100, fig. 91; p. 150, cat. no. 23. The form was also produced in Sheffield plate; see Bradbury, *History of Old Sheffield Plate*, pp. 835–36; see also Drawing 10. See

Wilton-Ely, *Giovanni Battista Piranesi*, pls. 820, 921, 931, 932–33, 937, 939; and Henry Moses, *A Collection of Antique Vases, Altars, Paterae, Tripods, Candelabra, Sarcophagi, &c.* (London: H. G. Bohn, 1814), pls. 40–45. Delicate vine ornament of this type occurs in ancient art as well as in border patterns for eighteenth- and early nineteenth-century creamware designed by Wedgwood; see Wilton-Ely, *Giovanni Battista Piranesi*, pls. 901, 938, 940, 943; and Wolf Mankowitz, *Wedgwood* (London: Spring Books, 1953), col. pl. 5. Wedgwood's first pattern book (ca. 1769–1814) is housed at the Wedgwood Museum in Barlaston, England. The Boulton wine coolers are Metropolitan Museum acc. nos. 66.192.12a-c, 66.192.13a-c.

25. My thanks to Joan Mertens for the observation about birds' heads; compare Dietrich von Bothmer, "A Greek and Roman Treasury," *The Metropolitan Museum of Art Bulletin* 42 (Summer 1984): figs. 65, 66, 76, 114, 115. This pitcher is nearly identical to another of the drawings (Drawing 14), which is shown without a handle. Although neither sheet is dated, Drawing 14 is rendered on paper watermarked J WHATMAN / TURKEY MILL, indicating that it probably dates from the 1820s or 1830s.

26. The indented lines are visible under the microscope; other drawings in this group display similar indentations. See Drawing 13.

27. On the double C-scroll handle, see Drawing 9.

28. For related porcelain dishes, see Donald C. Pierce, *English Ceramics: The Frances and Emory Cocke Collection* (Atlanta: High Museum of Art, 1988), cat. nos. 135, 173. For the fan-shape thumbpiece, see Geoffrey A. Godden, *An Illustrated Dictionary of British Pottery and Porcelain* (New York: Bonanza Books, 1965), figs. 100, 542, pl. 13.

29. For the border, see Drawing 10; Drawing 11; cat. no. 39; cat. no. 41; and cat. no. 42. For the handle, compare Drawing 31 and Drawing 32. For a similar handle treatment on a Fletcher & Gardiner flagon, see cat. no. 52. For French examples, see a drawing from the workshop of Henri Auguste in McCormick., *Vasemania*, cat. no. 65. For leaf-capped paw feet, compare cat. no. 24; cat. no. 46; and cat. no. 47.

30. For the designs, see Richard H. Randall, "Sword Designs by Thomas Fletcher," *The American Arms Collector* 1, no. 4 (October 1957): 103–5; cat. no. 79. Fletcher Papers, Athenaeum.

31. For watermarks dated 1835, see Drawings 22, 24, 29, and 30. Similar handles are found on extant ewers marked by the firm; see cat. nos. 52 and 80. A silver pitcher of this design without the extra chasing survives in a private collection; it weighs just under 40 troy ounces (39 oz. 16 dwt.) and has an inscription dated 1838.

32. For 1830s design elements, see Michael Clayton, *The Collector's Dictionary of the Silver and Gold of Great Britain and North America* (New York: World Publishing Company, 1971), pl. 147. For an overview of European chalices, see Carl Hernmarck, *The Art of the European Silversmith, 1430–1830*, 2 vols. (London: Sotheby Parke Bernet, 1977), I:306–13, II:319–27; see also Arthur Grimwade, "Georgian Church Plate," *Proceedings of the Society of Silver Collectors* 2 (Spring 1982): 222–26.

33. For silver owned by the Park Street Church, see E. Alfred Jones, *The Old Silver of American Churches* (Letchworth, Eng.: Privately printed, 1913), pp. 89–90. I am most grateful to Bethany Sayles for searching the church's records for documented church silver by the firm; see also Jones, *Old Silver*, pp. 88–90, 368.

34. The style appears in English church plate by the 1820s; see the altar service of 1822/23 marked by Paul Storr belonging to St. Pancras, Euston Road, illustrated in Timothy Schroder, *Silver and the Church* (London: Silver Society, 2004), fig. 45.

35. An 1818 notice in *Poulson's American Daily Advertiser* advised that LaFourcade had just imported from England "a large quantity" of watercolors and other painting equipment, and "where also may be had, an elegant edition of the New Testament, just published . . . a large variety of Drawing Paper," and "printing of all kinds neatly executed at the shortest notice" (*Poulson's American Daily Advertiser*, February 19, 1818, p. 2).

36. See Drawings 23 and 24.

37. Compare cat. nos. 62 and 83. For ceramic tureens, see Peter Walton, *Creamware and Other English Pottery at Temple Newsam House, Leeds* (Bradford, Eng.: Manningham Press, 1976), pp. 94–95; and Godden, *Illustrated Dictionary of British Pottery and Porcelain*, figs. 502, 607.

38. The profile of the domed cover is very similar to the tureen in Drawing 26.

39. For Clinton vases, see cat. no. 43. For egg-and-dart borders, see Drawings 10 and 11. For banding, compare Drawing 10.

40. See Drawing 30. The banded ornament recalls Sheffield plate designs as well; see Bradbury, *History of Old Sheffield Plate*, p. 364, for tea urns of similar design.

41. Clayton, *Collector's Dictionary*, p. 308. Thomas Fletcher described the form as the "fluted" style; see cat. no. 88. For the Metropolitan Museum's teapot (acc. no. 33.120.530), see C. Louise Avery, *American Silver of the XVII and XVIII Centuries: A Study Based on the Clearwater Collection* (New York: Metropolitan Museum of Art, 1920), p. 172, cat. no. 425. For flower finials, see Drawings 35 and 31 and cat. no. 88. Bradbury, *History of Old Sheffield Plate*, p. 419.

42. See Bradbury, *History of Old Sheffield Plate*, p. 260, coffeepot by M. Fenton & Co.; and Anneke Bambery, "Richard Morton, Sheffield Silversmith," *Antique Collector* 58 (June 1987): fig. 3.

43. On Worth, see John A. Garraty and Mark C. Carnes, eds., *American National Biography*, vol. 23 (New York: Oxford University Press, 1999), pp. 884–85. It is possible that this drawing was prepared for the New York State Assembly, which wrote to Thomas Fletcher on April 17, 1835, to request that a "suitable sword with appropriate devices and emblems thereon" be made for Colonel Worth (Fletcher Papers, Athenaeum). Randall, "Sword Designs by Thomas Fletcher," pp. 105–7.

44. Like the oak leaves depicted on the drawing of a wine cooler, these leaves are drawn without lobes, suggesting a Holm or Holly Oak; see Drawing 10.

45. On Bennett, see Chapter 3.

46. Randall, "Sword Designs by Thomas Fletcher," p. 108.

47. Letter, Thomas Fletcher to Daniel W. Coxe, Esq., December 10, 1836, Thomas Fletcher Papers, Joseph Downs Collection of Manuscripts and Printed Ephemera, Winterthur Library. Postponement of the final polishing until the vessels were to be placed in their cases sheds instructive light on the silversmiths' practice. Drawings for most of the service are not known to survive. By February 1838, when prominent merchant Philip Hone, one-time mayor of New York City, saw the service at "the shop of Messrs. Fletcher & Co., in Chestnut street," he proclaimed it "the most superb service of plate I ever saw . . . It is to cost $15,000" (Bayard Tuckerman, *The Diary of Philip Hone, 1828–1851*, 2 vols. [New York: Dodd, Mead and Company, 1889], 1:288).

48. For the Biddle service, see Drawing 35. The graphite inscription below the drawing is a later addition, and the inscription on the verso referring to S. Bonn & Sons has not been deciphered. Similar ornament occurs on early nineteenth-century designs for French silver, for instance on a mustard pot designed by Charles Percier; see Anthony Phillips and Jeanne Sloane, *Antiquity Revisited: English and French Silver-Gilt, from the Collection of Audrey Love* (London: Christie's, 1997), p. 109, fig. 54. For English silver baskets, see G. B. Hughes, "Pierced Silver Table Baskets," *Country Life* 108 (November 10, 1950): 1603–6. Similar diaperwork appears on Sheffield plate baskets as well; see Bradbury, *History of Old Sheffield Plate*, pp. 80, 205.

Catalogue

Cat. no. 1
1. Martha Gandy Fales, *Jewelry in America* (Woodbridge, Eng.: Antique Collectors' Club, 1995), p. 100, pl. 60.

2. Richard D. Birdsall, *Berkshire County* (New Haven: Yale University Press, 1959), p. 117. The initials "A.E." are believed to be those of Abigail Ellery, née Shaw; the owner of the initials "L.C.E." was Lucy Channing Ellery.

Cat. no. 2
1. Jones pictures a beaker marked by Jacob Hurd, dated 1743, and donated by Isaac Lothrop, and an unmarked beaker given by Deacon Jona Diman, dated 1797, both approximately 6 inches high with molded upper lips, bellied bowls, and low molded feet. The Fletcher & Gardiner cup follows the same general form, although with different proportions and molding ornament; see E. Alfred Jones, *The Old Silver of American Churches*, vol. 2 (Letchworth, Eng.: Privately printed, 1913), pp. 374–76. Fletcher & Gardiner produced a pair of two-handled cups for the Second Baptist Church in Boston, given by Joseph Shed, dated 1811, similar to the Plymouth cup, but with another hand for the engraving.

2. This engraved dedication is unusual in its anonymity; most documented silver from this congregation bears a giver's name; see Jones, *Old Silver*, pp. 374–76. The idiosyncratic variation of an ampersand (&) in the inscription is not unlike one used by Fletcher and Gardiner in an early mark; see Appendix 1, fig. 2a.

Plymouth Church Records 1620–1859, vol. 3 (New York: New England Society, 1923), p. 556 (December 9, 1807).

Cat. no. 3
1. Ellis Paxson Oberholtzer, *Philadelphia: A History of the City and Its People*, 4 vols. (Philadelphia: S. J. Clarke Publishing Company, 1912), 2:35, 339.

Cat. no. 4
1. Fletcher & Gardiner ecclesiastical silver is recorded in Boston and Hadley, Mass.; Wilmington, Del.; Philadelphia and Pittsburgh, Pa.; and possibly in Virginia, from 1808 to 1835. The known patrons were Congregationalist, Baptist, and Episcopal congregations.

2. Karen Parsons recently published an investigation of Elizabeth Phelps's personal commitment to the Hadley congregation and her contributions to their new meeting house; see Karen Parsons, "'We owe something more than prayers': Elizabeth Porter Phelps's Gift of Church Silver and Her Quest for Christian Fellowship," in *New England Silver & Silversmithing, 1620–1815*, ed. Jeannine Falino and Gerald W. R. Ward (Boston: Colonial Society of Massachusetts, 2001), pp. 91–112. For family documents, see *Porter-Phelps-Huntington Family Papers (1698–1968)*, Amherst College Archives & Special Collections.

Cat. no. 5
1. Samuel Adams and Sarah Adams, *The Complete Servant* (London: Knight & Lacey, 1825), pp. 282–83.

2. The Sheepshanks set, made in Philadelphia and so stamped, could not date prior to 1811, when the partners settled there. Therefore, it was made to commemorate rather than celebrate the marriage; for Dyer's ad, see *Columbian Centinel*, October 23, 1805.

3. The Fletcher & Gardiner advertisement is in *Columbian Centinel*, October 6, 1810. A French casserole with identical handles is illustrated in Henri Bouilhet, *L'Orfèvrerie Française aux XVIIIᵉ et XIXᵉ siècles* (Paris: H. Laurens, 1910), p. 169.

Cat. no. 6
1. Such a mill was included in an auction notice of the estate of Boston silversmith Isaac Hull in the *Columbian Centinel*, May 8, 1811.

2. Auction catalogue, Parke-Bernet Galleries, New York, no. 2888, September 16–18, 1969, lot 851.

Cat. no. 7
1. Ian M. G. Quimby, *American Silver at Winterthur* (Winterthur, Del.: Henry Francis du Pont Winterthur Museum, 1995), p. 452, ent. 473.

2. Frederic L. Billon, *Annals of St. Louis* (St. Louis: By the author, 1888), p. 260.

Cat. no. 8
1. On the round style, see Letter, Charles Fletcher to Thomas Fletcher, July 8, 1815, Collection 39, Thomas Fletcher Papers, Athenaeum of Philadelphia (hereafter Fletcher Papers, Athenaeum). The single exception to the ornament is the collar of oak leaves encircling the finial on the teapot lid, which was chased. For then-current fashion, see E. Hessling, *Dessins d'Orfèvrerie de Percier* (Paris: By the author, 1912).

Cat. no. 9

1. Goodwin appears in Boston directories from 1800 until his death; see *The Boston Directory* (Boston: John West, 1803), p. 56; *Boston Directory* (Boston: J.H.A. Frust, 1818), p. 102. Ozias Goodwin was reelected as a Boston Marine Society officer in 1804; *Boston Gazette*, November 8, 1804, p. 2, citation used with the permission of NewsBank/Readex and the American Antiquarian Society (hereafter NewsBank/Readex/AAS). Quoted in *Federal Republican*, March 31, 1813, p. 1. The Massachusetts House of Representatives request for depositions appears in the *Federal Republican*, March 26, 1813, NewsBank/Readex/AAS. Ozias Goodwin is linked to the New England Insurance Office on State Street in a classified advertisement and likely worked with the company. His son Ozias was listed as a director in 1831; see *Newburyport Herald*, March 12, 1811, p. 3, NewsBank/Readex/AAS; *Stimpson's Boston Directory* (Boston: Stimpson & Clapp, 1831), p. 25.

2. American silver pitchers were uncommon for table services before 1800 although Liverpool jugs of similar shape, a ubiquitous English creamware export to North America, enjoyed great popular use. Another pitcher using the same construction is marked by George Carleton, now at Winterthur, acc. no. 1956.12. Pitchers made by Ebenezer Moulton are sympathetic comparisons to Goodwin's, such as the 1811 presentation pitcher for Isaac Harris in the Museum of Fine Arts, Boston, acc. no.1913.560; see also Philip H. Hammerslough II, *American Silver Collected by Philip H. Hammerslough II* (Hartford, Conn.: Privately printed 1960, 1961), 2:44–45.

Cat. no. 10

1. Weight given includes the silver liner (69 oz. 6 dwt. Troy), thus the urn and lid together weigh 492 oz. 4 dwt. Troy. In a letter to his brother James dated January 19, 1814, Thomas Fletcher reported the urn's weight as nearly 502 oz. Troy. The liner was likely a later addition. Isaac Hull may refer to it in his letter to Thomas Fletcher dated December 7, 1829: "Sir, I have determined not to have the bason belonging to the urn made over at present" (Fletcher Papers, Athenaeum). The tremendous size of Hull's urn exceeded all precious-metals scales available to the authors, who used a postal scale. We attribute the ten-ounce weight disparity to the scale not being calibrated for fine measurements.

2. Isaac Hull subscription list, September 3, 1812, Collection 1343, Thomas Fletcher Papers, Historical Society of Philadelphia (hereafter Fletcher Papers, HSP). Announcement, *Commercial Advertiser*, September 8, 1812, p. 3; and *Pennsylvania Gazette*, September 9, 1812; see also Elizabeth I. Wood, "Thomas Fletcher: A Philadelphia Entrepreneur of Presentation Silver," in *Winterthur Portfolio III*, ed. Milo M. Naeve (Winterthur, Del.: Henry Francis du Pont Winterthur Museum, 1967), pp. 138–40. Wood cites items similar to those in the *Aurora*, September 4, 1812, and *Niles' Weekly Register*, September 12, 1812; the initial committee included Richard Dale, William Jones, George Harrison, Charles Biddle, Thomas W. Francis, and John Sergeant. One classical emblem for the god Zeus was an eagle clutching a thunderbolt; an eagle perched on a spiraling thunderbolt was central in Napoleon Bonaparte's imperial coat of arms. His eagle, with two flanking winged figures, was incorporated into a design by Chaudet for Empress Marie-Louise, in 1810, pictured in Jean-Marie Pinçon and Olivier Gaube du Gers, *Odiot l'Orfèvre* (Paris: Sous le Vent, 1990), p. 91.

3. Elizabeth Wood first noted this connection; see Wood, "Thomas Fletcher," pp. 143–44; and Charles Percier and Pierre-François-Léonard Fontaine, *Recueil des décorations intérieurs* (Paris: Chez les Auteurs, 1812), pls. 46, 72. The figures personifying Fame and History (or Victory) likely were influenced by engravings of Emperor Trajan's column in Rome; see "Trofei de Daci de Sarmati ed altri Popoli Alleati . . .," in Giovanni-Battista Piranesi, *Trofeo o Sia Magnifica Colonna Coclide* (1774–79); and L. D. Ettlinger, "The Pictorial Source of Ripa's 'Historia,'" *Journal of the Warburg and Courtauld Institutes* 13, no. _ (1950): 322–23. For engravings of ram's-head handles, which derived from Roman sculpture, see Giovanni-Battista Piranesi, *Diverse maniere d'adornare I cammini . . . e toscana* (Rome: Salomoni, 1769), "Tavola I, pag 31"; and "A Vase from Piranesi Published by H. Moses, Oct. 1, 1811," in Henry Moses, *A Collection of Antique Vases, Altars, Paterae, Tripods, Candelabra, Sarcophagi, etc.* (London: Privately printed, 1814), pl. 34 (see chap. 4, fig. 11). Piranesi's collection of motifs in "Tavola I," nos. 45, 55, 60, 87, and 93 illustrates ornament similar to that on the Hull urn.

4. Letter, Thomas Fletcher to Timothy Fletcher, December 19, 1813, Fletcher Papers, Athenaeum.

Cat. no. 11

1. Thomas Sheraton, *The Cabinet Dictionary* (1803; reprint, 2 vols., New York: Praeger Publishers, 1970), 2:328.

2. Sheraton, *Cabinet Dictionary*, p. 296.

Cat. no. 12

1. *Poulson's American Daily Advertiser*, June 29, 1814; and *Pennsylvania Gazette*, "Tribute to Merit," July 6, 1814. The letter, dated April 21, 1814, acknowledges public awards given Biddle (as in the urn's dedication) and names the committee of Biddle's friends: Thomas Cadwalader, Charles Ross, George Reinholdt, Bernard Henry, and Condy Raguet. The silver urn was also announced in newspapers from several cities. "Tribute to Merit"; see also Benson Lossing, *A Pictorial Field Book of the War of 1812* (New York: Harper & Brothers Publishers, 1862), p. 453.

Cat. no. 13

1. "A HAPPY NEW-YEAR TO COMMODORE RODGERS, OR, HUZZA FOR THE PRESIDENT AND CONGRESS. A SONG Composed on the arrival of these Frigates in BOSTON, yesterday (December 31, 1812) with a good supply of the READY RHINO"; Massachusetts Historical Society, *The War of 1812* (Boston: By the society, 1962). The citizens of Philadelphia purchased a silver urn for Jones from the workshop of Jean Simon Chaudron, now in the New-York Historical Society collection, acc. no. 1952.103. Chaudron's urn for Jones includes sculptural handles featuring the head of Neptune, an element similar to that on Fletcher & Gardiner's urns for James Biddle and Oliver Perry and on ewers made by Harvey Lewis in the 1820s. One Lewis ewer is in the Maryland Historical Society collection; see Beatrice B. Garvan et al., *Philadelphia: Three Centuries of American Art* (Philadelphia: Philadelphia Museum of Art, 1976), p. 224. For the Delaware quote, see *American Watchman*, February 20, 1813, p. 2; and "Tribute to Valor," *Boston Daily Advertiser*, March 17, 1813, p. 2, NewsBank/Readex/AAS.

Cat. no. 14

1. *Village Record*, August 14, 1833, www.accessible.com. For advertisements, see *Poulson's American Daily Advertiser*, March 13, 1813, p. 3; *Salem Gazette*, March 19, 1813, p. 2; *Boston Daily Advertiser*, March 19, 1813, p. 2; *America Advocate*, March 25, 1813, p. 3; and *Democratic Republican*, March 29, 1813, NewsBank/Readex/AAS.

2. Presentation urns were made by Fletcher & Gardiner for William Bainbridge and Charles Morris in 1814. The Morris urn is currently unknown. For a sketch of Bainbridge's, see Lossing, *Pictorial Field Book,* p. 463. Lossing saw the urn and reported it standing 18 inches high with an eagle finial and Neptune's head handles. He recorded the inscription: "Presented by the citizens of Philadelphia to Commodore William Bainbridge, of the U.S. frigate *Constitution*, as a testimonial of the highest sense they entertain of his skill and gallantry in the capture of the British frigate *Java*, of 49 guns and 500 men, and of their admiration of his generous and magnanimous conduct toward the vanquished foe. Loss in the action of 29th December, 1812 – C., 9 killed, 25 wounded; J., 60 killed, 101 wounded."

3. A similar and slightly later basket is now in the National Museum of American History, Smithsonian Institution, acc. no 326,501. A similar Fletcher & Gardiner basket is privately held.

Cat. no. 15

1. See gifts of silver for Perry in "Valuable Gift," *Pennsylvania Gazette*, June 8, 1814 (no. 4355), quoting the *Boston Gazette*; *Columbian Centinel*, May 25, 1814. Michel Felice Corné's watercolor views of the battle on Lake Erie were reproduced as engravings by printers in several cities. One by Francis Kearny in Philadelphia was the source for William Hooker's work on the Perry urn. Thus, "Kearny DEL.T" and "Hooker SC" are inscribed below the battle scene.

2. See subscription list for additional funds in five-dollar increments, United States Naval Academy Museum files. Letter, Oliver Perry to the Newport award committee of Asher Robbins, Christopher Fowler, Jno., P. Mann, William Ellery, and Benjamin Hazard, December 28, 1814, United States Naval Academy Museum files.

Cat. no. 16

1. On Houstoun, see David B. Warren, Katherine S. Howe, and Michael K. Brown, *Marks of Achievement: Four Centuries of American Presentation Silver* (New York: Harry N. Abrams, 1987), p. 118, cat. no. 147. The bill, dated November 15, 1815, is in a private collection. It states: "1 Silver Pitcher, round on square pedistal & claw feet/chased leaves on the body & lid, with dolphin top} $150.00/Engraving Inscription on do.... 4.00" (information courtesy of Michael K. Brown, curator, Bayou Bend Collection, Museum of Fine Arts, Houston). For a nearly identical, non-presentation example of this form by Fletcher & Gardiner, see the Museum of Fine Arts, Boston, acc. no. 1995.45.

2. Jennifer Goldsborough noted similarities of the leaf pattern as well as the rose-and-leaf border in "Silver in Maryland," *The Magazine Antiques* 125, no. 1 (January 1984): 261, figs. 9–10.

Cat. no. 17

1. Benton Seymour Rabinovitch, *Antique Silver Servers for the Dining Table* (Concord, Mass.: Joslin Hall Publishing, 1991), pp. vii, viii.

Cat. no. 18

1. Thomas Fletcher executed a preliminary drawing for this rose border in his notebook about 1815 (chap. 3, fig. 14), Fletcher Papers, Athenaeum.

Cat. no. 19

1. Letter, Thomas Fletcher to Samuel Smith, February 11, 1837, Fletcher Papers, Athenaeum.

2. For Smith, see Dumas Malone, ed., *Dictionary of American Biography*, 20 vols. (New York: Charles Scribner's Sons, 1935), 17:341–42. A pitcher made by Fletcher & Gardiner engraved with the Smith arms is in the collection of the Maryland Historical Society, acc. no. 49.96.23.

3. Notebook, Fletcher Papers, Athenaeum. For a piece of Philadelphia silver that may have influenced the cast ornament on this pot, see Charles E. Buckley, *The St. Louis Art Museum* (St. Louis: By the museum, 1975), p. 216.

Cat. no. 20

1. Thomas's brother Charles wrote to him: "Mr. Bridport has just completed the drawings for Col. Armsted's urn–in the form of an shell supported on 4 Eagles standing upon a round foot: the body without any chasing" (Letter, Charles Fletcher to Thomas Fletcher in Liverpool, 1815, Fletcher Papers, Athenaeum). The attribution to George rather than Hugh Bridport is made upon the basis of the latter's arrival in Philadelphia in 1816. Thomas replied to Charles from Paris: "If you can send me a sketch of the urn you are making and some other matters & things that I can turn to advantage–such as the portraits of our naval officers &c. it will be well" (Letter, Thomas Fletcher to Charles Fletcher, August 31, 1815, Fletcher Papers, Athenaeum). The workshop may have known a presentation vase supported by four eagles perched on ball feet made by J. Simon Chaudron's workshop for Peter Dobel, ca. 1808; see Dobel vase, Metropolitan Museum of Art, drawings collection, acc. no. 1953.652.7 (Chap. 6, Drawings 1, 2). For comparison of the engraving, see *View of the Bombardment of Ft. McHenry* (Philadelphia: John Bower, 1816).

2. The event was listed in *Niles' Weekly Register*, May 18, 1816, pp. 185–86; "Honor to the Brave . . . The design for the plate, adopted by the committee as most appropriate, was a Vase, of the shape and size of the largest bomb thrown by the enemy into Fort McHenry during the bombardment, being thirteen inches in diameter, supported by four eagles with wings expanded . . . The workmanship of the vase and swords [for George Armistead, John Webster, and Henry Newcomb] is executed in a very superior style, by Messrs. Fletcher & Gardiner, of Philadelphia" (*Niles' Weekly Register*, May 18, 1816, p. 185). Award committee: John E. Howard, William H. Lorman, Robert Gilmore, Jr., Thomas Tennant, Isaac McKim, and Fielding Lucas, Jr. A description of the presentation ceremony, in the same issue of *Niles'*, reports that the tray was part of the original service: "The vase was accompanied by silver cans and ladle, and the whole placed on a large silver stand or tray."

Cat. no. 21

1. Robert Rowe, *Adam Silver* (New York: Taplinger Publishing Company, 1965), pls. 20, 21, 22a, 23, 52, 53, 93; Véronique Alemany-Dessaint, *Orfèvrerie Française* (Paris: Les Éditions de l'Illustration, 1998), p. 83, fig. 2; p. 88, fig. 1; p. 159, fig. 4.

2. Faith Dennis, *Three Centuries of French Domestic Silver*, 2 vols. (New York: Metropolitan Museum of Art, 1960), 1:220, fig. 329; Olivier Quéant, *Styles de France* (Paris: Le Rayonnement Français, 1950), p. 118. The Chaudron sauceboats are in the collection of the Philadelphia Museum of Art, acc. no. 1991–1–1, 2; Beatrice B. Garvan, *Federal Philadelphia, 1785–1825, The Athens of the Western World* (Philadelphia: Philadelphia Museum of Art, 1987), p. 59, fig. 37. Another pair of this type bearing Chaudron's mark is pictured in Sotheby's sale catalogue, New York, January 18, 2001, lot 280. A related serpent-handle pair by Anthony Rasch is illustrated in Wendy A. Cooper, *Classical Taste in America, 1800–1840* (New York: Abbeville, 1993), p. 155, fig. 113.

Cat. no. 22

1. The urn has not been weighed by the authors; a contemporary newspaper reported its weight as "14 lb. 10 oz." (*Boston Gazette*, September 26, 1816, p. 2).

2. One of Paul Storr's tureens for Rundell, Bridge & Rundell, dated 1805–6, has a related handle design; see tureen and stand, Winterthur acc. no. 1996.4. Examples of tureens and serving pieces with bifurcated snake-head handles abound in French silver; see the service made for Napoleon by Henri Auguste and a tureen by Jean-Baptiste-Claude Odiot, reproduced in Bouilhet, *L'Orfèvrerie Française*, p. 119. South Carolina State Museum files record an incident of vandalism in 1905 with a repair of modest eagle replacements; the surviving drawing offers their original design, see Chap. 6, Drawing 5. An eyewitness recorded: "On each corner of the pedestal is a spread eagle, in *frosted silver*, grasping a thunderbolt" (*The Union*, August 2, 1816, p. 3).

3. Letter extract dated October 5, 1815, from Mr. Strobel, reprinted in *American Beacon and Commercial Advertiser*, November 9, 1815, pp. 2–4; see also *Baltimore Patriot*, November 9, 1815, p. 2.

4. *The Union*, August 2, 1816, p. 3; *Boston Gazette*, September 26, 1816, p. 2; *Salem Gazette*, September 27, 1816, p. 3; *The Providence Gazette*, September 28, 1816, p. 3; *Newburyport Herald*, September 27, 1816, p. 2. The urn was completed and sent to Charleston in June 1816; see *The National Advocate*, June 29, 1816, p. 2. It may not have reached Jackson until Colonel Hayne and Major Gadsden delivered it; see *Niles' Weekly Register*, March 15, 1817, p. 48. Andrew Jackson bequeathed it, through his adopted son, to the last surviving member of the South Carolina Palmetto Regiment; see A.W. Salley, Jr., "The Jackson Vase," *Bulletins of the Historical Commission of South Carolina*, no. 1 (1915).

Cat. no. 23

1. Minor Myers, Jr., *The Insignia of the Society of the Cincinnati* (Washington, D.C.: Society of the Cincinnati, 1998), p. 9.

2. Letter, Winfield Scott to Thomas M. Randolph, July 9, 1821, quoted in Jay P. Altmayer, *American Presentation Swords* (Mobile, Ala.: Rankin Press, 1958), p. 18. Fletcher & Gardiner likely executed the goldwork, set the ruby, and enameled the wreath of leaves in their manufactory; the partners probably imported the enamel medallions from France.

3. Letter, Thomas Fletcher to Eustis Prescott, June 9, 1830; Letter, Thomas Fletcher to Nathan Towson,

December 12, 1834, Collection 278, Thomas Fletcher Papers, Joseph Downs Collection of Manuscripts and Printed Ephemera, Winterthur Library (hereafter Fletcher Papers, Winterthur Library).

Cat. no. 24

1. Baltimore was generous to its defenders; another committee commissioned a significant silver service for Stephen Decatur from Andrew Ellicott Warner, valued at $6,000. For the anniversary, see *Niles' Weekly Register*, Sept. 20, 1817.

2. *American Beacon and Commercial Diary*, June 16, 1817. Fielding Lucas, Jr. sold books and stationery on Market Street in Baltimore. Three months later his store displayed Andrew E. Warner's silver presentation service awarded to Stephen Decatur; see Warren, Howe, and Brown, *Marks of Achievement*, p. 109, quoting *Baltimore Gazette and Daily Advertiser*, September 5, 1817. *Niles' Weekly Register*, June 14, 1817, p. 245. *American Beacon and Commercial Diary*, June 16, 1817.

3. For comparison of French work, see works by Henri Auguste in Bouilhet, *L'Orfèvrerie Française*, p. 51. The mate to the Rodgers tureen is in the Smithsonian Institution, National Museum of American History. One wonders if Thomas Fletcher knew Sir Joshua Reynold's oft-quoted opinion: "Invention, strictly speaking, is nothing more than a new combination of those images which have been previously gathered and deposited in the memory"; see the title page of Charles Heathcote Tatham, *Designs for Ornamental Plate, Many of Which Have Been Executed in Silver, from Original Drawings* (London: Printed for Thomas Gardiner by John Barfield, 1806).

4. Baron Vivant Denon's publications in French and English with copperplate images of his travels in Egypt, and Napoleon Bonaparte's Imperial Press images of the Egyptian campaign, *Description de l'Egypte*, broadly influenced decorative arts. Winged animal feet similar to those on the Rodgers basket appear on other contemporary Philadelphia silver as well as French silver; see Anthony Rasch's sauceboats, Metropolitan Museum of Art acc. nos. 1959.152.1–.2 (Chap. 2, fig. 9); sauceboat and waste bowl by Thomas Whartenby (Chap. 5, fig. 9). One design influence may be Charles Percier; see mustard pot in Anthony Phillips and Jeanne Sloane, *Antiquity Revisited: English and French Silver-Gilt from the Collection of Audrey Love* (London: Christie's, 1997), p. 109, fig. 54. "It is a most superb service of plate intended for the dinner table, and consists of a large fish dish: four large meat and four smaller dishes: four covered vegetable dishes; two soup tureens and ladles: two large pitchers, four sauce boats and ladles; a bread basket, and a dozen forks . . . The service of plate cost $4000" (*Niles' Weekly Register*, June 14, 1817, p. 245).

Cat. no. 25

1. Warren, Howe, and Brown, *Marks of Achievement*, p. 89, ent. 95; p. 92, ent. 101; p. 93, ent. 103; p. 100, ent. 114; p. 101, ent. 116; p. 102, ent. 117; p. 113, ent. 137; p. 119, ent. 147; p. 124, ent. 155; p. 126, ent. 157.

2. E. McClung Fleming, "From Indian Princess to Greek Goddess: The American Image, 1783–1815," in *Winterthur Portfolio III*, ed. Milo M. Naeve (Winterthur, Del.: Henry Francis du Pont Winterthur Museum, 1965), p. 50, fig. 11; p. 51, fig. 13; p. 53, fig. 15.

Cat. no. 26

1. Thomas Webster, *An Encyclopaedia of Domestic Economy* (New York: Harper and Brothers, 1845), p. 335.

2. For a design for a French ewer with closely related handle, see Pinçon and du Gers, *Odiot l'Orfèvre*, p. 127, fig. 204; and Charles C. Gillespie and Michel Dewachter, eds., *Monuments of Egypt*, 2 vols. (Princeton, N.J.: Princeton University Press, 1987),1:pl. 29.

Cat. no. 27

1. Letter, Thomas Fletcher to Benjamin Gorham, August 21, 1830; Letter, Thomas Fletcher to Benjamin Gorham, October 26, 1830, Fletcher Papers, Winterthur Library.

2. Letter, Thomas Fletcher to Benjamin Gorham, June 10, 1831, Fletcher Papers, Winterthur Library.

Cat. no. 28

1. Letter, J. Curice Duncan to Thomas Fletcher, June 2, 1841, Fletcher Papers, HSP.

2. Representative examples are in Kathryn Buhler and Graham Hood, *American Silver: Garvan and Other Collections in the Yale University Art Gallery*, 2 vols. (New Haven: Yale University Press, 1970), 2:113, ent. 678; 124, ent. 695; 185, ent. 833; 216, ent. 887.

3. *Wrightson's Annual Directory of Birmingham* (Birmingham, Eng.: R. Wrightson, 1829), p. 37; Letter, Thomas Fletcher to Goddard & Bibby, October 7, 1829, Fletcher Papers, Winterthur Library.

Cat. no. 29

1. For grape-leaf border Chinese export porcelain with American provenance, see the plate for Thomas ap Catesby Jones pictured in David Sanctuary Howard, *Chinese Armorial Porcelain*, vol. 2 (Wiltshire, Eng.: Heirloom & Howard Ltd., 2003), p. 672; see also the David M. Perine family porcelain serving pieces in the Baltimore Museum of Art collection.

2. "Records of the Committee on Manufacturers (1819–1911)," *Guide to the Records of the U.S. House of Representatives at the National Archives, 1789–1989*, chp. 7,7.11, www.archives.gov/records_of_congress/house_g uide. Lord later served as president of the Erie Railroad, founded religious and educational institutions, and wrote extensively on the subjects of banking and theology; see Malone, *Dictionary of American Biography*, 11:406.

3. Petition, November 27, 1819, Fletcher Papers, Athenaeum of Philadelphia. Wood screws are iron wire screws used in wood construction. Citizens in Wilmington, Delaware, commissioned a Fletcher & Gardiner presentation pitcher for Mathew Carey "as a testimony of their gratitude for his writings upon political economy" (*Niles' Weekly Register*, July 28, 1821). This pitcher is now at the Athenaeum of Philadelphia. The inscription identifies the donors as "friends of National Industry."

Cat. no. 30

1. Gisela M. A. Richter and Marjorie J. Milne, *Shapes and Names of Athenian Vases* (New York: Metropolitan Museum of Art, 1935), pp. 55–59; Cooper, *Classical Taste in America,* p. 246, fig. 198; Garvan, *Three Centuries of American Art*, p. 347, ent. 332. A pair of Fletcher &

Gardiner beakers is illustrated in Letitia Hart Alexander, "The Myth of the Julep Cup," *The Magazine Antiques* 8, no. 6 (December 1925): 364, fig. 2.

2. Nicholas B. Wainwright, ed., *A Philadelphia Perspective: The Diary of Sidney George Fisher Covering the Years 1834–1781* (Philadelphia: Historical Society of Pennsylvania, 1967), p. 122.

3. The Insurance Company of North America, *American Fire Marks* (Philadelphia: By the company, 1933), pp. 43–53.

Cat. no. 31

1. Henry Simpson, *The Lives of Eminent Philadelphians, Now Deceased*, 2 vols. (Philadelphia: William Brotherhead, 1859), 2:867–72.

2. Letter, Charles Fletcher to Thomas Fletcher, January 12, 1828, Fletcher Papers, Athenaeum; Bill, Thomas Fletcher to J. I. Middleton, January 6, 1830, Fletcher Papers, Winterthur Library.

Cat. no. 32

1. *Aurora General Advertiser*, September 7, 1812.

2. *Niles' Weekly Register*, April 23, 1825, p. 121. Letter, Isaac Hull to Thomas Fletcher, December 7, 1829, Fletcher Papers, Athenaeum. The illustrated salver survives with a 9-inch diameter mate.

Cat. no. 33

1. Representative examples are illustrated in Quimby, *American Silver at Winterthur*, p. 349, ent. 335.

2. Katharine Morrison McClinton, *Collecting American 19ᵗʰ Century American Silver* (New York: Charles Scribner's Sons, 1968), pp. 13, 33.

Cat. no. 35

1. Harry B. Weiss and Grace M. Weiss, *The Early Snuff Mills of New Jersey* (Trenton: New Jersey Agricultural Society, 1962), p. 15.

2. Letter, Thomas Fletcher to James Lloyd, January 15, 1831, Fletcher Papers, Winterthur Library.

Cat. no. 36

1. These and other condiments are identified in a trade catalogue of plated wares that originated in Sheffield, England, about 1790, NK7199Y78★TC, Winterthur Library.

2. The scallop shell at the tops of the legs was stamped with the die the partners used on their thread-and-shell spoons and forks. Frederick Bradbury, *A History of Old Sheffield Plate* (London: Macmillan and Company, 1912), pp. 67–69. English glassmakers who appear in Fletcher manuscript material are Pellatt & Green, Brueton Gibbons, and Biddle & Loyes, Fletcher Papers, HSP. Some believe these bottles may be of American make; see "A Kensington Connection," *Pittsburg Glass Journal* 3, no. 2 (October 1990): 2, 3.

Cat. no. 37

1. Bradbury, *History of Old Sheffield Plate*, p. 73.

Cat. no. 38

1. Myers, *Society of the Cincinnati*, p. 60. This badge is constructed in the same manner. Additionally, the

word CINCINNATORUM on the reverse is misspelled CINCINATORUM, as is the case with the Rhode Island badge illustrated as ent. 19, p. 60 in Myers.

2. Myers, *Society of the Cincinnati*, p. 30. Advertisement, *Columbian Centinel*, November 9, 1808.

3. Letter, William S. Peirce to W. H. McCarer, November 4, 1835, Fletcher Papers, Winterthur Library.

Cat. no. 39

1. Robert Means Lawrence, *The Site of St. Paul's Cathedral, Boston, and Its Neighborhood* (Boston: Gorham Press, 1916), pp. 94, 95, 144, 145; Justin Winsor, *The Memorial History of Boston*, 4 vols. (Boston: James R. Osgood and Company, 1882), 3:455.

2. Jones, *Old Silver*, p. 90.

3. Title page, trade catalogue, George Brinley & Company, Boston, c. 1812, no. 24935, Massachusetts Historical Society.

Cat. no. 40

1. A graphic illustration may be seen in E. McSherry Fowble, *Two Centuries of Prints in America, 1680–1880* (Charlottesville: University Press of Virginia, 1987), p. 460, ent. 324.

2. For representative examples of the cornucopia, see David B. Warren et al., *American Decorative Arts and Paintings in the Bayou Bend Collection* (Princeton, N.J.: Princeton University Press, 1998), p. 123, ent. F198; J. Michael Flanigan, *American Furniture from the Kaufman Collection* (Washington, D.C.: National Gallery of Art, 1986), p. 233, ent. 96; Arlene Palmer, *Glass in Early America* (New York: W.W. Norton, 1993), p. 256, ent. 221; p. 257, ent. 222; Melinda Zongor, *Coverlets and the Spirit of America* (Atglen, Pa.: Schiffer Publishing, 2002), p. 150, fig. 70. Related cornucopia handles on a cake basket by Fletcher & Gardiner's neighbor and competitor Harvey Lewis are illustrated in Quimby, *American Silver at Winterthur*, p. 385, ent. 382.

Cat. no. 41

1. Claude C. Robin, *New Travels through North America* (Boston: Privately printed, 1781), p. 23.

2. Letter, Sullivan Dorr to Thomas Fletcher, May 29, 1833, Fletcher Papers, HSP.

3. The borders of this tea set, those of the hot-water urn in cat. no. 42, and a drawing identified as a "coffee urn" in Chap. 6, Drawing 11, were made en suite.

Cat. no. 42

1. An insightful instance of how casual owners were about all tea and coffee vessels matching is seen in a three-piece set made by Philadelphia silversmiths Joseph and Nathaniel Richardson and Joseph Anthony; see Quimby, *American Silver at Winterthur*, p. 330, ent., 311; p. 439, ent. 459. For another set, see Quimby, *American Silver at Winterthur*, pp. 428–29, ent. 446.

2. Donald L. Fennimore, "Thomas Fletcher and Sidney

Gardiner: The Stylistic Development of Their Domestic Silver," *The Magazine Antiques* 102, no. 4 (October 1972): 643, fig. 1; 647, fig. 10; 649, fig. 17. Letter, Thomas Fletcher to Alfred Welles, September 18, 1832, Fletcher Papers, Winterthur Library. Memo, record of purchases by Mrs. Richard Ashhurst, Collection 290, 689x22.2, Winterthur Library.

3. A drawing identified as "coffee urn" is among the Fletcher drawings in the Department of Drawings and Prints, Metropolitan Museum of Art, acc. no. 53.652.28 (Chap. 6, Drawing 11). The borders of this urn and those in cat. no. 41 were made *en suite*.

Cat. no. 43

1. A modern, internal conservation support accounts for the significant variation in weights between the vases.

2. "The premium of $100 for the best design for the Clinton Vases, has been awarded to Messrs. Fletcher & Gardiner, of Philadelphia" (*Independent Chronicle & Boston Patriot*, January 21, 1824). The vases were on public view in Philadelphia and New York City before going by steamboat to Albany for the March 19, 1825, award ceremony, after which they were displayed in Knickerbocker Hall. Newspaper coverage in 1825 and again after Clinton's death in 1828 spread their fame; see *Independent Chronicle & Boston Patriot*, March 23, 1825 (quoting the *New York Statesman*); *Niles' Weekly Register*, April 23, 1825; see also Ann Wagner, "Fletcher and Gardiner: Presentation Silver for the Nation" (Master's thesis, University of Delaware, 2004), pp. 72–77.

3. Thomas Fletcher and Isaac S. Hone, "Description of the Vases," handbill, Fletcher Papers, Winterthur Library; Letter, Thomas Fletcher to Melina Fletcher, March 12, 1825, Fletcher Papers, Athenaeum. Text was reprinted by the *New York Commercial Advertiser*, March 18 and 22, 1825; *Independent Chronicle & Boston Patriot*, March 23, 1825; and *Niles' Weekly Register*, April 23, 1825. The Warwick vase was assembled by Giovanni-Battista Piranesi and Antoine Guillaume Grandjacquet and acquired by Sir William Hamilton, who took it to England and persuaded his nephew George Greville, Earl of Warwick, to purchase it; see Bent Sørensen, "Piranesi, Grandjacquet, and the Warwick Vase," *The Burlington Magazine* 145, no. 1208 (November 2003): 792–95. The vase measures 5.57 feet (1.70 m) high and 6.39 feet (1.95 m) in diameter; see *Vitruvius Britannicus* (London: John Weale, 1827–44), pp. 33–36. From 1810 to 1821 Paul Storr created pairs of wine coolers inspired by the Warwick for Rundell, Bridge & Rundell. Fletcher's letterbook records visiting the London shop in 1815 and seeing "a fine vase copied from one in the possession of the Earl of Warwick . . . which was dug from the ruins of Herculaneum. [It] is beautifully made–it is oval, about ¾d the size of that made for Hull, the handles are grape stalks and a vine runs all around covered with leaves & clusters of grapes–below are heads of Bacchus &c. finely chased–some wine coolers in the same style" (Letterbook, June 14, 1815, Fletcher Papers, Athenaeum). The Clinton vases are nearly double the height of Storr's wine coolers and incorporate a non-Warwick grape-leaf border similar to one used by Rundell, Bridge & Rundell; see the salver in James Lomax, *British Silver at Temple Newsam and Lotherton Hall* (Leeds, Eng.: Leeds Art Collections Fund and W. S. Maney and Son Ltd., 1992), pp. 105–6, fig. 99.

4. Fletcher and Hone, "Description of the Vases."

5. Source engravings by James Eights were identified by Berry Tracy, "Late Classical Styles in American Silver," *The Magazine Antiques* 86, no. 6 (December 1964): 703. Three of Eights's (Bights) views were reproduced in Cadwallader D. Colden, *Memoir, prepared at the request of a committee of the Common Council of the city of New York* (New York: W. A. Davis, 1825); see also Patricia Anderson, *The Course of Empire: The Erie Canal and the New York Landscape, 1825–1875* (Rochester: Memorial Art Gallery of the University of Rochester, 1984), nos. 17–18. Fletcher described these as "the wild animals who haunted our western region before the industry and enterprize of our brethren made 'the wilderness to rejoice and blossom as the rose'" (Fletcher and Hone, "Description of the Vases").

6. A watercolor by Hugh Bridport depicts the 1824 vase standing on a royal blue textile with thick gold fringe; Metropolitan Museum of Art, acc. no. 53.652.2; see Catherine Hoover Voorsanger and John K. Howat, eds., *Art and the Empire City: New York, 1825–1861* (New York: Metropolitan Museum of Art, 2000), p. 356, fig. 290. *Albany Daily Advertiser,* May 24, 1828, quoted in the *Niles' Weekly Register,* June 7, 1828, pp. 233–34; see also *Niles' Weekly Register,* June 14, 1828, p. 252. The vases reportedly cost $3,500 when created (*Niles' Weekly Register,* April 23, 1825, p. 120).

Cat. no. 44

1. Samuel Prioleau, appointed intendant of the city of Charleston in 1824, served as the spokesman of the group; for further discussion on this miniature and its history, see Martha R. Severens and Charles L. Wyrick, Jr., comp. and ed., *Charles Fraser of Charleston* (Charleston, S. C.: Carolina Art Association, 1983), p. 2.

2. The white metal may be platinum, called platina at the time, with which the partners worked, as recorded in the *Baltimore Patriot*, October 11, 1823.

Cat. no. 45

1. Letterbook, p. 124, 1815, Fletcher Papers, Athenaeum. A downfall press of this type is illustrated in "The Americans at Work, Among the Silver-Platers," *Appleton's Journal* 31 (December 1878): 484.

2. A jug with cast-and-applied grapevine border by Fletcher & Gardiner's competitor Edward Lownes is illustrated in McClinton, *Collecting American 19th Century Silver*, p. 34.

Cat. no. 46

1. Letter, Charles Fletcher to Thomas Fletcher, January 19, 1829, Fletcher Papers, HSP. Letter, Charles Fletcher to Thomas Fletcher, February 28, 1829, Fletcher Papers, Athenaeum.

2. Cornelius C. Vermeule, *Roman Imperial Art in Greece and Asia Minor* (Cambridge, Mass.: Harvard University Press, 1968), p. 124, figs. 53–56. Morrison H. Heckscher and Leslie Greene Bowman, *American Rococo, 1750–1775: Elegance in Ornament* (New York: Metropolitan Museum of Art, 1992), p. 88, fig. 54; p. 100, fig. 62; p. 102, fig. 63. The phrase OLD SILVER 141 was probably stamped on the underside of each by Tiffany & Company early in the twentieth century, when that firm traded in antique silver.

Cat. no. 47

1. David L. Barquist, " 'The Honours of a Court' or 'The Severity of Virtue': Household Furnishings and Cultural Aspirations in Philadelphia," in *Shaping a National Culture: The Philadelphia Experience, 1750–1800*, ed. Catherine E. Hutchins (Winterthur, Del.: Henry Francis du Pont Winterthur Museum, 1994), p. 330.

2. Bradbury, *History of Old Sheffield Plate*, p. 359. The burner, a replacement, is stamped incuse on the underside "TIFFANY & Co/T2437/STERLING."

Cat. no. 48

1. Record of purchases of Mrs. Richard Ashhurst, January 27, 1836, Collection 290, 68x22.11, Winterthur Library.

2. Bill, Fletcher & Gardiner to Mrs. Richard Ashhurst, January 31, 1820, Collection 290, 68x22.8, Winterthur Library; see Quimby, *American Silver at Winterthur*, p. 249, ent. 213; pp. 374–75, ent. 370.

3. Fletcher described repoussé as "basso relievo"; see Letterbook, January 1830, Fletcher Papers, Winterthur Library.

Cat. no 49

1. Their father, John, built Andalusia, later owned by the Biddle family.

2. For a double-bellied coffeepot made by Thomas Shields in Philadelphia about 1765, see Buhler and Hood, *American Silver*, p. 205, fig. 872. The Richardson's coffeepot spout is illustrated in Quimby, *American Silver at Winterthur*, p. 437, ent. 457.

3. Letter, Thomas Fletcher to John B. Jones, September 25, 1829, Fletcher Papers, Winterthur Library.

Cat. no. 50

1. David Drakard, *Printed English Pottery* (London: Jonathan Horne Publications, 1992), p. 242; see also Robert H. McCauley, *Liverpool Transfer Designs on Anglo-American Pottery* (Portland, Me.: Southworth-Anthoensen Press, 1942), pl. 11, fig. 8. John A. Garraty and Mark C. Carnes, eds., *American National Biography*, 24 vols. (New York: Oxford University Press, 1999), 1:902–4.

2. In 1814 Bainbridge was given a service of plate (cat. no. 14) and an urn made by Fletcher & Gardiner, which was probably why he asked Fletcher to make this jug.

Cat. no. 51

1. On the conspiracy case, see *Niles' Weekly Register*, November 24, 1827, p. 96, and December 20, 1828, pp. 261–62. Henry Eckford's vase is in the New-York Historical Society collection, acc. no. 1951.71. *Connecticut Mirror*, July 14, 1828, p. 2; see "A silver vase, weighing 730 [sic] ounces, and said to be a most splendid article, not surpassed in design and finish in this country, was, on Tuesday last week, presented to Hugh Maxwell, esq., by a committee of merchants" (*Niles' Weekly Register*, October 3, 1829, p. 90); also "A superb silver vase . . . The vase weighs 370 ounces, and cost one thousand dollars. The money was raised by subscription of two dollars each; no person being allowed to contribute a larger sum" (*Connecticut Mirror*, September 26, 1829, p. 3).

2. Letter, Baldwin Gardiner to Thomas Fletcher, August 29, 1828, Fletcher Papers, Athenaeum. The letter also mentions a pair of pitchers for a total commission costing $800 to $1,000 and requests drawings for proposed designs immediately for Mr. [John S.] Crary. The pitchers are not known, and announcements of the vase do not include them; see *Connecticut Mirror*, September 26, 1829, p. 3. The committee of merchants included John S. Crary, John Haggerty, and Henry Wyckoff. Their certificate to Maxwell, dated August 22, 1829, is in the manuscript department of the New-York Historical Society; see also Wagner, "Fletcher and Gardiner," pp. 78–79; and Margaret K. Hofer, "Celebrating Two Centuries of Collecting," *Antiques & Fine Art* 5 (January 2005), pp. 233–34, fig. 5.

3. In early nineteenth-century decorative arts, winged sphinxes are typically female. Eighteenth-century designs by Giovanni-Battista Piranesi have male sphinxes with pharaonic headdresses like Fletcher's design. For Greek types, see Jean-Baptiste-Claude Odiot's design in Pinçon and du Gers, *Odiot l'Orfèvre*, p. 170, fig. 267. Paul Storr produced a dessert stand with four sphinxes that combined Egyptian and Greek features, see Sotheby's New York sale, *Fine English and Continental Silver*, October 12, 1990, lot 247. Perhaps the male sphinx was dictated by Fletcher's design for putting an American face on antiquity—the head resembles George Washington.

Cat. no. 52

1. Letter, Rev. John H. Hopkins to Fletcher & Gardiner, June 9, 1829, Fletcher Papers, Athenaeum. St. Stephen's Church is in Philadelphia. Information about the chalices is extrapolated from a letter from Thomas Fletcher to Mr. W. Norvell, Esq., of Lynchburg, February 4, 1834, Fletcher Papers, Winterthur Library. For a similar Fletcher & Gardiner pitcher made for household use, see the New-York Historical Society collection, acc. no. 1951.313.

2. Letter, Thomas Fletcher to Rev. John H. Hopkins, July 16, 1829, Fletcher Papers, Winterthur Library.

Cat. no. 53

1. Recounting Fletcher & Gardiner's swords made for Captain Ballard and Lieutenants Mayo and Cross, *Niles' Weekly Register*, April 25, 1829, p. 131, quoted the *U.S. Gazette*, "The swords are something smaller than those formerly worn, but are comfortable to the mode." At present count, 24 presentation swords made by Fletcher & Gardiner are documented.

2. Swords for Henry Ballard, Isaac Mayo, and Joseph Cross were ordered in August 1828 and completed in 1829. Mayo's sword was published in an auction catalogue: Butterfield & Butterfield, *Historic American Swords*, sale 3149X, November 20, 1989, lot 6149; see Peter Tuite, *U.S. Naval Officers: Their Swords and Dirks* (Lincoln, R.I.: Andrew Mowbray, Inc., 2004), pp. 148–50. Joseph Cross's sword is in the Maryland State Archives collection. A related sword was made by the firm for George W. Rodgers in 1832; see Fletcher Papers, Athenaeum; and Maryland Historical Society, vertical file.

3. *Niles' Weekly Register*, July 25, 1829, p. 355 (quoting the *Maryland Republican*, July 21, 1829).

Cat. no. 54

1. Chauncey's initials are engraved on the obverse of the footed salver.

2. Rush's table is illustrated in Louise C. Belden, *The Festive Tradition* (New York: W.W. Norton, 1983), p. 84, figs. 2:47, 2:48. Drawings for the two sauce turcens and stands and the four lidded oblong vegetable dishes in this service are illustrated in Chap. 6, Drawing 9.

Cat. no. 55

1. Dennis, *Three Centuries*, 1:114, fig. 144. For thread-and-shell, see Michael Snodin and Gail Belden, *Spoons* (London: Pitman Publishing, 1976), pp. 46–47.

2. D. Albert Soeffing, "An Interesting Letter to Thomas Fletcher, Philadelphia Silversmith, from Benjamin Gratz," *Silver* 34, no. 2 (March/April 2002): 14–15.

3. Letter, Thomas Fletcher to Richard S. Smith, February 11, 1837, Fletcher Papers, Winterthur Library.

Cat. no. 56

1. Silversmith Harvey Lewis created a vase awarded in 1822 to Frederick Graff, the superintendent responsible for improving Philadelphia's Fairmount Water Works. It is now in the Atwater Kent Museum collection (Chap. 2, fig. 5). The cartouche is loosely based upon an engraving by William Birch, *Bank of the United States, in Third Street*, as published in *The City of Philadelphia* (Philadelphia, 1804); see Garvan, *Three Centuries of American Art*, fig. 142.

2. Semi-annual meeting of stockholders on March 1, 1830, as reported in Atwater Kent Museum object files. It is not known whether 11 trustee awards were also created or if some selected cash gifts. My thanks to Jeffrey Ray for sharing this information. See cat. nos. 57, 58; see "Philadelphia Thursday, January 13, 1831," *National Gazette and Literary Register*, January 13, 1831. The upper collar of Fisher's vase, below the egg-and-dart molding, is formed from two separate sections of silver seamed together on the sides. The Cadwalader Evans vase does not have this construction.

Cat. no. 57

1. The *Baltimore Patriot*, June 10, 1830, and the *Republican Star and General Advertiser*, June 15, 1830, both reported: "*a piece of plate* was unanimously voted to JAMES C. FISHER, Esq. and a committee appointed to have it prepared and presented." *The Ariel: A Semimonthly Literary and Miscellaneous Gazette*, March 20, 1830, quotes *Poulson's Daily Advertiser* to report a near tragedy on the opening of the Chesapeake and Delaware Canal. Alfred Bennett of Philadelphia saved a member of the Washington Grays from drowning. The paper describes the vase presented to Bennett: "The Committee appointed for this purpose procured an Etruscan Vase, executed by Mr. Thomas Fletcher, bearing the following emblems and inscriptions. On one side encircled by an Oak Wreath, is the inscription 'pro Cive Servato'–and above it is a chased tablet, representing the scene of the occurrence–the Canal, Toll House and Lock, at St. George's–the several canal boats, and their positions at the time–and on the other side are the following words: 'TRIBUTE OF GRATITUDE. / The / WASHINGTON GRAYS, / To / ADFRED BENNETT, / Of the / PHILADELPHIA GRAYS. At

the imminent peril of his life, he rescued a member of the Corps from drowning, in the Chesapeake and Delaware Canal, Sept. 19th, 1829.'" "The whole is surmounted by a lid bearing a piece of field ordinance, emblematic of the Corps." The location of this vase is unknown.

2. Letter, Thomas Fletcher to James Fisher, February 8, 1831, Fletcher Papers, Winterthur Library.

Cat. no. 58

1. One announcement described the vase: "This Vase is of Etruscan form, on a square plinth or pedestal, the four sides of which are ornamented by four views, in basso relievo, of the principal works on the Schuylkill. It cost 540 dollars" (*National Gazette and Literary Register*, January 13, 1831). Evans's will inventory, dated March 23, 1838, lists a "Silver Urn" valued $200 located in one of the parlors.

Cat. no. 59

1. Harold L. Peterson, *American Silver-Mounted Swords, 1700–1815* (Washington, D.C.: Privately printed, 1955), pp. 31–46; see also E. Andrew Mowbray, *The American Eagle-Pommel Sword* (Lincoln, R.I.: Man at Arms Magazine, 1997), p. 215; Harold L. Peterson, *The American Sword, 1775–1945* (Philadelphia: Ray Riling Arms Books Company, 1973), p. 59.

2. Wagner, "Fletcher and Gardiner," pp. 100–132, 212. Quoted in *Columbian Centinel*, April 20, 1811.

Cat. no. 60

1. In 1830 both Nicholson and Warrington contacted Thomas Fletcher about designs for naval devices and ornament such as epaulettes, buttons, belt buckles, and regulation sword patterns; see Letter, Thomas Fletcher to Commander Daniel Patterson, May 1, 1830, Fletcher Papers, Winterthur Library. Donors: Isaac Chauncey, Lewis Warrington, William M. Crane, Charles G. Ridgeley, John Downes, George C. Read, Henry E. Ballard, and Joseph J. Nicholson.

2. Letter, Thomas Fletcher to Captain Henry E. Ballard, March 4, 1831, Fletcher Papers, Winterthur Library. This letter indicates the vase cost more than $135.62.

Cat. no. 61

1. Letterbook, January 8 and 19, 1832, Fletcher Papers, Winterthur Library; also photocopy, inventory of Richard Singleton's silver, May 1850, lists "2 silver wine coolers Phil^d," 04x147, Downs Collection, Winterthur Library.

Cat. no. 62

1. Patricia A. Halfpenny and Donald L. Fennimore, *Campbell Collection of Soup Tureens at Winterthur* (Winterthur, Del.: Henry Francis du Pont Winterthur Museum, 2000), p. 2, fig. 2; p. 11, ent. 2. The earliest American silver soup tureen presently known was made by Lancaster, Pennsylvania, silversmith Peter Getz, about 1750. It is illustrated in Beatrice B. Garvan and Charles F. Hummel, *The Pennsylvania Germans: A Celebration of Their Arts, 1683–1850* (Philadelphia: Philadelphia Museum of Art, 1983), p. 47, fig. 23. Philip D. Zimmerman and Jennifer Faulds Goldsborough, *The Sewell C. Biggs Collection of American Art* (Dover, Del.: Biggs Museum of American Art, 2002), pp. 164, 165, ent. 133, Halfpenny and Fennimore, *Campbell Collection*, p. 68, ent. 23; p. 71, ent. 35; p. 72, ent. 36.

2. Thomas Fletcher to John Linton, June 18, 1830, May 24, 1834, Letterbook, Fletcher Papers, Winterthur Library.

3. The mate is in the collection of the New-York Historical Society, acc. no. 1951.311a,b. For French counterparts, see Clement E. Congor, *Treasures of State* (New York: Harry N. Abrams, 1991), fig. 223, facing p. 352; and Jacques Helft, *French Master Goldsmiths and Silversmiths* (New York: French & European Publications, 1966), p. 218, fig.1; p. 223, fig. 1; p. 313, fig. 1.

Cat. no. 63

1. An example of similar size by Paul Revere is illustrated in Jonathan Fairbanks et al., *Paul Revere's Boston, 1735–1818* (Boston: Museum of Fine Arts, 1975), pp. 190–91, ent. 296.

2. Letter, Thomas Fletcher to Mark Peirce, May 13, 1833, Fletcher Papers, Winterthur Library; Letter, Mark W. Peirce to Thomas Fletcher, June 4, 1833, Fletcher Papers, HSP.

Cat. no. 64

1. Bradbury, *History of Old Sheffield Plate*, p. 283. Letterbook, p. 161, Fletcher Papers, Athenaeum.

2. Letterbook, p. 161, Fletcher Papers, Athenaeum.

3. Bradbury, *History of Old Sheffield Plate*, p. 157. Three other closely related vegetable dishes made by Fletcher & Gardiner are in the collection of the New-York Historical Society, acc. no. 1951.285a–f. Letter, Thomas Fletcher to Daniel Coxe, April 6, 1837, Fletcher Papers, Athenaeum. Drawings in plan and elevation for this vegetable dish are illustrated in Chap. 6, Drawing 9.

Cat. no. 65

1. Fletcher & Gardiner advertised "cake and fruit baskets" in the *Columbian Centinel*, November 9, 1808, and October 6, 1810; Belden, *Festive Tradition*, p. 169.

2. Advertisement, John C. Dyer, *Columbian Centinel*, October 23, 1805.

3. Letter, Mark W. Peirce to Thomas Fletcher, June 4, 1833, Fletcher Papers, HSP.

Cat. no. 66

1. Letter, Thomas Fletcher to Mark Peirce, May 13, 1833, Fletcher Papers, Winterthur Library.

2. Newton W. Elwell, *Colonial Silverware of the 17th and 18th Centuries* (Boston: George H. Polley & Co., 1899), pl. 16; McClinton, *Collecting 19th Century American Silver*, p. 38; Sotheby Parke Bernet auction catalogue, New York, November 19, 1976, log 586; Cooper, *Classical Taste*, p. 181, fig. 139.

Cat. no. 67

1. William Elder, "Philip Syng Physick, M.D.," in Simpson, *Lives of Eminent Philadelphians*, 2:797–98.

Cat. no. 68

1. Dedication inscriptions engraved on Fletcher & Gardiner presentation silver frequently invoke the word "testimony" to refer to the physical and visual presence of an award. Its use for this vase appears to be a direct quotation from Thomas Biddle's will, although the wording of his will in the St. Louis probate court states "memorial

of my affection" (Nicholas B. Wainwright, "Major Thomas Biddle's Silver Vases," *The Magazine Antiques* 115, no. 1 [January 1979]: p. 180, n. 1, p. 183). Nicholas Wainwright, who possessed Fletcher's bill for the order, dated July 27, 1832, identifies Biddle's wife placing the order via Thomas's siblings, Mary Biddle and William S. Biddle, after she visited Philadelphia in 1831–32. Wainwright transcribes the bill: "Mrs. Ann Biddle Executrix of Thomas Biddle decd. Bought of Thomas Fletcher 10 silver cups richly chased with Dolphin handles & c. @ $60—$600" (Wainwright, "Biddle's Silver Vases," p. 181).

2. Dueling, an ancient mode of defending one's honor, was publicly discouraged yet practiced in the United States among men of various social stations. Fletcher & Gardiner fashioned a silver pitcher given to Dr. Philip S. Physick by another duelist, Commodore James Barron, who mortally wounded Commodore Stephen Decatur in 1820. One extended account of "THE LATE BLOODY DUEL," quotes a letter to the editor of the *Louisville Advertiser,* August 29, 1821, in *Eastern Argus*, September 20, 1831, p. 2; see also "Fatal Duel in the West," *New-York Journal of Commerce*, September 20, 1831; *The Farmers' Cabinet*, September 17, 1831; "The Affair of Pettis & Biddle," *Eastern Argus*, September 20, 1831; "Affair of Honor," *Vermont Gazette,* September 20, 1831; NewsBank/Readex/AAS.

Cat. no. 69

1. William G. Mason engraved his and Thomas Fletcher's names on the bottom edge of the base; the "sc" following Mason's name is an abbreviation for "sculp," indicating he was the engraver. Mason worked in Philadelphia primarily as an engraver of prints and a painter; see George C. Groce and David H. Wallace, *The New-York Historical Society's Dictionary of Artists in America, 1564–1860* (New Haven: Yale University Press, 1957), pp. 428–29.

2. Thomas Hayes, Henry W. H. Darley, John Neagle, and others joined by 1829. Thomas Sully's name appears on the bowl base as a founding and associate member. Sully sketched club archers but rarely participated; see *The United Bowmen of Philadelphia, 1828–1953, Commemorating the 125th Anniversary,* (Philadelphia: United Bowmen of Philadelphia, 1953); and Robert B. Davidson, *History of the United Bowmen of Philadelphia* (Philadelphia: Allen, Lane & Scott's Printing House, 1888), pp. 2–6. Davidson recounts Titian Peale's reminiscences in 1881 of the club's origin: "After returning from Long's Expedition to the Rockey Mountains, feeling the want of outdoor exercise, and disliking billiards, tenpins, &c., a few friends joined in choosing archery before breakfast … six young men of social disposition and scientific proclivities, in the spring of the year 1828 agreed to associate themselves together as a Club."

3. *Hazard's Register of Pennsylvania*, September 12, 1835, p. 175. *Constitution and Regulations of the United Bowmen of Philadelphia: Founded September 1828* (Philadelphia: Hogan & Thompson, 1844), reg. X, p. 10. This practice is borne out by the varied chasing of leaves and slightly irregular spacing. Concentric circles and radiating lines were lightly inscribed on the bowl to guide alignment for the leaves and placement of bolts. Many leaves have roman numerals inscribed on the back.

4. The following names are engraved on the left side of the base after a club symbol (left column): "Franklin Peale, elected Sept. 3rd, 1828/Titian R. Peale, …/R.

Eglesfeld Griffith, …/Sam. P. Griffitts, Jr., …/Jacob G. Morris, …/Thomas Hayes, …Oct.ʳ 6th 1828/W.H. W. Darley, …/Alexander Krumbhaar, … July 9th 1830/Thomas F. Betton, … Sept. 2nd 1831"; (right column) Lewis Krumbhaar Jr., … Sept. 2nd 1831/Elhanan W.Keyser, … April 6th 1832/[erased: John P. Griffith, … June 3rd 1832]/Henry Bohlen, … 8th 1832/William Norris, … May 10th 1833/[erased: George B. Hall, … Aug. 9th/Harvey D. Sellers, … Sept. 3rd]/Ambrose W. Thompson, … June 15th 1834/Mark M. Reeve, … July 11th 1834." The right side of the base lists founders as both Peales, Griffith, Griffitts, Jr., Morris, and Sully. Associate members are Thomas Sully, Cephas G. Childs, John K. Kane, and Mord. L. Dawson, with Dr. R. M. Patterson the only honorary member engraved on the base; *United Bowmen of Philadelphia,* pp. 23–24.

Cat. no. 70

1. Letter, Thomas Fletcher to John Sergeant, Esq., January 14, 1833, Fletcher Papers, Winterthur Library. The vase for Joshua Lippencott is in a private collection.

2. *Hazard's Register of Pennsylvania*, January 18, 1834, p. 36.

Cat. no. 71

1. Letter, Thomas Fletcher to Timothy Fletcher, March 15, 1815, Fletcher Papers, Athenaeum. Letter, Welles, Williams & Green to Thomas Fletcher, October 10, 1815, Fletcher Papers, HSP.

2. Virtually identical examples by Parisian silversmiths can be seen in Alemany-Dessaint, *Orfèvrerie Française*, p. 139, fig. 3; and Dennis, *Three Centuries*, 1:88, fig. 91.

Cat. no. 72

1. Vanessa Brett, *The Sotheby's Dictionary of Silver* (London: Sotheby's Publications, 1986), p. 377, figs. 1790, 1791. For French prototypes, see Alemany-Dessaint, *Orfèvrerie Française*, p. 156, fig. 1; p. 157, fig. 195; p. 177, fig. 3.

2. See Dominique Vivant Denon, *Voyage dans la Basse et Haute Égypte* (Paris: De L'Imprimerie de P. Didot l'Aîné, 1802), p. 130, fig. 3; p. 137, fig. 83; p. 140, fig. 8.

Cat. no. 73

1. Letterbook, Fletcher Papers, Athenaeum.

2. The vases presented to Clinton are illustrated in cat. no. 43; see also Warren, Howe, and Brown, *Marks of Achievement*, pp. 90, 91, figs. 96–99; and Voorsanger and Howat, *Art and the Empire City*; Deborah D. Waters, "'Silver Ware in Great Perfection': The Precious Metals Trades in New York City," in *Art and the Empire City*, pp. 355–75. The phrase OLD SILVER was probably stamped on the underside by Tiffany and Company in the early twentieth century, when that firm traded in antique silver.

Cat. no. 74

1. Eliza Acton, *Modern Cookery for Private Families* (London: Privately printed, 1845), p. 105. Eneas S. Dallas, *Ketter's Book of the Table* (London: Privately printed, 1877), pp. 418–19.

2. Richter and Milne, *Shapes and Names*, p. 24, fig. 152.

Cat. no. 75

1. Richter and Milne, *Shapes and Names*, pp. 6–7, figs. 55–59.

2. Letterbook, Fletcher Papers, Athenaeum.

Cat. no. 76

1. Charles H. Carpenter, *Gorham Silver* (New York: Dodd, Mead & Company, 1982), pp. 74, 75, fig. 61.

2. David L. Barquist, *Myer Myers* (New Haven: Yale University Press, 2001), pp. 119–22, figs. 35, 36. *Columbian Centinel,* April 20, 1811; Bradbury, *History of Old Sheffield Plate,* p. 157.

3. Bill, Thomas Fletcher to George Cadwalader, March 10, 1832, Fletcher Papers, HSP. English fixtures of this type are pictured in Nicholas Goodison, *Ormolu: The Work of Matthew Boulton* (London: Phaidon, 1974), figs. 82, 84, 162c,e. Their French counterparts are pictured in Hans Ottomeyer and Peter Pröschel, *Vergoldete Bronzen,* 2 vols. (Munich: Klinkhardt & Biermann, 1986), 1:328–37, figs. 5.2.2–5.2.19. Letter, Thomas Fletcher to John Skinner, January 6, 1834, Fletcher Papers, Winterthur Library.

Cat. no. 77

1. Bayard Tuckerman, *The Diary of Philip Hone,* 2 vols. (New York: Dodd, Mead and Company, 1889), 1:289.

2. Closely related design elements on Parisian metalwork are pictured in Pinçon and du Gers, *Odiot l'Orfèvre,* p. 55; fig. 62; p. 67, fig. 87; p. 127, fig. 204.

Cat. no. 78

1. Thomas Fletcher named his eighth child, born 1834, Daniel Webster Fletcher.

2. Letter, Thomas Fletcher to Daniel Webster, April 17, 1833, Fletcher Papers, Winterthur Library. A large hot-water urn that Fletcher & Gardiner made for Webster is illustrated in Katharine Morrison McClinton, "Fletcher and Gardiner, Silversmiths of the American Empire," *The Connoisseur* 173, no. 697 (March 1970): 221, fig. 15.

Cat. no. 79

1. Janice Carlson of Winterthur's Scientific Research and Analysis Laboratory used semi-quantitative energy-dispersive X-ray fluorescence to determine that Towson's sword hilt ranges from 14 to 24kt gold, with most elements between 22 and 24kt. Variations in the color of yellow and red gold were achieved by changing the copper or silver in the alloy. The scabbard is gilded using a mercury gilding process on silver; the mounts are 23kt gold.

2. The tapered grip has a vertical seam and was fashioned from one sheet of gold. The design, suggesting a miniature Trajan's column, was also used by Phillip Hartmann for a sword given to Stephen Decatur by Philadelphia in 1814; see Tuite, *U.S. Naval Officers,* pp. 127–28. Thomas Fletcher used a similar grip at least one more time in a sword design for William Worth (Chap. 6, Drawing 32).

3. Thomas Culbreth to Thomas Fletcher, December 13, 1833, Fletcher Papers, Athenaeum. Towson's sword was set to cost $500, by the State of Maryland, but as work progressed Fletcher sent prices for gold versus silver scabbards, and the final value was closer to $700. Donald Fennimore transcribed an undated itemized bill comparing the costs of Towson's and John Gallagher's swords, accounting for materials and labor. Towson's sword is listed at $605.16 and Gallagher's at $508.75; see Donald L. Fennimore, "Elegant Patterns of Uncommon Good Taste: Domestic Silver by Thomas Fletcher and Sidney Gardiner" (Master's thesis, University of Delaware, 1971), p. 45; and Fletcher Papers, Athenaeum. For Gallagher's sword, Fletcher explained methods for achieving a rich look

without higher costs: "The scabbard may be silver gilt with the ornaments on relief of gold soldered on which will look about as well as if the whole were of gold, and they would cost $130 less" (Letter, Thomas Fletcher to Thomas Culbreth, May 8, 1834, Fletcher Papers, Winterthur Library). Watercolor-and-ink drawing, Maryland Historical Society, Gift of Mr. Joseph Katz, acc. no. 1952.124.3.

Cat. no. 81

1. Dennis, *Three Centuries,* 1:210, fig. 311. For the King's pattern, see Rabinovitch, *Antique Silver Servers,* p. 189, fig. 87.

2. Letter, Robert Campbell to Thomas Fletcher, April 20, 1831; Letter, Thomas Fletcher to Robert & Andrew Campbell, July 23, 1831, Fletcher Papers, Winterthur Library.

3. Photographs of spoons and forks with handles in the King's Pattern marked by Thomas Fletcher are on file in the Decorative Arts Photographic Collection, Winterthur Library, 78.2923.

Cat. no. 82

1. Letter, Rezin D. Shepherd to Thomas Fletcher, October 28, 1831, Fletcher Papers, HSP.

2. Two more salts identical to these that bear the same engraved crest are recorded in Zimmerman and Goldsborough, *Sewell C. Biggs Collection,* 1:191, ent. 166. The identity of the owner of the crest has not been determined, but it may have been a member of the Mercer family of Pennsylvania.

3. Percy Hennell, *Hennell Silver Salt Cellars* (East Grinstead, Eng.: BLA Publishing Ltd., 1986), p. 33, fig. 10. Letterbook, undated entry, Fletcher Papers, Athenaeum. John Bodman Carrington and George Ravensworth Hughes, *The Plate of the Worshipful Company of Goldsmiths* (Oxford, Eng.: Oxford University Press, 1926), p. 139.

Cat. no. 83

1. The applied, stamped anthemion-and-feather motif measures identically to the motif ornamenting the lip of the pierced cake basket (cat. no. 87). Lewis's tureens and the cake basket were presumably fashioned after these dies were cut for the presentation table service designed by Thomas Fletcher and given by the Second Bank of the U.S. to Nicholas Biddle; see drawing of a cake basket with this motif identified as "For Nicholas Biddle Presented to him by United States Bank," Chap. 6, Drawing 36. The anthemion-and-feather motif also appears on two surviving tea and coffee services in private collections; see cat. no. 88.

2. The mate to Lewis's tureen is now in the collection of the Philadelphia Museum of Art, acc. no. 1972-38-1; resolution reported to the public in *Niles' Weekly Register,* April 4, 1835, p. 76.

3. Letter, Isaac Hull, Washington Naval Yard, to Thomas Fletcher, December 7, 1829, Fletcher Papers, Athenaeum.

Cat. no. 84

1. For a concentrated treatment of the subject, see Heather Jane McCormick et. al., *Vasemania: Neoclassical Form and Ornament in Europe, Selections from The Metropolitan Museum of Art* (New Haven: Yale University Press, 2004).

2. Alters, Taylor & Dewey are listed at 325 High Street,

Philadelphia; *A. McElroy's Philadelphia Directory for 1839* (Philadelphia: Isaac Ashmead & Co., 1839), p. 5.

Cat. no. 85

1. Janice Carlson of Winterthur's Scientific Research and Analysis Laboratory used semi-quantitative energy-dispersive X-ray fluorescence to determine that Kennedy's sword hilt ranges from 14 to 23kt gold, with most elements testing at 23kt gold. The scabbard mounts and tip were analyzed as between 14 and 23kt. Variations in color of yellow and red gold were achieved by changing the copper or silver in the alloy. Additional red colorant on the hilt was not identifiable.

2. The overall cross-guard and elliptic eagle-guard design is related to those used by the firm for Maryland swords given to David Geisinger, Joseph Smoot, and John Contee in 1831. Geisinger's sword is now in the U.S. Naval Academy Museum, and Smoot's is at the New-York Historical Society.

3. Letter, Thomas Veazey to R. H. Goldsborough, January 22, 1836, Maryland State Archives, MSA SC 2085-B71-F22.

Cat. no. 86

1. Letter, Thomas Fletcher to Daniel W. Coxe, April 6, 1837, Fletcher Papers, Winterthur Library. Additional objects were made for Biddle at the time, but they were not enumerated on the document. "The service of plate voted to . . . Nicholas Biddle . . . is now exhibiting in Chesnut Street . . . a full service for two dozen persons, made of silver of the purity of coin, highly burnished, and exquisitely wrought and embossed . . . It attracts crowds of visitors, and it should call forth serious reflections," in New Hampshire Patriot and State Gazette, April 9, 1838.

2. Letter, Thomas Fletcher to Daniel W. Coxe, December 10, 1836, Fletcher Papers, Winterthur Library. The initials *NJB* stand for Nicholas Biddle and his wife, Jane. The initial *B* in a circle stands for the surname Biddle. The blade on the table knife is a replacement. The handles of the fish knife, carving fork and knife, and table knife are made of two thinly stamped halves of silver that were soldered together and pitch filled. While handles of this type had been made in England since the eighteenth century, these are among the first known to have been made in the United States.

Cat. no. 87

1. Wood, "Thomas Fletcher," pp. 136–71.

2. Edward Wenham, *Domestic Silver of Great Britain and Ireland* (New York: Oxford University Press, 1931), pl. 73; Heckscher and Bowman, *American Rococo,* p. 122, fig. 82; see also a rococo cake basket made about 1765 by London silversmith William Plummer, Winterthur acc. no. 61.210.

3. Wainwright, *Philadelphia Perspective,* p. 74; see also Garvan, *Three Centuries of American Art,* p. 293, ent. 248. This basket is said to have been made for a member of the Wetherill family of Philadelphia.

Cat. no. 88

1. Letter, Thomas Fletcher to Daniel W. Coxe, December 10, 1836, Fletcher Papers, Winterthur Library.

2. Letter, Thomas Fletcher to Daniel W. Coxe, April 6, 1837, Fletcher Papers, Winterthur Library. Tuckerman, *Diary of Philip Hone,* 1:288.

APPENDICES

Appendix 1
Marks of the Firm and Its Associates

This appendix lists all the variants of marks known to have been used on silver and gold by the firm of Fletcher & Gardiner in Boston (1808–11) and Philadelphia (1811–ca. 1827). About the time of Sidney Gardiner's death (1827), Thomas Fletcher had new marking dies made, which he used in Philadelphia (ca. 1827–42). For a few years, Fletcher took his nephew Calvin W. Bennett into partnership in Philadelphia (1835–37). The mark used during that partnership is also illustrated.

Most of the silver produced by the firm is not dated, so one must assign specific dates to the use of any marking die with care. Nevertheless, marks can generally be placed in a chronological order, thanks to the firm's presentation silver and gold that is dated and, to a lesser degree, the stylistic attributes of the work on which the various marks are stamped.

The presentation silver and gold made by the firm usually bears stamped marks. It also sometimes carries the hand-engraved name of the firm, following a practice by the most prominent silversmithing establishments in London and Paris at the time. Each of these hand-engraved marks is one of a kind, as opposed to stamped marks, which, by definition, are replicates.

The illustrated stamped marks are the best-preserved examples that could be found. These must be considered representative of the hundreds of the firm's stamped marks that a reader could potentially encounter. Stamped marks cited in each catalogue entry refer to an example in this appendix and not necessarily the exact mark on the object. In a few instances where they are accompanied by varying secondary marks, they are pictured in duplicate, so that readers will have as complete a reference to all the primary and secondary marks as possible.

By contrast, every engraved mark on silver and gold produced by the firm, and known to the authors, is pictured. Stamped and engraved marks are illustrated separately, each organized as a unit and arranged in chronological order.

Thomas Fletcher and Sidney Gardiner, both members of large families, had siblings as well as relations by marriage who were involved with the firm. In some instances, these relatives acted as traveling agents who sold goods in various markets throughout the country. In others, they established independent businesses and sold goods made in Philadelphia by Fletcher & Gardiner, later Fletcher, and other Philadelphia manufacturers as well. These independent firms sometimes had silver marks of their own, which are listed as a separate group.

Stamped marks used by Thomas Fletcher and Sidney Gardiner, by Thomas Fletcher alone, and by Thomas Fletcher and Calvin W. Bennett, in conjunction with secondary marks.

Fig. 1a, b

Two marks used by Fletcher & Gardiner consisting of (a) F&G in rectangle and (b) spread-eagle with shield-shape body stamped incuse. These may have been used exclusively on jewelry. There is no dated silver or gold bearing these marks. They are tentatively assigned a date range of 1808 to about 1815.

Fig. 2a, b

Two marks used by Fletcher & Gardiner consisting of (a) F&.G. in rectangle, and (b) PHILAD.^{A} in rectangle. This F&.G. mark was used as early as 1811, evidenced by a pair of two-handle church cups given to the Second Baptist Church in Boston by Joseph Shed. The mark also appears on the urn presented to Oliver H. Perry dated 1814. Mark (a) was probably first used when the firm was in Boston.

Fig. 3

Mark used by Fletcher & Gardiner consisting of F&G in rectangle. A fish slice given to Ruth Gibbs when she married William Ellery Channing in 1814 establishes the only date context for this mark. It was probably used by the firm from about 1811 through the 1820s.

Fig. 4a–d

Four marks used by Fletcher & Gardiner consisting of (a) F&G in a clipped-corner rectangle, (b) spread eagle with shield-shape body on demi-globe in rounded-corner square, (c) spread eagle in clipped-corner square, and (d) the letter P in clipped-corner square. No dated silver from the firm has been located with these marks, which were probably used during the 1810s and 1820s. Mark (a) has been found only on flatware.

Fig. 5

Mark used by Fletcher & Gardiner consisting of FLETCHER & GARDINER. in rectangle. The punch bowl presented to George Armistead in 1816 and a soup tureen presented to John Rodgers in 1817 bear this mark. It was probably used from about 1815 to about 1820.

Fig. 6a, b

Two marks used by Fletcher & Gardiner consisting of (a) FLETCHER & GARDINER. in circular band and (b) PHIL^A in rectangle. The dinner service presented to John Rodgers in 1817 and vases presented to James C. Fisher in 1830 bear these marks, which were used by the firm from about 1815 to about 1830.

Fig. 7a, b

Two marks used by Fletcher & Gardiner consisting of (a) FLETCHER & GARDINER. in a Z-shape banner and (b) PHIL^A in rectangle. The vases presented to DeWitt Clinton in 1825 are the only silver bearing mark (a); the die was probably cut specifically for this commission and may have never been used again.

Fig. 8

Mark used by Fletcher & Gardiner consisting of F&G in ellipse. This mark, used from about 1815 to 1830, appears only on gold coins of foreign manufacture counterstamped by Fletcher & Gardiner to certify their purity.

Fig. 9a, b

Two marks used by Thomas Fletcher consisting of (a) •T. FLETCHER. PHILAD. in an elliptical band and (b) CROWNS in a rectangle. The CROWNS mark (b) references English coins of that denomination, indicating that the object is of English sterling purity. The three-part mark within (a) with the profile head, letters JB, and spread eagle probably belonged to Jacob Bennett, older brother of Calvin W. Bennett, who worked for and with Fletcher during the 1830s. Jacob was listed as a jeweler and silversmith in the Philadelphia directories during the 1830s. A new plate, paten, and chalice dated 1825 and presented to Christ Church, Philadelphia by Sarah Redman bears mark (a). While it might be presumed that these objects were made and marked in 1825, historically a delay often occurred between the time of a monetary bequest to a church and its execution, suggesting that the Christ Church silver was probably made after Gardiner's death. Mark (a) was probably used from about 1827 until about 1842.

Fig. 10

Mark used by Thomas Fletcher consisting of a profile head in belted circle, the letters T and F, each in a shield with diagonally striped ground, spread eagle with shield-shape body in belted circle, and the letter P in shield with diagonally striped ground. The letters T and F stand for Thomas Fletcher, and P stands for Philadelphia. This mark resembles individually struck English hallmarks but was cut as a single die. Fletcher may have used this mark in response to a general attempt to restructure the marking system for precious metals in the United States during the second quarter of the nineteenth century, best evidenced by the hallmarking used on Maryland and New York silver at that time.★ These marks appear on the two vases presented to James C. Fisher in 1830. They may be presumed to have been used from about 1827 to 1842.

Fig. 11a, b

Two marks used by Thomas Fletcher consisting of (a) T. FLETCHER and (b) PHILA., each in a rectangle. No dated silver has been found bearing mark (a), although it is on the United Bowmen's bowl, which is known to date before 1834. It was probably used from about 1830 to 1842. The mark may also have appeared on silver sold by Fletcher during the 1840s and 1850s after his manufactory was closed.

Fig. 12a–c

Three marks used by Thomas Fletcher and Calvin W. Bennett consisting of (a) F&B in a rectangle, (b) PHILA. in a rectangle, and (c) spread eagle in clipped-corner square. No dated silver has been found bearing mark (a). It is presumed to have been used only during the time of the partnership between Fletcher and Bennett, 1835 to 1837. *Photo with PHILA. courtesy of Spencer Marks, Ltd*

Fig. 13

Stamped mark of T.F in rectangle. Appears on spoons of light weight, atypical of Thomas Fletcher's work. When Fletcher was in business, there were at least 11 silversmiths with those initials, 3 in Philadelphia. Attribution is unresolved. *Photo courtesy of Dr. Richard Weiss.*

Engraved marks on presentation silver and gold made in the manufactory of Thomas Fletcher and Sidney Gardiner and, later, Thomas Fletcher.

Fig. 14

Mark engraved on the urn made for Isaac Hull in 1813.

Fig. 15

Mark engraved on the urn presented to Oliver Hazard Perry in 1814.

Fig. 16

Mark engraved on the punch bowl presented to George Armistead in 1816.

Fig. 17

Mark engraved on the urn made for Andrew Jackson in 1816.

Fig. 18

Mark engraved on the pair of vases presented to DeWitt Clinton in 1825.

Fig. 19

Mark on gold miniature frame presented to the Marquis de Lafayette in 1825.

Fig. 20 Mark engraved on the sword presented to David Geisinger in 1831: "FLETCHER" (photo unavailable).

Fig. 21

Mark engraved on the United Bowmen's bowl ca. 1830–34.

Fig. 22

Mark engraved on sword presented to Nathan Towson in 1834.

Fig. 23

Mark engraved on sword presented to John Webster in 1843.

Stamped marks used by individuals associated with Thomas Fletcher and Sidney Gardiner's manufactory.

Fig. 24a, b

Two marks used by Lewis Veron in Philadelphia between 1826 and 1841 consisting of (a) L.V. & CO. in rectangle and (b) L.VERON & Co. in rectangle.

Fig. 25a-h

Eight marks used by Baldwin Gardiner in New York City between 1827 and 1847 consisting of (a) B. GARDINER in serrated arc, (b) NEW·YORK in serrated arc, (c) B. GARDINER in rectangle, (d) B·GARDINER in serrated rectangle, (e) B.G in rectangle, (f) B•G in rectangle, (g) B.G.& C.º in rounded-corner rectangle, and (h) B G in rectangle.

Fig. 26

Mark used by Charles and George Fletcher in Philadelphia between 1819 and 1824 consisting of C & G. F in rectangle. *Photo courtesy of Cliff Nunn*

Fig. 27a, b

Two marks used by Henry Fletcher in Lexington, Kentucky (1817–29) and Louisville (1829–66) consisting of (a) H. FLETCHER in rectangle and (b) H. FLETCHER. stamped incuse.

Fig. 28

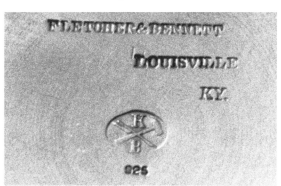

Mark used by partners Henry Fletcher and Charles Fletcher Bennett between 1843 and 1854 consisting of FLETCHER & BENNETT / LOUISVILLE / KY. stamped incuse. Here it appears in conjunction with marks of the Philadelphia silver manufacturing firm of Peter L. Krider and John W. Biddle.

Fig. 29a, b

Two marks on the blades of some presentation swords hilted by Fletcher & Gardiner consisting of (a) W.ROSE and (b) ROSE, both stamped incuse. William Rose and his sons, William and Joseph, were celebrated swordsmiths and cutlers who worked in Blockley Township, West Philadelphia, through the early nineteenth century.

★ The hallmarking system used in Maryland during the early nineteenth century is explored in Jennifer Faulds Goldsborough, *Maryland Silver* (Baltimore: Baltimore Museum of Art, 1975), pp. 7–22; and Patrick M. Duggan, "Marks on Baltimore Silver, 1814–1860: An Exploration," in *Silver in Maryland*, ed. Jennifer Faulds Goldsborough (Baltimore: Maryland Historical Society, 1983), pp. 26–37. Marks used on New York silver at the same time are pictured in Herbert F. Darling, *New York State Silversmiths* (Eggertsville, N.Y.: Darling Foundation, 1964) and compiled in John R. McGrew, *Manufacturers' Marks on American Coin Silver* (Hanover, Pa.: Argyros Publications, 2004).

Appendix 2
Genealogy for the Fletcher, Bennett, Gardiner, and Veron Families

The following information seeks to aid the reader with a summary of four families wonderfully entwined over two generations. Many of the details were gleaned from family records as well as letters and unpublished documents in archive collections, which preference male descendants. We provide this Appendix as reference for the catalogue and ask the Fletcher, Bennett, Gardiner, and Veron families to pardon any omissions.

Fletcher genealogy was kindly shared by Mrs. Frank J. Bowden, Jr. (Marjorie Fletcher Thomson Bowden), Thomas Fletcher's great-great granddaughter. We also consulted Edward H. Fletcher, *Fletcher Genealogy: An Account of the Descendants of Robert Fletcher, of Concord, Mass.* (Boston: Alfred Mudge & Son, 1871). The publication by Curtiss C. Gardiner, *Lion Gardiner and His Descendants* (St. Louis: A. Whipple, 1890), provided Gardiner genealogy details.

I. FLETCHER
Timothy Fletcher (1751–1823) married Hannah Fosdick (1757–1832) on March 30, 1775. They had fourteen children, the first nine born when the family lived in Alstead, New Hampshire, and the latter five born in Lancaster, Massachusetts. Timothy died in Lancaster; Hannah died in Philadelphia of cholera.

Children:
Hannah (1776–1838)
[*See* FLETCHER–BENNETT]
Polly (1778–79)
Betsey (1779–1863)
Timothy (1781–1811, d. New Orleans) married Sally (Sarah) White of Boston in 1805; three children
Joshua (1783–1844) married Nabby Warren of Boston in 1811; eight children
James Fosdick (1785–1820, d. New Orleans) married Felicitie du Corneau; 2 children
Thomas Charles (1787–1866, d. Delanco, N.J.) [*See* FLETCHER–VERON]
Henry (1789–1866, d. Louisville)
Martha (1791–94)
Charles (b. 1794) married Louisa Lovett October 4, 1831
George (b. 1796) married Sophia Eliza Cunningham, November 28, 1820; ten children

Mary Ann (b. 1798)
Levi (1800–1837, d. Mobile, Ala.)
Martha (1803–29)

II. FLETCHER–BENNETT
Hannah Fletcher (1776–1838) married Calvin Bennett, Sr. (ca. 1777–1814), May 8, 1798

Children:
Elvira (b. 1799)
Sophia (1800–1814)
Jacob (b. 1804)
Alfred (1806–51)
Calvin Wilder (b. 1808)
Thomas Sidney (b. 1810)
James (1812–39)
Charles Fletcher (b. 1814)

II. FLETCHER–VERON
Thomas Charles Fletcher (1787–1866) married Melina de Grasse Veron (1797-1849), September 29, 1818

Children:
Lewis Veron (1820–63)
Melina Veron (1822–24)
Eliza Anne Sigourney (1824-96)
Melanie De Grasse (b. 1825)
Thomas Sidney (1827–1905)
William Henry (1829–66)
Martha (b. 1832)
Daniel Webster (1834–63)
Charles Edward (b. 1837)

I. GARDINER
John Gardiner (1752–1823) married Abigail Worth (d. 1800) and had six children. He married Margaret Moore in 1803 and had two boys who died in childhood. John Gardiner, a descendant of Lion Gardiner of Long Island, practiced as a doctor in Mattituck and Southold, New York.

Children with Abigail Worth:
Rejoice (1783–90)
John W. (1785–1801)
Sidney (1787–1827, d. Vera Cruz)
[*See* GARDINER–VERON]

Laura (1789–1860)
Baldwin (1791–1869) [*See* GARDINER–VERON]
Mary Reeve (b. 179?)

II. GARDINER–VERON
Sidney Gardiner (1787–1827) married Mary Holland Veron (d. 1875) in Boston, 1811

Children:
Algernon S.
John W.
Ellen M.
John H.
Adelaine
Mary-Louise

Baldwin Gardiner (1791–1869) married Louise-Leroy Veron (d. 1849) in 1815

Children:
Louise L.
Melanie V.
Laura
John B.
Rosalie
Robert S.
Celestine
Charles Chauncey
Etienne

I. VERON★
Etienne Veron married (Abial/Elizabeth?), both were from St. Malo, France. The Thomas Fletcher papers connect Mrs. Veron to a boarding house at No. 59 Cornhill Street in 1811 and 1812; this was the address of the Fletcher & Gardiner firm in Boston (1810–11).

Children (possibly incomplete):
Lewis (1793–1853)
Stephen (d. 1819/20)
Timothy (b?)
Mary Holland (d. 1875)
Melina de Grasse (1797–1849)
Louise-Leroy (d. 1849)

★ In the Thomas Fletcher Papers at the Athenaeum of Philadelphia, the last name of the females in the Veron family often appears as "Vernon" although letters to Lewis and Timothy use "Veron." Boston city directories do not list Etienne Veron. However, the following names do appear: Abiah Verron (1805, 1806); Abiel Veron (1809, 1810); Elizabeth Veron "schoolmistress" (1813); Elizabeth Vernon "schoolmistress" (1816, 1818). If Elizabeth is Etienne Veron's wife/widow, her name appears as "Vernon" twice and is then not published after 1818.

Appendix 3
Description of the Clinton Vases

The following is a photographic reproduction of a two-sided handbill composed by Thomas Fletcher and Isaac S. Hone to narrate the pair of vases presented to DeWitt Clinton in Albany, New York, on March 19, 1825 (F&G cat. no. 43).★ The text was printed in *Niles' Weekly Register* and newspapers such as the *Independent Chronicle & Boston Patriot* (March 23, 1825) which prefaced the description:

> Two magnificent silver vases, about to be presented to De Witt Clinton, by the merchants of Pearl street, New-York City, have been completed by Messrs. Fletcher & Gardiner Philadelphia, and have been recently exhibited in New York, to gratify public curiosity. Having seen them, we can pronounce the following description of them which is copied from the New York Statesman, to be generally correct. Any description however could hardly fail to give an inadequate idea of these rich and splendid specimens of art.

DESCRIPTION OF THE VASES

Presented to **Governor Clinton** *by the* MERCHANTS OF PEARL-STREET, *in the city of New-York, in testimony of their gratitude and respect for his public services.*

THE form of these vases is copied from the celebrated antique vase, found among the ruins of the Villa of Adrian, and now in the possession of the Earl of Warwick. The handles and some of the ornaments are also similar to those upon that beautiful specimen of ancient art; but all the tablets and figures in *bas relief* are different, and exhibit scenes upon the Grand Canal, or allegorical illustrations of the progress of the arts and sciences.

The vases are twenty-four inches in height, twenty-one inches between the extremities of the handles, and the diameter of the body in the largest part is fourteen and a half inches; the weight of silver in each is about four hundred ounces.

Their form is circular, except that the lower part is slightly elliptical, as are also the covers, each of which is surmounted by an Eagle standing upon a section of the Globe, upon which is traced part of the outline of the state of New-York; he bears in one talon the arms of the state, and in the other a laurel wreath. The pedestal is square, and supported by four claws; two sides of the pedestal of the first vase are ornamented with foliage and scroll-work, with an oval medallion bearing a river Deity leaning on an inverted vase. The third contains the inscription,

"TO THE HONORABLE *DE WITT CLINTON*, WHO HAS DEVELOPED THE RESOURCES OF THE STATE OF NEW-YORK, AND ENNOBLED HER CHARACTER, THE MERCHANTS OF PEARL-STREET OFFER THIS TESTIMONY OF THEIR GRATITUDE AND RESPECT."

The fourth exhibits a number of figures, which in connection with those on the corresponding section of the other vase are intended to represent the progress of the Arts and Sciences from their rude origin to their present improvement. On the right of the spectator appears a pastoral group listening to the pipe of Mercury; next to these is a husbandman leaning upon his spade, and gazing upon a hive; while a female figure points to the labors of the industrious bee; then appears Minerva without her helmet and shield, directing the attention of the spectator to a bust which Sculpture is chisseling. The concave belt around the middle of this vase bears six tablets in *bas relief*; the two centre tablets exhibit views of the Cohoes Falls, and of the Little Falls of the Mohawk, with the stone aqueduct and bridge, and parts of the Canal. The figures on each side of the former are Fame and History; on one side of the latter is an Indian contemplating the stump of a tree recently felled, and the

ax lying at its root; and on the other, Plenty with her cornucopia—A head of Neptune with his trident, dolphins and shells, is placed at each extremity of this belt, under the grape-vine handles.

On the second vase, two sides of the pedestal are ornamented with foliage, &c. as on the first: the third contains the inscription,

"TO THE HONORABLE *DEWITT CLINTON*, WHOSE CLAIM TO THE PROUD TITLE OF PUBLIC BENEFACTOR IS FOUNDED ON THOSE MAGNIFICENT WORKS, THE NORTHERN AND WESTERN CANALS."

On the fourth side is Architecture leaning upon a column, with a level at its base.—Then a youth holding a drawing board with a diagram of one of the first problems in mathematics, and an old man directing his attention to the figures beyond, which denote the sciences still unexplored, and encouraging him to persevere. The next group is composed of two aged persons, contemplating a globe held by a female, who points to some lines upon its surface; next is a figure with a torch in the right hand, and a star on the head, and holding in the left hand a tablet with a diagram; by his side is a sun-dial, an athletic figure beyond holds a pair of dividers, and gazes attentively upon the female with the globe. This group is intended to indicate the study of the sciences. The concave belt around this vase is also embellished with six tablets. The front view is the Guard Lock and part of the basin at Albany, where the Canal is connected with the Hudson, together with the mansion of Mr. Van Rensselaer and the adjacent scenery, and Canal boats passing. The plate on the right of this tablet exhibits Ceres with the emblems of agriculture; that on the left Mercury, with the emblems of commerce. The reverse centre tablet contains a view of the aqueduct at Rochester, and a boat passing, drawn by horses; below are seen the Falls of the Genessee, and a number of unfinished buildings.—This view is supported on the right and left by Minerva and Hercules, indicating wisdom and strength.

The lower compartment of the body of each vase is ornamented with Acanthus leaves, intermingled, at proper distances, with small shrubs, among which are seen the wild animals who haunted our western region before the industry and enterprize of our brethren made "the wilderness to rejoice and blossom as the rose."

These vases were made by Messrs. FLETCHER & GARDINER of Philadelphia, and designed by their MR. FLETCHER.

★ Fletcher wrote to his wife, Melina, on March 12, 1825, that he had arrived with the silver vases in New York City: "There is to be a meeting of the subscribers this evening in the City Hotel where the vases will be exhibited ... to the public on Monday and Tuesday and I shall have to attend and explain the work ... I shall dine with Mr. Hone tomorrow and after dinner he and I shall draw up the description for publication" (Thomas Fletcher Papers, Athenaeum of Philadelphia).

Appendix 4
Fletcher & Gardiner's Correspondents

Surviving records in public and private collections document that Thomas Fletcher and, to a lesser extent, Sidney Gardiner, as well as several of their administrative employees (Calvin W. Bennett and George W. South, for instance) carried on an extensive business correspondence throughout the United States, England, France, and Mexico. Indeed, their correspondents were as far distant as Venezuela, Brazil, and Chile on occasion.

The names of the individuals with whom they corresponded, most of which are not recorded in the body of this catalogue, provide a potentially valuable resource for those interested in early American silver, manufacturing and mercantile history, trade relationships, economic history, cultural geography, and other disciplines. The names of the correspondents are listed alphabetically, with their location when known.

Adams, J. T.

Adams, Thomas F.; Philadelphia, Pennsylvania

Addison, Wilmarth & Co.; New York City

Allamand & Hersent

Allan & Johnston

Allan, William & Son; Charleston, South Carolina

Alleond, A.

Alofsen, S.

Alpin, James W.

Alsop, Samuel; Burlington County, New Jersey

Alsop, Wetmore & Cryder; Lima, Peru

Anderson, James F.

Andrews, J.

Armstrong, Jane W.; New York City

Ashhurst, Mrs. Richard; Philadelphia, Pennsylvania

Ashhurst, Richard; Philadelphia, Pennsylvania

Aspinwall, W. H.

Atherton, Humphrey; Philadelphia, Pennsylvania

Backus, E.; Fort Columbus, Governor's Island, New York

Bailey, Eben

Bainbridge & Brown

Ballard, Captain Henry E.; Baltimore, Maryland

Barlow, James & Thomas; Sheffield, England

Beatty, George

Beaty, Robert; Alabama

Bell, C. & R.; New Orleans, Louisiana

Bennett, Calvin W.; Philadelphia, Pennsylvania

Bennett, W. A.; Charleston, South Carolina

Berrett, W. H.

Berry, J.; New Orleans, Louisiana

Biddle & Loyes; Birmingham, England

Bill, S. C.; New Orleans, Louisiana

Bingham, Mrs.; New Orleans, Louisiana

Binny, Archibald; St. Mary's County, Maryland

Bolton, C.; New York City

Bolton, Fox & Levingston

Bonnefoux, L.; New York City

Boulegny, D.

Boyce & Henry; Charleston, South Carolina

Boyd, William; Harrisburg, Pennsylvania

Bradburn, Colonel

Bradlee, Josiah; Boston, Massachusett

Bradley, B.; New Haven, Connecticu

Bradley, General H.

Bray, Paul A.; New York City

Breed, E. & J.; Boston, Massachusetts

Bres, P. A.; New York City

Bretz, Jacob; Philadelphia, Pennsylvania

Brewer, C. & Co.

Brooks, Elijah

Brower, John; New York City

Brown, John A.; Liverpool, England

Brown, John Carter; Providence, Rhode Island

Brown, William & James & Co.

Buchanan, Frank; Philadelphia, Pennsylvania

Buehler, H.

Burrows, Thomas H.; Harrisburg, Pennsylvania

Cadwalader, George; Philadelphia, Pennsylvania

Campbell, Robert & Andrew; Baltimore, Maryland

Carnes, F. & N. G.; New York City

Carpenter, L. H.

Casey, Mr.

Chadwick, Capt.

Clark, A. H.; Vera Cruz, Mexico

Clawes, Thomas; Birmingham, England

Clay, Henry; Ashland, Tennessee

Coburn, John

Collins, John W.; Portsmouth, Virginia

Comstock, Capt.

Corbin, Robert B.; Caroline County, Virginia

Cornell, G., Jr.

Cortez, Eugenio; Philadelphia, Pennsylvania

Cox, Thomas & Co.; Birmingham, England

Coxe, Daniel W.; Philadelphia, Pennsylvania

Crabb, William A.; Harrisburg, Pennsylvania

Craven, Alfred; Yorkville, South Carolina

Crocker, Richmond & Co.; Taunton, Massachusetts

Cruse, S.

Cryder, John; Valapriso, Mexico

Culbreth, Thomas; Annapolis, Maryland

Curtis, Peter; Newbern, South Carolina

Cushing, Augustus

Cushing, George; Boston, Massachusetts

Custis, Peter

Dallas, Capt. Alexander James; Philadelphia, Pennsylvania

Dalton, Samuel; Sheffield, England

Danforth, J.

Darte, L. S.; Paris, France

Darwin, John & Samuel; Sheffield, England

Davis, John D.; Pittsburgh, Pennsylvania

Deguerre, Joseph; New York City

Delvey, R. C.; Philadelphia, Pennsylvania

Denny, H.

Dick, Nathaniel

Dickinson, Samuel

Dillingham, W. H.; West Chester, Pennsylvania

Dorr & Allen; Boston, Massachusetts

Dorr, Sullivan; Providence, Rhode Island

Downes, John

Duane, William J.

Dubbs, William; Maracaibo, Venezuela

Duncan, Dr. Stephen; New Orleans, Louisiana

Duncan, J. Curice; New Orleans, Louisiana

Dunn, Thomas; Sheffield, England

Durand, Calvin; New York City

Dyer, Joseph C.; Boston, Massachusetts & Manchester, England

Eaton, John A.

Eccleston, John B.

Emerson, G. B.

Eustis, General Abraham

Ewing, L.

Faber & Moore

Farley, Frederick A.; Boston, Massachusetts

Farnum, Henry

Fletcher, Martha

Fisher, James C.

Fletcher, Charles; Sheffield, Massachusetts

Fletcher, Fidelte; New Orleans, Louisiana

Fletcher, Hannah; Lancaster, Massachusetts

Fletcher, Henry; Boston, Massachusetts; Washington, D.C.; Baltimore, Maryland; New York City; Louisville & Lexington, Kentucky

Fletcher, James Fosdick; New Orleans, Louisiana

Fletcher, Levi; Cambridge, Massachusetts

Fletcher, Melanie; Philadelphia, Pennsylvania

Fletcher, Melinda; Philadelphia, Pennsylvania

Fletcher, Peter; Alstead, New Hampshire

Fletcher, Timothy; Lancaster, Massachusetts

Fletcher, Veron; Pawtucket, Rhode Island

Fondt, John P.; Washington, D.C.

Forman, General T. M.; Cecilton, Maryland

Francis, Richard; Alvaredo, Mexico

Fraser, John & Co.; Charleston, South Carolina

French, Mr.; London, England

Gadsby, Mr.

Gale, Wood & Hughes; New York City

Gandahl, Joseph; New York City

Gardiner, Baldwin; New York City

Gardiner, Dr. John; Mattituck, New York

Gates, Jacob; Boston, Massachusetts

Gideon, J., Jr.; Washington, D.C.

Gill, Bennington; Birmingham, England

Gill, John, Jr.

Gillingham, Thomas; Philadelphia, Pennsylvania

Gilmor, Robert, Jr.

Girard, A. & Co.; Mobile, Alabama

Goddard & Bibby; Birmingham, England

Goddard, George S.; Boston, Massachusetts

Goddard, S. A.; Birmingham, England

Goff, C. & R. S.; New York City

Goodman & Miller; Charleston, South Carolina

Goodman, Duke; Charleston, South Carolina

Gorham, The Honorable Benjamin; Boston, Massachusetts

Gorham, Mrs.; Boston, Massachusetts

Grace, J. A.; Newport, Rhode Island

Graham, D.; Philadelphia, Pennsylvania

Gray, B.

Gray, J. B.; near Fredericksburg, Virginia

Green, Thomas; Richmond, Virginia

Grillet, Francis, J.

Grillet, M.

Grinnell, M. H.

Grummere, Samuel; Burlington County, New Jersey

Gummere, John; Burlington County, New Jersey

Gunton, William

Haldeman, C.

Hall & Hewson; Albany, New York

Hall, D. W.

Hamilton, General

Hamilton, P.

Harrison, Major Thomas

Haw, John S.; Georgetown, South Carolina

Hayes & Colton; Newark, New Jersey

Hayne, Colonel; South Carolina

Hayward, William; Charleston, South Carolina

Heisely, George J.; Harrisburg, Pennsylvania

Heyward, William, Jr.; Pocosalig, South Carolina

Hillman & Co.; Sheffield, England

Hook, C. H.; Washington, D.C.

Hopkins, The Reverend John H.; Pittsburgh, Pennsylvania

Hopkiss, John H.

Hoppin, T. C.; Providence, Rhode Island

Hoskins, E. W.; New York City

House of Representatives of the State of Pennsylvania

Houston, Lady Ann Moodie; Savannah, Georgia

Howard, Abi; Baltimore, Maryland

Hubbard, Christopher S.; New York City

Hull, Isaac; Washington, D.C.

Hunter, Alfred; New York City and Newark, New Jersey

Hurtus, H. S.

Hutton, James; Washington, D.C.

Iturbide, Madame Ana Maria de Huarte, Washington, D.C.

Ives, Moses B.; Providence, Rhode Island

Jacobs, Coleman R.

Jacobs, F.; New York City

Jaudon, Samuel; Philadelphia, Pennsylvania

Johnson, R.; Baltimore, Maryland

Jolly, Thomas; Norristown, Pennsylvania

Jones, John B.; Boston, Massachusetts

Jones, Miller & Co.

Justice, Alfred Bunting

Kane, John K.; Philadelphia, Pennsylvania

Kearney, Joseph; Washington, D.C.

Keating, William H.

Keeling, C.; New York City

Kendall, Amos; Washington, D.C.

Kennon, Beverley; Norfolk, Virginia

Kirkby, Waterhouse & Co.; Sheffield, England

Kirkpatrick, John & Co.; Charleston, South Carolina

Konkle, Aaron, Elmira, New York

Lags, Gumain; Bordeaux, France

Lancaster, Richard; Sterling, Pennsylvania

Laws, John & Richard; Sheffield, England

Lecount, Peter; New York City

Leech, Richard T.; Pittsburgh, Pennsylvania

Leftwich, Robert; Russellville, Alabama

Legoux & Plunkett; New York City

LeSassur, L.; New Orleans, Louisiana

Leslie, Colonel Thomas J.; West Point, New York

Levingston, J.; New York City

Linton, John; New Orleans, Louisiana

Lloyd, James; Boston, Massachusetts

Lohse & Keyser; New York City

Lombard, Daniel; Boston, Massachusetts

Long, Peter; New Orleans, Louisiana

Loring, Thomas; Wiscasset, Maine

Lovett, Robert; New York City

MacDonald, Mr.; Baltimore, Maryland

Mackie & Murdock

Maires, Henry

Mantin, Martin; New York City

Marcy, W. L.; Albany, New York

Marquand & Brothers; New York City

Martin, Robert; Charleston, South Carolina

Masi, Seraphim; Washington, D.C.

Mason, Jabez; Staten Island, New York

Masson, C. A.

Mayo, Joseph; Annapolis, Maryland

Mayo, Lieutenant Isaac

McCahan, Mr.

McCarer, W. H.

McCarrlle, Peter; Washington, D.C.

McClellin, Arthur

McGrew, Alexander; Cincinnati, Ohio

McRa, Powell; Hyde Park, New York

Mearbeck, S.; Sheffield, England

Meigs, M. C.

Melly, Brothers

Meriam, William; Richmond, Virginia

Messenger, Thomas & Son (s); Birmingham, England

Messenger, Thomas, Birmingham, England

Middleton, J. Izaard; Charleston, South Carolina

Middleton, O. H.; Charleston, South Carolina

Miller, The Honorable Stephen D.; Washington, D.C.

Minor, Leo

Molly, Brothers; New York City

Moore, Colonel Samuel

Mordecai, A.; Washington, D.C.

Morey, George & Henry H. Fuller

Morfit, H. M.

Morlot, C.; New York City

Morrall & Bouland

Morris, Commodore Joseph L.

Morton, George C.

Murray, James; Annapolis, Maryland

Musselman, John; Lancaster, Pennsylvania

Myers, Lawrence; New York City

Myers, Tompkins & Fisher

Newbold, George; New York City

Nicoll, John D.; New York City

Norton, Charles E.; New Orleans, Louisiana

Norvelle, W.; Lynchburg, Virginia

Nowill, Thomas; Sheffield, England

Ogden, Abraham; New York City

Panther & Jacobs

Parker, Samuel H.; Boston, Massachusetts

Parker, Theodore S.; Boston, Massachusetts

Parrott & Willson; Mexico City, Mexico

Parrott, W. S.; Mexico City, Mexico

Patterson, Daniel T.

Paul, James W.; Philadelphia, Pennsylvania

Peabody, Augustus; Boston, Massachusetts

Peckham, Benjamin T.

Peel, H. H.; New York City

Peirce, Levi; New Orleans, Louisiana

Peirce, Mark W.; Portsmouth, New Hampshire

Pelham, William; Zanesville, Ohio & Philadelphia, Pennsylvania

Pellatt & Green; London, England

Pelletreau, Maltby; Newark, New Jersey

Perret, A.; New York City

Phillips, William; Philadelphia, Pennsylvania

Pierce, William S.; Philadelphia, Pennsylvania

Poirer & Bouge; Paris, France

Pool, L.

Pouchet, A.; Paris, France

Powis, R.; London, England

Pratt, George W.

Prentiss, W.

Prescott, Eustis

Ralston, A. Girard.; Paris, France

Read, Captain

Redon, C.; New Orleans, Louisiana

Reed, R.

Rees, Eben S.

Rhoads, W.; Baltimore, Maryland

Rice, Henry; Boston, Massachusetts

Ridgeway, John

Riou, E.; Paris, France

Rixon, Samuel A.; Bordentown, New Jersey

Roberts, Cadman & Co.; Sheffield, England

Roberts, George; Philadelphia, Pennsylvania

Robertson, James; London, England

Rodgers, Joseph & Loud; Sheffield, England

Rodgers, Joseph & Sons; Sheffield, England

Ronaldson, James; Philadelphia, Pennsylvania

Rose, J. & Co.

Ruggles, Nathan

Rundell, Bridge & Rundell; London, England

Russell, Joseph; Boston, Massachusetts

Sands, Spooner & Sands

Sansom, P. & Son

Sargeant & Brooks

Schenck, Peter; New York City

Scherpf, G. A.; Newark, New Jersey

Schlatter, Mr.

Schmetz, G.; Pottsville, Pennsylvania

Scott, General Winfield

Sergeant & Brooks

Sergeant, John; Philadelphia, Pennsylvania

Sewall, James

Sewall, Thomas R.

Shepherd, R. D.; Boston, Massachusetts

Shoemaker, John; Pottsville, Pennsylvania

Shoemaker, Joseph

Short, Dr. C. W.; Lexington, Kentucky

Sicard, Trigueros & Co.; Vera Cruz, Mexico

Sigourney, Andrew; Boston, Massachusetts

Sigourney, John C.; New York City

Silsbee, Nathaniel; Salem, Massachusetts

Singleton, Richard; Sumpter County, South Carolina

Skinner, J.; Baltimore, Maryland

Smith, George; Philadelphia, Pennsylvania

Smith, Mr.

Smoot, Joseph; Alexandria, Virginia

Snead, Mr.; Baltimore, Maryland

Snyder, John

South, George W.; Philadelphia, Pennsylvania

Spooner, Clowes & Co; Birmingham, England

Spooner, Painter & Co.; Sheffield, England

Standbridge, J. C.; Philadelphia, Pennsylvania

Stanley & Co.; Baltimore, Maryland

Stevens, E. A.

Stoddart, John; Philadelphia, Pennsylvania

Taliaferro, Charles C.

Taylor & Baldwin; Newark, New Jersey

Taylor & Pelletreau; Newark, New Jersey

Taylor, George; Richmond, Virginia

Taylor, Sicard & Co.; Vera Cruz, Mexico

Taylor, William; Vera Cruz, Mexico

Thibault, Felix; Philadelphia, Pennsylvania

Thompson, Ann

Thompson, Charles W.; Philadelphia, Pennsylvania

Thompson, P.; Philadelphia, Pennsylvania

Thorndike, Mr.

Tilford, John W.; Paris, Kentucky

Tomes, Francis; New York City

Tompkins, Edward W.; Richmond, Virginia

Towson, General Nathan

Tuttle, Lieutenant S.

Tyzack, Mark; Sheffield, England

United States Patent Office

Veron, Lewis; Philadelphia, Pennsylvania

Veron, Mrs.; Boston, Massachusetts

Veron, Timothy

Vickers, John; Sheffield, England

Vincent, Frederick

Voss, Maurice; Vera Cruz, Mexico

Warr, John & William W.; Philadelphia, Pennsylvania

Watson & Bradbury; Sheffield, England

Watson, & Co.; Sheffield, England

Watson, Ed.; Boston, Massachusetts

Watson, George & Son

Watson, Pass & Co.; Sheffield, England

Webster, The Honorable Daniel; Boston, Massachusetts

Welles & Co.

Welles & Greene; Havre, France

Welles, Alfred; Boston, Massachusetts

Welles, R. W.

Wells, Williams & Greene; Havre, France

White, Josiah; Philadelphia, Pennsylvania

Whitfield, Thomas B.

Wickham, John; Richmond, Virginia

Wiggin, Timothy; London, England

Williams, Charles G.; Norfolk, Virginia

Williams, F. J.

Williams, John; London, England

Williams, Samuel; London, England

Williamson, John P.

Willink, D. & J. A.; Liverpool, England

Wilmarth, Moffat & Curtis; New York City

Wilson, B; Washington, D.C.

Wilson, Hugh; Charleston, South Carolina

Wilson, J. M.

Winchester, Maria; Baltimore, Maryland

Wittberger, C. H.

Wolf, Spies & Clark

Woodward & Hale

Woodward, C. & Co.

Woodward, George; Philadelphia, Pennsylvania

Woodworth, S. H. & F. A.; New York City

Wright, Jonathan; Tampico, Mexico

Wright, W. W.

Yorke, McAllister & Co.

Young & Veal

Zacharie, J. W. & Co.

Selected Bibliography

Ackermann, Rudolph. *Repository of the Arts.* London: By the author, 1817–19.

Acton, Eliza. *Modern Cookery for Private Families.* London: Privately printed, 1845.

Alemany-Dessaint, Véronique. *Orfèvrerie Française.* Paris: Éditions de l'Illustration Baschet, 1988.

Allen, Henry Butler. *The Franklin Institute of the State of Pennsylvania.* Transactions of the American Philosophical Society, n.s., 43, Philadelphia, 1953.

Altmayer, Jay P. *American Presentation Swords.* Mobile, Ala.: Rankin Press, 1958.

"The American at Work, Among the Silver-Platers." *Appleton's Journal* 31 (December 1878): 483–94.

American Fire Marks. Philadelphia: Insurance Company of North America, 1933.

The American Neptune. Special supp. to vol. 54 (1994).

Anderson, Leslie J. "Isaac Hull Memorabilia at the USS Constitution Museum." *The Magazine Antiques* 125, no. 7 (July 1984): 119–23.

Anderson, Patricia. *The Course of Empire: The Erie Canal and the New York Landscape, 1825–1875.* Rochester: Memorial Art Gallery of the University of Rochester, 1984.

Artemis Group. *Valadier, Three Generations of Roman Goldsmiths: An Exhibition of Drawings and Works of Art.* London: David Carritt Limited, 1991.

Bancroft Woodcock, Silversmith. Wilmington, Del.: Historical Society of Delaware, 1976.

Baranoff, Dalit. "Fire Insurance in the United States." In *EH Net Encyclopedia*, edited by Robert Whaples. http://eh.net/encyclopedia/article/Baranoff.Fire .final.

Barquist, David L. "'The Honours of a Court' or 'The Severity of Virtue': Household Furnishings and Cultural Aspirations in Philadelphia." In *Shaping a National Culture: The Philadelphia Experience, 1750–1800,* edited by Catherine E. Hutchins, 313–34. Winterthur, Del.: Henry Francis du Pont Winterthur Museum, 1994.

———. *Myer Myers: Jewish Silversmith in Colonial New York.* New Haven: Yale University Press, 2001.

Beasley, Ellen. "Samuel Williamson: Philadelphia Silversmith, 1794–1813." Master's thesis, University of Delaware, 1964.

Belden, Louise C. *The Festive Tradition.* New York: W. W. Norton, 1983.

Bell, Witfield J. Jr., ed. *Francis Hopkinson's Account of the Grand Federal Procession Philadelphia 1788.* Boston: Old South Association, 1962.

Billon, Frederic L. *Annals of St. Louis.* St. Louis: By the author, 1888.

Birch, William. *The City of Philadelphia.* Philadelphia, 1800.

Birdsall, Richard D. *Berkshire County.* New Haven: Yale University Press, 1959.

Blumin, Stuart. "Mobility and Change in Antebellum Philadelphia." In *Nineteenth-Century Cities*, edited by Stephen Thernstrom and Richard Sennett. New Haven: Yale University Press, 1969.

Bouilhet, Henri. *L'Orfèvrerie Française aux XVIIIe et XIXe siècles.* Paris: H. Laurens, 1910.

Boultinghouse, Marquis. *Silversmiths, Jewelers, Clock and Watch Makers of Kentucky, 1785–1900.* Lexington: By the author, 1980.

Bowen, Abel. *The Naval Monument.* Boston: By the author, 1816.

Bower, Peter. *Turner's Later Papers: A Study of the Manufacture, Selection, and Use of His Drawing Papers, 1820–1851.* New Castle, Del.: Oak Knoll Press, 1999.

Bradbury, Frederick. *A History of Old Sheffield Plate.* London: Macmillan and Company, 1912.

Brett, Vanessa. *Sotheby's Dictionary of Silver.* London: Sotheby's Publications, 1986.

Brix, Maurice. *List of Philadelphia Silversmiths and Allied Artificers from 1682 to 1850.* Philadelphia: Privately printed, 1920.

Buckley, Charles E. *The St. Louis Art Museum.* St. Louis: By the museum, 1975.

Buhler, Kathryn C. *American Silver, 1655–1825, in the Museum of Fine Arts, Boston.* 2 vols. Boston: By the museum, 1972.

Buhler, Kathryn C., and Graham Hood. *American Silver: Garvan and Other Collections in the Yale University Art Gallery.* 2 vols. New Haven: Yale University Press, 1970.

Bushman, Richard L. *The Refinement of America: Persons, Houses, Cities.* New York: Alfred A. Knopf, 1992.

Carpenter, Charles H. *Gorham Silver.* New York: Dodd, Mead & Company, 1982.

Carrington, John Bodman, and George Ravensworth Hughes. *The Plate of the Worshipful Company of Goldsmiths.* Oxford, Eng.: Oxford University Press, 1926.

Catalogue of the Books. Philadelphia: C. Sherman and Co., 1837.

Childs, Cephas G. *Views in Philadelphia and Its Environs.* Philadelphia: C. G. Childs, 1827.

Chrysler Museum. *Treasures for the Table: Silver from the Chrysler Museum.* New York: Hudson Hills Press, 1989.

Clifford, Helen. *Silver in London: The Parker and Wakelin Partnership, 1760–1776.* New Haven: Yale University Press, 2004.

Congor, Clement E. *Treasures of State.* New York: Harry N. Abrams, 1991.

Cooper, Wendy A. *In Praise of America.* New York: Alfred A. Knopf, 1980.

———. *Classical Taste in America, 1810–1840.* New York: Abbeville, 1993.

Coxe, Tench. *A Statement of the Arts and Manufacturers of the United States of America for the Year 1810.* Philadelphia: A. Cornman Jr., 1814.

Crescent City Silver. New Orleans: Historic New Orleans Collection, 1980.

Dallas, Eneas S. *Ketter's Book of the Table.* London: Privately printed, 1877.

D'Ambrosio, Anna Tobin, ed. *Masterpieces of American Furniture from the Munson-Williams-Proctor Institute.* Utica, N.Y.: By the institute, 1999.

Davidson, Robert B. *History of the United Bowmen of Philadelphia.* Philadelphia: Allen, Lane & Scott's Printing House, 1888.

Dennis, Faith. *Three Centuries of French Domestic Silver.* 2 vols. New York: Metropolitan Museum of Art, 1960.

Denon, Dominique Vivant. *Voyage dans la Basse et la Haute Égypte.* Paris: Imprimerie de P. Didot l'Aîné, 1802.

———. *Description de l'Egypte; ou, recueil des observations et des recherches qui ont été faites en Egypte pendant l'Expédition de l'Armée Française.* Paris: L'Imprimerie Imperiale & L'Imprimerie Royale, 1809–13.

Deutsch, Davida Tenebaum. "Washington Memorial Prints." *The Magazine Antiques* 111, no. 2 (February 1977): 324–31.

Drakard, David. *Printed English Pottery.* London: Jonathan Horne Publications, 1992.

Eckhardt, George H. *Pennsylvania Clocks and Clockmakers.* New York: Devin-Adair Company, 1955.

Elwell, Newton W. *Colonial Silverware of the 17th and 18th Centuries.* Boston: George H. Polley & Co., 1899.

Fairbanks, Jonathan, et al. *Paul Revere's Boston: 1735–1818.* Boston: Museum of Fine Arts, 1975.

Fales, Martha Gandy. *Early American Silver for the Cautious Collector.* New York: Funk & Wagnalls, 1970.

———. *Joseph Richardson and Family: Philadelphia Silversmiths.* Middletown, Conn.: Wesleyan University Press, 1974.

———. *Jewelry in America.* Woodbridge, Eng.: Antique Collectors' Club, 1995.

Falino, Jeannine, and Gerald W. R. Ward, eds. *New England Silver & Silversmithing, 1620–1815.* Boston: Colonial Society of Massachusetts, 2001.

Fearon, Henry Bradshaw. *A Narrative of a Journey of Five Thousand Miles through the Eastern and Western States of America.* London: Longman, Hurst, Rees, Orme & Brown, 1818. Reprint, New York: Augustus M. Kelley, 1970.

Federico, Jean Taylor. "An Unfinished Tale of Three Cities." *Washington Antiques Show Catalogue* (1980): 87–90.

Fennimore, Donald L. "Elegant Patterns of Uncommon Good Taste: Domestic Silver by Thomas Fletcher and Sidney Gardiner." Master's thesis, University of Delaware, 1971.

———. "Thomas Fletcher and Sidney Gardiner: The Stylistic Development of Their Domestic Silver." *The Magazine Antiques* 102, no. 4 (October 1972): 642–49.

———. "Chaudron's & Rasch Tea and Coffee Set." *Silver* 17, no. 3 (May–October 1984): 20–22.

Ferguson, Eugene S. *Early Engineering Reminiscences (1815–1840) of George Escol Sellers.* Washington, D.C.: Smithsonian Institution Press, 1965.

Flanigan, J. Michael. *American Furniture from the Kaufman Collection.* Washington, D.C.: National Gallery of Art, 1986.

Fleming, E. McClung. "From Indian Princess to Greek Goddess: The American Image, 1783–1815." In *Winterthur Portfolio III*, edited by Milo M. Naeve, 36–66. Winterthur, Del.: Henry Francis du Pont Winterthur Museum, 1967.

Fletcher, Edward H. *Fletcher Genealogy: An Account of the Descendants of Robert Fletcher, of Concord, Mass.* Boston: Alfred Mudge & Son, 1871.

Fletcher, Henry, ed. *Descendants of Robert Fletcher: The First Six Generations.* 1950.

Fowble, E. McSherry. *Two Centuries of Prints in America, 1680–1880.* Charlottesville: University Press of Virginia, 1987.

Franklin Institute. *First Annual Report of the Proceedings of the Franklin Institute.* Philadelphia: J. Harding, 1825.

———. *Annual Report of the Exhibition (1825–38).* Philadelphia: J. Harding, 1838.

———. *Journal of the Franklin Institute* 53, no. 1. (January 1867).

Gardiner, Curtiss C. *Lion Gardiner and His Descendants.* St. Louis: A. Whipple, 1890.

Garraty, John A., and Mark C. Carnes, eds. *American National Biography.* 24 vols. New York: Oxford University Press, 1999.

Garrett, Wendell. "*Novus Ordo Seclorum*: A New Order of the Ages." In *Neo-Classicism in America.* New York: Hirschl & Adler Galleries, 1991.

Garvan, Beatrice B. *Federal Philadelphia, 1785–1825: The Athens of the Western World.* Philadelphia: Philadelphia Museum of Art, 1987.

Garvan, Beatrice B., and Charles F. Hummel. *The Pennsylvania Germans: A Celebration of Their Arts, 1683–1850.* Philadelphia: Philadelphia Museum of Art, 1983.

Garvan, Beatrice B., et al. *Philadelphia: Three Centuries of American Art.* Philadelphia: Philadelphia Museum of Art, 1976.

Gillingham, Harrold E. "The Cost of Old Silver." *Pennsylvania Magazine of History and Biography* 54, no. 1 (1930): 50–51.

———. "Cesar Ghiselin." *Pennsylvania Magazine of History and Biography* 57, no. 3 (July 1933): 248–49.

Glanville, Philippa. *Silver in England.* London: Unwin Hyman, 1987.

Goldsborough, Jennifer. "Silver in Maryland." *The Magazine Antiques* 125, no. 1 (January 1984): 258–67.

Gordon, Ralph C. *West Indies Countermarked Gold Coins.* Erik Press, 1987.

Gottesman, Rita Susswein. *The Arts and Crafts in New York, 1800–1804.* New York: New-York Historical Society, 1965.

Gravell, Thomas L., and George Miller. *A Catalogue of Foreign Watermarks Found on Paper Used in America, 1700–1835.* New York: Garland Publishing, 1983.

———. *American Watermarks, 1690–1835.* New Castle, Del.: Oak Knoll Press, 2002.

Groce, George C., and David H. Wallace. *The New-York Historical Society's Dictionary of Artists in America, 1564–1860.* New Haven: Yale University Press, 1957.

Guide to the Records of the U.S. House of Representatives at the National Archives, 1789–1989. http://www.archives.gov/records_of_congress/house_guide.

Gura, Judith B. "The Anthony Rasch Sauceboats: A High Point of American Neoclassical Style, Part I." *Silver* 31, no. 2 (March/April 1997): 28–33.

———. "The Anthony Rasch Sauceboats: A High Point of American Neoclassical Style, Part II." *Silver* 31, no. 3 (May/June 1997): 28–32.

Halfpenny, Patricia A., and Donald L. Fennimore. *Campbell Collection of Soup Tureens at Winterthur.* Winterthur, Del.: Henry Francis du Pont Winterthur Museum, 2000.

Halsey, R. T .H. *American Silver.* Boston: Museum of Fine Arts, 1906.

Hamilton, Sir William. *Collection of Etruscan, Greek, and Roman Antiquities.* Naples, Italy: F. Morelli, 1766.

———. *Sir William Hamilton's Vases.* 2d ed. London: T. McLean, 1814.

Hammerslough, Philip H. *American Silver Collected by Philip H. Hammerslough.* Vol. 2. Hartford, Conn.: Privately printed, 1960.

Harris, Theresa Fairbanks, and Scott Wilcox. *Papermaking and the Art of Watercolor in Eighteenth-Century Britain.* New Haven: Yale University Press, 2006.

Hartop, Christopher. *Royal Goldsmiths: The Art of Rundell & Bridge, 1797–1843.* Cambridge, Eng.: John Adamson, 2005.

Haviland, John. *The Builder's Assistant, Containing the Five Orders of Architecture.* Vol. 1. Philadelphia: John Bioren, 1818.

Heckscher, Morrison H., and Leslie Greene Bowman. *American Rococo, 1750–1775: Elegance in Ornament.* New York: Metropolitan Museum of Art, 1992.

Helft, Jacques. *French Master Goldsmiths and Silversmiths.* New York: French & European Publications, 1966.

Hennell, Percy. *Hennell Silver Salt Cellars.* East Grinstead, Eng.: BLA Publishing Ltd., 1986.

Hessling, E. *Dessins d' Orfèvrerie de Percier.* Paris: By the author, 1912.

Hiatt, Noble W., and Lucy F. Hiatt, *The Silversmiths of Kentucky, 1785–1850.* Louisville: Standard Publishing Company, 1954.

Hicks, James E. *Nathan Starr: U.S. Sword and Arms Maker, 1776–1845.* Mt. Vernon, N.Y.: James E. Hicks, 1940. Reprint, Phoenix, Ariz.: Restoration Press, 1976.

Hofer, Margaret K. "Celebrating Two Centuries of Collecting." *Antiques & Fine Art* 5 (January 2005): 230–35.

Hope, Thomas. *Household Furniture and Interior Decoration*. London: Printed by T. Bensley for Longman, Hurst, Rees & Orme, 1807. Reprint, New York: Dover, 1971.

Howard, David Sanctuary. *Chinese Armorial Porcelain*. Vol. 2. Wiltshire, Eng.: Heirloom & Howard Ltd., 2003.

Jackson, Joseph. *Encyclopedia of Philadelphia*. Harrisburg, Pa: National Historical Association, 1931–33.

Johnson, Marilynn A. "John Hewitt, Cabinetmaker." In *Winterthur Portfolio 4,* edited by Richard K. Doud, 185–205. Winterthur, Del.: Henry Francis du Pont Winterthur Museum, 1968.

Jones, E. Alfred. *The Old Silver of American Churches*. Vol. 2. Letchworth, Eng.: Privately printed, 1913.

Kane, Patricia E. *Colonial Massachusetts Silversmiths and Jewelers*. New Haven: Yale University Press, 1998.

Kirtley, Alexandra Alevizatos. "George Bridport." *The Magazine Antiques* 169, no. 5 (May 2006): 76–80.

———. "The Painted Furniture of Philadelphia: A Reappraisal." *The Magazine Antiques* 169, no. 5 (May 2006): 134–45.

Klapthor, Margaret Brown. *Presentation Pieces in the Museum of History and Technology, Smithsonian Institution*. Washington, D.C: By the institution, 1965.

Latrobe, Benjamin H. *Anniversary Oration Pronounced before The Society of Artists of the United States, by Appointment of The Society, On the Eighth of May, 1811.*

Laurie, Bruce Gordon. "The Working People of Philadelphia, 1827–1853." Ph.D. diss., University of Pittsburgh, 1971.

———. *Working People of Philadelphia, 1800–1850*. Philadelphia: Temple University Press, 1980.

Lawrence, Robert Means. *The Site of St. Paul's Cathedral, Boston, and Its Neighborhood*. Boston: Gorham Press, 1916.

Layton, Rachel E. C. "Samuel Williamson's Presentation Silver: Important New Discoveries." *Silver* 25, no. 1 (January–February 1992): 8–13.

Le Corbeiller, Clare. "The Construction of Some Empire Silver." *Metropolitan Museum Journal* 16 (1982): 195–98.

Letzer, Mark B., and Jean B. Russo, eds. *The Diary of William Faris: The Daily Life of an Annapolis Silversmith*. Baltimore: Maryland Historical Society, 2003.

Lindsay, Jack L. *Worldly Goods: The Arts of Early Pennsylvania, 1680–1758*. Philadelphia: Philadelphia Museum of Art, 1999.

Lindstrom, Diane. *Economic Development in the Philadelphia Region, 1810–1850*. New York: Columbia University Press, 1978.

Lomax, James. *British Silver at Temple Newsam and Lotherton Hall*. Leeds, Eng.: Leeds Art Collections Fund and W. S. Maney and Son Ltd., 1992.

Lossing, Benson. *A Pictorial Field Book of the War of 1812*. New York: Harper & Brothers Publishers, 1862.

McCauley, Robert H. *Liverpool Transfer Designs on Anglo-American Pottery*. Portland, Me.: Southworth-Anthoensen Press, 1942.

McClinton, Katherine Morrison. *Collecting 19th Century American Silver*. New York: Charles Scribner's Sons, 1968.

———. "Nineteenth-Century American Presentation Silver." *The Connoisseur* 167, no. 673 (March 1968): 192–94.

———. "Fletcher and Gardiner: Silversmiths of the American Empire." *The Connoisseur* 173, no. 697 (March 1970): 211–21.

McCormick, Heather Jane, et al. *Vasemania: Neoclassical Form and Ornament in Europe, Selections from the Metropolitan Museum of Art*. New Haven: Yale University Press, 2004.

McElroy, A. *McElroy's Philadelphia Directory for 1839*. Philadelphia: Isaac Ashmead & Co., 1839.

Mack, Norman. *Missouri's Silver Age: Silversmiths of the 1800s*. Carbondale: Southern Illinois University Press, 2005.

Malone, Dumas, ed. *Dictionary of American Biography*. 20 vols. New York: Charles Scribner's Sons, 1935.

Marks, Richard, and Brian J. R. Blench. *The Warwick Vase: The Burrell Collection*. Glasgow, Scot.: Glasgow Museums and Art Galleries, 1979.

Massachusetts Historical Society. *The War of 1812*. Boston: By the society, 1962.

Mease, James. *The Picture of Philadelphia*. Philadelphia: B. & T. Kite, 1811.

Miller, Nathan, *The U.S. Navy: An Illustrated History*. New York: American Heritage Publishing Company, 1977.

Moses, Henry. *A Collection of Antique Vases, Altars, Paterae, Tripods, Candelabra, Sarcophagi, &c.* London: H. G. Bohn, 1814.

Mowbray, E. Andrew. *The American Eagle-Pommel Sword*. Lincoln, R.I.: Man at Arms Magazine, 1997.

Myers, Minor, Jr. *The Insignia of the Society of the Cincinnati*. Washington, D.C.: Society of the Cincinnati, 1998.

Neo-classicism in America: Inspiration and Innovation, 1810–1840. New York: Hirschl & Adler Galleries, 1991.

New York City Chamber of Commerce. *Proceedings of the Chamber of Commerce*. Fifty-first Annual Report. Part 1. May 7, 1908.

Oberholtzer, Ellis Paxson. *Philadelphia: A History of the City and Its People*. 4 vols. Philadelphia: S. J. Clarke Publishing Company, 1912.

O'Gorman, James F., et al. *Drawing toward Building: Philadelphia Architectural Graphics, 1732–1986*. Philadelphia: Pennsylvania Academy of the Fine Arts, 1986.

Oman, Charles. "A Problem of Artistic Responsibility: The Firm of Rundell, Bridge & Rundell." *Apollo* 83 (March 1966): 174–83.

Palmer, Arlene. *Glass in Early America*. New York: W. W. Norton, 1993.

Penzer, Norman M. *Paul Storr: The Last of the Goldsmiths*. London: B. T. Batsford, 1954.

Percier, Charles. *Recueil des décorations intérieures*. Paris: A. Guérinet, 1801.

Percier, Charles, and Pierre-François-Léonard Fontaine. *Recueil des décorations intérieures*. Paris: Chez les Auteurs, 1812.

Peterson, Howard L. *American Silver Mounted Swords, 1700–1815*. Washington, D.C.: Privately printed, 1955.

———. *The American Sword, 1775–1945*. Philadelphia: Ray Riling Arms Books Company, 1973.

Philadelphia in 1824; or, A Brief Account of The Various Institutions and Public Objects in This Metropolis. Philadelphia: H. C. Carey and I. Lea, 1824.

Phillips, Anthony, and Jeanne Sloane. *Antiquity Revisited: English and French Silver-Gilt from the Collection of Audrey Love*. London: Christie's, 1997.

Pinçon, Jean-Marie, and Olivier Gaube du Gers. *Odiot l'Orfèvre*. Paris: Sous le Vent, 1990.

Pitkin, Timothy. *A Statistical View of the Commerce of the United States*. Hartford, Conn.: By the author, 1816.

Piranesi, Giovanni-Battista. *Diverse maniere d'adornare i cammini … e toscana*. Rome: Salomoni, 1769.

Pleasants, J. Hall, and Howard Sill. *Maryland Silversmiths, 1715–1830*. Baltimore: Lord Baltimore Press, 1930.

Plymouth Church Records, 1620–1859. Vol. 3. New York: New England Society, 1923.

Pursell, Carroll Wirth. *Early Stationary Steam Engines in America.* Washington, D.C.: Smithsonian Institution Press, 1969.

Quéant, Olivier. *Styles de France.* Paris: Le Rayonnement Français, 1950.

Quimby, Ian M. G. *American Silver at Winterthur.* Winterthur, Del.: Henry Francis du Pont Winterthur Museum, 1995.

Rabinovitch, Benton Seymour. *Antique Silver Servers for the Dining Table.* Concord, Mass.: Joslin Hall Publishing, 1991.

Randall, Richard H. Jr. "Sword Designs by Thomas Fletcher." *The American Arms Collector* 1, no. 4 (October 1957): 103–8.

Richter, Gisela M. A., and Marjorie J. Milne. *Shapes and Names of Athenian Vases.* New York: Metropolitan Museum of Art, 1935.

Robin, Claude C. *New Travels through North America.* Boston: Privately printed, 1781.

Robinson, James, ed. *Philadelphia Directory for 1816.* Philadelphia, 1816.

———. *Robinson's Original Annual Directory for 1817.* Philadelphia, 1817.

Rowe, Robert. *Adam Silver.* New York: Taplinger Publishing Company, 1965.

Sally, Alexander S. "The Jackson Vase." *Bulletin of the South Carolina Historical Commission* 1 (1915): 1–8.

Sellers Family Association. *Descendants of Samuel Sellers.* Ardmore, Pa., 1962.

———. "The Sellers Homes." *Proceedings of the Fourth and Fifth General Meetings of The Sellers Family Association Held in the Years 1916 and 1920.*

Sheraton, Thomas. *The Cabinet Dictionary.* London: By the author, 1803. Reprint, 2 vols. New York: Praeger Publishers, 1970.

Simpson, Henry. *The Lives of Eminent Philadelphians, Now Deceased.* 2 vols. Philadelphia: William Brotherhead, 1859.

Sinclair, Bruce. *Philadelphia's Philosopher Mechanics: A History of the Franklin Institute, 1824–1865.* Baltimore: Johns Hopkins University Press, 1974.

"Sixteenth Quarterly Report, 17 January 1828." *The Franklin Journal and American Mechanics' Magazine* 5, no. 2 (February 1828).

Smith, George. *A Collection of Ornamental Designs after the Manner of the Antique.* London: J. Taylor [n.d.].

Snodin, Michael. "J. J. Boileau: A Forgotten Designer of Silver." *The Connoisseur* 198, no. 196 (June 1978): 124–33.

———. "Some Designs for English Gold and Silver." In *The V&A Album 4,* 147–53. London: Associates of the V&A, 1985.

Snodin, Michael, and Gail Belden. *Spoons.* London: Pitman Publishing, 1976.

Snyder, Martin P. *City of Independence: Views of Philadelphia before 1800.* New York: Praeger Publishers, 1975.

Soeffing, D. Albert. "An Interesting Letter to Thomas Fletcher, Philadelphia Silversmith, from Benjamin Gratz." *Silver* 34, no. 2 (March/April 2002): 14–15.

Sørensen, Bent. "Piranesi, Grandjacquet, and the Warwick Vase." *The Burlington Magazine* 145, no. 1208 (November 2003): 792–95.

Southwick, Leslie. "The Silver Vases Awarded by the Patriotic Fund." *Silver Society Journal* (Winter 1990): 27–49.

Stimpson's Boston Directory. Boston: Stimpson & Clapp, 1831.

Stollenwerck, Frank, and Dixie Orum. *The Stollenwerck, Chaudron & Billon Families in America.* Privately printed, 1948.

Tatham, Charles Heathcote. *Designs for Ornamental Plate, Many of Which Have Been Executed in Silver, from Original Drawings.* London: Printed for Thomas Gardiner by John Barfield, 1806.

Taylor, George Rogers, ed. "'Philadelphia in Slices' by George G. Foster." *Pennsylvania Magazine of History and Biography* 93, no. 1 (January 1969): 23–72..

Teeters, Negley, K. "What is Known from Fact and Fiction Concerning Hugh and Jane Stretch Lownes." Typescript, Department of Sociology, Temple University, 1957.

Thernstrom, Stephen, and Richard Sennett, eds. *Nineteenth-Century Cities.* New Haven: Yale University Press, 1969.

Tracy, Berry. *Classical America, 1815–1845.* Newark, N.J.: Newark Museum Association, 1963.

———. "Late Classical Styles in American Silver." *The Magazine Antiques* 86, no. 6 (December 1964): 702–6.

Tuckerman, Bayard. *The Diary of Philip Hone, 1828–1851.* 2 vols. New York: Dodd, Mead and Company, 1889.

Tuite, Peter. *U.S. Naval Officers: Their Swords and Dirks.* Lincoln, R.I.: Andrew Mowbray, 2004.

[United Bowmen]. *Constitution and Regulations of the United Bowmen of Philadelphia, Founded September 1828.* Philadelphia: Hogan & Thompson, 1844.

The United Bowmen of Philadelphia, 1828–1953, Commemorating the 125th Anniversary.

Philadelphia: United Bowmen of Philadelphia, 1953.

Verlet, Pierre. *Les Bronzes Dorés Français.* Paris: Grands Manuels Picard, 1987.

Vermeule, Cornelius C. *Roman Imperial Art in Greece and Asia Minor.* Cambridge, Mass.: Harvard University Press, 1968.

Voorsanger, Catherine Hoover, and John K. Howat, eds. *Art and the Empire City: New York, 1825–1861.* New York: Metropolitan Museum of Art, 2000.

Wagner, Ann K. "Fletcher and Gardiner: Presentation Silver for the Nation." Master's thesis, University of Delaware, 2004.

Wainwright, Nicholas B. *Philadelphia in The Romantic Age of Lithography.* Philadelphia: Historical Society of Pennsylvania, 1958.

———, ed. *A Philadelphia Perspective: The Diary of Sidney George Fisher Covering the Years 1834–1871.* Philadelphia: Historical Society of Pennsylvania, 1967.

Ward, Barbara McLean. "Boston Goldsmiths, 1690–1730." In *The Craftsman in Early America,* edited by Ian M. G. Quimby, 126–57. New York: W. W. Norton, 1984.

Warren, David B., et al. *American Decorative Arts and Paintings in the Bayou Bend Collection.* Princeton, N.J.: Princeton University Press, 1998.

Warren, David B., Katherine S. Howe, and Michael K. Brown. *Marks of Achievement: Four Centuries of American Presentation Silver.* New York: Harry N. Abrams, 1987.

Waters, Deborah Dependahl. "Of Pure Coin: The Manufacture of American Silver Flatware, 1800–1860." In *Winterthur Portfolio 12,* edited by Ian M. G. Quimby, 19–20. Winterthur, Del.: Henry Francis du Pont Winterthur Museum, 1977.

———. "The Workmanship of an American Artist: Philadelphia's Precious Metals Trades and Craftsmen, 1788–1832." PhD diss., University of Delaware, 1981.

———, ed. *Elegant Plate: Three Centuries of Precious Metals in New York City.* New York: Museum of the City of New York, 2000.

Watson, John Fanning. *Annals of Philadelphia.* 3 vols. Philadelphia: Edwin S. Stuart, 1887.

Webster, Thomas. *An Encyclopaedia of Domestic Economy.* New York: Harper and Brothers, 1845.

Weiss, Harry B., and Grace M. Weiss. *The Early Snuff Mills of New Jersey.* Trenton: New Jersey Agricultural Society, 1962.

Wenham, Edward. *Domestic Silver of Great Britain and Ireland.* New York: Oxford University Press, 1931.

Wilton-Ely, John. *Giovanni Battista Piranesi: The Complete Etchings.* Vol. 2. San Francisco: Alan Wofsy Fine Arts, 1994.

Winsor, Justin. *The Memorial History of Boston.* Vol. 3. Boston: James R. Osgood and Company, 1882.

Wood, Elizabeth Ingerman. "Thomas Fletcher: A Philadelphia Entrepreneur of Presentation Silver." In *Winterthur Portfolio III*, edited by Milo M. Naeve, 136–71. Winterthur, Del.: Henry Francis du Pont Winterthur Museum, 1967.

Wrightson's Annual Directory of Birmingham. Birmingham, Eng.: R. Wrightson, 1829.

Young, Hilary. "Sir William Chambers and John Yenn: Designs for Silver." *Burlington Magazine* 128 (January 1986): 30–35.

———. "A Further Note on J. J. Boileau: 'a Forgotten Designer of Silver.'" *Apollo* 124 (October 1986): 334–37.

———. "Neo-Classical Silversmiths' Drawings at the Victoria and Albert Museum." *Apollo* 129 (June 1989): 384–88.

Zimmerman, Philip D., and Jennifer Faulds Goldsborough. *The Sewell C. Biggs Collection of American Art.* Dover, Del.: Biggs Museum of American Art, 2002.

Zongor, Melinda. *Coverlets and the Spirit of America.* Atglen, Pa.: Schiffer Publishing, 2002.

Manuscript and Archival Collections

Contributionship Insurance Company of Philadelphia.

County Tax Assessment Ledgers. Philadelphia City Archives.

Dubois, Abraham. Letterbook, 1803–7. Eleutherian Mills Historical Library, Wilmington, Del.

Fletcher, Thomas. Drawings. Maryland Historical Society, Baltimore, Md.

Fletcher, Thomas. Drawings. Department of Drawings and Prints, Metropolitan Museum of Art.

Fletcher, Thomas. Papers. Collection 39. The Athenaeum of Philadelphia.

Fletcher, Thomas. Papers. Collection 1343. Historical Society of Pennsylvania, Philadelphia.

Fletcher, Thomas. Papers. Collection 278. Joseph Downs Collection of Manuscripts and Printed Ephemera, Winterthur Library, Winterthur, Del.

Franklin Institute Membership Roll, 1824. Philadelphia.

Harvey, Isaac Jr., Diary. Historical Society of Pennsylvania, Philadelphia.

Hildeburn and Woolworths. Letterbook Am 9321. Historical Society of Pennsylvania, Philadelphia.

Indentures. Philadelphia City Archives.

Index. Records of Aliens' Declarations of Intention and/or Oaths of Allegiance, 1789–1880. WPA typescript.

Loudoun Papers. Historical Society of Pennsylvania, Philadelphia.

Morris Family Papers. Historical Society of Pennsylvania, Philadelphia.

Norris Manuscripts. Historical Society of Pennsylvania, Philadelphia.

New Jersey Register of Wills.

"Old Loan" Ledger. Bureau of The Public Debt, 1790–1836. National Archives.

Pennsylvania Abolition Society Papers. Historical Society of Pennsylvania, Philadelphia.

Philadelphia Deed Registry.

Philadelphia Monthly Meeting Southern District Minutes, 1781–93.

Philadelphia Register of Wills.

Richardson, Joseph Jr., Collection. Historical Society of Pennsylvania, Philadelphia.

Sellers, John Jr., Diary. American Philosophical Society, Philadelphia.

Stauffer Collection. Historical Society of Pennsylvania, Philadelphia.

U.S. Bureau of the Census. National Archives.

Williamson, Samuel. Daybooks, 1803–13. Joseph Downs Collection of Manuscripts and Printed Ephemera, Winterthur Library, Winterthur, Del.

Wister, Charles. Papers. Joseph Downs Collection of Manuscripts and Printed Ephemera, Winterthur Library, Winterthur, Del.

Index